# THE EVOLUTION OF THE THEORIES AND TECHNIQUES OF STANDARD COSTS

# THE EVOLUTION OF THE THEORIES AND TECHNIQUES OF STANDARD COSTS

by

Ellis Mast Sowell

The University of Alabama Press

University, Alabama

The publication of this volume is a long-thought-about endeavor, and I write this brief foreword with especial pleasure because of my admiration both for its author and for the monument of scholarship that he has left us.

Dr. Ellis Mast Sowell, whom it was my privilege to know well, passed away in the prime of life after making many contributions to the fields of education, professional accounting, educational administration, scholarly writing, and as a friend and advisor to countless young people. Yet his greatest work of scholarship has long remained unknown to all but a few.

Dr. Sowell, who served as Dean of the Texas Christian University School of Business for several years, became interested in the historical development of cost accounting in the early 1940's, under the inspiration of his mentor and friend, Dr. G. H. Newlove, of the University of Texas, who himself had collected many items of interest on the subject. Following the suggestion of Dr. Newlove, Ellis Sowell undertook the researches preliminary to writing the manuscript now published herein, in order to complete the historical survery of cost accounting which I had begun in my own research and writing some years previously. In my study of the evolution of cost accounting, I purposely omitted exhaustive treatment of standard costing matters, hoping that some other scholar would take up this particular challenge. Ellis Sowell, inspired by Professor Newlove to accept the challenge, within a few years completed research whose fruits will now be available to students and readers throughout the English-speaking world.

Publication of Dr. Sowell's magnum opus fills a real need. Over the past two decades or more, professional acquaintances have often asked me where copies of the Sowell manuscript could be obtained. Dr. Newlove, Professor Emeritus in Accounting, and a most eminent authority in the field, recently declared that Dr. Sowell made "a unique contribution to the history of the development of cost accounting. The Sowell study is particularly important as it traces the evolution of cost standards (especially for material cost) back to the Guild System in England."

For publication of this significant document, and a worthy tribute to the memory of Dr. Sowell, we owe a debt of gratitude to the generous financial sponsors of the project, the late Clara Bowman Worthington, an alumna of Texas Christian University and her son, William B. Worthington, who assisted in the financial arrangements for the publication of the book by the University of Alabama Press. The accomplishment of this objective provides a major addition to the growing body of literature on the historical development of accounting, a science described by Goethe as "one of the finest achievements of the human mind."

January, 1973
Paul Garner<br>Professor and Dean Emeritus<br>University of Alabama

# TABLE OF CONTENTS

# ACKNOWLEDGMENT

The writer of this dissertation desires to express his appreciation to all of the individuals who have contributed to making this study possible. First, to Professor George Hillis Newlove, of the University of Texas faculty, he acknowledges a debt of gratitude for the original suggestion of the problem, for his continual cooperation and assistance during its development, for the unselfish lending of his library, and for his timely expressions of encouragement. To Professor C. Aubrey Smith, also of the University of Texas faculty, he is indebted for valuable advice and pertinent comments. And, finally, to the writer's wife, Irma Alford Sowell, he bestows a generous amount of credit for her patience, sacrifice, and encouragement during the time that this study was being consummated.

Ellis Mast Sowell

The University of Texas
    May, 1944

x

CHAPTER I

INTRODUCTION


> For which of you, intending to build a
> tower, sitteth not down first, and counteth
> the cost. . . .                 St. Luke 14:28


In contemplation of the subject "The Evolution of the Theories and Techniques of Standard Costs," some clearness of objectives has been deemed possible through a definition of terminology and, based upon such delimitations, by a statement of the problem.

Standard Costs may be defined in the language of Harrison, an outstanding authority on this subject, as ". . . used in its broad meaning as applying to costs that are scientifically determined in advance, in contrast to historical costs which are accumulated after the event."[1]

The other terms, as employed to designate this study, may be expressed according to the definitions recorded in Webster's New International Dictionary:

1. Technique.--"Expert method in execution of the technical details of accomplishing something."

2. Theory.--"A general principle, formula, or ideal construction, offered to explain phenomena and rendered more or less plausible by evidence in the facts or by the exactness and relevancy of the reasoning."

---

[1] Harrison, G. Charter, Standard Costs, New York, The Ronald Press Company, 1930, pp. 3-4.

1

3. _Evolution_.--"A manifestation of related events or ideas in an orderly succession."

After taking into consideration these explanations of the subject's terminology, an adequate statement of the problem has been incorporated in the following summary of objectives:

1. To present, in a chronological succession, those related events, forces, individuals, and ideas that have contributed to and/or have developed into:

2. A group of general principles--theories offered as explanations and recognized as more or less plausible because of practical applications or reasonable conclusions--

3. And a body of specialized accounting procedures--techniques devised as cost methods and accepted as more or less adequate--that are commonly referred to as

4. Scientific predetermined costs--Standard Costs--of raw materials, labor, and overhead, with adequate analyses of the difference (variance) between such costs and the actual or historical costs.

As a means of evidencing the relative importance of Standard Costs for a practical investigation of this nature, attention is directed to the fact that this subject has been deemed worthy of treatment as a complete volume by several authors, notably Downie (1927), Harrison (1930), Camman (1932), Kearsey (1933), Gillespie (1935), and Gregory (1940).[2]

---

[2] Downie, Thomas, Jr., _The Mechanism of Standard (or Predetermined) Cost Accounting and Efficiency Records_, London, Gee and Company, 1927; Harrison, _op. cit._; Camman, Eric A., _Basic Standard Costs_, New York, American Institute Publishing Company, 1932; Kearsey, H. E., _Standard_

Harrison, Camman, and Gillespie were American writers; Downie and Kear-

sey were English; and Gregory was an Australian author.

In addition to these publications, there is a great amount of lit-

erature relating to Standard Costs in cost accounting textbooks, in the

National Association of Cost Accountants Yearbooks and Bulletins, and in

other printed material of a fugitive nature. However, the writers of

these articles have presented their ideas in accordance with three rather

distinct patterns: (1) textbook material for students of cost account-

ing, (2) case studies of applications to specific enterprises, and

(3) discussions of controversial issues.

Although the available material on Standard Costs represents a

rather large store of information, there has not been, so far as the

present writer has ascertained, an adequate treatment of the evolution-

ary aspects of this subject. In view of the significance of this ac-

counting procedure in the industrial field of endeavor, this phase of

Standard Costs has been deemed worthy of consideration in this manner.

Therefore, this dissertation has been dedicated to the remedying of the

paucity of literature of this nature and to the presentation of the

development of the theories and techniques underlying Standard Costs.

The locale of this investigation has been confined to the United

States and England, with occasional reference to other countries as the

---

Costs, London, Sir Isaac Pitman & Sons, 1933; Gillespie, Cecil Merle, *Accounting Procedure for Standard Costs*, New York, The Ronald Press Company, 1935; Gregory, Gerald H., *Accounting Control by Use of Standard Costs*, Sydney (Australia), The Law Book Company of Australasia Pty. Ltd., 1940.

opportunity developed.  This concentration has been found to have considerable justification.  Standard Costs represent the combined efforts of American industrial engineers and American cost accountants, as has been disclosed in the subsequent chapters of this study, while the treatment of the early problems associated with manufacturing by English cost accounting authorities affords the logical background for the general subject under consideration.

In addition to these explanatory statements, the general outline of the study has been made a part of the introduction.  The second chapter undertakes to trace, somewhat in detail, the development of the theories and techniques associated with the Cost Estimate through early British Industrial Organization--including the guild system, the domestic system, and the early factory system--through early English engineering procedure, and through cost accounting literature to the present time.  This portion of the investigation represents the evolution of non-scientific predetermined costs, one of the important contributory factors to Standard Costs or scientific predetermined costs.

The third chapter presents the evolution of the Cost Estimate Variation as has been evidenced in early cost accounting literature and in current publications treating this field of endeavor.  In view of the fact that the Cost Estimate Variation applies to the difference between the actual cost figures and the estimated cost values (as predetermined on a non-scientific basis), this device represents a forerunner of the Standard Cost Variance--one of the important phases of Standard Costs.

Chapter Four, "The Background of Standard Costs," contains an evolutionary treatment of the industrial engineer's and the cost accountant's contributions to Standard Costs, with particular attention being devoted to Harrington Emerson's principles of efficiency and ideas of standards. During this period (1835-1918), the industrial engineer begot time and motion studies, incentive wage payment plans, and the Principle of Exceptions, while the cost accountant devised burden allocation schemes and procedures for recording cost information and for presenting pertinent data to management.

The fifth chapter undertakes to summarize G. Charter Harrison's original presentation of his standard cost ideas as an aid to production and to suggest that these efforts represented the initial attempt to present Standard Cost theories and techniques in a unified and concise series of articles. An effort has been made to restate the author's concepts and to provide original illustrations for each.

The sixth chapter attempts to develop those theories and techniques that have been practiced since Harrison's original treatment of this subject in 1918 and that have been associated, more or less commonly, with Standard Costs. Particular attention has been given to Basic and Current Standard Costs--the two types of standards--to the methods for recording standard cost information in the accounting records, to the Principle of Exceptions, and to the disposition of Standard Cost Variances.

The three subsequent chapters apply Standard Cost theories and techniques to the disposition of the three cost components--raw materials, direct labor, and burden--in manufacturing enterprises. This

segment of the study is especially interested in the setting of standards for raw materials, direct labor, and burden, in the presentation of
these factors in the accounting records, in the final disposition of
variances between actual and standard costs, and in certain problems
that are peculiar to direct labor and burden.

And, finally, Chapter Ten proposes to summarize this study, "The
Evolution of the Theories and Techniques of Standard Costs," with a
rather brief restatement of those factors that have gained significance
and to present certain inductions that have seemed justified by this
rather extensive investigation.  In view of the fact that Standard Cost
evolution, according to its inherent nature, is dynamic rather than
static, these assertions should not be considered as conclusions.

## CHAPTER II

THE EVOLUTION OF THE COST ESTIMATE

The cost estimate--sometimes termed "specification costs," "formula costs," "predetermined costs," and "estimating cost accounting"--is an effort to count the cost before the money is spent or, to be more specific, is an attempt to predetermine for each product, process, or class of products, the cost figures which may be used by management as a guide to or a basis for establishing selling prices and/or for fixing production cost controls during a succeeding fiscal period. When properly prepared and intelligently used, the cost estimate may form the basis for many decisions as to policy and business conduct and may supplement, or even replace, other procedures for collecting and controlling costs.

These cost estimates may vary from a rather perfunctory guess by an official of the producing institution to a very careful computation based upon past experience or upon formulas and engineering specifications. These estimates may range from a forecast of total costs only to costs in terms of the elements of raw materials, direct labor and manufacturing expenses--from a calculation of total costs by departments to a rather detailed predetermination of the three cost elements by departments.

A practical definition of "cost estimating" describes this procedure as:

The process of compiling a cost of articles made or to be made, where experience supplies no complete figures. In compiling

the estimated cost, use may be made of actual cost figures,
past or present, and of facts concerning the available plant
and equipment, labor and burden rates, present and future
market prices of material, knowledge of the processes to be
performed, and good judgment applied to all these.[1]

The use of cost estimates probably dates to an early era of productive enterprise and record-keeping--Blocker[2] suggests that "various
forms of estimate cost accounting plans have been in use since the in-
fancy of cost accounting," while Langer[3] believes that "the practice of
estimating costs is much older than any system of cost accounting or
bookkeeping."

Estimate Costs in Early British Industrial Organization.--The
greater portion of productive endeavor in Great Britain may be considered to have passed through three stages from the standpoint of industrial organization--the guild system, the domestic system, and the
factory system.

Under the guild system, extending from the twelfth to the sixteenth
century, the various classes of artisans or independent craftsmen produced finished goods with their own machines from their own raw materials and, thus, sold the products of their own efforts rather than
their labor.  In many instances, these artisans joined themselves to-

_________________

[1]Alford, L. P., Cost and Production Handbook, New York, The Ronald
Press Company, 1934, p. 1273.

[2]Blocker, John G., Cost Accounting, New York, McGraw-Hill Book Company, 1940, p. 526.

[3]Langer, Charles H., Accounting Principles and Procedures, Chicago,
Walton Publishing Company, 1938, p. L. 23 - 1.

gether into Craft Guilds, urban institutions which not only influenced
the social, political and religious activities of their members but also
controlled the respective industries concerned by inspecting the
finished products and by regulating both wages and prices.[4]

> Instead of allowing a master to pay what wages he pleased, and
> to charge what prices he liked, many gilds fixed the remunera-
> tion of the artisans and determined the prices of commodi-
> ties.[5]

In fixing these prices of manufactured commodities and in setting
the wage scale, it is quite probable that some simple scheme of cost
estimating was devised in order that the majority, at least, of the
masters, who composed the Craft Guild, might recover their actual costs
and receive some remuneration for their own efforts.

> The Weavers' records provide an admirable illustration of the
> way in which the gilds regulated charges for labour by mutual
> agreement, though the right to fix prices resided ultimately
> in the civil authorities.  On June 29th, 1456, the Bailiff of
> the gild and all the Weavers met to consider the charges for
> weaving which "it hath been used and accustomed of time out of
> mind for to take."  They, "pondering and considering the said
> usage and custom of such taking for weaving to be a reasonable
> sustenance to the said Bailiffs and Weavers of the foresaid
> gild toward their said living and bearing of their said ferm
> and a common avail unto the King and his liege people, assent
> and grant that the said taking for weaving in the form above-
> said used, be, continued and had among them from the time for-
> ward."[6]

------------

[4]Lipson, E., _The History of the Woolen and Worsted Industries_,
London, A. & C. Black, Ltd., 1921, pp. 27-31.

[5]_Ibid._, p. 32.

[6]Consitt, Frances, _The London Weavers' Company_, Oxford, Clarendon
Press, 1933, I, 83-84.

Accompanying this statement was a schedule of charges which were to
be paid to master weavers and journeymen.  A careful interpretation of
this quotation indicates that the estimate of labor charges, one of the
components of the finished product, was based upon the cost of living
and the tax levy upon the class of labor under consideration.

> In the second year of Elizabeth's reign an ingenious Venetian
> exhibited before the Court of the Clothworkers a certain gin
> devised for the rowing (shearing) of broad cloths, and offered
> to teach the company his feat of workmanship, on condition
> they would provide him his necessaries.  Whereupon the master
> and wardens called the most expert men of the company and
> showed them the device, and gave them time to advise them;
> who, after deliberate advice taken thought it would be a great
> decay unto the company.[7]

In ascertaining the utility of this mechanical device, the committee of experts probably estimated the current investment in equipment
that would have to be discarded under a new system of production, the
cost of operation under the method in use, and the economic position of
the members of the Clothworkers Guild as well as the effect of the introduction of this new process upon the industry.  After whatever forecasting procedures that may have been available at the time had been
employed, the experts rejected the device and the inventor went his own
way.

> The Pewterers' Court in 1583 thought good to choose twelve,
> i.e., four of the assistants, four of the clothing and four
> of the yeomanry "to sit and determine as well the prices of

---

[7]Unwin, George, The Guilds and Companies of London, London, Methuen
& Co., Ltd., 1925, p. 222.

wares as also any other matter which they shall find necessary and good for the company."[8]

In performing its various functions, it is highly possible that this committee sought and obtained data from the members of this Craft Guild and, upon the basis of this information, prepared its estimates for the purpose of fixing prices and forming other decisions concerning the affairs of this guild.

However, the principle of the guild system was preserved only so long as the members of the guild remained independent capitalists, approximately equal in wealth and social standing. As some craftsmen became more successful and amassed more capital than others, it was only natural that they sought opportunity for investment which could not be found in the old system. These individuals sought a stable supply of raw materials and a market for their finished products. The rise of this capitalist-merchant-craftsman-employer marks the beginning of the downfall of the guild system.

The guild system gradually merged into the domestic system by an easy and natural process of evolution as the craftsman, while still a guild artisan in the sense that he processed his own materials, came to accept work from customers who paid a fee or wage to have their products completed in accordance with their own instructions.[9]

In the beginning, this "outwork"--orders accepted from customers--

-----

[8]Ibid., p. 223.

[9]Lipson, op. cit., p. 36.

might have been considered as a by-product or a supplement to the operations under the guild system.  Although the guilds, in attempting to check this method of production, came to forbid journeymen from taking work home or from producing for more than one master, eventually the domestic system prevailed and "outwork" became the predominant--although never the sole--form of capitalistic industrial organization in Great Britain.[10]

Under the pure domestic system, the merchant, customer, or enterpriser furnished the raw materials--and sometimes the machines upon which they were processed as well--while the artisan supplied the labor for the manufacture of the products.  Thus there was introduced the capitalistic or industrial system of production whereby the merchant or enterpriser assumed the risk of production when he purchased raw materials and contracted with the artisans to fashion them according to order.[11]

Under the capitalistic phase of the domestic system, a form of estimate was employed.  As the artisan carried the raw material or semi-processed commodity from the merchant's or enterpriser's warehouse, a careful check was made on the quantity delivered.  Specifications for production were given to the workman and both the owner of the materials and the producer understood the amount of finished product that should

---

[10] Clapham, J. H., _An Economic History of Modern Britain_, Cambridge, Cambridge University Press, 1930, pp. 178-180.

[11] Milner, Frederic, _Economic Evolution in England_, London, Macmillan and Company, Ltd., 1931, pp. 210-222.

be returned and the wages of production that should be paid.  Thus the
enterpriser was able to determine from week to week not only the quantity of finished products that he would be able to offer the trade but
also the cost per unit of such products.

Wells, in describing the "Capitalistic Domestic System" in the
British hosiery trade, suggests the procedure for issuing the materials
and machines in this particular industry:

> The worsted for the week is given out by the hosier, who lets
> frames and employs, every Monday morning.  Stockingers go for
> it about eleven and get home about twelve or one, then some
> has to be damped and wound.  They begin work about two on
> Monday and finish at two on Saturday to take the work back to
> the hosier.  It must be in by four; sometimes they have to
> wait till six as all the work is weighed.[12]

In view of the fact that embezzlement of materials was one of the
great faults of the domestic system, the enterpriser ordinarily employed
some method of estimates to determine the amount of product that should
be returned.  In this particular trade, the finished products were all
weighed and the weights were compared with the schedule of predetermined
amounts of finished products that should be returned.

Evelyn Gibson Nelson, in describing the "Putting-Out System"--
another term for "outwork"--has suggested the use of the cost estimate:

> Each Saturday the workman would bring his finished stock of
> knitted goods to the hosier's warehouse, . . . where it was
> carefully and critically inspected by the hosier or his

---

[12] Wells, F. A., _The British Hosiery Trade_, London, George Allen &
Unwin, Ltd., 1935, p. 71.

trusted clerk.  Deductions were made for any kind of defect
in texture or cleanliness before payment was made on the
basis of the wage-scale which the hosier kept posted outside
of his warehouse.  After all the financial arrangements had
been completed, the stockinger then received his orders for
the next week's or fortnight's work.  These were very specific concerning the number of threads to be used, the gauge
of knitting, size, fashioning, and decorations, if any.  The
raw material for filling this order was then exactly weighed
out and a slight amount allowed for unavoidable wastage.
This thread or yarn, with any other frame-parts for repair or
for modification of the looping, were then taken off by the
stockinger to his cottage in the country where actual manufacture of the completed article was carried on.[13]

Ronald S. Edwards has reproduced some of the accounting records as

prepared by Wardhaugh Thompson, "many years an Accomptant in London," in

his 1777 publication, The Accomptants' Oracle.  The example submitted

was a "thread-hosiery" manufacture and depicted pages from a spinners'

book and a weavers' book, which were required to relieve the ledger of

the great amount of detail which would appear if each spinner and weaver

had had a separate account.  Edwards observed that Thompson was dealing

with the domestic system and that he was assuming that the spinners and

weavers brought in their work weekly.  The journal entries indicate that

the spinners' accounts were charged with the cost of the flax delivered

to them and were relieved of this cost when the yarn was returned.[14]

Although no detailed system of estimates is recorded, the implication of

----

[13]Nelson, Evelyn Gibson, "The Putting-Out System in the English
Framework-Knitting Industry," The Journal of Economic and Business History, II (1930), 470-471.

[14]Edwards, Ronald S., "Some Notes on the Early Literature and Development of Cost Accounting in Great Britain," The Accountant, XCVII
(August 14, 1937), 228-230.

a simple predetermination of manufacture is suggested and additional

credence is given to Miss Nelson's findings.

Just as the guilds were displaced by the domestic system--the pre-

vailing economic system from the sixteenth until the close of the

eighteenth century--so was this productive scheme superseded by the fac-

tory system, a system involving the substitution of power-driven machin-

ery for simple hand tools and the housing of these machines in factories

rather than in the homes of the workers, as the changes associated with

the industrial revolution came into operation. Again the successful

merchant-capitalists had an opportunity to become the industrial leaders

because they had the capital and credit with which to build the facto-

ries, install the new machines, buy the raw materials, advance the wages

to workers, and hold the finished goods until a favorable market could

be found.

However, this transformation was a gradual process and the early

developmental stages of the factory system were contemporary with the

decadent stages of the domestic system. The first undertaking worthy of

the name factory was a silk mill, which was begun in 1715 by John Lombe.

Lombe went to Italy, gained employment in the silk mills, prepared draw-

ings of the Italian machinery, smuggled these to England, and returned

to his homeland to establish a silk industry there. Cooke-Taylor de-

clared that this undertaking was "without doubt the first English fac-

tory in the modern sense. It was the first, that is, where the motive

power was supplied from outside, where operations of manufacture, hither-

to performed by human hands, were performed by inanimate machinery thus set in motion, and where work-people congregated in one building, were

occupied about this machinery."[15]

However, the transition really was initiated after 1760 and was

witnessed first in the textile industry with Hartgraves' spinning jenny

(1767), Arkwright's "water-frame" (1769), Crompton's spinning mule (1779),

and Cartwright's power loom (1787).[16]  With the application of Watt's

steam engine to the driving of the new textile machines about 1785, the

manufacturing of cloth on a large scale really began.  Although these

initial steps were all taken in England, the first factory in which all

of the manufacturing processes were carried on by power in one establish-

ment was at Waltham, Massachusetts, in 1814.[17]

During the period under consideration, the business enterprises

were relatively small and the demands for records of operation were

rather insignificant.  However, the progress of the textile industry was

marked by an English writer employing a phase of it as an illustration

for the first "Manufacturer's Books" in England.  F. W. Cronhelm pre-

sented _Double Entry by Single_ in 1818 and therein exhibited, as Set III,

the books of John Henderson, woolen manufacturer at Leeds, for the month

-----

[15] Cooke-Taylor, R. W., _The Factory System_, London, Methuen and
Company, 1912, pp. 21-25.

[16] Kydd, Samuel, _The History of the Factory Movement_, London, Simpkin, Marshall and Company, 1857, pp. 7-19.

[17] _Encyclopaedia of the Social Sciences_, New York, The Macmillan
Company, 1931, VI, 52-53.

of March, 1817.[18]

Although Cronhelm displayed a satisfactory understanding of the essential elements of double entry in his other illustrations, it is somewhat disappointing to find his "Manufacturer's Books" to be of such an inferior grade. The manufacturing records were built around the "Merchandise Book"[19]--a book in which purchases and other charges were entered on the debit side and were offset by contra entries in the cash book or in ledger accounts for creditors and in which sales and other income items were recorded on the credit side and were posted contra to cash book or personal accounts of debtors in the ledger.

By recording the inventory of goods and materials on hand at the beginning of the period as well as all costs--purchased materials, salaries, taxes, stamps and stationery, bankers' charges, carriage, millwrights' work, coal, dyeing for the month--on the debit side and by entering the final inventory as well as the sales, consignments and discount income on the credit side, he produced a book which contained a remainder that represented the profit or loss for the period. This item was entered contra on the profit or the loss account, depending upon its nature, and was finally recorded in the proprietor's "Stock" (capital account).

Although the financial phase of the "Manufacturer's Books" was

---

[18] Cronhelm, F. W., Double Entry by Single (A New Method of Bookkeeping, Applicable to All Kinds of Business; and Exemplified in Five Sets of Books), London, Longman, Hurst, Rees, Orme, and Brown, 1818, pp. 125-164.

[19] Ibid., pp. 136-145.

nothing more than the application of the mercantile procedure to cost

data and failed to provide an analysis of costs by processes or by

orders of goods, Cronhelm did devise a method of accounting for quanti-

ties that is of particular interest to this study.

> It is a common prejudice that, from the very nature of his
> business, and the numerous processes through which his goods
> pass, the Manufacturer is unable to keep his accounts on the
> same systematic principles as those of the Wholesale Dealer or
> the Merchant. The difficulty, however, applies solely to the
> Quantities of goods, and in respect to the Accounts, which in
> all businesses are composed of expenditures and returns, re-
> ceipts and payments. These particulars the Manufacturer can
> ascertain as easily as the Merchant; and, therefore, he may
> with equal facility systematize his accounts.[20]

Recognizing the danger of embezzlement of goods in the warehouse

and the difficulty of proving the quantity of materials, Cronhelm pro-

posed that three accounts--"An Account of the Raw Materials, An Account

of the Goods in Process of Manufacture, and An Account of the Manufac-

tured Goods"--"be kept either in one Book or in separate Books, accord-

ing to the system of Manufactory, and the number of overlookers em-

ployed."[21]

The Account of Raw Materials (the Wool Book), which has been repro-

duced herein, was debited, in quantities and by grades of wool, for all

purchases and was credited "with all applications to the Manufactory."

The balance of this account showed the quantity of unused materials on

hand. A careful consideration of this account will suggest its

---

[20]Ibid., p. 125.

[21]Ibid., p. 45.

application as a model for the present store's account.

WAREHOUSE LEDGER[22]

Dr.          Wool*

| | | Total | | | A | | | D | | |
|---|---|---|---|---|---|---|---|---|---|---|
| | Purchases | Pks. | Sc. | Lb. | Pks. | Sc. | Lb. | Pks. | Sc. | Lb. |
| 1817 | | | | | | | | | | |
| Feb. 28 | To Balance | 81 | 2 | 9 | 22 | 8 | 15 | 15 | 6 | 8 |
| Mch. 3 | To S. Marsh | 19 | 5 | 2 | | | | 6 | 0 | 18 |
| 5 | To Welch & Co. | 13 | 5 | 12 | 13 | 5 | 12 | | | |
| 7 | To T. Bruce | 17 | 1 | 7 | | | | | | |
| 10 | To Gill & Co. | 22 | 7 | 8 | | | | 9 | 0 | 15 |
| 11 | To D. Carew | 22 | 7 | 5 | | | | | | |
| 12 | To Holt & Co. | 13 | 6 | 17 | 13 | 6 | 17 | | | |
| | | 190 | 0 | 0 | 49 | 9 | 4 | 30 | 8 | 1 |
| Mch. 31 | To Balance | 53 | 4 | 11 | 12 | 7 | 10 | 8 | 8 | 11 |

(1)          Per Contra*

| | | Total | | | A | | | D | | | For | |
|---|---|---|---|---|---|---|---|---|---|---|---|---|
| | Applications | Pks. | Sc. | Lb. | Pks. | Sc. | Lb. | Pks. | Sc. | Lb. | Pieces | Numbers |
| 1817 | | | | | | | | | | | | |
| Mch. 8 | By Manufac-tory | 35 | 2 | 15 | 9 | 3 | 7 | 5 | 3 | 16 | 170 | 1,802 to 1,971 |
| 15 | By Ditto | 33 | 2 | 5 | 9 | 10 | 13 | 5 | 1 | 12 | 172 | 1,972 to 2,143 |
| 22 | By Ditto | 33 | 6 | 16 | 8 | 2 | 10 | 5 | 7 | 8 | 167 | 2,144 to 2,310 |
| 29 | By Ditto | 33 | 7 | 3 | 9 | 5 | 0 | 5 | 9 | 5 | 163 | 2,311 to 2,473 |
| | | 135 | 6 | 19 | 36 | 9 | 10 | 21 | 10 | 1 | 672 | |
| 31 | By Waste | 1 | 0 | 10 | | 4 | 4 | | 1 | 9 | | |
| 31 | By Balance | 53 | 4 | 11 | 12 | 7 | 10 | 8 | 8 | 11 | | |
| | | 190 | 0 | 0 | 49 | 9 | 4 | 30 | 8 | 1 | | |

*Commodities "B" and "C" have been omitted for brevity.

The Account of Goods in process deserves the major attention in this study of the evolution of cost estimates. This account, which has been presented also, was debited, according to the following procedure,

---

[22] *Ibid.*, pp. 130-131.

with the raw material as it was put in process:

> . . . not, however, in the quantity of that material, but in
> the quantity of manufactures which it ought to produce, ac-
> cording to those rules and proportions which are established
> in all regular and well managed concerns.  This account being
> credited with all manufactured goods, its Balance shows the
> quantity of goods in process of manufacture.[23]

MANUFACTORY[24]

Dr.

| 1817 | Applications | Total Pieces | Cloths | | | | Casimirs | | | | Numbers |
|---|---|---|---|---|---|---|---|---|---|---|---|
| | | | A | B | C | D | L | M | N | O | |
| Feb. 28 | To Balance in process | 477 | 78 | 102 | 60 | 51 | 39 | 87 | 39 | 21 | |
| Mch. 8 | To Wool | 170 | 28 | 36 | 24 | 16 | 16 | 24 | 16 | 10 | 1,802 to 1,971 |
| 15 | To Wool | 172 | 32 | 32 | 18 | 14 | 20 | 28 | 16 | 12 | 1,972 to 2,143 |
| 22 | To Wool | 167 | 27 | 35 | 21 | 18 | 14 | 30 | 14 | 8 | 2,144 to 2,310 |
| 29 | To Wool | 163 | 30 | 38 | 22 | 17 | 12 | 20 | 12 | 12 | 2,311 to 2,473 |
| | | 1149 | 195 | 243 | 145 | 116 | 101 | 189 | 97 | 63 | |
| Mch. 31 | To Balance in process | 459 | 86 | 95 | 52 | 48 | 39 | 85 | 34 | 20 | |

(2)                     Per Contra

| 1817 | Manufactures | Total Pieces | Cloths | | | | Casimirs | | | |
|---|---|---|---|---|---|---|---|---|---|---|
| | | | A | B | C | D | L | M | N | O |
| Mch. 8 | By Merchandise | 183 | 32 | 38 | 26 | 18 | 14 | 26 | 17 | 12 |
| 15 | By Merchandise | 165 | 25 | 34 | 22 | 17 | 15 | 31 | 13 | 8 |
| 22 | By Merchandise | 174 | 28 | 38 | 25 | 15 | 17 | 23 | 18 | 10 |
| 29 | By Merchandise | 168 | 24 | 38 | 20 | 18 | 16 | 24 | 15 | 13 |
| | | 690 | 109 | 148 | 93 | 68 | 62 | 104 | 63 | 43 |
| 31 | By Balance in process | 459 | 86 | 95 | 52 | 48 | 39 | 85 | 34 | 20 |
| | | 1149 | 195 | 243 | 145 | 116 | 101 | 189 | 97 | 63 |

The author was quite convinced of the practical value of his

---

[23] Ibid., p. 45.

[24] Ibid., pp. 132-133.

procedure for the purpose of ascertaining discrepancies.

> In an extensive Manufactory, the very difficulty of checking the goods renders it but the more desirable; for they undergo so many transformations, and lie scattered in such a variety of states, that the Proprietor is ever exposed to accidental, as well as fraudulent, losses. In the following example of the Warehouse Ledger, its jurisdiction will be found so comprehensive, that no deficiency of any magnitude in the raw material, nor the deficiency of a single piece after being once put in process, can possibly occur undetected, unless the entries be designedly falsified.[25]

Although Cronhelm did not devise a system of cost accounting, he did suggest an estimating scheme that might be employed to determine the number of pieces of cloth which the quantity of wool put into process should produce. That this estimate was based upon more than mere guesswork is intimated by the assertion, "according to those rules and proportions which are established in all regular and well managed concerns." Cronhelm's procedure may be recognized as an early application of one phase of the cost estimate to a process cost industry.

In addition to the development of the textile industry, the evolution of progress in iron and steel manufacture deserves consideration as a means of establishing a background for modern industry and cost literature. Fleming and Brocklehurst[26] declared that, although improvements were made from time to time, the modern iron industry may be considered to have commenced with the enterprises of the Darby family and the

---

[25] _Ibid._, pp. 125-126.

[26] Fleming, A. P. M., and Brocklehurst, H. J., _A History of Engineering_, London, A. & C. Black, Ltd., 1925, pp. 171-204.

successful and continued use of coal as a fuel by this group.  Abraham

Darby I, the founder, and one assistant developed the process one night

and "the process they had evolved was practiced in the works owned by

the Darby family in secret, behind locked doors, for over 100 years."[27]

In view of the fact that the elder Darby took out a patent for "Casting

Iron-bellied Pots" in April, 1707, leased two furnaces and forges at

Coalbrookdale in 1708, and sold pig iron, pots, kettles and other iron

wares in sizable quantities, according to the Journal of Abraham Darby

for 1708 and 1709, it may be assumed that the coke-smelting of iron was

established on a commercial scale as early as 1709.[28]

Another discovery of importance to the development of the iron and

steel industry was the method of producing steel by the crucible process.

Benjamin Huntsman devised this procedure in 1740 and opened a works,

which was maintained in strictest secrecy, to exploit his process.[29]

However, knowledge of his methodology passed to other manufacturers and,

by 1787, there were twenty firms described in the Sheffield Directory as

Steel Converters and Refiners.  Seven of these enterprises used the

crucible process.[30]

During the eighteenth century, this industry was under the control

of small operators of the Darby and Huntsman type.  An index of the

---

[27]Ibid., p. 175.

[28]Ashton, Thomas Southcliffe, Iron and Steel in the Industrial Revolution, Manchester, University of Manchester Press, 1924, pp. 24-31.

[29]Fleming and Brocklehurst, op. cit., p. 177.

[30]Ashton, op. cit., p. 57.

industry's magnitude at the close of the century is suggested by the
production of 68,000 tons of pig iron in Great Britain by eighty-five
furnaces during 1788.  After the middle of the century, there was some
evidence of organized efforts to control prices.  In 1762, Abraham
Darby II and Isaac and John Wilkinson entered into an agreement whereby
their companies--Coalbrookdale, Willey and Bersham--were to charge uniform prices for their products.  By 1777, an organization, which regu-
lated the iron trade until well into the nineteenth century, was determining prices and conditions of sales and was participating in the
discussion of political questions.[31]

> To the British ironmaster the situation must, indeed, have
> appeared far from displeasing.  Pitt's attempt to find a new
> source of revenue for a straitened exchequer by imposing a tax
> on pig iron had failed; and the only result of the proposal
> had been an increase in the import duty imposed on foreign
> iron, while the English ironmasters, thanks to their capacity
> for organized propaganda, had escaped untouched.[32]

Ashton suggests two reasons for the apparent success of such organizations:  first, that the most successful and progressive group of such
ironmasters was that of Quakers; and, second, that matrimonial alliances
were practiced among ironmasters' families.  (He used the Darby family
as an illustration of both of these factors.)[33]

> It will suffice to say that a close study of such pedigrees
> helps to explain the longevity of the iron concerns owned by

---

[31] Ibid., p. 164.

[32] Ibid., p. 145.

[33] Ibid., pp. 208-232.

the Quakers, and perhaps to some extent also the relative ease
with which trading agreements and price associations were effected in this industry.[34]

Although Ashton was not interested in the bookkeeping procedure of

the iron industry, he presented several extracts from the Darby book

that indicated the use of a simple journal or daybook for recording ex-

penditures in chronological order.

|  |  |  |  | £ | s. | d. |
|---|---|---|---|---|---|---|
| 1709 | June 4 | By Cash pd. for 8 horsloads of lime | | 00 | 06 | 08 |
| | Aug. 24 | By Cash pd. Mary Cope for Laying and drawing Lime | | 00 | 06 | 07 |
| | Oct. 18 | Henry ffox for Getting Limestone | | 2 | 00 | 00[35] |

There is some evidence in Ashton's publication to suggest that the trade

prices were roughly determined from the available costs plus a rather

sizable amount of profit.  That the domestic producers operated in a

sellers' market is evidenced by the fact that import duties on bar iron

ranged from £2.1s.6d. per ton in 1695 to £3.15s.5d. in 1796.[36]  Since

Great Britain absorbed all the iron products that the industry made and

imported additional amounts, these producers found a ready market for

their maximum production at their trade prices and, therefore, experi-

enced little need for detailed cost statistics and estimates during the

eighteenth century.[37]

---

[34] Ibid., p. 217.

[35] Ibid., p. 31.

[36] Ibid., pp. 105, 145.

[37] Ibid., pp. 104-159.

Advancing into the nineteenth century, the influence of the industrial revolution became evident in the iron and steel industry--coke was applied to the manufacturing processes and water power was displaced by the steam engine. As the tendencies of the eighteenth century, which had kept the industrial enterprises small and scattered, were removed, there developed the typical concern of the new era--an integrated unit which mined ore and coal and which smelted, refined and rolled iron into its finished forms of plates and rods. In 1812, a typical Birmingham ironworks required an investment of £50,000 and employed three hundred men while, by 1833, a manufacturing plant with a productive capacity of three hundred tons of bar iron per week represented an expenditure of from £50,000 to £150,000.[38]

The war period, 1793-1815, had witnessed the establishment of vast productive capacity in the British iron industry--a capacity which greatly exceeded the peacetime needs of the country. Ashton has described the next seven years (1816-1823) as a period in which ironworks were closed and liquidated under ruinous conditions to both owners and workers. There followed three years of improvement with subsequent collapse and stagnation during the latter years of this decade.[39]

These cyclical fluctuations prompted an analysis of the iron and steel industry. It was reported that in 1833 about one-fourth of the cost of bar iron consisted of royalties on raw materials and interest on capital invested in the plant. The operators of the period realized the

---

[38]Ibid., pp. 95-103, 163.

[39]Ibid., pp. 142-156.

financial danger of withdrawing from the industry during a depression,
when the plant would realize little from a forced sale, as well as the
cost of ceasing operation even for a short period of time.

> In time of bad trade, works were continued so long as the
> selling price of the iron would cover even a little more than
> the prime costs of production--raw material and labour.[40]

By this time, the iron and steel industry in Great Britain had
passed the stage in which one man could supervise all the activities of
a production unit, had reached the capacity to supply the country's demand, and had realized the importance of production costs, particularly
during a period of depression.

As an indication of the status of cost accounting procedure at this
time, the publication of Frederick Charles Krepp, _Statistical Book-
keeping_, of 1858 is cited. This author--after "fifteen years' personal
observation and practical experience in English, American, and German
Counting Houses"--presented a book containing a Simple System, a Com-
pound System, Auxiliary Statistics, and seven Special Systems. Under
the classification Special Systems, he included seven pages as a description of an adequate Manufacturers' System.[41]

The author prefaced his Manufacturers' System with the statement
that "The Manufacturers' System, in its main features, is identical with
that drawn up for Tradesmen, except for more extensive Manufacturers,

---

[40] _Ibid._, p. 164.

[41] Krepp, Frederick Charles, _Statistical Book-keeping_, London, Longman, Brown, Green, Longmans, and Roberts, 1858, pp. 151-158.

who will probably find it to their advantage to follow the Merchants'
System."

Krepp provided for recording the purchase of raw materials, for "an
exact estimate of the actual value of the Stock" at the end of the period,
and for the "Manufacturers' Central Statistics"--Raw Materials, Produce,
Settlement (Purchases with balances owed to sellers and Sales with balances due from buyers), Expenditure, Loss, Assets, Net Profit, and Private Expenditure.  However, he failed to undertake any method of ascertaining cost of production.

The writer employed a rather simple method of recording market
fluctuations of raw materials, which he commended in the following
manner:

> An occasional study of the fluctuations of the Market, as
> clearly exhibited by these Statistics, will sometimes enable
> a Merchant to make a shrewd, and perhaps, very profitable
> guess into the future, which otherwise might have escaped his
> attention.[42]

As a device for assisting the manufacturer in his estimating procedure,
this statistical technique represents the primary contribution of Krepp.

THE COST ESTIMATE IN NINETEENTH-CENTURY ENGINEERING PROCEDURE.--
Knowles has pointed out that the Industrial Revolution involved six
great interdependent developments:  the application of mechanical devices to textile processing; the improvements in iron-making; the expansion of coal mining; the creation of the great chemical industry; the

_______________

[42]Ibid., pp. 128-129, 159.

improvement of transportation facilities; and the formation of engineering.[43]

While the textile and metallurgical industries were being trans-
formed, engineering was being made possible.  Allen has very aptly summarized the evolution of engineering in England:

> Engineering can scarcely be regarded as a single industry.  It
> consists rather of a group of separate trades which differ
> from one another in age and origin.  Reference to a few of
> them will bring out their diversities.  The manufacture of
> stationary steam-engines may be regarded as having achieved
> the status of an industry during the last quarter of the
> eighteenth century, and its expansion followed on the adoption
> of steam-power by a succession of trades.  Textile machinery
> began to be produced by specialists firms in the first quarter
> of the nineteenth century.  The industries producing locomo-
> tives, rolling stock and other railway equipment appeared with
> the advent of railways in the thirties.  The construction of
> steamships and of marine engines became a large branch of en-
> gineering after 1850.  The last quarter of the nineteenth cen-
> tury saw the creation of many new branches.  The expansion of
> machine-tool production led to the appearance of several dis-
> tinct trades, and the adoption of mechanical methods of pro-
> duction by a number of small metal industries which had hither-
> to been handicrafts brought many of them within the sphere of
> engineering.  The production of gas engines in substantial
> quantities began in the seventies.  The cycle trade and elec-
> trical engineering became important in the eighties.  The
> motor industry appeared in the late nineties.[44]

Allen stated that there was no place for the engineer prior to
1760,[45] whereas Clapham declared that "the material" for engineering

---

[43] Knowles, L. C. A., The Industrial and Commercial Revolution in
Great Britain During the Nineteenth Century, London, George Routledge
and Sons, Ltd., 1930, pp. 20-25.

[44] Allen, G. C., British Industries and Their Organization, London,
Longmans, Green and Company, 1933, pp. 134-135.

[45] Ibid., p. 134.

"was assured in abundance by 1815."[46] During the developmental period--while the industrial technique was simple and the size of the enterprise was small--there was little difficulty experienced in recording transactions involved with the purchase of raw materials, the hiring of a few workers, and the handling of small workshop expenses. However, with the development of textile processing, iron manufacturing, coal mining, and engineering, industrial problems for both the engineer and the accountant came into existence rather rapidly.

Charles Babbage, an English engineer and mathematician, seemed to have gained a keen insight into industrial problems rather early and to have presented his impressions in a pioneer work, On the Economy of Machinery and Manufactures, in 1832. A later edition,[47] which has been used in this study, contains the following problems that are of interest to this study: advantages from the use of machinery in manufacture, together with the mechanical aspects involved in the control, regulation, and application of power; the registering of operations; methods of observing manufacturing processes and forms for recording the investigator's findings (a forerunner of time studies); the importance of considering the fluctuations of prices as measured by money in making comparisons at different times; and the advantages of determining the separate costs of each process in a manufacturing enterprise.

Babbage employed the manufacture of pins as an example and

---

[46] Clapham, op. cit., p. 151.

[47] Babbage, Charles, On the Economy of Machinery and Manufactures, London, Charles Knight and Company, 1841.

ascertained not only the time and cost required for the making of one
pound of pins but also the workmen's earnings per day and the cost of
making each part of a single pin.  These calculations, which have been
reproduced,[48] suggest a device that might have been employed for ascertaining either the cost of future production or the efficiency of labor
in this particular enterprise.

ENGLISH MANUFACTURE

| Name of the Process | Workmen | Time for making 1 lb. of Pins | Cost of making 1 lb. of Pins | Work-man earns per Day | Price of making each Part of a single Pin, in Millionths of a Penny |
|---|---|---|---|---|---|
| | | Hours | Pence | s.  d. | |
| 1. Drawing Wire (#224) | Man | .3636 | 1.2500 | 3  3 | 225 |
| 2. Straightening Wire (#225) | Woman | .3000 | .2840 | 1  0 | 51 |
| | Girl | .3000 | .1420 | 0  6 | 26 |
| 3. Pointing (#226) | Man | .3000 | 1.7750 | 5  3 | 319 |
| 4. Twisting and Cutting Heads (#227) | Boy | .0400 | .0147 | 0  $4\frac{1}{2}$ | 3 |
| | Man | .0400 | .2103 | 5  $4\frac{1}{2}$ | 38 |
| 5. Heading (#228) | Woman | 4.0000 | 5.0000 | 1  3 | 901 |
| 6. Tinning, or Whitening (#229) | Man | .1071 | .6666 | 6  0 | 121 |
| | Woman | .1071 | .3333 | 3  0 | 60 |
| 7. Papering (#230) | Woman | 2.1314 | 3.1973 | 1  6 | 576 |
| | | 7.6892 | 12.8732 | | 2320 |

Number of persons employed:--Men, 4; Woman, 4; Children, 2;
Total, 10.


The author not only anticipated the idea of efficiency but also the

---

[48] *Ibid.*, p. 184.

principle of depreciation, as may be substantiated by the following

quotation:

> The great competition introduced by machinery, and the appli-
> cation of the principle of the subdivision of labour, render
> it necessary for each producer to be continually on the watch,
> to discover improved methods by which the cost of the article
> he manufactures may be reduced; and, with this view, it is of
> great importance to know the precise expense of every process,
> as well as of the wear and tear of machinery which is due to
> it.[49]

Diemer pointed out that this work was a most remarkable production,

especially in view of the fact that it was written so soon after the

establishment of the factory system in England:

> . . . and the fact that nothing more was produced upon the
> subject for more than fifty years indicates the extent to
> which the ideas of Babbage was in advance of those of his con-
> temporaries.[50]

Church also found Babbage's publication to be significant to his

study of overhead distribution. The early writer, according to Church,

had recognized the importance of competition introduced by machinery and

of the application of the principle of the division of labor as well as

the necessity for improved methods in manufacture, for means of deter-

mining the cost of each process, and for a method of ascertaining the

wear and tear of machinery due thereto. In pointing out that this was

probably the earliest reference by any writer either to costs or to

---

[49]Ibid., p. 203.

[50]Diemer, Hugo, Factory Organization and Administration, New York,
McGraw-Hill Book Company, 1910, p. 289.

establishment charges (burden), Church shared with Diemer the conception

of Babbage's pioneer efforts and of the scarcity of cost literature for

a relatively long period of time.

> Yet notwithstanding that the importance of such matters was
> realized by Babbage so early in the development of manufactur-
> ing industries, the lesson for various reasons fell upon deaf
> ears, and it is only today, when the principle of competition
> has attained its full growth, that the commercial organization
> of manufactories is felt to have a matter of prime urgency.[51]

During this time, the engineer was called upon not only to prepare

drawings and specifications for the multitudinous machinery that was

being constructed but also to assist in determining estimates of costs

of such equipment.  Although Edwards believed that the engineering

trades should have been the principal fields for cost accounting prob-

lems because of the importance of estimating and tendering for contracts,

yet he found little literature during this particular period (1820-1885).

He proposed two explanations for this condition.[52]  In the first place,

he found a British tradition which indicated that as little information

should be disclosed as possible in order to hinder competition.  Apply-

ing this attitude to cost accounting, the manufacturer developing satis-

factory methods was under no obligation to act as a benefactor to the

remainder of the business world by disclosing these processes.  From

another standpoint, business was so satisfactory in general during the

---

[51] Church, A. Hamilton, "The Proper Distribution of Establishment
Charges," _The Engineering Magazine_, XXI (1901), 508-509.

[52] Edwards, _op. cit._, p. 283.

first seventy-five years of the nineteenth century that manufacturers
paid little attention to cost methods and information.  "While the demand for machinery was great and the supply of engineers limited, there
was no pressing for economy, but in the course of time brains and capital were attracted, and competition became keener."

An index of the relative accuracy of engineers' estimates during
the nineteenth century is suggested by Edwards' quotation from a leading
article in The Engineer of 1869:

> ". . . right within 20 per cent. of the actual cost, is, how-
> ever, regarded as a very good estimate, and one reflecting
> much credit on the engineer and all concerned."  There is no
> good treatise on the subject. . . ."[53]

For the American engineer's technique of this period, the following
data have been reproduced, in a somewhat simplified form, from an analysis of the cost of producing one ton of iron ore in the Marquette Iron
Region, Lake Superior, Michigan, in 1874.[54]

---

[53] Ibid., p. 283.

[54] Brooks, Major T. E., "An Analysis of the Cost and Description of
the Methods of Mining Employed in the Marquette Iron Region, Lake
Superior, Michigan," Transactions, American Society of Civil Engineers,
II (1874), 15-32.

| General Heads Under which Cost of Mining is Classified | Elements of Cost, not Including Royalty or Depreciation | Approximate Cost of Each Item* | | | |
|---|---|---|---|---|---|
| | | Per Cent | Total | Labor | Supplies |
| I. Dead Work (Preparation) | Explorations, sinking shafts, drifts and tunnels, roads, &. | .281 | $ .742 | $ .620 | $ .122 |
| II. Mining Proper (Labor) | Drilling and other work | .398 | 1.050 | 1.050 | |
| III. Mining Materials and Implements ("Mine Costs") | Explosives, tools, and repairs | .119 | .313 | .103 | .210 |
| IV. Handling Ore from Miners' Hands to Cars, and Pumping | By horses, men, and steam | .156 | .413 | .272 | .141 |
| V. Management and General Expenses | Salaries, office expenses and taxes | .046 | .122 | .062 | .060 |
| | | 1.000 | $2.640 | $2.107 | $0.533 |

*Based on total cost of $2.64 per ton.

The writer stated that the approximate total cost of $2.64 was determined by dividing the total expenditures at the mine for the year by the number of tons of ore produced. The mining processes were divided into five divisions, which, in turn, were subdivided into as many elements of costs as were deemed necessary. Percentages were then ascertained for each of these classifications and were applied to the total unit cost for analysis purposes--for instance, Exploration was given a per cent of .006 and a total cost of $0.015 per ton while Powder and Fuse received a per cent of .036 and a cost of $0.095.

As a measure of efficiency, Brooks compared some of his costs with like figures for mines in New Jersey, New York, and Sweden. (Figures are costs per ton.)

| Type of Cost | Marquette | New Jersey | New York | Sweden |
|---|---|---|---|---|
| Total Cost | $2.64 | | $3.12 | $2.20 |
| Drilling | 1.05 | $0.60-$0.80 | 1.25 | .40 |
| Salaries, Office Expenses and Taxes | .122 | | | .36 |

Although the total cost per ton ($2.64) might be considered as an example of historical costs, the application of the percentages for sub-division rates represents an instance of estimating cost procedure.

Somewhat later (1878), Thomas Battersby, a public accountant of Manchester, England, published a treatise on bookkeeping, The Perfect Double Entry Bookkeeper and the Perfect Prime Cost and Profit Demonstrator (on the Departmental System) for Iron and Brass Founders, Machinists, Engineers, Shipbuilders, Manufacturers, &c., and, according to Edwards, enumerated therein some of the techniques that were practiced at the time. In order that additional evidence may be presented with respect to the rather crude methods that were employed by engineers during this time, the portions pertaining to cost estimates have been reproduced from Edwards' findings.

The workmen are rated at the actual wages paid them, and 100 per cent. is added for the use of tools and all expenses; and 25 per cent. is added on the total and materials purchased for profit, which gives the selling price.

The lathes and tools are rated at a uniform price, viz., the workman's wages plus 2s. per day for the lathe or tool; and all the workmen--pattern makers, fitters and carpenters--are rated at the wages paid them; and 25 per cent. is added on the total for indirect expenses and profit, and 25 per cent. is also added on materials purchased, which gives the selling price.

The rates for lathes and tools are fixed by the managing partner, according to the purchase price, and these rates are used as the selling prices, both for contract work and jobbing work. In fixing the rates the principal has no further data than the purchase price, and his own opinion to guide him, and he does not consider it necessary to have other than selling rates, for the simple reason that every contract is made up at these rates, and a deduction taken off the total, in estimating contract work. This deduction, no doubt, varies according to circumstances, the object being to secure the order with the least possible deductions. . . .

These various methods have been first adopted for want of a correct system; and they are continued because they are in keeping with the old styles, and are the easiest ways of arriving at general results. . . . in short, there is no true theory brought to bear upon the application of the expenses and profit, and the consequence is that whilst the nature of the work and the expenses are similar in all engineering establishments there is great variety in the methods in general use, and many of these methods do not even approach to correctness.[55]

As late as 1902, Bardsley, an Englishman, stated that, although the responsible technical manager usually established a cost system that fulfilled the requirements as he recognized them, these techniques fell short of complete efficiency because of the difficulty of verification with the financial books. He stated also that he had not seen any engineer's system which fully satisfied this prerequisite; that is, possessed the capacity of tying in with the financial records of the concern.[56]

---

[55] Edwards, op. cit., p. 285.

[56] Bardsley, John B., "Hints to Students in Devising System of Engineers' Cost Accounts," The Accountant, XXVIII (1902), 1055.

As the nineteenth century drew towards a close, production facilities tended to be able to supply the demands of purchasers. When competition became keener, the inefficiency of the current cost estimates became more apparent and several different attempts were made to improve the procedures. Some of these efforts, as revealed in cost literature, will be considered first.

Estimate Costs in Early Cost Accounting Literature.--With the publication of Factory Accounts by Garcke and Fells, two English writers, in 1887, a new era in industrial competition and in cost accounting literature may be considered to have dawned. Coincident with the development of manufacturing to this time, the cost records and cost estimates had been considered as independent and separate analyses from the commercial transactions and ordinarily had been only tested with certain data from the financial records. This situation is readily understood when a retrospective consideration of the development of double entry bookkeeping during a period of exchange--and until the nineteenth century remaining in an environment of trade--suggests the difficulty of bringing any manufacturing or non-exchange transactions into the financial records.

However, when these authors suggested that there might be a complete coördination of commercial and manufacturing records, they indicated a new trend in thought concerning the application of double entry methods:

Factory books must not, however, be considered, as is generally the case, to be merely memoranda books, which are not

necessarily required to balance.  They should so assimilate to
the books of the counting-house that the obvious advantage of
having a balance-sheet made up from the General Ledger, em-
bracing the balances of the ledgers and books kept in the
stores and warehouses, is not sacrificed.  No matter how far
the subdivision of departments of an establishment be carried,
or to whatever extent the principle of localising the bookkeeping be applied, the concentration of the accounts--the
merging of the departmental books in the General Ledger--
should be kept constantly in view.[57]

For Garcke and Fells, the cost estimate was deemed to be a neces-

sity in order to produce economy in cost of production.  Before any

order should be manufactured, they declared that the person who was best

acquainted with the details of the manufacturing process should estimate

the probable cost of materials and wages for the product under consider-

ation.[58]  However, since the authors did not suggest a system of cost

estimates for the manufacturing books, it must be supposed that such

statistical analyses were outside the manufacturing records of the con-

cern.

In describing the bookkeeping procedure, the authors made the fol-

lowing explanations with respect to the recording of completed goods.

The finished product was credited to the Prime Cost Ledger--a book which

ordinarily collected materials and wages only but which was flexible

enough to include the indirect factory expenses also--with the actual

cost except in those cases when some of the articles made under a stock

order were transferred before the order was completed.  In those

-------------------------

[57]Garcke, Emile, and Fells, J. M., *Factory Accounts*, London, Crosby
Lockwood and Son, 1893, pp. 7-8.

[58]*Ibid.*, p. 51.

instances, the prime cost clerk prepared calculations (estimates) which formed the basis for the entries in the "Stock Received Book" (in the stock warehouse) and the credits in the "Prime Cost Ledger."[59]

A review of this publication in The Accountant of 1888, as reported by Edwards, maintained that "the book was more· theoretical than practical, that it was pedantic and involved, 'in the nature of a work on political economy.'"[60] However, Factory Accounts by Garcke and Fells has come to be considered an important landmark in English cost accounting literature.

Captain Henry Metcalfe, an officer in the Ordnance Department of the United States Army, presented a treatise on the administration of public and private workshops--The Cost of Manufactures--in 1885. Although this author did not set up a system of cost estimates, he recognized the importance of this procedure by stating that "success in manufacturing depends almost entirely upon accuracy of estimate" and by pointing out that "the greater the details of past expenditures the more certainly may estimates of future cost be based on what is already known and established."[61]

This publication has not been given the same significance as that by Garcke and Fells because the author was primarily concerned with the management of a shop in a government arsenal where the problems of

------

[59] Ibid., pp. 59-74.

[60] Edwards, op. cit., p. 316.

[61] Metcalfe, Captain Henry, The Cost of Manufactures, New York, John Wiley and Sons, 1907, p. 17.

profit and loss on private investments are not involved and because he
admitted that he had not been able to present a system in which the cost
books might be reconciled with the financial records.[62]

In 1889, George P. Norton, an English practicing accountant, published the next important work on cost accounting, Textile Manufacturers'
Book-keeping. According to the author's statement in the preface to the
first edition (which was included in the fourth edition), he had attained a large audit practice among manufacturers and had served as
auditor for the Creditors' Association of Manufacturers. He declared
that, in these capacities, he had studied and devised many accounting
systems and that, in his text, he had sought to present only that which
was essential for a successful manufacturing system.

His publication followed the usual practice of the time by maintaining the manufacturing books separate and apart from the financial
records and by considering the manufacturing account as purely supplementary to the trading account.[63]

This author advocated the use of estimate costs, which were based
upon the prices that other concerns of like nature were charging for the
particular processes that might be under consideration.[64]

When discussing the procedure for a departmentalized factory,
Norton condemned the practice of charging each successive department

---

[62] Ibid., p. 289.

[63] Norton, George Pepler, Textile Manufacturers' Book-keeping, London,
Simpkin, Marshall, Hamilton, Kent and Company, Ltd., 1900, p. 219.

[64] Ibid., p. 224.

with the value of the goods transferred to it by the preceding department and proposed a satisfactory plan to be as follows:

> The foreman of each department keeps a record of work done in
> the processes under his supervision, and the profit or loss is
> ascertained by comparing in each case the value of such work
> done, when calculated at trade prices . . ., with the propor-
> tion of wages and expenses chargeable against the respective
> department.[65]

Norton was very emphatic in stating that prices of special orders
and goods manufactured for all other purposes than for stock were always
based on estimates:

> Except in the case of goods made for stock, the cost is calcu-
> lated and orders are taken long before the pieces are put into
> work. It is, however, very essential for future guidance, as
> well as for checking purposes, that the _actual_ cost should be
> calculated after the goods are made.[66]

In 1891, Child pointed out that the state of the market, and not
cost accounts and estimates, determined how much would be obtained for
manufactured goods, but he declared that cost accounts and estimates
should indicate the lowest price at which such goods could be sold without suffering a loss.[67] Thus Child recognized a third function--to
determine whether or not to manufacture a product--of estimated costs
which might be added to those of setting sales or tender prices and of

---

[65] _Ibid._, p. 220.

[66] _Ibid._, p. 254.

[67] Child, F. W., "Is the Value of Bookkeeping Appreciated," _Engi-
neering Magazine_, I (August, 1891), 601.

promoting economy or efficiency in the manufacturing process.

The Accountant of 1894 contained two rather important treatises on cost accounting:  a series of four articles by the Editor treating a system of cost accounts for general purposes, and a prize essay by a chartered accountant relating cost accounting to auditing.

After briefly reviewing the development of cost accounting to the status in which the cost records and financial books could be reconciled --the writer suggested that the two be separate in order that at periodic stock-taking, the Trading Account (financial books) and the Cost Account Summary (cost records) might form a sort of check upon any errors that may have entered into the preparation of either or both[68]-- the Editor exhibited a set of pro forma accounts, with a short explanation of each, that was applicable to disclosing the cost of manufacture in a general business.

With respect to estimated costs, the author presented a Cost of Manufacture Sheet and an Annual Working Statement, which, although ordinarily prepared annually, were equally applicable for interim statements by the use of estimated expenses rather than actual figures.[69] His Cost Book was a compilation of Tabular Ledger Sheets which contained not only the cost for each department or process of manufacturing but also accumulated the costs by classes or by qualities of goods completed or by each separate division or portion of such work.[70]

---

[68]"Cost Accounts, III," The Accountant, XX (August 11, 1894), 687.

[69]Ibid., pp. 656-657, 674.

[70]Ibid., p. 689.

For manufacturers who made their goods to put into stock awaiting sale, this section (writer's note: Section II of the Cost Book form) is to be used as a means of ascertaining the difference, from time to time, of the cost of making various classes of goods; while in trades, such as millwrights, where estimating for contractual work is very extensive, this section is arranged to show the cost of making each portion of a job separately; to be used as a means of reference to facilitate estimating, and to show fluctuations in the cost of making the same portions of work, as a guide to future costing.[71]

At the end of the year, the totals of each job were transferred to the Cost Account Summary (as herein shown),[72] which accumulated the Total Cost, the Contract Price and the Profit or Loss.

COST ACCOUNT SUMMARY
For ____ Ending ____ 189_

| Date | Name | Fo. | Cost | Manage-ment & Charges | Depre-ciation & | Departments -- -- -- | Total Cost | Contract Price | Profit | Loss |
|---|---|---|---|---|---|---|---|---|---|---|
|  |  |  |  |  |  |  |  |  |  |  |

According to the author, the difference between the totals of the Profit and Loss columns should agree with the balance of the Profit and Loss Account (financial books); however, there would usually be a difference due to clerical inaccuracies and/or the use of estimated figures for management expenses, depreciation and other cost items. A trial balance

---

[71] Ibid., p. 703.

[72] Ibid., p. 703.

(as presented below),[73] rather unique in that it contained cost figures

only in the comparative columns, was finally prepared in order that the

results from the financial records might be compared with those of the

cost books.

> The clerical differences, unless of trifling amount, should
> be sought for and eliminated; while, if the percentages of
> management expenses and depreciation, etc., have been care-
> fully fixed, the differences between the estimates and the
> actual results will not be large. . . .[74]

TRIAL BALANCE OF THE COST ACCOUNTS

For _________ 189_

| | £ s d | £ s d | | £ s d | £ s d |
|---|---|---|---|---|---|
| **Profit and Loss** | | | **Cost Accounts:** | | |
| **Account:** | | | | | |
| Sales ........ | 96 14 2 | | Total Cost (from | | |
| Less Gross | | | Summary) ........ | | 76 19 4 |
| Profit .... | 19 14 10 | 76 19 4 | Percentages charged | | |
| Management and | | | (from Summary): | | |
| Establishment | | | Management and | | |
| Expenses .... | 1 2 0 | | Establishment .. | 10 8 2 | |
| Depreciation . | 2 0 0 | | Depreciation and | | |
| Interest on | | | other charges .. | 6 0 0 | |
| Capital ..... | 5 0 0 | 8 2 0 | | 16 8 2 | |
| | | | Less (Over- | | |
| | | | estimated) ..... | 8 6 2 | 8 2 0 |
| | | £85 1 4 | | | £85 1 4 |

This comparative statement and explanation, although rather crudely

presented, represent an early recognition by the Editor of The Accountant

that the financial and manufacturing records might not disclose identical

---

[73]Ibid., p. 704.

[74]Ibid., p. 704.

results and an attempt to dispose of any difference that might exist.
George P. Norton had presented already two sets of books and separate
statements prepared from each, but his method of disclosure did not
bring to the attention of the reader the result of the comparison of the
actual and the estimated figures as in this case.

In the second significant article of 1894, R. Whitehill, the English Chartered Accountant, presented the cost accounts of an iron
founder and, in discussing the procedure that would be followed in
auditing these accounts for the purpose of preparing a balance sheet
that the auditor might sign, he also disclosed the procedure with respect to the debits and credits in these accounts.[75]

From the standpoint of the cost estimate, the "Production Account"
is quite significant in view of the fact that the products finished during the year, as well as the goods in process at the beginning and the
ending of the year, were valued for transfer and inventory purposes at
an estimated figure--fixed cost values as determined from the Cost Book,
which was "kept for the purpose of working out quotations for customers,
controlling wages, expenditures, etc."[76]

Cudworth, an English Chartered Accountant, writing in 1896, indicated the degree of dispersion in understanding of terminology when he
stated that the term "Cost Account" was wide enough to cover:

------------

[75]Whitehill, R., "Cost and Production Accounts and Their Uses for
the Purposes of an Audit," The Accountant, XX (December 15, 1894), 1097-
1113.

[76]Ibid., p. 1103.

1. A memorandum of the supposed cost of producing an article;
   or
2. An account showing the application of the estimated cost
   of producing an article to the number of articles made or
   sold during a particular period; or
3. An account showing, after stock has been taken and the
   actual profit or loss ascertained, the average cost per
   article made or sold, divided under such headings as may
   be most convenient.[77]

The writer recognized also three functions of a cost account, where
it is in the nature of an estimate:

> . . . to enable the manufacturer to form a judgment as to
> price at which he can afford to sell the article when made;
> or, in the event of the selling price being fixed, whether he
> can make the article at a reasonable profit. And, further,
> after the article has been manufactured, it affords an oppor-
> tunity of comparing the estimated with the actual cost, and,
> if necessary, revising the estimated cost for future use.[78]

Although other writers had intimated the possibility of revising the
estimate, this is the first statement that has been found suggesting the
basis for such action.

J. Slater Lewis, an engineer, presented his publication, The Commercial Organisation of Factories, in 1896 as a handbook for manufacturers, auditors, engineers, estimate clerks and others. This book is
a rather voluminous presentation of the various forms and procedures,
including the bookkeeping for recording manufacturing data, of an industrial concern. Although the author recognized the importance of

---

[77] Cudworth, A. J., "Some Notes on Cost Accounts," The Accountant,
XXII (1896), 313.

[78] Ibid., p. 312.

estimating and devoted a chapter to this subject, he attempted rather
vaguely to describe the procedure in the Estimating Department rather
than to portray any cost accounting technique.  A suggestion of the
thinking of the writer is gained from his explanation with respect to
determining estimated labor:

> Each manufacturing operation, or each set of operations,
> should, when an Estimate is being prepared, be carefully dis-
> sected and entered on foolscap paper, or in a rough estimate
> book. . . . When this information has been so extracted and
> checked, so that nothing may be overlooked, the prices should
> be added to each item.  These prices should be arrived at by
> the manager, the Estimate Clerk and the Foreman conjointly.
> Each one should write down privately his price or rate for
> each operation, immediately after which they should be com-
> pared and a definite figure arrived at:  a·very safe method
> being that of adopting the mean of the three rates.[79]

Although Lewis presented an "Estimate Form"[80] for collecting the
predetermined costs of materials, labor and establishment charges and an
"Estimates Given Book"[81] for recording every estimate which was given to
a customer, these books were considered as adjuncts to the bookkeeping
records.  When he came to record costs, he transferred the finished
goods to the warehouse at actual cost and listed the unfinished products
on the balance sheet at the end of the fiscal period at accumulated
costs according to the Manufacturing Prime Cost Books.[82]

---


[79] Lewis, J. Slater, _The Commercial Organisation of Factories_,
London, E. & F. N. Spon, 1896, p. 107.

[80] Ibid., p. 112.

[81] Ibid., p. 240.

[82] Ibid., pp. 352-384.

Horace Lucian Arnold, an American writing under the _nom de plume_ of
Henry Roland, presented two series of articles in the _Engineering Maga-
zine_ during 1897-98 and recognized therein the significance of accurate
cost estimates for the purpose of submitting prices in a competitive
market.  In the first articles, his primary contribution to cost estimate literature was the reproduction of an estimate form of foundry
costs as taken from actual practice--the Builder's Iron Foundry:

1. Estimate fully time cost of core-makers, moulders, and
   helpers.
2. Estimate fully cost of pig iron piled in the yard, adding
   for waste 9.13 per cent.
3. Examine melting book to determine average cost per gross
   ton for the last four weeks; to this average cost add 34.2
   per cent., which will make a total equal to the cost of
   melting each net ton, covering waste and remelting.
4. For cartage add 88 cents per short ton.
5. Moulding materials equal 36.13 per cent. of producer's
   wages.
6. Foundry labor, $3.75 per ton.
7. Yard expenses, cleaning and shipping $3.50 per ton.
8. Fixed charges.  These will vary with number of producers--
   moulders, moulders' helpers and core-makers.  The number of
   these men on the time book is taken as the base, as the
   average output per same number of producer's names is almost constant.
       With 100 names in work, on order under estimate add for
   fixed charges 50 per cent. of total producers' wages.
       For 90 names add 55.5 per cent.
       For 80 names add 62.5 per cent.
       For 70 names add 71.5 per cent.
       For 60 names add 83.33 per cent.
       For 50 names add 100 per cent.
       For 40 names add 125 per cent.
       For 30 names add 166 per cent.[83]

The first series of articles prompted requests from several very

---

[83] Roland, Henry, "Cost-Keeping in Machine Shop and Foundry," _Engi-
neering Magazine_, XIV (1897-98), 632.

successful concerns for easily installed cost-keeping systems. The

author complied in part by submitting the second series of articles, "An

Effective System of Finding and Keeping Shop-Costs," in 1898 and by pre-

senting his publication, The Complete Cost-Keeper, in 1899.

The second series of articles depicted practices in shops which had

come under Arnold's observation. In describing that of Strieby and

Foote, Newark, New Jersey, he presented the "Beecher rule" for making

drop-forging cost-estimates as introduced here in 1883:

> The "Beecher rule" . . . devised by Beecher, of Meriden,
> Conn., one of the early American drop forgers, . . . gave in
> average work a wonderfully close approximation to accuracy.
> Beecher's rule was to add the stock cost, the weight of the
> rough stock being one-third more than that of the finished
> work, and the flat labor-cost, and double the sum of these two
> items for the selling cost. If the work is of about the aver-
> age description, the rough and ready Beecher rule gives re-
> sults very nearly correct, but, if the work is very simple and
> so uses a large weight of stock for the labor involved, the
> Beecher rule makes the selling price too high, while with
> little stock and much labor the price is too low.[84]

This system was superseded by a well-indexed plan of filing one

sample of each piece of work completed as well as the job-ticket under

which this particular work was made. With a new piece of work under

consideration, a highly reliable estimate could be prepared readily by

seeking the samples (and the corresponding job-tickets) that corre-

sponded most closely with the work to be constructed.

Arnold (Henry Roland) found a similar system existing in the Newton

---

[84] Roland, Henry, "An Effective System of Finding and Keeping Shop-Costs," Engineering Magazine, XV (1898), 241.

Machine-Tool Works, Philadelphia:

> Every machine, as finished by the Newton Works, has its cost
> sheet complete in the locked cost-books, and an estimate for
> a new machine materially differing from anything previously
> manufactured can be readily made from such a record, as the
> same elements appear throughout the whole line of Newton
> machines with surprising frequency.[85]

Arnold's book contained a rather exhaustive presentation of various forms, together with the application of each, in several factory accounting systems rather than a treatise on cost principles. The author recognized estimate costs primarily as of assistance in preparing bids or tenders to potential customers.[86]

He stated that the cost records should be separate and apart from the commercial accounting records and gave one illustration whereby the two had no relation or modifying influence on each other. In this case, the commercial office paid the factory for finished goods completed during the year. The prices for products were fixed each year from records of the factory books for the previous year--a use of estimate costs. In case of a profit or loss as shown by the factory receipts, the commercial offices took over the surplus or assumed the deficit.[87]

In the case of the foundry records, Arnold pointed out that it was not practicable to accumulate the cost of castings but that the average

---

[85] Ibid., p. 620.

[86] Arnold, Horace Lucian (Henry Roland), The Complete Cost-Keeper, New York, The Engineering Magazine Press, 1901, pp. 21, 32-33, 49, 53, 110-116, 205.

[87] Ibid., p. 53.

cost was determined periodically and, as castings were received from the foundry, the stores  account was debited and the foundry account was credited at a fixed rate determined as follows:

> The cost per pound of the mixture in the cupola; the cost per pound for fuel and power, unproductive labor, and material; the cost per pound for waste between the cupola and the finished castings; the cost per pound for moulding each specific article, which is easily determined, either from time-rate or price per piece.[88]

The author ignored any variation that might arise in the foundry account as the result of using this procedure.  In setting up inventories at the end of the year, the variation would finally arrive in the trading accounts but no importance was placed in this feature.

THE COST ESTIMATE DURING THE FIRST TWO DECADES OF THE TWENTIETH CENTURY.--At least three significant additions were made to estimated cost literature during the first two years of the twentieth century.  In the first instance, Francis G. Burton presented his book, _Engineering Estimates and Cost Accounts_ (a portion of which was published in 1894 in the English journal _Engineering_), and recognized therein that the increasing keenness of competition in the engineering trades warranted the proper compilation of estimates for tenders.  He advocated a standard estimate for each standard type of machine but failed to develop this thesis as adequately as subsequent writers.[89]

---

[88] _Ibid._, p. 205.

[89] Burton, Francis G., _Engineering Estimates and Cost Accounts_, Manchester, The Technical Publishing Company, 1900, pp. 18-28.

Burton would organize both his cost and estimate records with the same degree of detail and would permit the recording of estimated figures in the cost records temporarily, but would make the necessary corrections as soon as practicable.[90]

Goode, a chartered accountant, suggested another service that might be performed with estimated costs--to assist the manufacturer in making a sufficiently accurate estimate of the result of his trading for any period, without taking stock and preparing the financial statements in the usual manner.[91]

This writer, who was considering a process cost system, advocated the preparation of a predetermined cost of producing a standard quantity or weight of each article, which would be revised for any change in price of materials or rate of wages.[92] However, his greatest contribution is found in his analysis of the differences between the estimated and actual cost of manufactured goods, which will be considered further in a chapter on variations.

In the third publication of this period, Lean, a chartered accountant, declared that a system of cost accounts should show the estimated, and subsequently the actual, production cost for each standard unit of weight, should indicate the profit and loss for a given period without

---

[90]Ibid., pp. 55-71.

[91]Goode, G. E., "The Methods of Ascertaining Costs in a Factory where a Variety of Articles are Made, which Mostly Pass Through Several Processes in the Course of Manufacture, and are Turned Out in Large Quantities," The Accountant, XXVI (June 30, 1900), 600-607.

[92]Ibid., pp. 601-603.

taking stock and closing the books, should disclose the detailed causes
that have contributed to the general results for the particular period,
and should facilitate the detection of fraud, theft of stock or errors
in bookkeeping and accounts.[93]

Lean's primary contribution was the development of a method for ascertaining the cost of a principal product and two by-products by employing the "Estimate Book"--a compilation of completed estimate forms
which had accumulated the predetermined cost of raw materials, wages and
general production expense for each standard unit of weight.[94]

The author recommended that, at the end of each six months, a careful inventory of stock be made and a comparison of operating results, as
determined by the cost and accounting departments, be prepared.  Any
discrepancy was to be reconciled and the ascertained differences were to
be investigated in order to indicate whether the bookkeeping, costing,
stocktaking or honesty of employees was at fault.[95]

The following year, Wilton C. Eddis and William B. Tindall, two
Canadian Chartered Accountants, published a book, Manufacturers' Accounts, for manufacturers, merchants, accountants and bookkeepers.  In
view of the fact that Mr. Eddis had been president of the Institute of
Chartered Accountants of Ontario, this publication may be deemed to reflect somewhat Canadian thinking at the turn of the century.

---

[93]Lean, F. W. LeBlount, "Cost Accounts," The Accountant, XXVII
(March 16, 1901), 331-345.

[94]Ibid., pp. 332-335.

[95]Ibid., pp. 342-345.

In recognizing the importance of estimate costs, the authors included in their accounting scheme an "Estimate Book," which was classified as outside of the Commercial Books (Purchase Journal and General Ledger) but as related to the Invoice Book, the Cost Ledger and the Summary Register. This Estimate Book was designed to provide for the cost elements of materials, labor and proportion of workshop and distributing expenses. In preparing the data for the Estimate Book, the writers suggested that the costs should be figured on an average output for several years rather than the present year's or last year's business.[96]

Under these writers' accounting procedure, the Factory Ledger (a subsidiary ledger) was controlled by the Cost Ledger Account in the General Ledger. As the products were completed and transferred to manufactured stock, their costs were recorded in a Summary Register. The columns in this register were totaled periodically and their sums were used to form the data for a journal entry, as indicated below, which was posted to the General Ledger:

```
Manufactured Stock                              Dr.
        To Cost Ledger Account
            Wages
            Material
            Factory Expenses (Estimated
              or otherwise)
            Direct Expenses[97]
```

At the end of each fiscal period, the actual expenses were

_______________

[96] Eddis, Wilton C., and Tindall, William B., *Manufacturers' Accounts*, Toronto, Canada, Warwick Brothers and Rutter, Ltd., 1902, pp. 19, 32.

[97] *Ibid.*, p. 45.

accumulated in the Factory Ledger and were compared with the estimated expenses that had been entered in the Summary Register. Any discrepancy was considered in the preparation of future estimates.

Another point of significance to this study was a hypothetical case which was presented to illustrate the current estimating procedure in the lumber industry. This problem, in brief, and the solutions (the authors presented three possible methods), in tabular form, have been reproduced as an indication of the accounting illustrations for estimating costs that were available for students at the beginning of the twentieth century.[98]

Problem. A manufacturer of lumber was requested to put in a tender (bid) for supplying one thousand articles which required twenty-five feet of lumber each. The lumber, in the rough, costs twenty dollars per thousand feet; the cost of manufacture amounts to five dollars per thousand feet; the waste is twenty per cent on the rough lumber; and the manufacturer desires to earn twenty-five per cent on his selling price. What price should he quote for each article?

Solution. (Tabulated from authors' answers.)

---

[98] Ibid., pp. 166-168.

| Cost Items | "A" Method | "B" Method | "C" Method |
|---|---|---|---|
| Lumber--One thousand feet | $20.00 | $20.00 | $20.00 |
| Labor | 5.00 | 5.00 | 5.00 |
| Waste | 4.00[a] | 5.00[b] | 6.25[c] |
|   Total Cost | $29.00 | $30.00 | $31.25 |
| Profit | 7.25[d] | 10.00[e] | 10.41[f] |
|   Total Quotation per Thousand Feet or Forty Articles | $36.25 | $40.00 | $41.66 |
| UNIT PRICE | $ 0.91 | $ 1.00 | $ 1.04 |

[a] 20% of $20.00 (Lumber only).
[b] 20% of $25.00 (Lumber and Labor).
[c] 200 (Waste in feet) ÷ 800 (Finished Lumber obtained from each thousand feet of Rough Lumber) x $25.00 (Lumber and Labor).
[d] 25% of $29.00 (Total Cost).
[e] 33 1/3% of $30.00 (Total Cost).
[f] 33 1/3% of $31.25 (Total Cost).

In approving "C" Method as the correct procedure, the authors observed that a great many manufacturers were figuring their estimates under "A" Method and were, therefore, not earning the profits on contracts that they had anticipated.

If it may be assumed that the volumes of The Accountants' Library --a series of fifty-one handbooks published by the Editor of The Accountant (1903-1909) and designed to give detailed information concerning the most approved methods of keeping accounts for those classes of industry requiring specialized accounting methods--were written by authorities in their respective fields, then the English thinking at the opening of the twentieth century with respect to estimated costs may be gained by considering the four volumes that deal with factory records.

Volume XLII, Multiple Cost Accounts by H. Stanley Garry, undertook to present a system applicable to organizations in which the manufacture of a number of products was involved but in which the costs or selling prices were unrelated. The author suggested that a detailed cost estimate be established for each machine or product manufactured and that one of these machines be set up as a standard unit of output into which all the products for any fiscal period might be converted for costing and comparative purposes.

Under the writer's procedure, the Manufacturing Account--an account in the factory records, which were separate from the commercial records --accumulated the actual cost of production as debits and the estimated value of production, in accordance with the predetermined cost schedule, as credits.[99]

Although a standard unit of output technique had been suggested already by Goode in his preparation of a predetermined cost of producing a standard quantity or weight of each article under a process cost system and by Lean in his determination of the production cost for each standard unit of weight (both heretofore mentioned), Garry was the first writor that has recorded sufficient information to permit a reproduction of the procedure followed.

In order to illustrate Garry's methodology, there has been prepared the following assumed schedule, which is designed to represent a detailed cost estimate of all the products manufactured by a concern. This detailed estimate has been adapted to the author's technique but has been somewhat abridged and has been priced in dollars rather than in pounds.

---

[99]Garry, H. Stanley, *Multiple Cost Accounts*, London, Gee and Company, 1906, p. 29.

SCHEDULE OF FACTORY COSTINGS[100]

| | | Factory Costs | | | |
|---|---|---|---|---|---|
| Product | Selling Price | Total | Materials | Wages | Factory Charges |
| M | $40 | $25 | $7 | $15 | $3 |
| N | 30 | 20 | 6 | 10 | 4 |
| P | 28 | 22 | 8 | 9 | 5 |
| S | 26 | 17 | 5 | 4 | 8 |
| T | 22 | 16 | 6 | 7 | 3 |
| V | 20 | 18 | 4 | 8 | 6 |

Continuing the author's scheme, Product M has been accepted as the standard unit of output and the other products have been converted into this unit by using the Total Factory Cost of the Standard Unit as the base or 1.000. The estimated costs of the other products, having been divided by this base cost figure, are thus expressed as percentages of the standard unit of output.

SCHEDULE OF FACTORY UNITS[101]

| | Factory Costs | | | |
|---|---|---|---|---|
| Product | Total | Materials | Wages | Factory Charges |
| M | 1.000 | .280 | .600 | .120 |
| N | .800 | .240 | .400 | .160 |
| P | .880 | .320 | .360 | .200 |
| S | .680 | .200 | .150 | .320 |
| T | .640 | .240 | .280 | .120 |
| V | .720 | .160 | .320 | .240 |

In determining the estimated production costs for any fiscal period, the actual production in units by products was converted into standard

---

[100] Ibid., p. 12.

[101] Ibid., p. 26.

units and the estimated cost of the standard unit was applied thereto.

The following table will indicate this procedure:

SCHEDULE OF PRODUCTION REDUCED TO
STANDARD UNITS OF PRODUCT

| Product | Actual Production | Conversion Ratio | Standard Units |
|---------|-------------------|------------------|----------------|
| M | 1,000 | 1.000 | 1,000 |
| N | 800 | .800 | 640 |
| P | 500 | .880 | 440 |
| S | 750 | .680 | 510 |
| T | 600 | .640 | 384 |
| V | 2,000 | .720 | 1,440 |
| | 5,650 | | 4,414 |

By applying the estimated factory cost per standard unit (see

Schedule of Factory Costing) to the total standard units of production,

the estimated cost of the actual production was obtained and was used

for the credit to the Manufacturing Account--in this case: $25.00 x

4,414 = $110,350. The author's Manufacturing Account, adapted to the

example herein, has been presented as an illustration of this state-

ment:

Manufacturing Account[102]

Debits:

    To Materials .......................... $32,000
    " Wages direct ....................... 66,000    $ 98,000

    " Salaries and Foremen .............. $ 2,400
    " Coal and Power Account ............ 5,000
    " Rent, Rates and Taxes ............. 2,000
    " Insurance and Compensation ........ 500
    " Maintenance of Works and
            Buildings ................... 600
    " Drawing Office Salaries ........... 1,000
    " Timekeepers and Works Office
            and Stores .................. 750
    " Patterns and Models ............... 250
    " Warehouseman and Carters .......... 300
    " Incidental Charges ................ 400
    " Packages Account .................. 1,200    14,400

    " Balance to Revenue Account ........           600
                                                $113,000

Credits:

    By Production Account ................           $110,350
    " Sundry Sales, Scrap, Ashes, &c. ... $ 1,650
    " Transfer to Renewals Account ...... 1,000     2,650
                                                $113,000

Note:  The author's text presented the usual "T" form of ac-
       count, but it is not practicable to prepare such an
       account with two columns each for debits and credits.


A careful consideration of Garry's efforts indicate that his con-

tribution to estimating costs has been the charging of production, less

any products that were put into stock, to the Trading Account at esti-

mated cost and the crediting of the Manufacturing Account with the same

sum.

Volume XLVI, Terminal Cost Accounts,[103] depicted a system for

---

[102]Ibid., p. 10.

[103]Nisbit, Andrew Gow, Terminal Cost Accounts, London, Gee and Company, 1906.

undertakings--engineers, shipbuilders and contractors--which enter into definite contracts so far as costs and completion dates are concerned. In each case, a detailed estimate of costs was usually prepared preceding the tender. As an illustration, the author presented an estimate for a railway bridge and included therein Shop Expenses and Establishment Charges based on the preceding year's actual figures--"it is more correct to work on actual figures of a previous year than on estimated figures for the current year."[104]

At the end of the fiscal period, the Cost Ledger was summarized in the Manufacturing Account, which indicated three classifications of contracts--those actually completed, those estimated as completed and those in progress. This account served also as a guide in the preparation of estimates for future tenders and permitted a comparison of estimated with actual costs--in the case of an underestimated contract, the account tended to disclose the location of the unfavorable differences.[105]

Thus, for Nisbit, estimated costs did not become a part of either the financial books or the cost records but served only as a foundation for tenders and as a basis for comparative purposes.

Volume XLVII, Single Cost Accounts,[106] was devised for those businesses (breweries, collieries and mines) with a natural cost unit--ton, barrel or other quantity. The author recommended the use of commercial

-----

[104] Ibid., p. 23.

[105] Ibid., pp. 34-41.

[106] Mitchell, George A., Single Cost Accounts, London, Gee and Company, 1907.

books with as few nominal accounts as possible and of factory records
with as many divisions as practicable in order that greater detailed information might be obtained for comparative purposes.

The cost records, as presented for a Malting Business, consisted of
various accounts, schedules and summaries for the 1904-05 season.  The
first section consisted of the "Estimated Total Malt Costing" (as prepared in October, 1904) and comprised an estimate of sales, of production, of purchases, and of kiln, sales and general expenses.  Finally,
all of these data were accumulated in "The Summary"--an antecedent of
the modern budget--which has been reproduced with figures rounded to
pounds.[107]

SUMMARY

(Estimated Total Malt Costing)

| Purchases | £ | Sales | £ |
|---|---|---|---|
| Barley and Carriage ....... | 13,237 | Malt ..................... | 17,249 |
| Kiln Expense .............. | 2,475 | Screenings ............... | 665 |
| Sales Expenses ............ | 520 | Culms .................... | 217 |
| General Charges ........... | 770 | | |
| Balance down ............. | 1,129 | | |
| | 18,131 | | 18,131 |
| Bank Interest ............. | 35 | Balance down ............. | 1,129 |
| Special Charges as per | | Net Rents as per last | |
| last Profit and Loss | | year's Accounts ........ | 530 |
| Account, estimated ...... | 59 | Sundry Receipts .......... | 10 |
| Income Tax, estimated ..... | 40 | | |
| Balance, or Profit down ... | 1,535 | | |
| | 1,669 | | 1,669 |
| Return on Capital employed | | Profit down .............. | 1,535 |
| representing: | | | |
| Interest at 5 per cent | | | |
| on £15,000 .......... | 750 | | |
| Profit, about 5-1/4 per | | | |
| cent on £15,000 ..... | 785 | | |
| | 1,535 | | 1,535 |

---

[107]Ibid., p. 41.

After compiling the actual costs during the year in accounts corresponding with the classifications in the estimates, the author brought
the predetermined and actual costs together in contiguous columns on a
"Reconciliation Statement," which will be considered in the following
chapter on variations.

For Mitchell, the cost estimate served not only as a standard for
annual comparative purposes but also as a basis for periodic checks on
sales, production and expenses--"if these are compiled at short intervals it will allow of time for efforts being made to redress the balance, or average, before stocktaking."[108]

The author presented also a costing system for an Engineering Business, which manufactured machines according to standard patterns. Under
this plan, an estimate was prepared as in the malting business. However,
the manufacturing accounts were included as controlling accounts in the
Nominal (Main) Ledger and the cost data were accumulated and compared
with the estimated figures. Since the actual figures were entered in
the cost records, the estimates served only as statistical devices. A
monthly check was provided for labor, materials and production in order
that the management might ascertain the position of the business periodically and might observe shortages in materials as well as efficiency of
labor.[109]

And, finally, Volume XLIX, Process Cost Accounts[110]--applicable to

----

[108]Ibid., p. 44.

[109]Ibid., pp. 65-101.

[110]Garry, H. Stanley, Process Cost Accounts, London, Gee and Company, 1908.

Chemical Industries, Food Products Manufacturers and Tanners--outlined a
system of accounting for a continuous process industry and applied the
author's "standard unit of production" theory, as heretofore explained,
to this type of production.

In the latter publication, the author reiterated the importance of
the cost estimate. In preparing his figures for the succeeding year,
Garry began with a volume of production sufficient to cover operating
costs and to yield the desired dividend on stock--in the case presented,
1,420 tons to produce revenue of £2,992. This volume was anticipated in
the following manner:

Standard Estimate of Output[111]

| Product | Last Year | Highest* | Estimated for Year | Gross Profit | Profit |
|---|---|---|---|---|---|
|  | Tons | Tons | Tons | £ | £ |
| M | 322 | 460 | 370 | 1.5 | 550 |
| N | 200 | 200 | 220 | .30 | 66 |
| O | 426 | 557 | 460 | 1.94 | 892 |
| P | 68 | 69 | 50 | 3.13 | 156 |
| Q | 91 | 174 | 120 | 3.07 | 368 |
| R | 140 | 140 | 200 | 4.80 | 960 |
|  | 1,247 | 1,600 | 1,420 | 2.21** | £2,992 |

*Highest production of each product during last three years.
**Average.

In preparing his estimates, Product R, which was the most profitable, was selected as his standard unit of output and was scheduled for
the greatest degree of increase in production. The estimated production
for the other items, except Product N, had been exceeded during the last

---

[111]Ibid., p. 95.

three years and appeared, therefore, to be feasible.

By way of summary, the author concluded that, once the standard of output was set up and the planning procedure was undertaken, the method would not be abandoned. However, his procedure, particularly with respect to estimating costs, was not nearly as clear-cut in this system as in his Multiple Cost Accounts.

When J. Lee Nicholson, an American writer, published his book, Nicholson on Factory Organization and Costs, in 1909, he presented for the first time a unified treatment of the "Estimated Cost System." This author undertook to devise three methods of handling estimated costs and prepared three chapters on this subject in his publication.

The first chapter on estimated costs, "Estimated Cost System Based on an Annual Verification of Material, Labor and Indirect Expenses,"[112] contains the simplest device for determining whether the material, the labor, and the expenses have been correctly stated in the estimates of cost and whether or not the manufacturer "would be justified in installing a cost system in his particular plant."

In setting up the system, the first step was to prepare an "Inventory Sheet" of the goods on hand, analyzed as to material, labor, and indirect expenses and priced according to the estimated cost price which was to be verified.

After all of the articles have been priced in this manner and the total ascertained, the inventory should be re-entered in

---

[112] Nicholson, J. Lee, Nicholson on Factory Organization and Costs, New York, Kohl Technical Publishing Company, 1911, pp. 232-236.

the Ledger to the debit of each of these three accounts--that
is, supposing the total inventory amounted to $10,000, of
which $6,000 was represented in the first cost of material,
$3,000 in labor and $1,000 in indirect expenses, these amounts
are the ones which should be entered in the Ledger to the
debit of these various accounts.[113]

In the second place, Nicholson devised a "Schedule of Estimated
Costs" to accumulate the estimated costs for all the articles manufactured.  These costs, which were analyzed according to material, labor
and indirect expenses, were used to price not only the beginning and
final inventories but also to determine the cost of sales for the period.
In applying these data to determine the cost of sales, he prepared an
"Analysis of Cost of Sales" for the fiscal period.  At the end of the
year, an inventory was computed under the same conditions as were used
for determining the initial inventory.

Nicholson then undertook a plan of verification.  Since the material account, the labor account, and the indirect expense account had
been charged with the initial inventory at estimated prices and with the
actual expenditures for these items during the period, then, if these
accounts were credited with the final inventory at estimated costs,
their balance, he reasoned, would represent the actual cost of material,
labor and indirect expenses consumed and expended in the manufacture of
goods actually sold.  The same items, at the estimated costs, would be
shown by the "Analysis of Cost of Sales."

----

[113] Ibid., p. 233.

Material Account

| | | | |
|---|---|---|---|
| Beginning Inventory--at | | Ending Inventory--at | |
| Estimated Cost | 5,000 | Estimated Cost | 8,000 |
| Purchases--Actual | 15,000 | | |
| (Balance 12,000) | | | |

Labor Account

| | | | |
|---|---|---|---|
| Beginning Inventory--at | | Ending Inventory--at | |
| Estimated Cost | 3,600 | Estimated Cost | 5,000 |
| Expenditures | 8,400 | | |
| (Balance 7,000) | | | |

Indirect Expenses Account

| | | | |
|---|---|---|---|
| Beginning Inventory--at | | Ending Inventory--at | |
| Estimated Cost | 3,200 | Estimated Cost | 4,800 |
| Expenditures | 5,800 | | |
| (Balance 4,200) | | | |

In order to illustrate Nicholson's methodology, hypothetical data have been recorded in ledger accounts and have been summarized in the following "Analysis of Cost Accounts."

ANALYSIS OF COST ACCOUNTS*

| | Debits to Accounts | | Credits | |
|---|---|---|---|---|
| Accounts | Beginning Inventory | Purchases or Expenditures | Ending Inventory | Account Balance |
| Material | $ 5,000 | $15,000 | $ 8,000 | $12,000 |
| Labor | 3,600 | 8,400 | 5,000 | 7,000 |
| Indirect Expenses | 3,200 | 5,800 | 4,800 | 4,200 |
| Totals | $11,800 | $29,200 | $17,800 | $23,200 |

*This schedule was devised by writer in lieu of posting to Ledger Accounts.

At the same time, the "Analysis of Cost of Sales" has been prepared in totals only with corresponding figures. In this case, the estimated

cost figures for materials were too high, those for labor were correct
and those for indirect expenses were too low.

ANALYSIS OF COST OF SALES
(Totals Only)

| | Material | Labor | Indirect Expenses | Total |
|---|---|---|---|---|
| Totals for Period | $13,000 | $7,000 | $4,000 | $24,000 |

It is rather interesting to note that when Nicholson published his
text, Cost Accounting Theory and Practice, in 1913, he employed the same
procedure for determining his inventories, Cost Estimates and Analysis
of Cost of Sales. However, he varied his verification technique. Instead of crediting the three ledger accounts--Materials, Labor and Indirect Expenses--with the final inventory and of comparing the resulting
actual cost of sales figures with the estimated cost of sales as in this
publication, he credited these accounts with the estimated cost of sales
and compared the balances (computed or book inventories) with the actual
inventories priced according to the estimated schedules.[114]

An application of the latter technique to the data heretofore used
for illustrating the procedure in the first publication will indicate
the change in the author's accounting method with respect to verification of estimated and actual figures.

---

[114]Nicholson, J. Lee, Cost Accounting Theory and Practice, New York,
The Ronald Press Company, 1913, pp. 168-169.

COMPARISON OF BOOK AND PERIODIC INVENTORIES

| Account | Debits to Accounts | | Credits | Balances | Physical |
| | Beginning | Purchases or | Cost of | Book | (Actual) |
| | Inventory | Expenditures | Sales | Inventory | Inventory |
| --- | --- | --- | --- | --- | --- |
| Material ... | $ 5,000 | $15,000 | $13,000 | $ 7,000 | $ 8,000 |
| Labor ...... | 3,600 | 8,400 | 7,000 | 5,000 | 5,000 |
| Indirect Expenses ... | 3,200 | 5,800 | 4,000 | 5,000 | 4,800 |
| Totals . | $11,800 | $29,200 | $24,000 | $17,000 | $17,800 |

From this schedule, it may be seen that, according to Nicholson's reasoning--"if any element in the book inventory exceeds the corresponding element in the physical inventory, it shows that the estimated costs were too low as regard that element, and if the reverse, the estimated costs were too high"[115]--the estimates for materials were too high, for labor correct and for indirect expenses too low. The results obtained by using either method are identical, but the significance arises from the change in crediting these accounts with an estimated figure for the cost of goods sold rather than with estimated final inventory--a procedure which might be varied somewhat further to charge the production accounts with actual costs and to credit these accounts with estimated figures for finished goods.

The second chapter on estimated costs in the original publication--"Estimated Cost System Based on an Annual Verification of Departmental Charges for Material, Labor and Indirect Expenses"[116]--undertook to

---

[115] Ibid., p. 169.

[116] Nicholson, Nicholson on Factory Organization and Costs, pp. 237-243.

subdivide and analyze materials by classes and labor expenditures by departments in order the better to disclose any inaccuracies that might exist between the estimated and actual costs. The indirect expenses were verified in the same manner as in the first system.

The procedure for verification followed the same general routine as in the first system except that columns were provided for subdividing the general classes of materials and/or the departments of labor on the Inventory Sheets for the initial and final inventories, on the Schedule of Estimated Costs, on the Analysis of Cost of Sales, in the Purchase Journal, and on the Pay Roll.

For illustrative purposes, it has been assumed that the data, heretofore used in totals, have been analyzed and recorded under the following conditions:

| | Materials | | Labor | | Indirect | |
| Information | Class.1 | Class.2 | Dept.1 | Dept.2 | Expenses | Total |
|---|---|---|---|---|---|---|
| Initial Inventory ... | $3,000 | $2,000 | $2,000 | $1,600 | $3,200 | $11,800 |
| Purchases or Expenditures | 8,000 | 7,000 | 5,000 | 3,400 | 5,800 | 29,200 |
| Analysis of Cost of Sales | 7,000 | 6,000 | 4,000 | 3,000 | 4,000 | 24,000 |
| Final Inventory | 5,000 | 3,000 | 3,200 | 1,800 | 4,800 | 17,800 |

The author stated that the following entries would be made in the Ledger accounts to record these facts (journal entries have been made for illustrative purposes rather than recording in Ledger accounts):

(1)

| | | |
|---|---|---|
| Material--Classification 1 | 3,000 | |
| Material--Classification 2 | 2,000 | |
| Labor--Department 1 | 2,000 | |
| Labor--Department 2 | 1,600 | |
| Indirect Expenses | 3,200 | |
|     Balancing Accounts* | | 11,800 |

  *Probably Inventories--see Entry 3--although
the credits were not suggested.

    To record the initial inventories,
analyzed as to materials, labor and
indirect expenses--actual units with
estimated prices applied.


(2)

| | | |
|---|---|---|
| Material--Classification 1 | 8,000 | |
| Material--Classification 2 | 7,000 | |
| Labor--Department 1 | 5,000 | |
| Labor--Department 2 | 3,400 | |
| Indirect Expenses | 5,800 | |
|     Accounts Payable, Cash, and/or Other<br>      Balancing Accounts | | 29,200 |

    To record the purchase of materials and
expenditures for labor and indirect expenses
during the period at actual figures.


(3)

| | | |
|---|---|---|
| Inventories: | | |
|   Material--Classification 1 | 5,000 | |
|   Material--Classification 2 | 3,000 | |
|   Labor--Department 1 | 3,200 | |
|   Labor--Department 2 | 1,800 | |
|   Indirect Expenses | 4,800 | |
|     Material--Classification 1 | | 5,000 |
|     Material--Classification 2 | | 3,000 |
|     Labor--Department 1 | | 3,200 |
|     Labor--Department 2 | | 1,800 |
|     Indirect Expenses | | 4,800 |

    To record the final inventory--actual
units with estimated prices applied.


When these journal entries had been posted, the account balances

were ascertained and were compared with the results as computed on the

Analysis of Cost of Sales.  In the case under consideration, the follow-

ing facts would have been obtained:

COMPARISON OF ACTUAL AND ESTIMATED COST OF SALES

| Accounts | Debits to Accounts | | Credits | Balance | Estimated |
| | Beginning Inventory | Purchases or Expenditures | Final Inventory | Actual Cost of Sales | Cost of Sales |
| --- | --- | --- | --- | --- | --- |
| Material: | | | | | |
|   Class. 1 | $ 3,000 | $ 8,000 | $ 5,000 | $ 6,000 | $ 7,000 |
|   Class. 2 | 2,000 | 7,000 | 3,000 | 6,000 | 6,000 |
| Labor: | | | | | |
|   Dept. 1 | 2,000 | 5,000 | 3,200 | 3,800 | 4,000 |
|   Dept. 2 | 1,600 | 3,400 | 1,800 | 3,200 | 3,000 |
| Indirect | | | | | |
|   Expenses | 3,200 | 5,800 | 4,800 | 4,200 | 4,000 |
|     Total | $11,800 | $29,200 | $17,800 | $23,200 | $24,000 |

In accordance with the author's proposals, the estimates for Mate-

rial--Classification 1 and Labor--Department 1 were too high, those for

Material--Department 2 were satisfactory and those for Labor--Depart-

ment 2 and Indirect Expenses were too low.  A careful consideration of

System One and System Two will disclose that the methods are the same

but that additional information is furnished in the latter plan.

When Nicholson came to his third estimated cost system--"Estimated

Cost System Based on a Monthly or Annual Verification of Estimated Cost

of Class of Product According to Departmental Material, Labor, and In-

direct Expenses"[117]--he not only analyzed the elements of cost by sub-

divisions as in System Two but also devised a breakdown of the costs

into the several classifications of products sold with provision made

_______________

[117] Ibid., pp. 244-255.

for each classification to consist of as many articles as might be manufactured.  There were several innovations in this system.

In the first place, Raw Materials Inventory (not related in any way
to goods in process or finished goods) was charged to a Raw Materials
Account on the General Ledger.  This account was charged also with purchases of raw materials and was credited with materials used as reported
by the "Material Requisitions" (a form peculiar to this system).

With respect to the initial and final inventories, a sheet (or several sheets as might be required) was used for each department and was
designed to accumulate not only the material and labor in accordance
with the plan of subdivision but also the indirect expenses as explained
below.

In completing the "Schedule of Estimated Costs" and the "Analysis
of Cost of Sales," the same form was used as in System Two but a separate sheet was prepared for each classification of product.  In like
manner, a "Pay Roll" sheet, with columns for distribution purposes according to the classifications desired, was prepared for each department.

Indirect Expenses, which had not been distributed at this stage of
the accounting procedure, were allocated to the various classifications
of products according to the labor costs of these departments.

At this time, each ledger account covering the various classifications of products contained the beginning inventory at estimated figures
and the materials used and/or labor and indirect expense expenditures at
actual costs.  When the author came to credit these accounts at the end
of the period, he varied from his procedure in Systems One and Two (he

had credited the final inventory at estimated values in these two systems).  However, under System Three, Nicholson credited these accounts with their respective cost of sales (as ascertained from the "Analysis of Cost of Sales"), and, thus, left in the accounts the final inventories at estimated values.[118]

A consideration of Nicholson's efforts, in comparison with today's Cost Estimate technique, will indicate that this author had gone a long way toward presenting this system in 1909.  A review of this publication in The Journal of Accountancy in 1909 will suggest the recognition that was given this work at the time.

> The first American treatise on cost accounting proper, dealing with the subject from an accountant's point of view.  The author, though keeping to the front in his treatment of important accounting principles applicable to the subject, has nevertheless written the book in clear and untechnical language.
>
> While it may be questioned whether the author has been successful in preparing a text-book for students, he has undoubtedly accomplished his prime object, that of supplying the manufacturer with a thorough treatise on a subject in which he is vitally interested, and that of giving professional accountants and cost specialists a valuable reference work.[119]

Webner, a certified public accountant and cost accounting specialist, pointed out that the estimate and test plan of cost finding was, in 1911, perhaps the oldest method of cost finding in practice and the most

---

[118] Ibid., pp. 250-252.

[119] "Review of J. Lee Nicholson's Factory Organization and Costs," The Journal of Accountancy, VIII (July, 1909), 222.

widely used at the time. Although this author was critical of the plan, even to the extent of stating that it was not to be recommended under any conditions, he did present a general plan which might be developed and improved into a somewhat adequate system.[120]

This author defined the estimate and test plan as follows:

> . . . any system under which cost calculations in the first place are based on estimates of the quantity of material, labor, and expense involved, and thereafter if the particular operation be of a more or less recurrent nature, a so-called test is applied in individual cases to measure as far as possible the correctness of the preceding estimates.[121]

Then he proceeded to present very briefly a rather elementary scheme for recording material, labor and expense charges and to develop a chart to illustrate the operations of the various records under the "Estimate and Test Plan of Cost Finding."[122]

Webner stated that physical tests were made periodically of material and other goods in process accounts and that calculations were undertaken of theoretical and actual consumption and rates of variations in order that the predetermined figures might be used in connection with cost tests on the products manufactured. However, he failed to develop this technique to the extent that Nicholson had done in 1909.

> The exact method of making cost tests under the estimate and test plan can hardly be outlined, as these tests will vary

---

[120] Webner, Frank E., _Factory Costs_, New York, The Ronald Press Company, 1911, pp. 247-251.

[121] _Ibid._, p. 247.

[122] _Ibid._, p. 357.

with the product.  Estimates of materials are easily verified.
Labor cost is much more difficult, as on a test the labor
conditions are entirely different from those of regular production work, and the results accomplished are not those
usually attained.  For this reason labor tests are apt to be
entirely inaccurate and unsatisfactory--a characterization
which may well be applied to the whole system of estimate and
test cost finding.[123]

When Webner wrote his second text, Factory Accounting, in 1917, he

was even less concerned with Estimated Costs than in the former publica-

tion.  In developing the specific order plan, he made the following sim-

ple comparison:

> It will be noted that the specific order plan and what is
> called the "estimate and test" plan of cost finding are al-
> most diametrically opposed.  Under the "estimate and test"
> plan the first estimates are usually but little more than
> guesses, not provable by balance and only subject to correc-
> tion by later tests. . . .[124]

In addition to this brief reference to estimating costs as such, he

presented "The Budget System" as one used extensively in the steel fab-

ricating industries.  Under this system, the cost figures were filed

carefully and were readily available for computing bids on similar

projects--to match past performance with present estimates.[125]

> Under the budget system it does not necessarily mean that the
> cost must not exceed the estimated amount, as the work must
> be produced under the contract, no matter what the cost.  It
> is a sharp and succinct method of watching the possible varia-
> tions between plan and performance.[126]

---

[123]Ibid., p. 251.

[124]Webner, Frank E., Factory Accounting, Chicago, LaSalle Extension
University, 1917, pp. 161-162.

[125]Ibid., pp. 217-221.

[126]Ibid., p. 221.

Upon the awarding of a contract, according to Webner, a "Notice of Work Order Issued," which contained a summary of the estimated cost, was prepared for the general manager. Somewhat later, a "Work Order," confirming the "Notice," was issued. As the work progressed, cost figures were recorded on the "Work Order" and were compared with the budget amount of each individual item. Tests were suggested, especially when costs seemed to be running too high, but the recording of the budget figures or other accounting procedure was not demonstrated.

In 1911, John R. Wildman, Professor of Accounting in New York University, also recognized estimated costs as hypothetical figures "founded on the assumption that the costs for the current period will be the same as those of the next preceding period."[127]

The author applied the principles of estimating costs to contract work and recorded the predetermined figures in the general ledger by using two accounts, "Costs of Contracts" and "Reserve for Cost of Contracts." The data for making entries in these accounts were taken from the contract book, in which was listed the estimated cost of each contract that was accepted. If the following schedule may be assumed to represent the contracts for a fiscal period,

SCHEDULE OF ESTIMATED COSTS

| Jobs | Total | Material | Labor | Overhead |
|---|---|---|---|---|
| X - 1 | $30,000 | $15,000 | $10,000 | $5,000 |
| Y - 3 | 21,000 | 7,500 | 9,000 | 4,500 |
| Totals | $51,000 | $22,500 | $19,000 | $9,500 |

---

[127]Wildman, John R., _Principles of Cost Accounting_, New York, New York University Press, 1911, p. 88.

then the journal entry for recording this information would be:

| | | |
|---|---|---|
| Cost of Contracts | 51,000 | |
|    Reserve for Cost of Contracts | | 51,000 |

     To record the estimated cost of
contracts accepted and undertaken
during the fiscal period.

If the actual expenditures for the period were \$42,000--Material \$17,500, Labor \$16,000 and Overhead \$8,500--the journal entry to record these figures, according to Wildman, would be:

| | | |
|---|---|---|
| Reserve for Cost of Contracts | 42,000 | |
|    Material | | 17,500 |
|    Labor | | 16,000 |
|    Overhead | | 8,500 |

     To record the actual expenditures on contracts during the
period.

The author realized that this information would be more pertinent if these principles were applied to the cost elements rather than to their total. Therefore, he varied these journal entries so that the various cost elements might be disclosed in the general ledger. This procedure is illustrated in the following manner:

(1)

| | | |
|---|---|---|
| Estimated Cost of<br>   Uncompleted Contracts | 51,000 | |
| Reserve for Material,<br>   Uncompleted Contracts | | 22,500 |
| Reserve for Labor,<br>   Uncompleted Contracts | | 19,000 |
| Reserve for Overhead,<br>   Uncompleted Contracts | | 9,500 |

     To record the estimated costs of
contracts (analyzed as to material,
labor and overhead) accepted and
undertaken during the fiscal period.

(2)

```
Reserve for Material,
   Uncompleted Contracts          17,500
Reserve for Labor,
   Uncompleted Contracts          16,000
Reserve for Overhead,
   Uncompleted Contracts           8,500
         Material                              17,500
         Labor                                 16,000
         Overhead                               8,500
   To record the actual expenditures
(analyzed as to material, labor and
overhead) on contracts during the
fiscal period.
```

The author stated that the only difficulty which arose from employing this scheme was with respect to uncompleted contracts. In such a case, the uncompleted contracts should be treated as inventories and the usual procedure followed. If it may be further assumed that Job Y - 3 had been completed during the period and that the inventory value of Job X - 1 was $20,700--Material $10,000, Labor $7,000 and Overhead $3,700--then the final journal entry would be:

```
Cost of Contracts                  21,300
   Estimated Cost of
      Uncompleted Contracts                    21,000
   Reserve for Overhead,
      Uncompleted Contracts                       300
   To transfer the actual cost of
Job Y - 3, which was completed,
to cost of contracts.
```

An analysis of these journal entries and the relevant data will indicate that the estimated costs and resulting variations between estimated and actual amounts were disclosed but that the figure for "Cost of Contracts," which would be closed into Profit and Loss, represented actual costs.  It is worthy of mention that this chapter on "Estimated

Costs" was published originally in The Journal of Accountancy, Volume XI,

April, 1911.

Toward the close of this period (1900-1920), Nicholson and Rohrbach

published a text, Cost Accounting, which contained many of the princi-

ples as advanced by Nicholson in his former books but which included

some refinements of technique and some new concepts with respect to esti-

mated costs.[128]

In the first place, these authors defined an estimating cost system

as "one in which the cost of production is checked and controlled by

means of estimates as to what the actual expenditures on certain arti-

cles or groups of products are expected to be."[129]

The writers stated that whereas the cost components (materials,

labor and overhead), under the order or process methods of cost-finding,

were compiled on separate sets of records for every job, order or pro-

cess as the work moved through the factory, in those cases involving the

use of cost estimates, these figures were accumulated for articles or

groups of articles by using as many records as might be required to ob-

tain the desired analysis of cost elements and the corresponding com-

parison with estimates.  In addition, they pointed out that "the esti-

mated costs are incorporated in the financial accounts through a simple

system of records, thereby establishing an accounting proof or check on

---

[128]Nicholson, J. Lee, and Rohrbach, John F. D., Cost Accounting,
New York, The Ronald Press Company, 1919, pp. 459-480.

[129]Ibid., p. 459.

the accuracy of the predetermined figures on which the selling prices are based."[130]  In the first two publications by Nicholson, this procedure was optional.

The following quotation represents a summary of procedure in the operation of an estimated cost system as prepared by Nicholson and Rohrbach:

1. Estimated costs are predetermined for every article manufactured and sold.  The figures may show the total cost only or the details of material, labor, and overhead.
2. The accounts showing the factory operations either as to the total cost of the lot or as to its elements are charged with the beginning inventory priced at the estimated figures and the actual material, labor, and overhead expenses incurred during the period.
3. The accounts showing the factory operations are credited with the total cost of the articles produced, priced at their estimated figures.  (The balance of the accounts showing factory operations represents the value of the closing inventory.)
4. A physical inventory is taken at the end of the period and is priced at the estimated figures.
5. A comparison is made between the book inventory as shown by the account balances with the total amount of the inventory based upon an actual physical stock-taking.  Any discrepancies between the two sets of figures indicate the extent of errors made in the predetermined estimates.[131]

These writers enumerated four methods or stages of development in cost-finding by means of predetermined estimates.  An analysis of these methods indicates that they somewhat overlap Nicholson's former treatment of this subject, in which he had presented only three plans.

Under the first method--"Verification of Estimated Costs in Total

---

[130] *Ibid.*, p. 459.

[131] *Ibid.*, p. 461.

Amount"--a step that was not recognized previously by Nicholson, the
writers undertook to verify only the total cost of articles manufactured.

Nicholson and Rohrbach prepared a "Schedule of Estimated Costs,"
which listed every article manufactured and the total estimated cost of
each. Likewise, they prepared a "Summary of Estimated Cost of Sales,"
the total of which became the basis for the following journal entry:

```
        Cost of Sales                               xxx
            Production (or Estimated) Cost               xxx
                To record the cost of sales
            for the fiscal period.
```

The initial inventory and purchases of materials and/or expenditures for labor and overhead expenses were charged to the Production
Cost account. The total of these debits less the credit, Cost of Sales,
represented the value of the book (estimated) inventory.

The authors' second method--"Verification of the Material, Labor
and Overhead Costs in Total"--was Nicholson's System One and disclosed
little improvement over the scheme as devised in the senior author's
text of 1913. Under their procedure of verification with respect to
this method, they observed that this plan of proving the estimates in
detail was a valuable means of revealing wastage of time, material, or
other inefficiencies.

> If, for example, the actual cost of material proves to be
> greater than the estimated cost, while it is an established
> fact that the amount of material used should not have ex-
> ceeded the estimated allowance, this is a clear indication
> that material must have either been stolen or wasted. If, on
> the other hand, there is some doubt as to the reliability of
> the estimated material cost, and the actual cost proves the

estimates to have been inaccurate, it may be advisable to
amplify the system by introducing material requisitions for
the purpose of more closely checking the consumption of material.  If the material costs are considerably underestimated,
it is probable that leaks of considerable importance exist
in the methods of handling and safeguarding it, or wastes may
be occurring in the different processes throughout the plant.

In the same way errors in the estimates for labor may disclose differences in the classifications of workers' time,
and it may be discovered that labor which is really direct
has been classified as indirect; or the discrepancies may
disclose that productive workers are not keeping up to the
time schedules on which labor costs are estimated; or that
the piece rates are vitiated by an excessive amount of
spoiled or defective work.  Also differences invariably appear between the estimated and actual overhead because in
comparatively few cases are all expense items included in the
estimate overhead.[132]

Under the third method--"Verification of Estimated Costs of the

Different Products Manufactured"--the writers followed Nicholson's

System Two with some refinement of the accounting procedure.  For exam-

ple, they recognized Raw Materials, Goods in Process, and Finished Stock

for inventory purposes and distributed factory overhead to the various

departmental accounts as Nicholson had done in his System Three.

And the fourth method--"Verification of Costs by Operating Depart-

ments"--undertook to control the costs of a plant carrying products

through several processes by developing predetermined costs for each

operation and by comparing estimated with actual results.  This method

was Nicholson's System Three somewhat revised.  A Raw Materials account,

as many Work in Process accounts as might be required, and a Finished

Stock account were opened on the General Ledger.

---

[132]Ibid., pp. 468-469.

The Raw Materials account was charged with beginning inventory and purchases of materials at actual costs and was credited with the materials used in the operating departments at actual costs likewise.

The Work in Process account for each department was charged with the beginning inventory at estimated values, with actual cost of raw materials received from the stores department, with the productive labor used therein, and with factory overhead distributed in accordance with the method of expense distribution employed in the factory. As goods were completed, this account was credited with the finished product valued at prices shown on the Schedule of Estimated Costs. The balance of the account represented the goods in process, which was compared with the physical inventory likewise valued at estimated costs.

The Finished Stock account was charged with finished goods on hand at the beginning of the period and with the cost of the products completed during the period. Estimated figures were used to determine the amount of each of these charges. The account was credited with the estimated Cost of Goods Sold; the debit for this entry being to Cost of Sales. The resulting balance of the Finished Stock account represented the book (estimated) value of the finished goods inventory at the end of a fiscal period. This inventory was compared with the physical (actual) inventory, which was priced at estimated costs.

THE COST ESTIMATE SINCE 1920.--During the early twenties, several authors considered the subject of Estimated Costs. Eggleston (1920)[133]

---

[133] Eggleston, DeWitt Carl, _Business Accounting_, New York, The Ronald Press Company, 1920, III, 349-362.

proposed the application of cost-finding by means of estimates to those industries manufacturing products with small intrinsic value or with slight differences in construction--he used manufacturers of cheap jewelry as an example in which numerous styles were made and were sold at many different prices.  In those industries to which he would apply this technique, the management would not find a complete cost system practicable but would get rather satisfactory results through the application of predetermined estimates.

The procedure that this author proposed was relatively simple.  In the first place, a schedule of estimates (analyzed as to material, labor, and indirect expense)[134] for each article to be manufactured would be prepared.  Applying these estimates to the inventory of finished goods at the time--work in process would be taken as a quantity of finished goods and any raw material on hand would be added to the material valuation of finished goods--the initial inventory would be determined and a journal entry would be made to open the factory ledger accounts.  In order to illustrate the procedure, it will be assumed that the beginning inventory for an establishment, as determined by Eggleston's methods, amounted to $14,810--Material $7,000, Labor $3,800, and Indirect Expense $4,010.  This information would be recorded as follows:

---

[134]In considering the contribution of the writers in this case, the account titles that they used for the three cost components will be employed.

                   Material                                    $7,000
                   Labor                                        3,800
                   Indirect Expense                             4,010
                        General Ledger Account                            $14,810
                        To record the opening inventory of
                   all goods analyzed as to material,
                   labor, and indirect expenses and valued
                   according to the estimated figures.


     At the close of the fiscal period, the actual expenditures for the

elements of manufacturing cost were summarized and were charged to the

respective accounts.  The figures used in the following journal entry

have been assumed for illustrative purposes:


                   Material                                    $82,000
                   Labor                                        45,000
                   Indirect Expense                             51,600
                        General Ledger Account                           $178,600
                        To charge the cost component
                   account with the actual expenditures.


     The final inventory would be determined and the estimated prices

would be applied thereto, in the same manner as followed in ascertaining

the initial inventory, and a journal entry would be made to record the

results:


                   General Ledger Account                      $22,950
                        Material                                         $10,560
                        Labor                                             5,910
                        Indirect Expense                                  6,480
                        To record the final inventory
                   valued at estimated figures.


     According to Eggleston, the balances of the three cost accounts--

Material, Labor, and Indirect Expense--represented the actual cost of

goods sold during the period, divided into the elements of material,

labor, and burden. By computing the estimated material, labor, and
burden costs of the products sold and crediting these three accounts
with these estimated figures, the author was able to get an idea of the
accuracy of his cost estimates.

```
Cost of Goods Sold                      $170,031
   Material                                        $78,210
   Labor                                            42,985
   Indirect Expense                                 48,836
      To record the estimated cost of
   sales.
```

The continuation of this author's technique, particularly with respect to the disposition of differences between actual and estimated
figures, will be considered in the next chapter.

The Simple Type Estimating Cost System, as presented by Newlove
(1922),[135] contained several improvements over Eggleston's plan.  In the
first place, he set up accounts for Raw Materials, Productive Labor,
Manufacturing Expense, Goods in Process, and Finished Goods.  As an
illustration of the contents of these accounts for the cost components,
the Raw Materials account will be reproduced:

-------

[135] Newlove, George Hillis, Cost Accounts, Washington, D. C., The
White Press Company, 1922, pp. 105-116.

| | |
|---|---|
| Initial Raw Material Inventory ............... $ .... | Raw Material in: Finished Goods Completed (a) ....... $ .... |
| Raw Material in Initial Inventory of Goods in Process (e) ............. $ .... | Final Inventory of Goods in Process (b) $ .... |
| Purchases of Raw Material . $ .... | Final Raw Material Inventory (c) ....... $ .... |
| | Balance to Profit and Loss (d) ............. $ .... |
| $ .... | $ .... |
| Raw Material Inventory (f) $ .... | |

Notes:
(a) Number of units of finished goods completed times raw material cost as per "schedule of estimated costs."
(b) Data from "analysis of inventory" for closing date; raw material cost times number of units.
(c) Ascertained by physical inventory.
(d) The balance, whether debit or credit, is closed to profit and loss.
(e) Same figure as (b) for the previous period.
(f) Same figure as (c); amount of asset to be shown in balance sheet.

The charges to this account represented the initial raw materials inventory, raw materials in initial inventory of goods in process, and purchases of raw materials as compared with Eggleston's debits of beginning inventory of materials--materials in the storeroom, in process, and in finished goods--and purchases of materials. A third improvement arises from the fact that the latter author credited the Raw Materials account, as well as the Productive Labor and Manufacturing Expense accounts, with the estimated cost of the finished goods and charged this

---

[136] Ibid., p. 107.

sum to a Finished Goods account.  And, finally, at the end of the fiscal

period, the Goods in Process Inventory was recorded in a separate ac-

count, thus leaving in the Raw Materials account only the inventory of

raw materials for balance sheet purposes.

It should be noted that this author applied his technique to a de-

partmentalized factory in order to verify the estimated unit cost of

each class of product.  He styled this method "Estimating Cost Systems--

Complex Type."[137]

Dohr (1924) devoted one chapter, "Estimating Cost Procedure,"[138] of

his text to a consideration of the estimating cost plan and exhibited

some differences in procedure from those already considered.

> During the cost period the various items of expense will be
> entered in the voucher register or the purchase book, and
> charged to ledger accounts for Raw Materials, Labor, and
> Burden.  The Raw Materials account is then credited for the
> materials issued to the factory, while the Labor account is
> divided by credits for the direct labor charged to the Goods
> in Process account and credits for indirect labor transferred
> to the Burden account.  This last account is balanced by
> credits for the burden applied to the Goods in Process.  In
> apportioning the expenses of the period as between materials,
> labor, and burden, care should be exercised to classify the
> expenses in the same manner as they are classified in the
> preparation of the estimated costs.  Unless this is done, the
> accuracy of the estimates cannot be properly measured by the
> accounts.[139]

In computing the cost of manufacture, Goods in Process accounts for

---

[137]Ibid., pp. 117-123.

[138]Dohr, James L., Cost Accounting Theory and Practice, New York,
The Ronald Press Company, 1924, pp. 494-507.

[139]Ibid., p. 497.

materials, labor and burden were charged as indicated by the quotation and were credited with the estimated cost of the goods completed during the period. The balances of these Goods in Process accounts represented the final inventory of goods in process and were compared with the totals as determined on the inventory sheets. To illustrate, ledger accounts, as employed by the author to demonstrate his plan, have been prepared.

Raw Materials

| | |
|---|---|
| 1. Opening Inventory at Actual Cost | 1. Material Used During the Period at Actual Cost |
| 2. Purchases at Actual Cost | |

Goods in Process--Materials

| | |
|---|---|
| 1. Opening Inventory of Material Content of Goods in Process at Estimated Cost | 1. Goods Completed During the Period at Estimated Material Cost |
| 2. Materials Used During the Period at Actual Cost | |

Finished Goods

| | |
|---|---|
| 1. Beginning Inventory | 1. Goods Sold During the Period Priced at Estimated Cost |
| 2. Goods Completed During the Period at Estimated Material, Labor, and Burden Costs | |

A consideration of this plan for handling estimated costs will indicate a rather concise system of recording cost information. The author was so well satisfied with this chapter that when he, together with Inghram and Love, revised the original publication in 1935,[140] this

---

[140] Dohr, James L., Inghram, Howell A., and Love, Andrew L., _Cost Accounting Principles and Practice_, New York, The Ronald Press Company, 1935, pp. 555-568.

chapter was incorporated in the new text almost intact.

Lawrence (1925)[141] recognized the value of an estimating cost system for manufacturers of chemicals, candy, and patent medicines--products that are based on definite formulas--and for makers of clothing and shoes.  This author believed that records might be maintained in such a manner that comparisons could be made of actual and estimated costs as to total cost, as to each element of cost, and as to each element with direct labor and manufacturing expenses divided according to departments.  He tended to follow Nicholson and Rohrbach's technique to such an extent that it has not been deemed necessary to illustrate his procedure.

When Lawrence revised his publication in 1937, he stated that the estimating cost system was seldom used but that it might serve a valuable purpose under some manufacturing conditions.  Evidently he found no innovations in this method of recording cost data during the interval since the first text was printed because he brought Chapter 25, "Estimating Cost Systems," practically without any changes into his later publication.[142]

Amidon and Lang (1928) thought that conditions might exist whereby a complete cost system would be impracticable and estimating costs might be installed as an alternative.[143]  In proposing the shoe and clothing

---

[141]Lawrence, W. B., Cost Accounting, New York, Prentice-Hall, Inc., 1925, pp. 360-375.

[142]Ibid., Revised Edition, 1937, pp. 381-395.

[143]Amidon, L. Cleveland, and Lang, Theodore, Essentials of Cost Accounting, New York, The Ronald Press Company, 1928, pp. 231-268.

industries as examples of plants using estimated costs, these authors

stressed the importance of style--a condition which requires the making

of samples, the quoting of selling prices, and the accepting of orders

far in advance of actual manufacturing--as a prime motive for using this

cost method to ascertain cost figures.  They followed the procedure ad-

vanced by Nicholson and Rohrbach, and reiterated by Lawrence, to such an

extent that additional consideration is not thought to be required.

That the practice of estimating costs was considered unimportant by

some authors of cost literature during this time may be suggested by the

fact that the following writers omitted this procedure entirely from

their publications:  Alford (1924); Jordan and Harris (1925); Schlatter

(1927); Maze and Glover (1929); Bangs (1930); and Reitell (1933).[144]

When Alford published his Cost and Production Handbook in 1934, he

devoted one section--Section 23, "Estimating Product Cost"[145]--to this

subject.  However, he was interested primarily in presenting accepted

practices and methods of estimating the cost of products for the purpose

of setting sales prices and/or for determining the practicability of

manufacturing a certain item rather than in the accounting procedure.

--------

[144]Alford, L. P., Management's Handbook, New York, The Ronald Press
Company, 1924; Jordan, J. P., and Harris, Gould L., Cost Accounting
Principles and Practices, New York, The Ronald Press Company, 1925;
Schlatter, Chas. F., Elementary Cost Accounting, New York, John Wiley
and Sons, 1927; Maze, Coleman L., and Glover, John G., How to Analyze
Costs, New York, The Ronald Press Company, 1929; Bangs, John R., Jr.,
Industrial Accounting for Executives, New York, McGraw-Hill Book Company,
1930; Reitell, Charles, Cost Accounting, Scranton, Pa., International
Textbook Company, 1933.

[145]Alford, Cost and Production Handbook, pp. 1273-1286.

Sanders (1934) recognized the significance of estimating by describing briefly the preparation of a cost estimate and by making the following statement:

> In a plant which secures much of its business in the form of orders obtained as a result of competitive bidding, an estimating department is required which can supply the sales department with the figures necessary for making bids.[146]

However, he was not concerned with the accounting procedure that might be necessary to furnish the required cost information or to verify the results of actual and estimated operations for a fiscal period.

That writers of periodical articles have been interested in subjects other than those relating to the accounting for cost estimates is attested by the paucity of this type of literature. In the few papers that are available, the writers have been interested, as in the cases of Alford and Sanders, with applying estimating to some particular purpose other than that of accounting. The following examples will tend to substantiate this statement.

R. E. Jacke presented a chart, together with appropriate explanations, that might be used by an individual authorized to set prices in the printing industry. The paper was classified as a technical document, which might be comprehended only by those with considerable experience. The following statement by the author is thought worthy of quoting:

> There can be no doubt that after a short practice in the use of this chart any person authorized to set prices will be

---

[146]Sanders, Thomas Henry, _Cost Accounting and Control_, New York, McGraw-Hill Book Company, 1934, p. 40.

able to determine costs as quickly and accurately as any
technical cost man with years of experience.[147]

This paper did not consider any accounting techniques.

Eugene R. Nevins presented a paper, including a set of forms and
working papers, dealing with the problem of estimating the cost of a
special job.[148] Another writer, J. C. White (Head of Estimating Department, Inland Manufacturing Division, General Motors Corporation),[149] followed the trend of thought by submitting a method of estimating factory
costs. He presented a broad general outline of this technique but failed
to include any accounting procedure. However, he did recognize the importance of the cost department:

> A good cost system is the foundation of sound estimating. Cost
> department records should form the proof of all estimates.
> Burden rates need to be correctly established for all existing
> centers. New operations, processes, or departments may re-
> quire new rates to be determined by cost studies. An energetic
> cost control activity is essential if sound estimates are to
> be met in actual production.[150]

George P. Cormack applied cost estimating to the determination of

---


[147] Jacke, R. E., "Printing Cost Estimating for Price Setting,"
National Association of Cost Accountants Bulletin, Vol. XV, No. 6,
Sec. I (November 15, 1933), pp. 325-335.

[148] Nevins, Eugene R., "Estimating the Special Order," National
Association of Cost Accountants Bulletin, Vol. XVI, No. 8, Sec. I
(December 15, 1934), pp. 434-443.

[149] White, J. C., "Estimating as a Science," National Association of
Cost Accountants Bulletin, Vol. XIX, No. 14, Sec. I (March 15, 1938),
pp. 820-828.

[150] Ibid., p. 822.

contract prices in the motor truck industry[151] but omitted the phase of accounting entirely from his thesis. George L. Williams (General Electric Company) presented a paper, "Technique of Estimating," before the Twentieth International Cost Conference. He was interested only in the methods required for proper estimating and accepted the cost department as an instrument for compiling such cost data as might be required by the estimator.[152] And, finally, Max F. Thompson offered some current features applicable to the estimating of government contracts, but recognized cost accounting only as a tool for supplying statistical information pertaining to material, labor, and overhead.[153]

A careful consideration of these articles will indicate that these writers of current literature relating to estimating costs were interested in procedures that would aid them in establishing prices of commodities rather than in the methods of recording actual and estimated costs in books and of comparing such actual and estimated results.

Van Sickle (1938), in recognizing the comparison of actual with estimated costs in an estimate cost system as the first step away from the purely historical type of actual cost system, offered three advantages that might accrue from the use of an estimate cost plan:

---

[151] Cormack, George P., "Cost Estimating for a Trucking Company," National Association of Cost Accountants Bulletin, Vol. XX, No. 6, Sec. I (November 15, 1938), pp. 315-332.

[152] Williams, George L., "Technique of Estimating," National Association of Cost Accountants Yearbook, 1939, pp. 60-73.

[153] Thompson, Max F., "Cost Estimating for Government Contracts," National Association of Cost Accountants Bulletin, Vol. XXIII, No. 21, Sec. I (July 1, 1942), pp. 1415-1428.

(1) The variances between the estimated cost of a job and its
    actual cost are set forth in accounts, and the differ-
    ences may be analyzed in terms of jobs, cost elements,
    departments and cost centers, which provide a check-up on
    the accuracy of estimating and a form of cost control.
(2) The use of predetermined estimates constitutes a forecast
    or prediction, which is in keeping with the more modern
    budgetary control procedure.
(3) The plan is simple and easy to operate where no great
    amount of details regarding variance are desired, and
    where the number of jobs worked on each month are rela-
    tively few.[154]

Van Sickle followed the usual procedure of presenting the cost esti-

mate in terms of cost elements, of cost elements according to products,

and of cost elements classified by products and departments through the

use of a single Work in Process account, an individual Work in Process

account for each cost element, or an individual Work in Process account

for each department.[155]

Neuner, another writer to incorporate a chapter on estimating costs

--"Estimated Cost Accounting Procedures"--in his publication,[156] has

summarized in a very accurate manner the accounting procedure for an

estimated cost system:

(1) Charge the Work-in-Process account with _actual_ cost of
materials, labor, and expenses used in production, (2) Charge
the Finished Goods account, crediting the Work-in-Process account for the _estimated_ cost of work completed, (3) Take a

---

[154] Van Sickle, Clarence L., _Cost Accounting_, New York, Harper &
Brothers, 1938, p. 412.

[155] _Ibid._, pp. 412-431.

[156] Neuner, John J. W., _Cost Accounting_, Chicago, Richard D. Irwin,
Inc., 1942, pp. 544-576.

physical inventory of work-in-process at <u>estimated</u> cost,
(4) Find the differences between the book and physical inventory of work-in-process and prorate the error over work-in-
process, finished goods, and cost of goods sold on the basis
of estimated cost of each or on the basis of equivalent production quantity of each.[157]

In addition to presenting the usual estimate cost systems--the gen-

eral principles of which were declared to be the same--Blocker summarized

a method that was used by a large paper manufacturing concern.[158] When

a production order was prepared, the estimated costs, in addition to the

specifications and job requirements, were recorded thereon in order that

a comparison might be made between the estimated and the actual costs as

each stage of work was completed. However, the ledger accounts were

maintained at actual costs and the estimates of costs and variances be-

tween the actual and estimated costs, as compiled on the production

orders, were used for statistical purposes only. Theorizing somewhat on

the possibilities of this device, the author made the following state-

ment:

> A variation of an improvement in the plan just explained can
> be effected by recording the total estimates of material,
> labor, and overhead costs in the Material in Process, Labor
> in Process, and Overhead Expense in Process accounts beside
> the actual costs; in this way the variance between the total
> estimates and the total actual costs for the period can be
> determined. The total estimates and variances are recorded
> in the general ledger accounts for work in process but are
> for comparative and statistical purposes only, and, conse-
> quently, no disposition need be made of the variances.[159]

---

[157]Ibid., p. 549.

[158]Blocker, op. cit., pp. 526-551.

[159]Ibid., pp. 533-534.

| | Materials in Process | | | | |
|---|---|---|---|---|---|
| Actual | Estimated | Variance | Actual | Estimated | Variance |
| $11.55 | $10.00 | $1.55 | $11.55 | $10.00 | $1.55 |

| | Labor in Process | | | | |
|---|---|---|---|---|---|
| Actual | Estimated | Variance | Actual | Estimated | Variance |
| $ 3.00 | $ 2.50 | $ .50 | $ 3.00 | $ 2.50 | $ .50 |

| | Overhead Expense in Process | | | | |
|---|---|---|---|---|---|
| Actual | Estimated | Variance | Actual | Estimated | Variance |
| $ 3.60 | $ 3.00 | $ .60 | $ 3.60 | $ 3.00 | $ .60 |

| Finished Goods |
|---|
| $18.15* |

*Sum of actual credits in the three work-in-process accounts.

A careful consideration of these accounts, with the general technique of Harrison and Camman for recording standard costs at both actual and standard values (as hereinafter presented) before the reader, will suggest that this author has passed out of the realm of estimated costs and has approached the territory claimed for standard costs.

It is rather interesting to note that when Blocker revised this publication in 1942 and edited the new text under another title, _Essentials of Cost Accounting_,[160] he failed to include the chapter, "Estimate Cost Accounting Systems," as found in the initial book. Other writers of this period who did not accept this subject as worthy of treatment in

---

160 Blocker, John G., _Essentials of Cost Accounting_, New York, McGraw-Hill Book Company, 1942.

their texts included Lawrence (1942), Neuner (1942), and Sherwood and
Chase (1942).[161]

During the last twenty-five years, the general technique for the
recording of estimated costs has passed from a condition of confusion to
a more or less state of agreement.  The accounts, as may be necessary to
record the expenditures and other costs, are maintained at actual values,
while the Work in Process, Finished Goods, and Cost of Sales accounts
accumulate the estimated figures.  At the end of the fiscal period, such
actual and estimated costs are brought together for comparison and any
differences are analyzed in accordance with the concern's policy and are
disposed of in the manners as brought out in the following chapter.

---

[161]Lawrence, W. B., *Cost Accounting for War Production*, New York,
Prentice-Hall, Inc., 1942; Neuner, John J. W., *Industrial Cost Account-
ing*, Chicago, Richard D. Irwin, Inc., 1942; and Sherwood, J. F., and
Chase, Franklin T., *Principles of Cost Accounting*, Cincinnati, Ohio,
Southwestern Publishing Company, 1942.

CHAPTER III

THE EVOLUTION OF COST ESTIMATE VARIATIONS

From the standpoint of this study, the Cost Estimate Variation will
be considered as the difference between the estimated or predetermined
cost (based primarily upon past experience and not on scientific methods)
of a factory product, or of any element of this product, and the corresponding actual cost of the same product, or any comparable element
thereof.

When the management of a concern adopts an estimate cost plan, an
attempt is made to establish a set of predetermined cost figures for
each product--a cost that will be as nearly representative as possible
of the actual costs to be incurred during the succeeding fiscal period.
The accuracy with which these estimates can be compiled will determine
the effectiveness of the system.  This accuracy may be ascertained at
the end of the period by computing the variations--the differences between the estimated and the actual costs.  If these variations indicate
that the estimates have been either greatly above or below the actual
production costs, then the management may find, by further investigation,
that it has been accepting a device so inaccurate as to be entirely use-
less or even of negative value.

The Cost Estimate Variations may arise from any one or more of the
following causes:

1. The estimates were computed incorrectly.

2. The estimates were based upon normal production, whereas the

actual production has been above or below normal.

3. The actual unit costs of the cost elements--material, labor, and overhead--were found to be greater or less than the estimated figures.

4. The actual costs were influenced by abnormal conditions which were outside the control of the factory management.

5. The operations were marked by inefficiencies which generated waste and spoilage in excess of the amounts included in the estimates.

From a historical point of view, the Cost Estimate was employed during early British industrial organization, particularly under the guild and domestic systems, as a means of checking the integrity of handicraftsmen. In those cases disclosing variations, the workman was rewarded for output in excess of the estimate and was penalized for deficits. Under the factory system, the cost estimate as a procedure for verifying quantities--a remedy for the embezzlement of raw materials --was adapted to a process cost industry by Cronhelm. However, the primary function of the cost estimate during that portion of the nineteenth century in which the engineer was responsible for the application of this technique, was to establish prices or to compute tenders for potential contracts. As the demand for products greatly exceeded the supply during this time, the price was fixed sufficiently high to cover costs, an allowance for errors that might arise, and a profit that actually depended upon the bargaining power of the two contracting parties. Variations were found to exist in those instances where any comparisons were made between the estimated and actual costs, but these factors were not considered seriously. However, as the nineteenth century closed and competition became keener, the cost estimate, and variations therefrom, became of increasing importance. About the same time, cost accounting came to receive greater emphasis, particularly from the standpoint of published material. It has, therefore, been deemed feasible to initiate this analysis of cost estimate variations with a consideration of early cost accounting literature.

Cost Estimate Variations in Early Cost Accounting Literature.--When Garcke and Fells presented the first important treatise on cost accounting in 1887, they advocated a complete coördination of the financial and cost records and accepted the cost estimate as an essential device. However, they found only one occasion in which they would record the estimated figures in the Commercial Books--when it was not practicable to proceed concurrently with the manufacture of all the articles included under a factory order but was desirable to complete and deliver a portion of the products covered by such order. Such a procedure, they reasoned, would cause some difficulty and would result in certain differences arising in the production accounts.

> But this difficulty is more apparent than real, inasmuch as
> any debit or credit balances which, upon completion of an
> order, may be found to exist, can be adjusted by the commodi-
> ties last produced to that order being taken into stock, at
> prices slightly reduced or increased to the extent of the
> difference; or the balance may, if preferred--and must neces-
> sarily if all the articles comprised in the Stock Order are
> disposed of--be at once carried to the debit or credit of
> trading account, or the sales account of any particular
> branch.[1]

---

[1] Garcke and Fells, op. cit., p. 70.

Thus, these two early writers of cost literature not only provided for recording cost estimates but also foresaw cost variations arising from the application of such a procedure and arranged for the disposition of such differences by employing one of the following methods:

1. By closing the variation into the final inventory of finished products.

2. By transferring the variation to Cost of Sales, in view of the fact that the Trading Account on the Commercial Books contained the cost of stock issued on the debit side and the proceeds of sales on the credit.[2]

3. By charging or crediting the variation to Branch Sales of the particular branch receiving the commodities (in the case of an establishment with branches).

G. P. Norton, as has been pointed out before, declared that the cost records should be separate from the financial books and that estimates, based on prices that other concerns were charging for performing the particular processes (labor and manufacturing expenses only) through which the raw materials must be put, should be recorded in the cost records only.

In order to present Norton's contribution to variation literature, his manufacturing account has been reproduced and hypothetical figures have been recorded therein. A brief explanation of each significant item will suggest the general intentions of the writer.[3]

-------

[2] Ibid., p. 239.

[3] Norton, op. cit., pp. 181-226.

| Dr. | Manufacturing Account[4] | | | Section I | | Cr. |
|---|---|---|---|---|---|---|
| 1884 | | | | 1884 | | |
| Jan. 1 | To Stock on Hand | £3,368 | | Dec.31 | By Sales | £ 9,372 |
| Dec.31 | " Material | 3,697 | | | " Commission Work | 36 |
| | " Outwork | 526 | | | " Stock on Hand | 3,220 |
| | " Packing Materials | 23 | | | | |
| | " Carriage | 94 | £ 7,708 | | | |
| | " Pattern Making (Cost | | | | | |
| | Exclusive of Material) | | 134 | | | |
| | " Processes of Manufacture, | | | | | |
| | at Trade Prices, viz.: | | | | | |
| | Dept. 1 | £1,131 | | | | |
| | Dept. 2 | 1,547 | | | | |
| | Dept. 3 | 1,088 | 3,766 | | | |
| | | | 11,608 | | | |
| | " Balance--Gross Selling | | | | | |
| | Profit to Section II | | 1,020 | | | |
| | | | £12,628 | | | £12,628 |

| | Manufacturing Account | | | Section II | | |
|---|---|---|---|---|---|---|

| Dr. | Manufacturing Account | | | Section II | | | | | Cr. |
|---|---|---|---|---|---|---|---|---|---|
| 1884 | | | | 1884 | | | | | |
| Dec.31 | To Warehouse & Office | | | Dec.31 | By Gross Selling Profit from | | | | |
| | Standing Expenses, viz.: | | | | Section I | | | | £ 1,020 |
| | Stables | £ 11 | | | | Dr. | Cr. | | |
| | Rent, Rates, Taxes, | | | | | Wages | Work | | |
| | Gas and Insurance | 36 | | | " Profit on | and | Done | | |
| | Incidentals | 20 | | | Depart- | Expenses | as Per | | |
| | Warehouse and Office | | | | ments, | as Per | Section | | |
| | Salaries | 53 | | | viz.: | Analysis | I | Profit | |
| | Traveller' Salaries | | | | | | | | |
| | and Expenses | 122 | | | Dept. 1 | 1026 | 1131 | 105 | |
| | Commission | 32 | | | " 2 | 1349 | 1547 | 198 | |
| | Depreciation of | | | | " 3 | 985 | 1088 | 103 | |
| | Fittings | 1 | £ 275 | | | 3360 | 3766 | 406 | 406 |
| | To General Charges, viz.: | | | | | | | | |
| | Bank Charges | £ 26 | | | | | | | |
| | Discount on Sales | 179 | | | " Discount on | | | | |
| | Bad Debts | 15 | 220 | | Purchases | | | | |
| | " Net Profit as Per | | | | | | | | 73 |
| | Trading Account | | 1,004 | | | | | | |
| | | | £1,499 | | | | | | £ 1,499 |

[4]Ibid., pp. 194-195.

In Section I, and on the debit side of the account, are found these items:

1. Stock on hand on January 1 of £3,363 represents the finished goods and goods in process at the beginning of the fiscal period. In valuing these inventories, the raw materials were included at cost and the processing costs were taken as the estimated figures--the trade-price for the manufacturing process.

2. Materials of £3,697 includes the actual cost of all the raw materials that were put in process during the period.

3. Outward of £526 comprises all the processes that were put out to work, either because the special process was not carried on in the mill or because it was not possible to process all the materials due to the rush of business. This amount was treated as extra cost of material.

4. Processes of Manufacture, at Trade Prices of £3,766 and ascertained by departments, represents the volume of the work, which was processed in the factory during the period, valued at the standard prices as established by the trade.

On the credit side of Section I of the Manufacturing Account is recorded the Net Sales, Income from Commission Work and the Final Inventory of Stock, which has been valued in the same manner as the Beginning Inventory (Item 1).

The difference between the debits and the credits of this account (Section I) was transferred to the credit of Section II as the gross selling profit--"corresponds in the aggregate with the margin allowed in calculating the prices of goods, between the <u>cost of production</u> and the sales price."[5]

In Section II, the debit side contains the Warehouse Expenses, the
Office Standing Expenses, and the General Charges--the selling, general,
and financial expenses of the present time.

In addition to the Gross Selling Profit from Section I and the Discount on Purchases--earned by the counting-house through its financial
arrangements--the credit side of Section II carried also the profit
(saving) on the Processes of Manufacture.  This portion of the account
tabulated the actual costs, which had been apportioned on a columnar
analysis sheet, and the estimated costs as recorded in Section I.  The
differences--variations from the Trade Prices--represent the saving that
the manufacturing department had made for the business because the management chose to perform these particular processes within the factory
rather than putting the work out to other processors.

The author recognized that the actual cost of manufacture might exceed the estimated rates and, in such an instance, the increased cost
would appear as a loss in the departments on the debit side of Section
II.[6]

Thus, in providing a scheme for indicating the profit (saving) or
loss that would arise from recording an estimated value for completed
processes in the manufacturing records of the textile industry, Norton
instituted a means of determining variations between actual costs and

---

[5]Ibid., p. 221.

[6]Ibid., p. 224.

estimated costs for wages and manufacturing expenses.

The Editor of The Accountant in 1894[7] recognized that there would

be a difference between the financial records and the cost books, due to

clerical inaccuracies and the use of estimates. He prepared a trial

balance of the cost accounts, as heretofore presented, which was de-

signed to disclose any discrepancy but, in view of the fact that the

cost figures were not recorded in the financial books, it was not neces-

sary to adjust these books. The variations did serve as a guide for

seeking inaccuracies or defalcations.

R. Whitehill, whose article[8] of 1894 has been referred to in the

chapter on "The Evolution of the Cost Estimate," employed an estimate

technique whereby the finished product was transferred to the Finished

Goods Stock Account at a fixed cost as determined from the Cost Book for

the previous year. He recognized that variations would arise and pro-

vided the "Difference Account," which has been abridged, adapted to as-

sumed data, and presented herewith, to accumulate the various discrepan-

cies. In order that his procedure with respect to variations may be

indicated, the following discussion, accounts, and journal entries in

connection with the assumed data have been presented.

The author began his system with a columnar sheet, Nominal Accounts,

which contained figures compiled from the Purchase Invoice Book, the

Wages Book, the Stock Book, and other records of initial entry. Among

the accounts included on this analysis sheet were the Melting Account,

---

[7]"Cost Accounts," op. cit., pp. 703-704.

[8]Whitehill, op. cit., pp. 1097-1113.

Sundry Stores, Sundry Working Expenses, Salaries, Sundry Processes,

Engine Expenses, Machinery and Plant, Buildings, Carriage, Commission

and Travelling Expenses, Warehouse Packing and Sundry Selling Expenses,

Rents, Rates and Insurance, Stationery and Sundry Office Expenses, Lists

and Advertising, General Expenses, Sales and Total.

DIFFERENCES ACCOUNT[9]

| Dr. | | | | Cr. |
|---|---|---|---|---|

| | | | | |
|---|---|---|---|---|
| To Sundry Stores Account-- Balance, being excess of sundry stores consumed over issues per Store Clerk's Issues Book ............... 16 | | By Melting Account-- Balance, being surplus in weight of iron ............. 22 | | |

To Sundry Stores Account--
  Balance, being excess of
   sundry stores consumed over
   issues per Store Clerk's
   Issues Book ................ 16

To Production Account--
  Balance, being excess of
   costs as shown by accounts
   over fixed costs .......... 55

To Expenses Account--
  Balance, being excess of
   production expenses over
   last year's percentages .... 43  114

To Finished Goods Stock
 Account--
 Amount to reduce stagnant
  stock:--
   Class A ................... 80
   Class D ................... 100  180

By Melting Account--
  Balance, being surplus in
   weight of iron ............. 22

By Transfer to Profits on
 Sales Account--
  Balance, being excess of
   costs as shown by accounts,
   over fixed cost values of
   goods sold (divided in
   proportion to weight of
   goods produced):--

| Tons | | |
|---|---|---|
| 580 | Class A | 20 |
| 225 | Class B | 8 |
| 290 | Class C | 10 |
| 870 | Class D | 31 |
| 435 | Class E | 15 |
| 220 | Class F | 8 |
| 2620 | | 92  114 |

By Transfer to Profits on
 Sales Account--
 Amount to reduce stagnant
  stock:--
   Class A ................... 80
   Class D ................... 100  180

         294                         294

The first ledger account to be considered is the Sundry Stores Ac-

count which was debited with a figure obtained from the Nominal Account

---

[9]Ibid., p. 1110, adapted.

and composed of the beginning inventory plus purchases less the final

inventory--the periodic plan of determining stores used.  The credits

included transfers to the Melting Account and the Sundry Processes Ac-

count in accordance with records kept by the Stores Clerk (Stores

Clerk's Issues Book)--the use of requisitions and the perpetual inven-

tory system of maintaining inventories.

## SUNDRY STORES ACCOUNT

| | | |
|---|---|---|
| To Transfer from Nominal Accounts:--<br>    Sundry Stores Consumed ... 636* | By Melting Account--Sundry Stores Issued, per Stores Clerk's Issues Book ........ 195 |
| | By Processes Account--Sundry Stores Issued, per Stores Clerk's Issues Book ........ 425 |
| (*Purchases less net increase in stock--Present writer's explanation.) | By Differences Account--Excess of Sundry Stores consumed, as shown by Accounts over Issues, per Stores Clerk's Issues Book ...................... 16 |
| 636 | 636 |

Any variation that might arise was disposed of as indicated by the fol-

lowing journal entry:

```
        Differences Account                 16.00
            Sundry Stores Account                   16.00
                To transfer to the Differences
            Account the excess of stores used,
            as shown by accounts, over issues
            as recorded in Stores Clerk's
            Issues Book.
```

The Melting Account accumulated the actual production costs--raw

materials (pig iron), coke, wages, engine expense and sundry stores--as

debits, and the average cost of the iron transferred to the Production

Account as a credit.

MELTING ACCOUNT

| | Tons | Amount | | Tons | Amount |
|---|---|---|---|---|---|
| To Sundry Transfers from Nominal Accounts:-- | | | By Production Account:-- Consumption of Iron, as per Stores | | |
| Pig Iron .............. | 2,720 | 6,187 | Clerk's Weight Book | 2,622 | 7,341 |
| Coke ................ | | 476 | By Loss in Weight by | | |
| Wages ............... | | 240 | Melting--at Fixed | | |
| Engine Expense ...... | | 221 | Rate of 5 per cent . | 138 | |
| To Transfer from Sundry Stores Account:-- | | | | | |
| Sundry Stores Issued, per Stores Clerk's Issues Book ....... | | 195 | | | |
| To Differences Account:- Balance, Being Surplus | | | | | |
| in Weight of Iron ... | 10 | 22 | | | |
| | 2,760 | 7,341 | | 2,760 | 7,341 |

The variation, which might be a surplus or a deficit in the weight of
iron, was carried to the Differences Account in accordance with this
journal entry:

| | | |
|---|---|---|
| Melting Account | 22.00 | |
| Differences Account | | 22.00 |

      To transfer surplus in weight of
iron, at average price, to the Differences Account.

The following account, Sundry Processes Account, appeared as an
antecedent Production Account and accumulated material, labor, and ex-
penses--cost items broken down according to the following departments:
Moulding, Dressing, Fitting, Painting and Japanning, and Finishing.  The
total of this account was transferred to the Production Account.

## SUNDRY PROCESSES ACCOUNT

| | | | |
|---|---|---|---|
| Transfer from Nominal<br>  Accounts:--<br>    Wages ................. | 5,450 | By Production Account:--<br>  Amount Transferred ....... | 7,782 |
| Transfer from Sundry Stores<br>  Account:--<br>    Sundry Stores Issued,<br>      per Stores Clerk's<br>      Issues Book .......... | 425 | | |
| Transfer from Expenses<br>  Account:--<br>    General Production<br>      Expenses--35 per cent<br>      on Labor (Rate as per<br>      last year's account) . | 1,907 | | |
| | 7,782 | | 7,782 |

An analysis of the Production Account indicates that it was charged
with the initial goods in process inventory valued at the estimated average cost of $3.50 per ton, with the cost of the iron consumed as re-
corded in the Melting Account, and with the conversion cost as accumulated in the Sundry Processes Account.  The Production Account was
credited with the Finished Goods completed, valued at $5.75 per ton (the
fixed cost value as predetermined from the preceding year's Cost Book),
and with the final inventory of Goods in Process, valued at the estimated cost of $3.50 per ton as employed in determining the initial in-
ventory.

## PRODUCTION ACCOUNT

| | Tons | Amount | | Tons | Amount |
|---|---|---|---|---|---|
| To Stock Account:--<br>Goods in Process<br>of Manufacture<br>on Hand at this<br>Date ............. | 165 | 577 | By Finished Stock<br>Account:--<br>Goods Finished at<br>Fixed Cost Values,<br>as Based on Records<br>of Weights, &c.,<br>and as per Cost<br>Books .............. | 2,620 | 15,061 |
| To Melting Account:--<br>Iron Consumed as<br>per Stores Clerk's<br>Weight Book ...... | 2,622 | 7,341 | By Stock Account:--<br>Goods in Process of<br>Manufacture on Hand<br>at this Date ....... | 167 | 584 |
| To Sundry Processes<br>(Including General<br>Production Expenses)<br>--Amount Transferred | | 7,782 | By Differences<br>Account:--<br>Balance, being excess<br>of Costs as shown by<br>Accounts over Fixed<br>Costs .............. | | 55 |
| | 2,787 | 15,700 | | 2,787 | 15,700 |

The variation of $55 was closed into the Differences Account in the following manner:

|  |  |  |
|---|---|---|
| Differences Account | 55.00 | |
| Production Account | | 55.00 |

> To transfer the excess of costs
> (actual costs) as shown by the ac-
> counts over fixed costs (estimated
> costs) to the Differences Account.

The Expenses Account, as employed by Whitehill, contained three columns--General Selling Expenses, General Production Expenses, and Total Expenses--on the debit side and columns for General Selling Expenses and General Production Expenses on the credit. Only the portion of the account that pertains to production costs has been reproduced here.

## EXPENSES ACCOUNT

| To Sundry Transfers from | | By Sundry Processes:-- | |
|---|---|---|---|
| Nominal Accounts:-- | | 35% on Labor-Rate, as per | |
| Sundry Working Expenses .. | 365 | Last Year's Accounts .... | 1,907 |
| Salaries ................. | 230 | By Differences Account:-- | |
| Engine Expenses .......... | 275 | Balance, being Excess of | |
| Machinery, Plant, &c.-- | | Production Expenses over | |
| Repairs, Renewals, &c. .. | 375 | Last Year's Percentages . | 43 |
| Buildings--Repairs, | | | |
| Renewals, &c. ........... | 209 | | |
| Rent, Rates, Taxes, | | | |
| Insurance, &c. .......... | 310 | | |
| Stamps, Stationery, and | | | |
| Sundry Office Expenses .. | 72 | | |
| General Expenses ........ | 114 | | |
| | 1,950 | | 1,950 |

The variation would be disposed of by an entry to the Differences Account:

```
            Differences Account                    43.00
                Expenses Account                              43.00
                    To transfer excess of production
            expenses (actual costs) over esti-
            mated figures (as charged to Sundry
            Processes on last year's percentages)
            to Differences Account.
```

In order that the final disposition of the Differences Account may
be ascertained, the other adjusting and closing entries, as recorded by
Whitehill, have been prepared:

```
            Differences Account                   180.00
                Finished Goods Stock Account                 180.00
                    Class A        80.00
                    Class D       100.00
                    To charge the Difference Account
            with the nonsalable stock at ordi-
            nary rates.
```

Profit on Sales Account[10]                       92.00
    Differences Account                                   92.00
        To transfer the excess of costs
    as shown by the accounts over the
    fixed cost values to the Profit on
    Sales Account.

Profit on Sales Account                           180.00
    Differences Account                                  180.00
        To charge Profit on Sales with
    the reduction of finished goods
    for nonsalable goods at ordinary
    rates.

Profit on Sales Account                        14,844.00
    Finished Goods Stock Account                      14,844.00
        To charge Profit on Sales
    Account with the fixed cost
    value of goods sold.

Sales Account                                  19,890.00
    Profit on Sales Account                           19,890.00
        To transfer Sales Account, less
    Carriage, Discounts, and General
    Selling Expenses, to Profit on
    Sales Account.

Profit on Sales Account                         4,778.00
    Profit and Loss Account                            4,778.00
        To transfer the net profit on
    Sales to Profit and Loss Account.


The net effect of all of these entries has been the accumulation in

a Differences Account of not only the variations that have arisen from

the use of estimated figures for recording finished goods as completed

---------------------------------

[10]This account is a multi-columnar form with a column for each
class of products and total on the left-hand page for debits and a like
ruling for the credits on the opposite page. Each entry is broken down
according to the various classes of products. These characteristics
apply also to the Sales Account and the Finished Goods Stock Account.

but also from any losses in inventory and in valuation of nonsalable stock. This Differences Account was closed into a summarizing account, Profit on Sales Account, which was ultimately closed into the Profit and Loss Account. A careful analysis of this technique will suggest that its importance merits the amount of space that has been devoted to its explanation and that Whitehill has made a great contribution to the presentation of cost estimates and their variations.

COST ESTIMATE VARIATIONS DURING THE FIRST TWO DECADES OF THE TWENTIETH CENTURY.--Goode, an English chartered accountant writing in 1900, undertook a rather detailed comparison of actual costs with estimated costs and a somewhat complete explanation of the differences that appeared.[11] At the end of the year, the writer prepared a "Summary of Cost Sheets," which disclosed the estimated net profit for the period. At the same time, he completed the "Trading Account," which revealed the actual net profit for the corresponding time. Finally, Goode presented a comparative statement, "Comparison of Cost Sheets' Summary with Trading Account," which has been reproduced in a somewhat modified manner.

---

[11] Goode, op. cit., pp. 603-607.

COMPARISON OF COST SHEETS' SUMMARY WITH TRADING ACCOUNT

| Description | Net Amount Charged to Trading Account* | Amount Charged on Cost Sheets | Surplus of Net Amount Charged to Trading Account Over Amount Charged on Cost Sheets | Surplus of Amount Charged on Cost Sheets Over Net Amount Charged to Trading Account |
|---|---|---|---|---|
| A. Materials .......... | £15,529** | £15,123 | £    406 | |
| B. Materials .......... | 27,933 | 28,744 | | £   811 |
| C. Materials .......... | 4,555 | 4,668 | | 113 |
| Wages, Process 1 ....... | 21,204 | 20,123 | 1,081 | |
| Wages, Process 2 ....... | 16,222 | 15,916 | 306 | |
| Wages, Process 3 ....... | 12,840 | 13,126 | | 286 |
| Expenses of Processes .. | 1,319 | 1,066 | 253 | |
| Tins, Boxes, Packets, &c. | 1,983 | 1,915 | 68 | |
| Expenses apportioned according to Weight of Sales ................ | 3,224 | 3,166 | 58 | |
| Expenses apportioned according to Amount of Sales ................ | 21,365 | 20,894 | 471 | |
| Discounts allowed ...... | 3,111 | 2,842 | 269 | |
| | | | £2,912 | £1,210 |
| Balance being excess of actual over estimated costs ............... | | | | 1,702 |
| | | | £2,912 | £2,912 |

*This column was headed "Net Amount" and represented the difference between the following two columns, which have been omitted: "Amount Charged to Trading Account" and "Less Increase in Finished Stock."
**Only pounds have been tabulated.

The balance of £1,702 represents also the difference between the Estimated Net Profits of £14,550 and the Actual Net Profits of £12,848, and, since the actual sales (£142,138) were used in both statements, this balance may be explained by the actual costs being in excess of the estimated costs. In order that this variation (£1,702) might be analyzed, the author prepared the Reconciliation Account which accumulated the

details that were necessary to bring the Cost Sheets into agreement with
the Trading Account.

RECONCILIATION ACCOUNT

| | | | | | |
|---|---|---|---|---|---|
| To Waste of Materials in excess of Estimate valued at .......... | | 248 | By Net Profit as per Cost Sheets' Summary | | 14,550 |
| To Net Under-estimate in Price of Materials | | 162 | By Value of errors in Estimating the Proportion of the different Materials Used: | | |
| To Deficiency in Charging Wages on Cost Sheets: | | | B. Materials over-estimated ....... | 1,135 | |
| Process 1 ......... 1,081 | | | C. Materials over-estimated ....... | 211 | |
| Process 2 ......... 306 | | | | 1,346 | |
| 1,387 | | | Less A. Materials under-estimated . | 418 | 928 |
| Less Surplus, Process 3 ....... 286 | 1,101 | | | | |
| To Deficiency in Charging Expenses of Processes ........... | | 253 | | | |
| To Deficiency in Charging Boxes, Tins, Packets, &c. ........ | | 68 | | | |
| To Deficiency in Charging Expenses: | | | | | |
| Apportioned according to Weight ... | 58 | | | | |
| Apportioned according to Amount ... | 471 | 529 | | | |
| To Deficiency in Estimating Discount . | | 269 | | | |
| To Balance, being Net Profit as per Trading Account ............ | | 12,848 | | | |
| | | 15,478 | | | 15,478 |

The author declared that the differences as disclosed in the Reconciliation Account should be thoroughly investigated and proposed a
rather detailed procedure for considering the discrepancies in raw materials.  Goode thought that the variations in materials might arise from
one or more of four causes:

1. Errors in bookkeeping or stocktaking.--His method of ascertaining errors under this classification may be summarized in four divisions:

(1) Check figures and calculations on each periodic Cost Sheet.

(2) Analyze purchases for correct classification of materials.

(3) Test stock for weights, amounts, and analysis.

(4) Examine late invoices for proper stock counting and recording.

The accountant will recognize these devices as good audit technique for raw materials at this time. In the case at hand, the author suggested that special attention might be extended to determine that no "A" Material was omitted from stock and that no "B" Material had been wrongly included.

2. Errors in estimating the cost price of materials.--The writer disclosed an analysis of this variation by compiling both the estimated cost and the actual cost per unit of the materials consumed, by ascertaining the variations by units between these two types of costs, by applying these variations to the actual units processed, and by recording the results in tabular form. The summation of the individual differences represented his "Errors in Pricing Materials." This procedure may be considered as an antecedent of the current methods of ascertaining the Price Variation of Materials. The following reproduction of Goode's example, in a somewhat different form, will tend to substantiate this statement.

SCHEDULE OF ERRORS IN PRICING MATERIALS

| Materials | Actual Tons Consumed | Estimated Cost Per Ton | Actual Cost Per Ton | Over- or Under*-Estimate Per Ton | Total Over- or Under*-Estimate |
|---|---|---|---|---|---|
| A | 15,123 | £1 | £0.19s.10$\frac{1}{2}$d. | 1$\frac{1}{2}$d. | £ 94.10s.4$\frac{1}{2}$d. |
| B | 7,186 | £4 | £4. 0s. 6 d. | 6 d.* | £179.13s.* |
| C | 3,112 | £1.10s. | £1.10s. 6 d. | 6 d.* | £ 77.16s.* |
| Net Under-estimate | | | | | £162.18s.7$\frac{1}{2}$d.* |

3. Errors in estimating shrinkage, waste, or theft of stock.--In the author's illustration, the actual deficiency in weight was 228 tons while the estimated amount was 95 tons. A comparison of the two figures discloses an under-estimated deficiency of 133 tons. This difference was analyzed as to various materials and the actual cost price per unit was applied in determining the amount of this particular variation.

SCHEDULE OF ERRORS IN ESTIMATING STOCK WASTE

| Materials | Net Deficiency in Tons | Actual Cost Per Ton | Amount of Net Deficiency |
|---|---|---|---|
| A | 83 | £0.19s.10$\frac{1}{2}$d. | £ 82. 9s.0d. |
| B | 36 | £4. 0s. 6 d. | £144.18s.0d. |
| C | 14 | £1.10s. 6 d. | £ 21. 7s.0d. |
| To Under-estimated Waste | 133 | | £248.14s.0d. |

4. Errors in estimating the weight of the various materials used in the manufacturing process.--In the hypothetical case, the author presented the following procedure for ascertaining the amount arising from this classification of potential errors. This variation was determined after taking into consideration the waste deficiency as already

calculated.

COMPARISON OF THE ESTIMATED WEIGHT OF MATERIALS
CONSUMED WITH THE ACTUAL (IN TONS)

| Mate-rials | Weight Con-sumed | Less Increase Finished Stock | Net Weight | Estimated Weight Consumed | Add Waste Defi-ciency | Net Weight | Over- or Under*- Weight Estimate |
|---|---|---|---|---|---|---|---|
| A | 15,712 | 85 | 15,627 | 15,123 | 83 | 15,206 | 421* |
| B | 6,980 | 40 | 6,940 | 7,186 | 36 | 7,222 | 282 |
| C | 3,002 | 15 | 2,987 | 3,112 | 14 | 3,126 | 139 |

Applying the actual costs to these variations in weight, the author arrived at a value of the errors in estimating the weight of the different materials used in the manufacturing processes. This difference has a tendency to parallel the Quantity Variation, which will be considered more completely in another section of this study.

COMPUTATION OF ERRORS IN WEIGHT OF MATERIALS CONSUMED

| Mate-rials | Over- or Under*- Weight Estimate (Tons) | Actual Cost Per Ton | Amount of Over- or Under*- Estimate |
|---|---|---|---|
| A | 421* | £0.19s.10½d. | £ 418. 7s.4½d.* |
| B | 282 | £4. 0s. 6 d. | £1,135. 1s.0 d. |
| C | 139 | £1.10s. 6 d. | £ 211.19s.6 d. |
| Net Over-estimate | | | £ 928.13s.1½d. |

A recapitulation of these tables will indicate that a net material over-estimate of £517.0s.6d. has been analyzed into three differences (variations)--over-estimate due to errors in estimating weight (a form of quantity variation) of £928.13s.1½d.; an under-estimate in cost price of materials consumed (a price variation type) of £162.18s.7½d.; and an under-estimate in shrinkage or waste of £248.14s.

The author recognized three causes for differences in the wages account--changes in the rates of wages (a price variation); errors in analyzing the wages paid; and payment of wages for work not actually done (might be considered as a forerunner of the quantity variation). However, he failed to include an illustration of the application of these forces as he had done in the explanation of the material differences.

Although Goode has indicated several other discrepancies in the Reconciliation Account, he has failed to make a detailed analysis of these items. However, this review of his efforts suggests that the English had recognized the importance of variations in presenting cost data as early as the beginning of the twentieth century.

Lean, another English writer of this period to make use of the cost estimate, followed the same general procedure as Goode. Lean prepared a Factory Trading Account from the Cost Records and a Factory Trading Account from the Financial Books. He brought these two compilations together on "The Comparative Statement of Estimated and Actual Costs as Per Trading Accounts." Finally, he prepared the Reconciliation Account as a means of disclosing the variations between the estimated and actual net profits.[12]

This writer, as in the case of Goode, gave more attention to the analysis of the material variations than to the other cost elements. He apportioned the material differences under three classifications--Errors

---

[12] Lean, op. cit., pp. 331-345.

in Pricing, Errors in Estimates of Different Proportions of Materials
Used, and The Actual Waste in Excess of the Estimate.  He recognized
that differences would arise in Wages and in General Production Expenses
but failed to consider these cost elements from the standpoint of determining the various factors within each.  As the Cost Records were maintained primarily as statistical devices, the variations prompted no adjusting entry in the Financial Books but served simply as a guide in
preparing future estimates.

In view of the fact that Lean's methods are so similar to those
proposed by Goode, a complete presentation of his forms and procedure
has been omitted.  Mention of Lean's article is made here to add credence to the earlier writer's contribution.

Garry, who charged his Manufacturing Account on the factory ledger
with actual expenses as incurred and credited this account with estimated cost of total products completed during the fiscal period, realized
that a variation or difference would usually arise as a result of actual
production differing from anticipated output or of inaccuracies of estimates.[13]  Therefore, he provided for the disposition of this difference
by closing it into the Revenue Account at the end of the year.  The
author's Manufacturing Account, greatly abridged, and Revenue Account
have been reproduced to substantiate this statement.

---

[13] Garry, _Multiple Cost Accounts_, pp. 5-29.

Manufacturing Account for Twelve Months,
December 31st, 1904

| | | | |
|---|---|---|---|
| To Prime Costs ........... | £17,889 | By Production Account .... | £24,435 |
| To Factory Charges ....... | 6,215 | By Sundry Sales, Scrap, | |
| To Balance to Revenue | | Ashes, &c. ............. | 39 |
| Account ................ | 370 | | |
| | £24,474 | | £24,474 |

Revenue Account to December 31st, 1904

| | | | |
|---|---|---|---|
| Directors' Remuneration ... | £  600 | By Trading Account ........ | £7,042 |
| Income Tax, Schedule D .... | 435 | By Manufacturing Account .. | 370 |
| Law Charges and Fees ...... | 130 | By Repairs Account ........ | 218 |
| Auditor's Fees ............ | 105 | | |
| Patents and Expenses ...... | 274 | | |
| Land Purchases Expenses ... | 247 | | |
| Balance to Profit and Loss | | | |
| Account ................ | 5,839 | | |
| | £7,630 | | £7,630 |

In commenting upon this phase of his procedure, Garry stated that

> . . . the crux of the whole system of Factory Accounting
> rests on the balancing of the production value with the con-
> sumption of raw material, wages, and expenses of producing
> same; and what we ask of the factory accountant is the carry-
> ing out of the cost system so that, excepting the ordinary
> fluctuations in the prices of raw material, savings in labour,
> coal, and charges, the factory production values on the
> credit side shall balance the purchases, wages, and charges
> incurred and debited to the Factory Account on the other
> side, with the result that the Factory Accounts will show
> cost, neither more or less.[14]

In 1909, when J. Lee Nicholson first proposed his three estimated

cost systems, he recognized that their application would result in cer-

tain differences remaining in the ledger accounts due to the fact that

---

[14] *Ibid.*, pp. 22-23.

the estimates would usually be inaccurate.  In this publication, the
author provided for a method of eliminating these differences.[15]

By way of review, it is called to the attention of the reader that,
under System One, the ledger accounts--Materials, Labor, and Indirect
Expenses--were charged with the beginning inventory at estimated prices
and with the purchases and expenditures at actual costs, and were credited with the final inventory at estimated figures.  The resulting
balance would be the Cost of Sales at actual prices which was compared
with the estimated cost of sales as determined by the completion of the
Analysis of Cost of Sales.

Again employing the data as assumed heretofore in the chapter on
Estimated Costs, the author's scheme for closing the differences in the
ledger accounts will be illustrated.

SCHEDULE OF LEDGER ACCOUNT BALANCES, ESTIMATED
COST OF SALES AND DIFFERENCES BETWEEN
ACTUAL AND ESTIMATED FIGURES

| Ledger Accounts | Debits to Accounts | | Credits | Balances Actual Cost of Sales | Estimated Cost of Sales | Differ- ences Debits* Credits |
| --- | --- | --- | --- | --- | --- | --- |
| | Beginning Inventory | Purchases or Expenditures | Final Inventory | | | |
| Materials | $ 5,000 | $15,000 | $ 8,000 | $12,000 | $13,000 | $1,000 |
| Labor | 3,600 | 8,400 | 5,000 | 7,000 | 7,000 | --- |
| Indirect Expenses | 3,200 | 5,800 | 4,800 | 4,200 | 4,000 | 200* |
| Totals | $11,800 | $29,200 | $17,800 | $23,200 | $24,000 | $ 800 |

Under Nicholson's closing procedure, the estimated cost of sales (from

---

[15]Nicholson, Nicholson on Factory Organization and Costs, pp. 232-
255.

the "Analysis of Cost of Sales") would be debited to the Sales Account

and credited to the three ledger accounts--Materials, Labor, and In-

direct Expenses:

```
Sales                                 24,000.00
     Materials                                    13,000.00
     Labor                                         7,000.00
     Indirect Expenses                             4,000.00
          To record the estimated cost
     of sales in accordance with the
     amounts determined in the
     Analysis of Cost of Sales.
```

When this journal entry had been posted, the Sales Account showed

the gross profit, based on estimated calculations, and the three ledger

accounts--Materials, Labor, and Indirect Expenses--contained any differ-

ences resulting from inaccuracies in the estimates.  In the case at hand,

the Materials Account has a credit balance of $1,000 (indicating that

the estimate was too high), the Labor Account has no balance (denoting

an accurate forecast), and Indirect Expenses has a debit balance of $200

(suggesting that the estimate was too low).  These differences would be

disposed of in the following manner:

```
Materials                             1,000.00
     Indirect Expenses                              200.00
     Sales                                          800.00
          To close the differences between
     the actual and estimated cost of
     sales to the Sales Account.
```

In the first publication, the author recognized the alternative

method of handling these accounts.  After debiting the Materials, Labor,

and Indirect Expenses Accounts with the initial inventories and purchases

and/or expenditures, he pointed out that these accounts might be credited with the total estimated costs as determined upon completion of the
Analysis of Cost of Sales. The corresponding debit was to Sales, which
would, as in the preceding procedure, now contain the gross profit based
on estimated cost calculations. The balances in the three ledger accounts (Materials, Labor, and Indirect Expenses) would represent the
theoretical inventories based on the estimated cost.[16]

The application of this last procedure to the data assumed in the
foregoing instance will give results as indicated below:

SCHEDULE OF LEDGER ACCOUNT BALANCES, ESTIMATED<br>
INVENTORIES, AND DIFFERENCES BETWEEN<br>
ACTUAL AND ESTIMATED FIGURES

| | The Ledger Accounts | | | | Physical | Differ-ences |
| Ledger Accounts | Debits to Accounts | | Credits | Balances | (Actual) | Debits* |
| | Beginning Inventory | Purchases or Expenditures | Cost of Sales | Book Inventories | Inventories | Credits |
|---|---|---|---|---|---|---|
| Materials | $ 5,000 | $15,000 | $13,000 | $ 7,000 | $ 8,000 | $1,000 |
| Labor | 3,600 | 8,400 | 7,000 | 5,000 | 5,000 | --- |
| Indirect Expenses | 3,200 | 5,800 | 4,000 | 5,000 | 4,800 | 200* |
| Totals | $11,800 | $29,200 | $24,000 | $17,000 | $17,800 | $ 800 |

In view of the inherent nature of estimates, inaccuracies will
usually arise and the three inventory accounts will ordinarily vary from
the physical inventories. These disclosed differences, arising from a
comparison of the book and physical figures, should be disposed of as in
the former case but the explanation for the current required journal
entry will be different from the explanation for the entry referred to.

---

[16] *Ibid.*, p. 236.

| | | |
|---|---|---|
| Materials | 1,000.00 | |
| Indirect Expenses | | 200.00 |
| Sales | | 800.00 |

To adjust the inventory accounts
for the difference between the book
(estimated) and the physical (actual)
figures.

When the author published his text, Cost Accounting Theory and Practice, in 1913, he ignored the first scheme of verification and included only the latter plan; that is, of crediting the ledger accounts (Materials, Labor, and Indirect Expenses) with the estimated cost of sales rather than with the final inventory.[17]

Nicholson stated that the amount of the differences would tend to guide the manufacturer in ascertaining the causes for the variations and the extent to which the estimates should be revised.

For instance, if the material costs are considerably underestimated, it is probable that leaks of considerable importance exist in the methods of handling and safeguarding the material, or that wastes occur in the processes. If the estimates for labor are much too low, the cause may lie in the classification of labor; that is, labor that is really direct may have been classed as indirect. The principal difference, however, is almost always found in the indirect expense account, since comparatively few manufacturers calculate all the phases of overhead cost in their estimates.[18]

After a careful study of the differences, together with an analysis of the contributing factors, the author stated that the estimates should be revised on the basis of known data if the causes of the differences

---

[17]Nicholson, Cost Accounting Theory and Practice, p. 169.

[18]Ibid., p. 169.

could not be found.  However, he was convinced that no revision would
give the correct figures but that the following rule, if the same
methods and routine of manufacture have been maintained since the original estimate was made, would result in fairly accurate figures:

> . . . if the differences between any corresponding elements
> in the book inventory and physical inventory be divided by
> the number of units of product manufactured during the period,
> the result will be, approximately, the amount to be added to
> or subtracted from the original estimate relating to that
> element.[19]

Nicholson pointed out in both publications that the manufacturer
might prepare monthly statements, based on his estimates of costs, and
might adjust the differences at the end of the fiscal period after the
physical inventory had been ascertained.

> If such a system of verifying and revising estimates is fol-
> lowed up, it will sooner or later bring the estimates close
> to the true costs.  But it will often be necessary to locate
> and correct seeming inaccuracies in the cost estimates.  To
> do this, the estimates will have to be made by departments or
> operations, and the plan of verification will have to be ex-
> tended to meet the divisions in the estimates.[20]

Under System Two, Nicholson provided for the departmental classification of material and labor but followed the same general procedure for
the verification of differences as in System One.  The only modification
of principle was in the number of accounts employed--a procedure which
tends to disclose compensating discrepancies that might be concealed

---

[19] Ibid., p. 170.

[20] Ibid., pp. 170-171.

under the simple plan.  By making use of the data as assumed in the
study of System Two in the first chapter of this study, an idea of the
significance of this improvement may be gained.

SCHEDULE OF LEDGER ACCOUNT BALANCES, ESTIMATED INVENTORIES<br>BY CLASSIFICATIONS, AND DIFFERENCES BETWEEN<br>ACTUAL AND ESTIMATED FIGURES

| | The Ledger Accounts | | | | Physical | Differ- |
| | Debits to Accounts | | Credits | Balances | (Actual) | ences |
| Ledger | Beginning | Purchases or | Cost of | Book | Inven- | Debits* |
| Accounts | Inventory | Expenditures | Sales | Inventories | tories | Credits |
|---|---|---|---|---|---|---|
| Materials: | | | | | | |
| Class 1 | $ 3,000 | $ 8,000 | $ 7,000 | $ 4,000 | $ 5,000 | $1,000 |
| Class 2 | 2,000 | 7,000 | 6,000 | 3,000 | 3,000 | --- |
| Labor: | | | | | | |
| Department 1 | 2,000 | 5,000 | 4,000 | 3,000 | 3,200 | 200 |
| Department 2 | 1,600 | 3,400 | 3,000 | 2,000 | 1,800 | 200* |
| Indirect | | | | | | |
| Expenses | 3,200 | 5,800 | 4,000 | 5,000 | 4,800 | 200* |
| Totals | $11,800 | $29,200 | $24,000 | $17,000 | $17,800 | $ 800 |

The additional analysis, which is subject to expansion sufficiently
to cover any number of classifications of materials and departments for
labor, tends to further the pursuit of discrepancies and their causes.
In the case under consideration, System One revealed an overestimate of
material costs of $1,000; System Two found this discrepancy in Material--
Classification 1 only.  In a study and revision of estimates, Material--
Classification 2 would not be involved.  Whereas System One indicated
the labor estimates to be accurate, System Two brought out compensating
differences of $200, which would be considered under the author's inves-
tigation and revision procedure at the end of the year.  The Indirect
Expenses were handled as in System One:  ". . . in order to avoid the

clerical work necessary for distributing and determining departmental

indirect expenses."[21]

The journal entry to remove the differences from the Ledger Ac-

counts, under System Two, would be, according to Nicholson, as follows:

```
        Materials--Class 1                      1,000.00
        Labor--Department 1                        200.00
           Labor--Department 2                                 200.00
           Indirect Expenses                                   200.00
           Sales                                               800.00
              To adjust the inventory accounts
           for the differences between the book
           (estimated) and the physical
           (actual) figures.
```

The author recognized that, although System Two tended to localize

estimates, costs, and differences to some extent, it failed to disclose

many significant facts.

> For example, it may be known that a profit is being made on
> the product as a whole, but it may also be expected that cer-
> tain articles or classes of products are being sold at a
> loss, and that this loss is being paid out of the profits on
> other goods.[22]

Estimating System Three was devised to remedy this deficiency, by

providing for an analysis of estimates and of actual costs according to

classes of products and operating departments.  In general, the proce-

dure followed was identical with that in System Two but the breakdown of

components was more complete--additional effort being made to localize

-----------------

[21] Ibid., p. 171.

[22] Ibid., p. 172.

estimates, costs, and differences.  There was some modification in the treatment of Indirect Expenses, which tends to reveal how errors in calculating indirect expenses have affected estimates and costs.  However, the additional flexibility afforded for analysis purposes does not warrant a presentation in this consideration of variations.

John R. Wildman, in presenting his chapter on Estimating Costs in 1911, stated that there would always be a difference between estimated costs and actual costs and enumerated two causes for these variations:

1. Inefficient material--material which is below the standard of quality and requires more than standard of quantity.
2. Inefficient labor, due to inefficient workmen, methods or conditions.[23]

The writer then set up a plan for reconciling estimated costs with actual costs.  To illustrate his procedure, the following data will be assumed for Job Y - 3:

| Cost Elements | Estimated Costs | Actual Costs |
|---|---|---|
| Materials | $ 7,500 | $ 7,500 |
| Labor | 9,000 | 9,000 |
| Overhead | 4,500 | 4,800 |
| Totals | $21,000 | $21,300 |

If these figures were recorded as totals only, the following journal entries would be made, according to Wildman:

---

[23]Wildman, op. cit., p. 88.

Cost of Contracts                                21,000.00
        Reserve for Cost of Contracts                        21,000.00
            To record the estimated cost
    of Job Y - 3.


Reserve for Cost of Contracts                    21,300.00
        Material                                              7,500.00
        Labor                                                 9,000.00
        Overhead                                              4,800.00
            To charge the Reserve for
    Cost of Contracts with the
    actual cost of Job Y - 3.


Cost of Contracts                                   300.00
        Reserve for Cost of Contracts                           300.00
            To charge the difference
    between estimated and actual
    costs of Job Y - 3 to Cost of
    Contracts.


A careful consideration of this procedure indicates that Wildman simply provided a method for recording estimated costs on the general ledger by using two accounts that did not affect the actual cost records. When the actual costs were ascertained upon the completion of a contract or at the end of a fiscal period, he compared these figures with the estimates by crediting the actual costs to their respective accounts and charging the estimating account that had originally received the credit entry. Any resulting variation was closed into the other account, which actually had the status of a cost of sales account. To be more specific, Wildman set up his estimates, disclosed the variation between actual and estimate, and closed this variation into the cost of contracts.

When Nicholson and Rohrbach revised the senior author's 1913 publication in 1919, they recognized the importance of carefully prepared

cost estimates and the certainty of differences between estimated and
actual figures.

> The figures which appear on the schedule of estimated costs
> are those on which the pricing of the inventories is based.
> They constitute the cost sheets of the articles priced there-
> on, in that they state the article cost which is used for
> making the selling prices.  Any errors in the estimated fig-
> ures necessarily affect the inventory valuations and throw
> the whole system of proof out of gear.[24]

The writers provided for the disposition of any differences that
might arise between their estimated and actual inventories and cost of
goods sold.  If the following data may be assumed for an enterprise
using Nicholson and Rohrbach's Method Two--"Verification of the Materials, Labor, and Overhead Costs in Total"--the author's scheme for
adjusting differences may be illustrated:

| | The Ledger Accounts | | | | Physical (Actual) Inven- tories | Differ- ences Debits* Credits |
| Ledger Accounts | Debits to Accounts | | Credits | Balances | | |
| | Beginning Inventory | Purchases or Expenditures | Cost of Sales | Book Inventories | | |
|---|---|---|---|---|---|---|
| Raw Material | $ 5,000 | $15,000 | $13,000 | $ 7,000 | $ 8,000 | $1,000 |
| Productive Labor | 3,600 | 8,400 | 7,000 | 5,000 | 5,000 | --- |
| Factory Overhead | 3,200 | 5,800 | 4,000 | 5,000 | 4,800 | 200* |
| Totals | $11,800 | $29,200 | $24,000 | $17,000 | $17,800 | $ 800 |

If, after discrepancies between estimated and actual figures have
been determined as in this case, an analysis of the estimated costs indicates that they have not been computed incorrectly, then the differences

---

[24] Nicholson and Rohrbach, *op. cit.*, p. 480.

are disposed of in accordance with the following rules:

> When discrepancies appear between the values of the book and
> the physical inventories, it is important to adjust the esti-
> mated costs and revalue the inventories at the close of the
> period. As regards the discrepancies in the accounts of the
> current period, if the value of the physical inventory is
> found to be less than that of the book inventory, the costs
> have been understated and the difference constitutes a loss;
> as such it is transferred to profit and loss. If the physi-
> cal inventory proves to be greater than the book inventory,
> the costs have been overestimated and the difference consti-
> tutes a profit which may be credited to either profit and
> loss or cost of sales.[25]

Applying these rules to the case at hand, the journal entries to
adjust the accounts would be as follows:

| | | |
|---|---|---|
| Raw Material | 1,000.00 | |
|     Profit and Loss _or_ | | |
|     Cost of Sales | | 1,000.00 |
|       To adjust the material component in final inventories for difference between estimated and actual value (Physical inventory greater). | | |
| | | |
| Profit and Loss | 200.00 | |
|     Factory Overhead | | 200.00 |
|       To adjust the indirect expense element in final inventories for difference between estimated and actual values (Physical inventory smaller). | | |

On the other hand, if a careful consideration of the estimated
costs indicated that they had been calculated incorrectly, then the
effect on the final inventories must be determined:

---

[25] _Ibid._, p. 480.

If the estimated costs are incorrect, the inventory values
based on them must also be incorrect.  Therefore, any adjustments also affect the closing inventories, the value of which
should be revised.[26]

In the case under consideration, if a careful check on the esti-

mated cost figures disclosed that an error in calculation has been made

in computing raw materials, which resulted in a net overstatement of

estimates of 4 per cent, then the Analysis of Sales (when the correct

figure was applied) would contain a figure of $12,480 instead of $13,000

and the final physical inventory would be $7,680 instead of $8,000.  The

book (estimated) inventory would be $7,520 instead of $7,000.  To cor-

rect and adjust the books for the revisions arising from correcting the

cost estimates, the following journal entries would be required:

```
Raw Materials                        520.00
    Cost of Sales                                520.00
        To correct the cost of sales of
    finished goods' component, raw
    materials, for 4 per cent net
    error in the cost estimate.


Raw Materials                        160.00
    Profit and Loss or
    Cost of Sales                                160.00
        To adjust the material compo-
    nent in final inventory for dif-
    ference between estimated and
    actual values.
```

The clearing of differences between estimated and actual figures

through Cost of Sales or Profit and Loss and the correcting of

---

[26]
    _Ibid._, p. 480.

Inventories and Cost of Sales for incorrect cost estimates at the end of
the fiscal period represent definite contributions contained in the 1919
publication of Nicholson and Rohrbach that were not in Nicholson's
earlier publications.

Cost Estimate Variations Since 1920.--As may be verified by another
consideration of the preceding division of this chapter, writers of accounting literature treating estimating cost principles recognized that
differences would arise between actual and estimated results and usually
provided for the disposition of such differences.  Eggleston,[27] whose
cost estimate plan has been presented in the preceding chapter by means
of the journalization of a hypothetical case, made provision for disposing of such difference through the Cost of Goods Sold account.

In order to illustrate the handling of variances by this author,
the journal entries, as just mentioned, have been posted to accounts in
this section:

Materials

| Beginning Inventory | 7,000 | Cost of Goods Sold | 78,210 |
| Purchases | 82,000 | Final Inventory | 10,560 |
| (Balance   230) | | | |

Labor

| Beginning Inventory | 3,800 | Cost of Goods Sold | 42,985 |
| Expenditures | 45,000 | Final Inventory | 5,910 |
| | | (Balance   95) | |

Indirect Expense

| Beginning Inventory | 4,010 | Cost of Goods Sold | 48,836 |
| Expenditures | 51,600 | Final Inventory | 6,480 |
| (Balance   294) | | | |

---

[27]Eggleston, op. cit., pp. 358-361.

A consideration of these ledger accounts will indicate that the
Material and Indirect Expense accounts have debit balances of $230 and
$294 respectively (the estimates for these cost items were too low)
whereas the Labor account has a credit balance of $95 (the estimate for
labor cost was too high).  According to Eggleston, if these discrepancies from period to period indicated that the estimates were strikingly
incorrect, they should be revised accordingly.  With respect to the disposition of these differences, the adjustment was made through the Cost
of Goods Sold account--the author's adjusting entries were made to Material, Adjustment; Labor, Adjustment; and Indirect Expense, Adjustment;
accounts, as indicated below, but were actually posted to the Material,
Labor, and Indirect Expense accounts in the ledger.

```
Cost of Goods Sold                       524.00
    Material, Adjustment                            230.00
    Indirect Expense, Adjustment                    294.00
        To adjust the Material and
    Indirect Expense accounts for dif-
    ferences due to estimates being
    too low.


Labor, Adjustment                         95.00
    Cost of Goods Sold                               95.00
        To adjust the Labor account for
    differences due to estimate being
    too great.
```

As the result of these entries, the differences between the actual
and estimated cost of the three cost components have been disclosed and
have been closed to Cost of Goods Sold, which, according to Eggleston,
now contained a balance equivalent to the total cost of goods sold.

Newlove,[28] another author to consider the problem of differences
between actual and estimated figures, would make the following correc-
tion adjustment to dispose of such variation (the figures in the hypothetical case have been used again for illustrative purposes):

```
Productive Labor                    95.00
Profit and Loss                    429.00
   Raw Materials                              230.00
   Manufacturing Expense                      294.00
      To close the balance in the
   three cost accounts to profit and
   loss.
```

In disclosing these three variations on the Statement of Profit and
Loss, the author included them as an adjustment to cost of sales.  "As
these balances affect net operating profit and yet do not constitute
selling or administrative items, the adjustment should be inserted in
the profit and loss statement as shown below."[29]

```
Sales                                                $10,000.00*
Cost of Sales                           $8,500.00*
Adjustments:
  Under-estimated Raw
    Material Cost         $230.00
  Under-estimated
    Overhead Cost          294.00
                          $524.00
  Over-estimated
    Direct Labor Cost       95.00         429.00        8,071.00
Gross Profit on Sales                                  $ 1,929.00
```

    *Amounts have been assumed for Sales and Cost of Sales;
       figures from the hypothetical case have been employed
       for the Adjustments.

---

[28] Newlove, op. cit., p. 113.

[29] Ibid., p. 111.

When Dohr came to the verification and adjustment of the cost estimates, he compared the balances of the Goods in Process accounts with
the final inventories of such components.  Any differences between such
values might be disposed of in either of two manners--(1) spread over
the goods completed during the period; or (2) allocated between the cost
of goods completed at estimated costs plus the closing inventory minus
the opening inventory.[30]  He thought that the second method was the more
accurate and presented it only in the revised edition.[31]

To illustrate this technique, the following data will be assumed
for the Goods in Process-Materials account:

Goods in Process-Materials

| Opening Inventory | | Goods Completed | |
|---|---|---|---|
| (Estimated) | 1,000.00 | (Estimate) | 5,600.00 |
| Materials Used | | | |
| (Actual) | 6,510.00 | | |
| (Balance 1,910.00) | | | |

When the physical inventory was valued at the estimated prices, the
amount was determined to be $1,600.00.  The corresponding account bal-
ance, as indicated above, was found to be $1,910.00.  Applying Dohr's
correcting method, the following result would be obtained for the Correcting Value in per cent:

---

[30]Dohr, _op. cit._, p. 499.

[31]Dohr, Inghram, and Love, _op. cit._, p. 560.

$$\frac{\text{Book Balance - Closing Physical Inventory Value}}{\text{Cost of Goods Completed + Closing Inventory - Initial Inventory}} = \text{Correcting Value (\%)}$$

$$\frac{\$1,910.00 - \$1,600.00}{\$5,600.00 + \$1,600.00 - \$1,000.00} = 5\%$$

If the estimate had been 5 per cent higher, the account would have been in balance.  Therefore, this adjusting per cent is applied to the estimated amounts in the Goods in Process-Materials account in order to obtain the adjusted balance.  After this adjusted balance has been determined, the following journal entry would be made to bring the book account to this amount:

```
Cost Adjustment Account                                    $230.00
   Goods in Process-Materials                                         $230.00
      To adjust the Goods in Process-Materials for
   the difference between actual and estimated
   values:
      Balance per Goods in
         Process-Materials be-
         fore adjustment                      $1,910.00
      Opening Inventory at
         Adjusted Estimate       $1,050.00
      Materials Used at
         Actual                   6,510.00
           Total                 $7,560.00
      Less Goods Completed
         at Adjusted Estimate     5,880.00
           Adjusted Inventory                 1,680.00
      Amount required to
         Adjust Account                       $   230.00
```

The balance of the Cost Adjustment Account ($230.00) would be allocated over the Cost of Sales for the period and the Finished Goods Inventory at the end of the period.[32]

_______________

[32] Dohr, _op. cit._, p. 500.

Lawrence[33] declared that the errors in the estimate should be apportioned between the finished goods and the work in process on the
basis of the estimated cost of each.  To illustrate his procedure, the
following data will be assumed:

1. Estimated cost of production:

|  | Amount | Per Cent |
|---|---|---|
| Finished Goods | $45,000.00 | 90 |
| Work in Process | 5,000.00 | 10 |
|  | $50,000.00 | 100 |

2. Differences between the inventory and the balances in the
   work in process accounts (as per hypothetical case):

| | |
|---|---|
| Material in Process | $230.00 |
| Labor in Process | 95.00* |
| Manufacturing Expense in Process | 294.00 |

    *Less than inventory; other
      items more than inventory.

The first journal entry would transfer these balances to the Adjustment account in the following manner:

| | | |
|---|---|---|
| Adjustment | 429.00 | |
| Labor in Process | 95.00 | |
|   Material in Process | | 230.00 |
|   Manufacturing Expense in Process | | 294.00 |

    To transfer the differences between
the balances of the work in process accounts and the amounts of the work in
process inventories valued at estimated
values to the Adjustment account.

After this entry had been posted, the balance in the Adjustment
account would be apportioned between Finished Goods and Work in Process
on the basis of the estimated cost of each--90 per cent and 10 per cent

---

[33] Lawrence, *op. cit.*, pp. 367-368.

respectively in this case--and the following journal entry would be made
to close the Adjustment account:

| | | |
|---|---|---|
| Finished Goods | 386.10 | |
| Material in Process | 23.00 | |
| Manufacturing Expense in Process | 29.40 | |
|     Labor in Process | | 9.50 |
|     Adjustment | | 429.00 |

      To close the Adjustment
account to Finished Goods and the
Work in Process accounts.

It is rather interesting that Lawrence transferred the balances in
total for all of the cost elements to the Adjustment account and immediately charged back to the Work in Process accounts their portion of
the variation (10 per cent here) rather than charge Finished Goods with
its share (90 per cent in this case) and debit and/or credit each Work
in Process account with amounts to offset this debit.  However, the
author was interested in disclosing not only the variation by using the
Adjustment account but also the range of the variation--$294.00 plus to
$95.00 minus or $389.00.  If the suggested entry had been made, the
variation account would not have been called to the management's attention and only $386.10 would have been carried to the Finished Goods ac-
count as a net figure.  The author did not vary this technique when he
revised his publication in 1937.

Amidon and Lang illustrated three methods of disposing of the variations between actual and estimated figures:  (1) charge to cost of sales;
(2) allocate to the goods completed during the period; and (3) spread
over the effective production for the period (Work in Process, Finished

Goods, and Cost of Sales) on the basis of the quantities of products in each classification or of the value represented by such quantities. The writers accepted the method of spreading the variation over the effective production according to quantities as the most logical and accurate of the plans.[34]

Van Sickle recognized that a cost variance might arise from one or more of four causes: (1) errors in the preparation of the cost estimate; (2) estimate based on normal production whereas actual production was above or below normal; (3) actual unit costs of cost elements differing from estimated unit costs; and (4) waste and spoilage being in excess of amount included in estimate.[35]

The variance, resulting from the entries in the Work in Process account, was transferred to a Cost Variance account at the end of the month. This account was closed to Work in Process, Finished Goods, and Cost of Goods Sold accounts according to the effective production represented by each account.[36] In making this transfer, he prepared three journal entries for reasons that he did not disclose.

If it may be assumed that the excess of actual cost over estimated cost was $96.00 and that the effective production contained in the three accounts was 4,800 units--Work in Process 800 units (2,400 units one-third completed), Finished Goods 1,000 units, and Cost of Goods Sold

---

[34] Amidon and Lang, _op. cit._, pp. 248-251.

[35] Van Sickle, _op. cit._, p. 417.

[36] _Ibid._, pp. 417, 422, 427.

3,000 units--then his procedure may be illustrated.

In the first place, he ascertained the Unit Cost Variance by dividing the Cost Variance by the Effective Production:

$$\frac{\text{Cost Variance,} \quad \$96.00}{\text{Effective Production,} \quad 4,800} = \$.02, \text{ Unit Cost Variance.}$$

He then prepared a schedule for the purpose of allocating the Cost Variance:

COMPUTATION OF COST VARIANCE CORRECTIONS
UNDER ESTIMATE COST PLAN

| | Units | Unit Cost Variance | Cost Variance Corrections |
|---|---|---|---|
| Work in Process | 800 | $.02 | $16.00 |
| Finished Goods | 1,000 | .02 | 20.00 |
| Cost of Goods Sold | 3,000 | .02 | 60.00 |
| Totals | 4,800 | | $96.00 |

After this information had been obtained, Van Sickle made the following journal entries:

| | | |
|---|---|---|
| Cost Variance | 96.00 | |
|     Work in Process | | 96.00 |

To record the transfer of the unfavorable cost variance, representing an excess of actual cost over estimated cost, to the Cost Variance account.

| | | |
|---|---|---|
| Work in Process | 16.00 | |
|     Cost Variance | | 16.00 |

To record the transfer of the unfavorable variance allocated to the Work in Process inventory.

```
Finished Goods                              20.00
    Cost Variance                                     20.00
        To record the transfer of the unfavora-
        ble variance allocated to the Finished
        Goods inventory.

Cost of Goods Sold                          60.00
    Cost Variance                                     60.00
        To record the transfer of the unfavora-
        ble variance allocated to Cost of Goods
        Sold.
```

Blocker[37] pointed out that the variances between actual and esti-

mated costs were of particular interest to management and declared that

it was desirable to transfer the variances from Work in Process accounts

to a separate variance account for each cost element--Material Variance,

Labor Variance, and Overhead Expense Variance.  He recognized that the

Variance accounts might have either debit or credit balances.

With respect to these balances, he stated that "Generally a debit

balance indicates that actual costs have exceeded estimated costs and

that production, whether it remains in process, in finished good stock-

rooms, or has been sold during the period, has been costed below the

actual production costs" and that a debit balance in a variance account

could be disposed of by one of the three following methods, with the

choice depending upon the cause of the variance:

a. The estimates have been incorrectly computed; therefore
   the variance should be apportioned to Work in Process Inventory, Finished Goods, and Cost of Goods Sold.
b. The variance may exist because of seasonal conditions of
   actual costs and/or production, owing to the fact that

---

[37]Blocker, *Cost Accounting*, pp. 540-543.

estimate costs have been set as normal costs to cover a
complete cycle of business activity, usually a year.  The
variance should be treated as a deferred charge to operations pending its adjustment during subsequent accounting
periods.
  c. The variance may have been caused by abnormal conditions
     which are beyond the control of factory management; the
     proper disposition of such a variance is to transfer it to
     either Profit and Loss or to Surplus.[38]

On the other hand, he accepted credit balances in the Variance ac-

counts as indicative that the estimates used in costing production were

greater than actual costs and that the Work in Process inventory, the

Finished Goods inventory, and the Cost of Sales were costed at too high

figures.  After an investigation of the causes, he would dispose of the

credit variances in one of two manners:  (1) if the estimates were com-

puted incorrectly, the variances would be used to reduce the value of

the Work in Process inventory, Finished Goods, and Cost of Goods Sold;

and (2) if the variances arose because of seasonal conditions, they

would be treated as deferred credits on the equity side of the balance

sheet.[39]

Neuner stated that the variations from estimates might be closed

out by apportioning the amounts of such variations, which were trans-

ferred to one account (Adjustment account or Estimated Cost Variation

account), to the Work in Process, Finished Goods, and Cost of Sales ac-

counts, or by transferring the entire amount to the Cost of Sales

account.  For the disposition of variations from estimates, this author

---

[38] Ibid., p. 541.

[39] Ibid., p. 543.

preferred the plan of allocating the differences to the three accounts as mentioned in the initial alternative.[40]

For those authors who have treated the Cost Estimate since 1920 and have recorded the estimated figures as credits in the Work in Process accounts, variances have been considered as indexes of accuracy in computing the original cost schedules and have been disclosed usually in one or more variation accounts. The variances from estimates have been allocated to Work in Process inventories, Cost of Sales, and Finished Goods inventory in most instances; however, these differences have been handled also as adjustments to cost of sales, profit and loss, or goods completed during the fiscal period in which the variances arose.

---

[40] Neuner, Cost Accounting, p. 564.

CHAPTER IV

THE BACKGROUND OF STANDARD COSTS

Before considering the early factors that contributed to the development of standard costs, it seems desirable to suggest the trend of events during this time with a quotation from G. Charter Harrison, one of the foremost proponents of this accounting concept:

> Until very recently, . . . the accountant regarded his sphere as being confined to the recording of past events. . . . The engineer, on the other hand, with his foreseeing mind, realized very fully that the accountant would never be a really constructive force in industrial progress until he embraced what we may call the engineering viewpoint of accounting, and some engineers expressed themselves very forcibly on this subject.[1]

According to this author, the credit for initiating the standard cost idea belongs to the engineer rather than to the accountant. This phenomenon can be readily reconciled when one considers that the accountant had, for many years, been auditing and preparing statements covering data for preceding periods of time--the functions of a historian--whereas the engineer had, for a greater number of years, been planning and estimating projects for succeeding eras of time--the business of a prophet. Therefore, the theme of standard costs was in close harmony with the engineer's habitual trend of thought but was in direct contrast with the accountant's line of training and practice.

Concurrently with the development of cost accounting literature,

----

[1] Harrison, *Standard Costs*, p. 24.

including the Cost Estimate, there arose a group of scientific engineers who developed distinct theories and procedures which were applicable to later demands on cost accounting and which were subject to either being used directly in or of influencing the growth of the standard cost accounting plan. It is not the purpose of this study to trace minutely the implications of these writers' efforts but to indicate only their contributions as such affect the problem at hand.

Evolution of the Industrial Engineer's Contribution to Standard Cost Accounting.--For recognizing the need of a revolution in the industrial order and for furnishing the stimulus to the development of improved technique, recognition should be given to the efforts of a group of members of the American Society of Mechanical Engineers. When Henry R. Towne, President of the Yale and Towne Manufacturing Company and a member of this professional organization, presented his paper, "The Engineer as an Economist,"[2] to the Society's annual meeting in 1885, he initiated a movement that has had marked effect upon industrial procedure.

Towne, in observing that productive labor must be directed and controlled by individuals possessing good executive ability and practical engineering knowledge, pointed out that industry required that such supervisors must be capable also of observing, recording, analyzing and comparing essential facts with respect to wages, supplies, expenses and other factors that affect the economy of production or the cost of the

---

[2]Towne, Henry R., "The Engineer as an Economist," Transactions, American Society of Mechanical Engineers, VII (1885-86), 428-432.

product.[3] This assertion seems to be a significant statement for the particular time and to represent thinking with far-sighted implications.

This author contended that the industrial problems of the time came under two distinct classifications:  shop management, with questions of organization, reports, wage payment systems, responsibility and other factors relating to the executive management of the factory; and shop accounting, with questions of determination of costs, distribution of expenses, methods of bookkeeping, and other influences that pertain to the manufacturing departments and to the recording of their results.[4] Approximately twenty-five years later, Towne's concepts were somewhat realized by the creation of "Scientific Management" from the first classification and "Standard Costs" from the second.

In the discussion that followed Towne's presentation, Frederick W. Taylor, who came to be regarded as the founder of a scientific technique in workshops, supported the speaker's thesis with an exposition, "Shop Order System of Accounts," covering the Midvale Steel Company's system of production control. According to Taylor, the manufacturing enterprise should be divided into a central office and as many departmental offices as may be required. The central office should issue authority for all work orders, should receive such information as may be required to keep the interested officials informed as to the progress and cost of work, and should keep such records as may be desirable to record properly

---

[3]Ibid., p. 428.

[4]Ibid., p. 429.

the information as received.  In the departmental offices, full informa-

tion should be accumulated and filed for each job, so that, when a new

piece of work was undertaken, the foreman might obtain the accumulated

record of the last job comparable with the one at hand and might deter-

mine the cost, the time of the operation and the workmen who performed

the services as well as any mistakes made or any suggestions relating to

the best procedure for accomplishing the task.[5]

Somewhat earlier than Towne's observations, Oberlin Smith had noted

that the nomenclature of machinery, tools and apparatus was in a state

of general confusion and that a reform movement was in great need for

this field.  In order to facilitate the manufacturing process, Smith

proposed that a specific name be adopted for each machine part simply

for the purpose of identification, which was required mechanically at

almost every stage of production.  This article, although of signifi-

cance in recognizing a neglected phase of scientific production, does

not have the general application of Towne's efforts and has not been

given the same degree of importance in this paper.[6]

In a pioneer work on wage systems as incentives, Towne explained a

scheme that he had devised for rewarding his factory employees for

greater than normal services.[7]  Under his plan, it was necessary to de-

---

[5]Ibid., p. 476.

[6]Smith, Oberlin, "Nomenclature of Machine Details," Transactions, American Society of Mechanical Engineers, II (1881), 366-377.

[7]Towne, Henry R., "Gain Sharing," Transactions, American Society of Mechanical Engineers, X (1888-89), 600-608.

termine the accurate cost of the product and to express this cost in
terms of those factors which could be influenced or controlled by those
employees who were to participate in the result.  All irrelevant factors
--the market value of raw materials, which are subject to fluctuation;
general expenses, whether relating to management of works or to commercial administration; and, in general, all items over which the workers
exercise no control--were excluded and, if the records did not disclose
sufficient information to ascertain the required values, proper books
must be installed and sufficient data must be accumulated before the
plan could be put into execution.

In arriving at any additional compensation that might be due the
employees, the author employed the account technique as a device for
making his computations.  The present writer has set up Towne's debits
and credits in a _pro forma_ account, which the author did not do in his
article, in order that this plan might be the more readily understood.

| Debits | Credits |
| --- | --- |
| Labor at cost ................ xxx | Volume of the products |
| Raw materials, measured by | manufactured measured by |
|   quantity only (arbitrary | the scale of values as |
|   fixed price might be | had been predetermined ..... xxx |
|   assumed) .................... xxx | |
| Incidental supplies (oil, | |
|   waste, tools and implements) | |
|   at cost ..................... xxx | |
| Power, light and water ....... xxx | |
| Renewals and repair of plant | |
|   at cost .................... xxx | |
| Superintendence, clerk hire | |
|   and other costs necessary to | |
|   operation of the department  xxx | |
| | |
| BALANCE--Resulting gain | |
|   (reduction in cost) shared | |
|   with employees on basis of | |
|   wages earned during year ... xxx | |
|                       xxx |                        xxx |

For this study, Towne's scheme is significant not only as a means of gaining greater efficiency in the factory through improved, employee-motivated use of raw materials, labor and manufacturing devices but also as a recognition of the possibility of valuing the periodical production at a predetermined--somewhat a standard--figure as a gauge for measuring the operating results.

Continuing the search for a definite basis on which gains in efficiency could be measured and, at the same time, on which these gains and the resultant bonuses for the employees could be presented effectively, Halsey, a Canadian, proposed his "Premium Wage Plan,"[8] which guaranteed to every worker, regardless of his productive effort, a day wage; which established a standard time for each operation or a standard day's accomplishment as based on past experience; and, finally, as an incentive to stimulate additional production, which effected a sharing between the employees and the employer of the savings due to increased output by giving the workman an arbitrary percentage of the time saved when he completed an operation in less than the standard as established.

Hess, in evaluating methods of compensating workmen, stated that "the merit of being the pioneer with a well worked out and competently introduced plan is due Mr. Halsey for his 'Premium Plan'"[9] and that from this scheme had sprung many modifications, particularly in Great Britain.

---

[8] Halsey, F. A., "The Premium Plan of Paying for Labor," Transactions, American Society of Mechanical Engineers, XII (1890-91), 755-780.

[9] Hess, Henry, "Wage-Paying Methods from the Viewpoint of the Workman," The Engineering Magazine, XXVII (April, 1904), 29.

He approved the plan because it induced more progressive and active men
to secure the returns that they knew were possible.

From the standpoint of this study, Halsey's plan (an attempt to
remedy the defects of profit sharing with its indefiniteness and of
piece rates with their concomitant possibility of decrease) may be considered a link in the developmental chain of standard costs--a rough
determination of a standard of individual performance for labor payments.
It should be stressed here, however, that the standard was merely an
average of past performance and was not a scientifically established
rate.

After several years of research with problems related to individual
and plant efficiency, Frederick W. Taylor presented a paper, "A Piece
Rate System,"[10] to the American Society of Mechanical Engineers and
therein proposed certain procedures that developed into the "Taylor
System." This paper contained a twofold message:  a general system of
management as related to the measurement and control of a day's work and
a method of wage payment as devised to gain the maximum production in a
factory.  The system, as outlined by the author, contained three principal elements:  (1) an elementary rate-finding department; (2) the differential rate system of piece work; and (3) a scheme characterized as
the best method of paying men who work by the day.[11]

His "Differential Piecework Wage Plan" is considered important to

_______________

[10] Taylor, Frederick W., "A Piece Rate System," Transactions, American Society of Mechanical Engineers, XVI (1894-95), 856-883.

[11] Ibid., p. 856.

this study because of the manner in which the rates were ascertained.

Under Taylor's rate-fixing procedure, a careful study was made of the

time required to perform each of the elementary operations into which

the manufacturing processes of a factory might be divided.  These simple

processes were classified, recorded and indexed so that the piece-rate

for new work might be computed by analyzing the particular job under

consideration and by applying the accumulated data thereto.  Thus a

standard of accomplishment for a required job might be obtained by the

application of scientific methods.

With respect to the wage payment, the differential rate system of

piece work provided for the offering of two different rates for the same

job:  a high price per piece if the standard was met (the work was fin-

ished in the minimum of time and in good condition) and a low price if

the standard of production was not met (the work was finished in a

longer time or in imperfect condition).

And the third phase of the author's scheme--the managing of men--

was accomplished by paying men and not positions, i.e., by rewarding

workmen according to the skill and energy with which they performed

their work and not according to the positions which they filled.  An

undertaking of this plan, according to Taylor, involved records for each

man--records that accumulated data concerning each workman's performance,

punctuality, attendance, integrity, rapidity, skill and accuracy.

The advantages of this system, as summarized from Taylor's paper,

include the following:[12]

---

[12]Ibid., pp. 872-875.

1. A decreased cost of production is coupled with increased wages for workmen.

2. A substitution of knowledge for guesswork tends to eliminate indifferent and careless efforts as workmen are treated with more uniformity and greater justice.

3. The co-operation of workmen and management becomes the common interest of both of these productive agencies.

4. Maximum production is attained and maintained automatically through the application of the differential rate.

5. The scheme attracts the best men, develops latent workmen into first-class employees and eliminates the inferior laborers.

6. Labor unions and strikes are less in evidence as friendly relations are promoted between employer and employee.

However, Taylor's paper was received rather critically and it was not until eight years later that the writer's views were presented again in an outright discussion of management, "Shop Management."[13]  This paper represented a considerable expansion of the earlier effort, "A Piece Rate System," and included a rather complete explanation of the detailed methods that he had developed during the intervening years, as well as an analysis of the industrial and economic implications of his system.  His methods of accurate scientific time study and his determination and application of standards in industry are of primary concern to this study.

---

[13]Taylor, Frederick W., "Shop Management," Transactions, American Society of Mechanical Engineers, XXIV (1902), 1337-1353.

Taylor's third publication, "On the Art of Cutting Metals,"[14] was

a report of his research efforts for more than twenty-five years in

machine shops with the fundamental purpose of determining the best con-

ditions for the utilization of available factory facilities.  He was

able to discover for many of the shop operations combinations of rela-

tively simple conditions, which, if established and maintained during

such operations, resulted in rather significant increases in output.[15]

Much space has been devoted to the "Taylor System" but this author's

steps of scientific procedure--(1) experiment or the measurement, clas-

sification, and filing of results; (2) standards or the formulation of

laws respecting the use of materials, labor, and machinery; (3) planning

of work or the systematic scheduling, designing, and directing work

through the processes; and (4) maintenance of standards or the develop-

ment of systematic inspection procedure covering performance and condi-

tions--have had their application in the development of standard cost

technique.

As a critic of Taylor's system, Church concluded that scientific

management presented nothing tangible except certain useful mechanisms--

time study, functional management, and the differential wage rate--that

the founder had brought to general notice again (Church insisted that

Taylor rediscovered Babbage's concepts of 1832-1946).[16]

---

[14]Taylor, Frederick W., "On the Art of Cutting Metals," Transactions, American Society of Mechanical Engineers, XXVIII (1906), 31-58.

[15]Ibid., pp. 54-55.

[16]Church, A. Hamilton, "Has 'Scientific Management' Science," American Machinist, XXXV (July 20, 1911), 108-112.

But in regard to this claim for the development of a "science"
or a philosophy of management, it is hard to avoid the conclusion either that Mr. Taylor is struggling unsuccessfully to
explain himself, or that he has mistaken a statement of aspirations for a statement of how to realize those aspirations.[17]

On the other hand, Professor Hugo Diemer approved Taylor's scien-

tific procedure and undertook to associate the duties of the industrial

engineer with those of the accountant:

> He [Taylor] considers a manufacturing establishment just as
> one would an intricate machine.  He analyzes each process
> into its ultimate, simple elements, and compares each of
> these simplest steps or processes with an ideal or perfect
> condition.  He then makes all due allowances for rational and
> practical conditions and establishes an attainable commercial
> standard for every step.  The next process is that of attain-
> ing continuously this standard, involving both quality and
> quantity, and the interlocking or assembling of all of these
> prime elements into a well-arranged, well-built, smooth-
> running machine.  It is quite evident that work of this char-
> acter involves technical knowledge and ability in science and
> pure engineering, which do not enter into the field of the
> accountant.  Yet the industrial engineer must have the ac-
> countant's keen perception of money values.[18]

Ennis (an engineer), in a rather elementary manner, anticipated a

cost keeping system that would assist the engineer in foreseeing, and

preventing, wastes rather than in disclosing these losses as historical

facts and attempting to cure them.  He desired that a ratio of costs to

output be calculated under ideal conditions, that this ratio be ap-

proached by bringing efficiency methods into the factory, and that

variations in efficiency be recorded and presented periodically to the

---

[17] *Ibid.*, p. 110.

[18] Diemer, *op. cit.*, p. 2.

management.[19]

H. L. Gantt, one of Taylor's colleagues, initiated his interpretation of factory efficiency with an incentive plan for rewarding wage earners--"A Bonus System of Rewarding Labor"[20]--which he had introduced into a large machine shop of the Bethlehem Steel Company.

Under his scheme, a skilled employee prepared a card indicating the best method of performing each of the elementary operations on any piece of work, the tools to be used, and the standard time, as determined by experiments, required to complete each operation. Employees who followed these instructions and performed their day's task were paid a bonus in addition to the day rate--the day wage was paid regardless of the output by the employee.

As an illustration of Gantt's procedure, the following schedule has been prepared by assuming a day's task--a standard day's work--of eight units, a basic day rate of four dollars and a bonus of 20 per cent on day rate wages for employees reaching or passing the standard.

SCHEDULE OF WAGE PAYMENTS ACCORDING TO GANTT PLAN

| Production (Units) | Day Rate | Wages at Day Rate | Worker's Bonus--20% | Total Wages | Labor Cost Per Unit |
|---|---|---|---|---|---|
| 6 | $4.00 | $4.00 | | $4.00 | $0.67 |
| 7 | 4.00 | 4.00 | | 4.00 | 0.57 |
| 8* | 4.00 | 4.00 | $0.80 | 4.80 | 0.60 |
| 9 | 4.00 | 4.50 | 0.90 | 5.40 | 0.60 |
| 10 | 4.00 | 5.00 | 1.00 | 6.00 | 0.60 |

*Standard.

---

[19]Ennis, William D., "The Engineering Management of Industrial Works," The Engineering Magazine, XXII (1901-02), 241-246.

[20]Gantt, H. L., "A Bonus System of Rewarding Labor," Transactions, American Society of Mechanical Engineers, XXXIII (1902), 341-372.

The wage scheme not only promoted factory efficiency by directly
rewarding the laborers but also provided for supervisory cooperation
through a system of bonus payments for foremen whose men attained standard performance.  As Gantt's wage scheme furnished an automatic punish-
ment for breakdowns--the workmen and foreman lost their bonuses not only
on the date of the breakdown but also for all subsequent days until the
machine was repaired--there was an inclination for the employees to
service machinery more carefully and to handle equipment with a greater
degree of responsibility.

Somewhat later, Gantt delivered two lectures at the Harvard School
of Business Administration and, subsequently, expanded his ideas into a
series of five articles under the heading "The Compensation of Workmen
and Efficiency of Operation."[21]

The author recognized only two means of substantially increasing
the profits on manufactured articles:  by increasing the selling price
or by reducing the cost of production.  Discarding the first method  as
a repetitive and cyclical process--increased selling prices result in
higher cost of living, followed by demands for higher wages and a still
greater cost of production--he attacked the other alternative, that of
decreasing the cost of production by employing labor incentives and en-
couraging operating efficiency.

In the first place, Gantt was interested primarily in labor efficiency and suggested that scientific procedures be adopted to determine

---

[21]Gantt, H. L., "The Compensation of Workmen and Efficiency of
Operation," The Engineering Magazine, Vols. XXXVIII and XXXIX (February-
June, 1910).

a standard method for performing factory operations--another plea for
his task and bonus scheme for rewarding laborers.  He also devised a
series of progress charts for recording the results attained by workers
and for disclosing quickly to management the cumulative records of the
factory employees.  These charts have been referred to frequently in
cost literature, particularly in The Cost and Production Handbook by
L. P. Alford.

Although the writer failed to undertake as careful a consideration
of the other manufacturing factors as labor, he did recognize that scientific methods could be applied to the handling of materials and the
absorption of overhead at an efficient rate of production.

> If the plant is a large one, or one doing a large variety of
> work, the advantage of controlling the material, planning the
> work, and increasing the efficiency of the individual, are so
> great that a little done in this direction soon makes itself
> felt, for the plant begins to run more smoothly, wastes
> diminish, and profits begin to increase, and we are on the
> road to our ideal, a self-perpetuating system based on the
> efficient utilization of scientific knowledge.[22]

Gantt combined his wage scheme and graphic records into a second
article, "A Practical Application of Scientific Management,"[23] and undertook to present a practical demonstration of factory operation through
the use of scientific management--its components, requirements, administration, and results.

---

[22]Ibid., XXXIX, 339.

[23]Gantt, H. L., "A Practical Application of Scientific Management,"
The Engineering Magazine, XLI (April, 1911), 1-22.

The author reiterated the importance of factory efficiency as the
means of gaining greater profits and again advocated Taylor's methods
for setting shop standards, which might be attained by employing the
author's task and bonus system for inciting laborers to maximum production and his system of graphics for assisting management in routing jobs
and eliminating idle capacity.  With respect to records, he made the
following comment:

> The essentials of a correct system are a store-keeping system
> and a time-keeping system suited to this method of control-
> ling work, a balance of work, a man record, and a system of
> expense and cost keeping that enables the superintendent to
> know each day what was done the day previous, who did it, and
> what the expense of it was.[24]

Gantt rejected the cost accounting method of making the output of
any month bear all the expenses for that month since such a policy
tended to confuse both management and salesmen, who undertook to base
their production and sales policies on costs as compiled by their accounting department.

> It is not surprising, then, that many managers have often
> gone ahead successfully regardless of the figures of their
> cost accounts, while others who have been guided by these
> figures have not been successful.  It also explains the fact
> that some concerns that have not had cost figures, but whose
> managers trusted to their common sense have been more suc-
> cessful than some with elaborate cost systems.  From this we
> may conclude that unless figures convey the correct idea they
> may be worse than useless.  This situation has been pretty
> generally recognized during the past few years and numerous
> attempts have been made to discover where the error lies.[25]

---

[24]Ibid., p. 11.

[25]Gantt, H. L., "Production and Sales," The Engineering Magazine,
L (January, 1916), 598.

He recognized a cost system ("the newer theory and the one which is rapidly finding acceptance") which allocated to factory output only that portion of the total factory expense required for such production.

> A cost system to fulfill the needs of competitive manufacture must then show not only what we are spending to obtain our product but also _what expense we are under day by day for that portion of the plant and equipment which is idle_. . . . Such expense is truly _non-productive_, and the great need of our industries today is a system that will continually bring this _non-productive_ expense, or loss, to the attention of the executive. Such a system has been devised and is in operation, with the result that the executives of those plants where it is in use are learning most illuminating things about their expenses.[26]

Clinton E. Woods, self-styled as an Industrial Engineer, presented _Unified Accounting Methods for Industrials_ first in 1917 and recognized industrial engineering as a new profession which had been effected by the actions of the industrial or factory accountant and the mechanical or efficiency engineer.[27] He was convinced that the two were interdependent--that the accountant's function was largely analytical ("and dealing only with results as a finality") while the engineer's was creative ("dealing almost wholly with causes").

> In other words, the one enables an executive to measure results obtained, while the other sets into activity causes that make possible a predetermination of results. One has worked from the top down by the process of deduction, while the other has worked from the bottom up by devising means for

---

[26] _Ibid._, p. 599.

[27] Woods, Clinton E., _Unified Accounting Methods for Industrials_, New York, The Ronald Press Company, 1919, pp. 3-24.

eliminating unnecessary waste; the combined effort of both
resulting in a standardization of factory operations.

Therefore, to qualify as an industrial engineer, a man must
not only be a master of both of these professions, but also
be able to reconcile the necessary workings of one with the
other.[28]

The author pointed out that through the development and standardi-

zation of a unified method of industrial accounting by the accountants,

together with the application of the engineer's analytical techniques,

the efficiency engineer had been able to predetermine the operating con-

ditions required for many kinds of industrial concerns.  Woods predicted

that out of the efforts of these two professions there had developed

"certain principles that will go a long way toward the required unified

code of standards."  The author was writing of accounting techniques,

expense distribution, unified output, stabilization of production, and

time and motion studies--those efficiency measures that Taylor, Gantt,

and Emerson had been propounding and that G. Charter Harrison was now

ready to bring together into "Standard Costs."

Other writers who recognized the great need for improvements in

factory techniques and who added their efforts to those considered in

this study, and some of their publications, have been enumerated below.

Charles U. Carpenter:
     "Money-Making Management for Work-shop and Factory," The
          Engineering Magazine, Vols. XXII-XXIV (1901-03).
     "Profit Making in Shop and Factory Management," The
          Engineering Magazine, Vols. XXXII-XXXIII (1907).
Charles Day:
     Industrial Plants, New York, Engineering Magazine Company,
          1911.

---

[28] Ibid., p. 6.

"Management Principles and the Consulting Engineer," _The Engineering Magazine_, Vol. XLI (1911).

Charles B. Going:
   _Principles of Industrial Engineering_, New York, McGraw-Hill Book Company, 1911.

H. K. Hathaway:
   "Prerequisites to the Introduction of Scientific Management," _The Engineering Magazine_, Vol. XLI (1911).

Dexter Kimball:
   _Principles of Industrial Organization_, New York, McGraw-Hill Book Company, 1913.

C. E. Knoeppel:
   "Cost Reduction Through Cost Comparison," _The Engineering Magazine_, Vols. XXXII-XXXIII (1907).
   "Maximum Production Through Organization and Supervision," _The Engineering Magazine_, Vol. XXXV (1908).
   "Systematic Factory Operation and Foundry Costing," _The Engineering Magazine_, Vol. XXXVI (1908-09).
   _Maximum Production in Machine-Shop and Foundry_, New York, Engineering Magazine Company, 1911.
   "Practical Introduction of Efficiency Principles," _The Engineering Magazine_, Vol. XLVI (1914).

A. C. Popke:
   "The Relations of Capital, Labor and Efficiency in Manufacturing," _The Engineering Magazine_, Vol. XLIII (1912).

Since these writers did not make original contributions to the trend of thought that has been followed herein, their publications have not been reviewed in detail.

_Evolution of the Cost Accountant's Contribution to Standard Cost Accounting_.--When George P. Norton presented his _Textile Manufacturers' Bookkeeping_ in 1889, he not only recognized Estimated Costs and Cost Estimate Variations but also demonstrated a technique that contained some semblance of the standard cost idea.

The author stated that, in the textile industry, there was a well-known trade price for almost every process of manufacture--a price at which goods could be completed upon the payment of recognized conversion costs.[29] The writer accepted these trade prices as a basis--a simple standard--for recording information in his Manufacturing Account (see chapter on Cost Estimate Variations) and for determining the relative efficiency of the particular manufacturing enterprise.

By way of review, Section I of the Manufacturing Account was charged with the beginning stock inventory, the total cost of materials consumed, the expense of pattern making, and the trade prices (Processes of Manufacture) for the goods completed. This account was credited with sales and final inventory. Under ordinary circumstances, Norton pointed out that a margin (gross profit) should arise upon the recording of these items. However, he could conceive of a deficiency due to incorrect calculations, to selling the manufactured goods too cheaply, and/or to purchasing the raw materials at too great a price.

> It should be clearly understood that this insufficiency cannot be attributed to unprofitable working of the processes of manufacture, as each process is charged at the standard trade price and not at its actual cost.[30]

To illustrate further the author's procedure, a portion of Section II of the Manufacturing Account (as presented in the Cost Estimate Variation chapter of this study) has been reproduced:

---

[29] Norton, *op*. *cit*., p. 222.

[30] *Ibid*., p. 221.

PROFIT ON DEPARTMENTS, VIZ.:--

| Depart-<br>ments | Wages and Expenses<br>as Per Analysis* | Work Done as<br>Per Section I** | Profit |
|---|---|---|---|
| 1 | £1,026 | £1,131 | £105 |
| 2 | 1,349 | 1,547 | 198 |
| 3 | 985 | 1,088 | 103 |
| Totals | £3,360 | £3,766 | £406 |

*Actual cost, as compiled in records, of work
processed.

**Trade prices, as calculated with recognized
prices, of work processed.

In this case, the production costs of the factory were compared
with a standard--accepted trade prices--and a method of gauging the efficiency of the organization was provided.  The writer was cognizant of
a further standard--the usual rate of profit as earned by departments in
this industry--as may be gleaned from the following extract:

The difference in each department represents the profit.  Inas-
much as in this account each department receives credit for
its work at the standard prices accepted by those who carry on
its special processes as a distinct trade, it should, other
things being equal, gain the usual rate of profit.  It sometimes happens, however, that a department is not fully employed, or is worked under other disadvantages, and any such
special reason for non-success must be taken into consideration.[31]

Edwards, the English writer, in discussing Norton's manufacturing
account, stated:

This method of bringing into the accounts the trade prices of
processes as a footrule to measure actual results is the

---

[31] Ibid., p. 222.

earliest example of standard costing which the present writer
has been able to discover.[32]

A variation of Norton's cost technique was suggested by George

Lisle in his text, Accounting in Theory and Practice, which was first

published in 1899.  In presenting cost accounting procedures, he made

the following statement:

> The third method is the most satisfactory, as by it the profit
> from the manufacture of goods is ascertained.  This is accom-
> plished by crediting the goods manufactured during the year at
> ordinary trading prices at which they could be purchased from
> their manufacturers to the Manufacturing Account, and debit-
> ing this sum to the Trading Account.  The Manufacturing Ac-
> count thus shows the profit on the manufacturing department,
> and the Trading Account the profit on trading.  The manufac-
> tured goods are charged at the same price as the finished
> goods could be purchased.[33]

These two examples indicate that certain English accountants and writers

of accounting literature were concerned with modifying historical cost

technique to such an extent that some comparative means could be estab-

lished.

H. Stanley Garry not only devised a standard unit of output and

provided for the conversion of the factory production into this unit for

estimate and actual cost purposes but also established a standard weekly

output equivalent to a certain number of these standard units for the

year of fifty weeks.

---

[32]Edwards, op. cit., p. 316.

[33]Lisle, George, Accounting in Theory and Practice, Edinburgh and
London, William Green and Sons, 1909, p. 255.

To illustrate Garry's procedure, a factory producing six products--styled herein as M, N, P, S, T, and V--has been taken as an example. Product M has been accepted as the standard unit of output with the other products having conversion ratios as follows:  N - .800; P - .880; S - .680; T - .640; and V - .720.

Using these figures, a Schedule of Weekly Production has been prepared with a standard week of 155 units of products, which are equivalent to 120 standard units of output.  Accepting fifty weeks, as suggested by Garry, for the operating year, a production of 6,000 standard units would be the factory's annual output.[34]

SCHEDULE OF WEEKLY PRODUCTION

| Time | Product | | | | | | Total* | Total Units** |
|---|---|---|---|---|---|---|---|---|
|  | M | N | P | S | T | V |  |  |
| Standard Week | 25 | 20 | 15 | 25 | 20 | 50 | 155 | 120.0 |
| Week 5 | 20 | 20 | 10 | 30 | 35 | 40 | 155 | 116.4 |
| Week 11 | 25 | 30 | 25 | 15 | 10 | 45 | 150 | 120.0 |
| Week 43 | 40 | 30 | 30 | 10 | 10 | 30 | 150 | 125.2 |

*Total of all units produced during the week.
**Total standard units produced during the week.

In view of the fact that the Factory Expenses have been allocated to production on the basis of a weekly output of 120 standard units, the efficiency of the factory for any week can be ascertained readily.  As this schedule indicates, the total number of units may be attained and yet result in a shortage of earning capacity (Week 5) while a smaller total number of products, assorted differently, may give an equal

---

[34]Garry, Multiple Cost Accounts, pp. 3, 28.

(Week 11) or even an increase (Week 43) in effective units of output.

Each week, a factory summary was prepared to present the current week's production as well as the total output for the fiscal period to date, which was compared with the standard for the corresponding time.[35]

FACTORY SUMMARY
Week Ending March 11, 1944

| Explanation | Total Units | Material Units | Wages Units | Oncost Units |
|---|---|---|---|---|
| Total to Last Week ....... | 1,018.320 | 285.1296 | 610.9920 | 122.1984 |
| Current Week . | 116.400 | 32.5920 | 69.8400 | 13.9680 |
| Total .... | 1,134.720 | 317.7216 | 680.8320 | 136.1664 |
| Standard Units for Period . | 1,200.000 | 336.0000 | 720.0000 | 144.0000 |
| Decrease on Standard ... | 65.280 | 18.2784 | 39.1680 | 7.8336 |

The author foresaw two causes for this situation:  either the work was not put through the shop as anticipated (ineffective labor) or the productive facilities were employed in processing the less remunerative output in the lower priced products.  His test for ascertaining which of these alternatives had operated was to determine the amount of wages paid, convert this sum into production wage units, and compare the result with the production units (see Schedule of Wage Returns) as computed on the Factory Summary.  This comparison, which indicates a variation of only 2 per cent, suggests that the discrepancy did not arise from ineffective labor but from the character of the work (lower priced

---

[35]Ibid., p. 59.

products) undertaken.

SCHEDULE OF WAGE RETURNS

| Explanation | Production Units | Cash Units |
|---|---|---|
| Total to Last Week | 610.992 | 623.892[a] |
| Current Week | 69.840 | 71.108[b] |
| Total | 680.832 | 695.000 |
| Loss on Units | 14.168 | |
| | 695.000 | 695.000 |

[a]$9,358.38 (Wages to date) ÷ $15 (Wages per standard unit).

[b]$1,066.62 (Wages current week) ÷ $15.

In addition to recognizing the significance of setting a standard amount of production per week for a year of fifty weeks and in providing a weekly means of reporting the operating results as compared with this standard, Garry also proposed a system of factory costs for the chemical industry which merits more than casual consideration in the background of standard costs.

In a paper delivered before the Society of Chemical Industry,[36] this author undertook to propose the subject of Factory Costs and Management as a part of the chemical engineering curriculum, with particular attention being devoted to the problem of profitable manufacturing.

When he came to consider raw materials from the standpoint of the comptroller, he raised two basic problems:  the conversion and manipulation of materials, and the fluctuations in material costs.  As a

---

[36]Garry, H. Stanley, "Factory Costs," The Accountant, XXIX (July 25, 1903), 954-961.

solution for these problems, he proposed "the provision of a normal

standard by which we can measure the effectiveness of the factory out-

put, which measure would be needlessly complicated by the introduction

of the fluctuation of market prices."[37]

> It may be assumed, therefore, that the proper provision of
> raw material for the period of return is a specified number
> of units.  This constitutes an effective working output, and
> for present purposes a normal standard price for same is
> assumed, based upon a sufficiently extended period of past
> experience and present prospects.  By this means there is
> obtained a standard against which may be measured the output,
> not only in quantity, but also in quality of material, as
> also in like manner the quality of the product.  By thus
> taking a normal standard for both quantity and quality, it is
> possible to show in the first place the results of the manage-
> ment; and, secondly, after this has been ascertained, the
> further effect on such cost of--
> (1) The increase or decrease in market price
> (2) Any decrease on standard in production.[38]

In order to illustrate Garry's procedure, Table A, which covers one

by-product (Product No. 1) and two main products (Products A and B), has

been adapted to the author's example.

---

[37] Ibid., p. 956.

[38] Ibid., p. 956.

TABLE A.--FACTORY PRIME COST SUMMARY IN TOTAL FIGURES[39]

| Maximum Standard Effective Output | | Revised Standard to Actual Output | | | Actual Working | | | Variations on Revised Standard | | |
|---|---|---|---|---|---|---|---|---|---|---|
| Quantity | Cost Value | Quantity | Cost Value | Description* | Quantity | Cost Value | Wages and Process | Quantity | Cost Value | Wages and Process |
| 400 | $ 360 | 300 | $ 270 | Raw Material | | | | | | |
| 120 | $ 60 | 90 | $ 45 | No.1 Material | 86 | $ 43 | | - 4 | $- 2 | |
| | 24 | | 18 | Wages | | | $ 19 | | | $+ 1 |
| | 12 | | 9 | Process Cost | | | 11 | | | + 2 |
| 136 | 136 | 102 | 102 | A. Material | 98 | 98 | | - 4 | - 4 | |
| | 272 | | 204 | Wages | | | 208 | | | + 4 |
| | 68 | | 51 | Process Cost | | | 60 | | | + 9 |
| 104 | 164 | 78 | 123 | B. Material | 90 | 142 | | +12 | +19 | |
| | 656 | | 492 | Wages | | | 540 | | | +48 |
| | 328 | | 246 | Process Cost | | | 280 | | | +34 |
| 40 | | 30 | | Shrinkage | 26 | | | | | |
| 400 | $1720 | 300 | $1290 | | 300 | $283 | $1118 | +12 | $+19 | $+98 |
| | | | | | | | | - 8 | - 6 | |
| | | | | | | | | + 4 | $+13 | |

*No. 1 represents the by-product; A and B are the two main products.

In the instance under consideration, the maximum standard output
was determined to be 400 units--120 units of by-product, 136 units of
Product A, 104 units of Product B, and Shrinkage of 40 units--at a material cost of $360, a conversion cost of $1,360, and a total cost of
$1,720. For comparative purposes, the level of production was revised
to actual output and a revised standard was prepared. Subsequently, the
variations from the revised standards were computed and were expressed
as quantity variation only for material and as total variation for wages

---

[39] Ibid., p. 959, adapted and expressed in dollars.

and process cost.

The author prepared also schedules for comparing Direct Costs
(Table D) and Indirect Costs (Table E) as to standard and actual figures.
These illustrations have not been reproduced; however, Table B--Schedule
of Excess Costs indicates the variation in unit cost between actual and
standard amounts divided as to Prime (actually wages and process costs),
Direct, and Indirect Costs.  Garry asserted that this variation was due
to partial output.

TABLE B.--SCHEDULE OF EXCESS COSTS[40]

| Description | Reference (Table) | Product No. 1 | Product A | Product B |
|---|---|---|---|---|
| Excess Cost: | | | | |
| Prime* | A | $.04[a] | $.13[b] | $ .91[c] |
| Direct | D | .01 | .08 | .19 |
| Indirect | E | .02 | .11 | .46 |
| | | $.07 | $.32 | $1.56 |

*Variations of Wages and Process Costs ÷ actual units
  produced:

[a] $ 3.00 ÷ 86 = $.04
[b] $13.00 ÷ 98 = $.13
[c] $82.00 ÷ 90 = $.91

By combining the data heretofore reproduced (Tables A and B) and
mentioned (Tables D and E), Garry prepared a Cost Summary (Table C) and
reconciled the actual unit cost with the standard unit cost.

---

[40] Ibid., p. 959, adapted.

TABLE C.--COST SUMMARY[41]

| Description | Reference (Table) | Product No. 1 | Product A | Product B |
|---|---|---|---|---|
| Prime Cost: | | | | |
| Material | A | $43.00 | $ 98.00 | $ 142.00 |
| Wages | A | 19.00 | 208.00 | 540.00 |
| Process Cost | A | 11.00 | 60.00 | 280.00 |
| Total Prime Cost | | $73.00 | $366.00 | $ 962.00 |
| Direct Cost | D | 6.00 | 48.00 | 61.00 |
| Indirect Cost | E | 10.00 | 63.00 | 129.00 |
| Depreciation | D | 3.00 | 44.00 | 68.00 |
| Total Cost | | $92.00 | $521.00 | $1,220.00 |
| Units Produced | | 86 | 98 | 90 |
| Cost Per Unit--Central | | $ 1.07 | $ 5.32 | $ 13.56 |
| Deduct Excess of Cost Due to Partial Output | B | .07 | .32 | 1.56 |
| Standard Cost Per Unit | | $ 1.00 | $ 5.00 | $ 12.00 |

The author pointed out that his procedure was applicable to con-

tinuous process industries in which raw materials emerge as finished

products from the factory at varying intervals and in which the varia--

tions in the inward raw materials tend to throw fluctuating outputs in

different departments.  He proposed a schedule, Standard Yield Adjust-

ment (Table F, below), for ascertaining these variations, which would be

disposed of in the following manner:

> If the standard units and wages and expenses are charged to
> each department, the output will give a contra to these fig-
> ures, and any variations would be treated as in Table F, and
> the differences brought down to the general cost.[42]

---

[41] Ibid., p. 959, adapted.

[42] Ibid., p. 961.

TABLE F.--STANDARD YIELD ADJUSTMENT

| Increase on Standard | | | | Period | Decrease on Standard | | | |
| Product | | | Shrink- | | Product | | | Shrink- |
| No. 1 | A | B | age | Ending | No. 1 | A | B | age |
| | | | | 1943 | | | | |
| 1 | 2 | 2 | 1 | Jan. 8 | | | | |
| 2 | 3 | | | 15 | | | 3 | 2 |
| | | 3 | 2 | 22 | 4 | 2 | | |
| | | 1 | 1 | 29 | 2 | 1 | | |
| 3 | 5 | 6 | 4 | 14- | 6 | 3 | 3 | 2 |
| | | | | 18+ | 3 | 5 | 6 | 4 |
| | | | | 4+ | -3 | +2 | +3 | +2 |
| Equation | | | | at | $.50* | $1.00* | $1.577* | |

*Standard unit cost of raw materials only.

```
-3 at $0.50   -$1.50
 2 at $1.00            $2.00
 3 at $1.577          $4.73
          -$1.50 +$6.73 = $5.23 (equal to difference in
```
working four weeks on standard yield.

The author recognized that there would arise some difficulty in
setting the standards, but, because of the methods of deduction and
analysis as practiced by chemists, he thought that this profession could
solve the problem for the chemical industry.  After the standards had
been set, a procedure which he neglected to disclose, the measure of the
variations from such standards would not only indicate the degree of accuracy of the figures but would also provide the basis for a revision of
the standards.

Church evidenced the influence of the scientific movement in factory organization when he pointed out that a satisfactory and complete
system would disclose daily results immediately, would provide in advance for the progress of work through the factory, and would present
the cost details, particularly indirect shop expenditures, according to

classes of work as well as to different portions of the factory itself.[43]

Thus, he sensed the importance of burden (indirect shop expenditures) and the current treatment of this cost element as inadequate.

Somewhat later, Church attacked the problem of distributing establishment charges[44] by rejecting the hourly-burden method, the percentage-on-wages plan, and the machine-rate method as inadequate and arbitrary and by proposing the elements of an ideal system.

Under his ideal system, the factory was divided into independent production centers--machines, benches, or floor space--and each of these production centers was charged with the costs that could be allocated reasonably thereto--rent, taxes, insurance, interest, depreciation, power, lighting, heating, and other shop charges that could be narrowed down to definite points of incidence. Other expenditures, which could not be associated directly with the production centers, were treated as general shop charges and were spread over production on an average basis.[45]

After the shop expenditures had been allocated to the production centers, the normal operating time per annum for each center was ascertained and was divided into the sum of such establishment charges for a machine-rate per hour--the author termed this rate as the "new machine

---

[43]Church, A. Hamilton, "The Meaning of Commercial Organisation," The Engineering Magazine, XX (1900-01), 391-398.

[44]Church, A. Hamilton, "Proper Distribution of Establishment Charges," The Engineering Magazine, XXI (1901), 725-727.

[45]Ibid., pp. 732-733.

rate" to distinguish his method from the old scheme.

As each production center was employed on production orders, these orders were charged with factory expense equal to the product of the new machine rate and the number of hours such jobs were in the production centers. At the end of the month, the total amount so allocated to production (earned by the machines according to Church) was deducted from the total shop expenses and any balance was distributed to these same production orders as a supplementary rate--this rate was determined by dividing the unallocated balance by the total number of hours operated by all of the production centers.[46] It is this supplementary rate which Church characterized as "the invaluable complement to the machine rate and which makes the great distinction between the new method and the old machine-rate method" and which this study is specifically interested in.

In order to illustrate Church's procedure,[47] hypothetical data have been assumed for a factory with nine production centers or machines and with machine rates, which have been ascertained according to the author's rules heretofore enumerated, as indicated in Table A.

---

[46] Ibid., pp. 907-911.

[47] Ibid., XXII, 235-240.

TABLE A.--MACHINE TIME MADE AND MACHINE EARNINGS

| Machine Number | New Machine Rate Per Hour--Cents | Total Hours Worked in Month | | Amount Debited to Jobs Per Machine Rates | |
|---|---|---|---|---|---|
| | | January | November | January | November |
| 1 | 10 | 250 | 160 | $ 25 | $ 16 |
| 2 | 12 | 250 | 150 | 30 | 18 |
| 3 | 16 | 250 | 200 | 40 | 32 |
| 4 | 8 | 250 | 200 | 20 | 16 |
| 5 | 8 | 250 | 150 | 20 | 12 |
| 6 | 8 | 250 | 250 | 20 | 20 |
| 7 | 20 | 250 | 180 | 50 | 36 |
| 8 | 20 | 250 | 245 | 50 | 49 |
| 9 | 20 | 250 | 125 | 50 | 25 |
| Totals | | 2,250 | 1,660 | $305 | $224 |

During the month of January, according to Table A, the production
centers were employed 2,250 hours and establishment charges of $305 were
carried to the "Shop-Charges Account," while, in November, the centers
operated 1,660 hours and the amount of $224 was charged to this account.
The actual shop expenses for January and November were $395 and $345
respectively.

Continuing the application of the author's proposition, the supplementary rate for January was determined to be four cents ($0.04) per
hour ($395 - $305 ÷ 2,250 = $0.04) and that for November was ascertained
to be seven and three-tenths cents ($0.073) per hour ($345 - $224 ÷
1,660 = $0.073).

SHOP-CHARGES ACCOUNT

| Debit | January | November | Credit | January | November |
|---|---|---|---|---|---|
| To Interest on Machines | $ 40 | $ 40 | By Machine Earnings (Table A) | $305[d] | $224[d] |
| To Depreciation on Machines | 60 | 60 | By Supplementary Rate | 90[e] | 121[f] |
| To Power | 70 | 50 | | | |
| To Wages | 75[a] | 55[b] | | | |
| To Process Sundries (Oil, &c.) | 35 | 25 | | | |
| To Debit for Floor Burden | 60[c] | 60[c] | | | |
| To Supervision | 55 | 55 | | | |
| | $395 | $345 | | $395 | $345 |

[a] Two operators and one supervisor.

[b] One operator and one supervisor.

[c] Three thousand square feet at two cents each.

[d] Being total of amount distributed to jobs by means of machine rates-- see Table A.

[e] Supplementary Rate--$90 ÷ 2,250 = 4¢ per hour.

[f] Supplementary Rate--$121 ÷ 1,660 = 7.3¢ per hour.

Note: Had an average hourly burden rate been applied, the following rates would have been used:

January --$395 ÷ 2,250 = 17.5¢ per hour.

November--$345 ÷ 1,660 = 20.8¢ per hour.

Applying these data to identical production orders under three conditions, as disclosed in Table B, the variation between total conversion costs may be ascertained readily. In the first place, identical orders were processed in January and November through the same machines with total conversion costs of $14.40 and $15.39 respectively. The variation of $0.99 was found in the amount allocated by the supplementary rate and was explained as additional costs arising from idle factory capacity.

In the second place, identical orders were processed during November but were routed differently. The variation in total conversion costs of $0.80 was apparent as the result of operating under improved methods.  When compared with January, the variation of $0.19 may be divided into two factors--the supplementary rate increase of $0.99 and the improved method decrease of $0.80.

TABLE B.--COST STATEMENT OF JOBS

| Hours | Machine Number | Machine Rate Per Hour--Cents | January | November | November Improved Method* |
|---|---|---|---|---|---|
| 20 | 3 | 16 | $ 3.20 | $ 3.20 | |
| 10 | 1 | 10 | 1.00 | 1.00 | $ 1.00 |
| 20 | 2 | 12 | | | 2.40 |
| | Total Machine Rates | | $ 4.20 | $ 4.20 | $ 3.40 |
| Add: Supplementary Rate: | | | | | |
| | 30 at 4¢ per hour | | 1.20 | | |
| | 30 at 7.3¢ per hour | | | 2.19 | 2.19 |
| Add: Wages: | | | | | |
| | 30 at 30¢ per hour | | 9.00 | 9.00 | 9.00 |
| | | | $14.40 | $15.39 | $14.59 |

*Altered Process.

A careful consideration of this procedure will disclose that all the shop charges will be distributed to production and that the supplementary rate will increase in proportion as the production centers are idle.  Thus this supplementary rate becomes somewhat of a significant index to the commercial efficiency of the factory.

> This factor has never been separated before from the general
> body of the costs.  On an averaging system, if we find a re-
> duced cost today as against the cost of the same article a
> year ago, we cannot, if the method has in the meantime been
> varied, say what is the reason of the reduction.  The manu-
> facturing efficiency due to method was intermixed with the
> commercial efficiency due to state of trade.  In the new
> method, the state of trade or the general efficiency of man-
> agement affect the supplementary rate alone, and a similar
> cost at two different periods might, if analyzed, show that
> what had been gained in method had been neutralized by a fall

in the volume of trade, or by a muddled condition of shop
organization.[48]

This author, in summarizing his scheme, pointed out its applica-
bility to heterogeneous processes, to heavy engineering work, to mass
production, and to most complex classes of work (even those processed by
automatic machines).  With respect to comparisons, Church declared that
the manufacturer employing this plan benefited in two ways:

> First, his normal rate being constant, he can compare costs
> of jobs worked on at different periods, and secondly the
> amount of the supplementary rate (its ratio to the normal
> rate) will serve as a very accurate barometer of the condi-
> tions under which he has been working at any period.[49]
>
> Again in the new machine rate we do get a factor of cost
> which is just as significant as the wages itself.  It is a
> factor which varies as method varies.  Cheaper methods of do-
> ing work will be promptly reflected in this factor.[50]

Church supplemented his early treatment of manufacturing expenses
with a series of articles entitled "Organisation of Production Factors."[51]
In these articles, the writer reiterated the importance of dividing the
factory into production centers, of determining his "new machine rate,"
and of employing his supplementary rate to dispose of any balance remaining in the factory expense account.

---

[48] Ibid., XXII, 40.

[49] Ibid., XXI, 908.

[50] Ibid., XXII, 40.

[51] Church, A. Hamilton, "Organisation by Production Factors," The
Engineering Magazine, Vols. XXXVIII and XXXIX (October, 1909-April, 1910).

> In the method of organisation by production factors it is
> sought to isolate as many as possible of the special func-
> tions exercised by the manufacturer, to determine their
> steady and regular rent-value, by foreseeing their fluctua-
> tions, and charge these rents as regular production factors
> of perfectly determinable value.[52]

These articles were primarily a restatement of his former concepts;

however, the author recognized the current trend in cost thinking to a

higher degree than before.

> The most noticeable tendency in engineering manufacture at
> the present time is a desire to reduce all operations to def-
> inite standards.[53]

He stated that the modern plan of predetermining costs and of comparing

estimated with actual results had a close relation to his form of organi-

zation--"since it permits every extension and every rearrangement to be

reduced to figures--definite, not as affecting particular groupings of

indirect charges, but as bearing on the hourly work of every single

machine or production centre."[54]

That Church was attempting to find a scientific and objective means

of treating manufacturing charges as Taylor and his colleagues had under-

taken to handle labor may be understood from the following rather

lengthy quotation:

> These developments are part of the general progress towards
> regarding manufacture as a step by step series of definite

---

[52] Ibid., XXXVIII, 189.

[53] Ibid., XXXIX, 85.

[54] Ibid.

predeterminable operations--a tendency that cannot be fully
realised until the vague incidence of indirect charges is,
once for all, got rid of and the maximum and minimum range
of incidence on definite production centres submitted for it.
When along with the "chip-removing" capacity and power absorption of every different type of machine we begin to
realise that it has a natural machine rate, which can be
forecast within certain limits even before it is actually
installed in a shop, a good step forward will have been made
in the direction of final standardisation.  Only the accumulation of records and of compared experience can make this
possible, but it will be allowed that _a general acceptance
of the principle of organisation by production factors would
have the effect of making known the usual or standard values
of such factors under conditions of good practice_, and that
therefore as soon as the elements of cost, power, durability,
space, and attendance of any new machine were determined, _its
normal rate under conditions of efficient and economical installation and working would also be predeterminable with
sufficiently close accuracy_.  In so far as such theoretical
rates were not realised in actual practice it would suggest
a prima-facie case for enquiry into causes.[55]

Thus, for Church, his "New Machine Rate" was a kind of standard for

manufacturing expenses--a method of allocating indirect charges accord-

ing to _normal_ production--and his "Supplementary Rate" was a variation

from this standard--a scheme for disclosing abnormal conditions and shop

inefficiency.  The author was not writing a treatise on standard costs

but he was developing a technique that could be devised into standard

cost procedure.

P. J. Darlington, another writer of this period to recognize idle

capacity, determined an indirect expense rate per hour for each square

foot of floor space, for each machine tool, and for each bench worker.

This rate was ascertained on the basis of a normal activity per month or

---

[55]_Ibid._, p. 86.  Italics are the author's.

other fiscal period.[56]

This author recognized that, if operation fell below normal, the total monthly indirect expenditures would not be charged against the production. In this case, he would dispose of this "idle indirect" balance by charging it directly as a loss against the profits for the month --as compared with Church's supplementary rate and charge to production orders.

> Such falling off of business does not raise the shop cost of product. There would seem to be no reason for changing indirect costs or percentages to keep pace with such varying activity of the works. Aside from the clerical cost and confusion that would result, it would destroy comparison and cover up valuable information in the monthly statements. It would also raise so-called shop cost in the face of reduced sales, when lower selling prices may be the remedy in filling up the shop and increasing total profits.[57]

Darlington also mentioned the "penalized job"--a term applied to a piece of work completed, from the exigencies of the moment, by a more expensive man or on a more expensive machine than normally used.

> A very large proportion of machine work is done on tools much larger than necessary for each operation. This is usually for good practical reasons, such as to keep otherwise idle equipment and operators profitably employed. . . . Evidently indirect cost must be based on the indirect rate normal to the operation, rather than on the rate of the tool on which the work happens to be done.[58]

---

[56] Darlington, P. J., "The Fundamental Principles of Works Organization and Management," The Engineering Magazine, Vols. XXXIV and XXXV (March-April, 1908).

[57] Ibid., XXXV, 65.

[58] Ibid., pp. 65-66.

Church, in discussing the penalized job somewhat later, rejected

Darlington's theory and declared that it was a dangerous procedure to

misrepresent in the actual costs what really took place in the factory:

> In view of the very grave dangers attending the permission to
> vary the truth of such records, it does not seem that the ad-
> vantages to be gained by smoothing down and rounding off
> "penalized" jobs are worth the trouble and risk, even were it
> proper from a theoretical point of view to do so.[59]

Webner, another writer to recognize the problem of allocating manu-

facturing expense to production, stated that this cost element

> . . . for a calendar month or four-week period should be
> equitably segregated over the various departments of the
> plant, then in turn the expense of each department segregated
> over each machine and bench in the department, and the ex-
> pense on each machine or bench divided by the number of work-
> ing hours in the month to find the cost per hour.[60]

This cost per hour, which Webner characterized as a constant per

hour, was applied to each job processed in the department by multiplying

the constant by the number of hours consumed.  The author foresaw unused

capacity, dead time of the machine for him, and provided that this dead

time "should be charged against a reserve account and finally find its

way back into the diffusion process as a cost like the cost of a work-

man's dead time."[61]  Thus Webner tended to follow Church's procedure but

------------------------------

[59] Church, op. cit., XXXVIII, 187.

[60] Webner, F. E., "Obtaining Actual Knowledge of the Cost of Production," The Engineering Magazine, XXXV (May, 1908), 255.

[61] Ibid., p. 255.

presented a much less adequate treatment of this phase of his subject.

John Whitmore, in a series of four lectures before the School of Commerce, Accounts and Finance of New York University (later published in The Journal of Accountancy),[62] anticipated certain principles that have been developed into a part of Standard Costs.

In the first place, this author stated that the purpose of factory accounting was to maintain records "in which waste should be plainly shown as waste."[63] Although he realized that this ideal could not be attained perfectly, he designated two factors of primary significance in reaching this goal--the full utilization of factory capacity and the development of mutual interests between the employer and the employee.

> It may almost be said that economy in production is attained if this single condition is fulfilled, namely, that factory capacity be fully utilized. This does not mean merely that every machine shall be in constant operation, but that it shall be constantly operated to the maximum advantage. If materials worked upon are spoiled the factory capacity that has been employed upon them is wasted. If a machine is employed upon less important work than that for which it was designed and is fitted, its capacity is partly wasted. If labor or management is inefficient and a machine is slackly operated, or the processes are ill arranged, capacity is wasted.[64]

Whitmore recognized the problem of handling idle time for factory equipment, criticized Church's "Supplementary Factory Rate," and declared that no factory accounting system which included the expense of

---

[62]Whitmore, John, "Factory Accounting as Applied to Machine Shops," The Journal of Accountancy, Vols. II and III (August, 1906-January, 1907).

[63]Ibid., II, 249.

[64]Ibid.

idle factory capacity in the cost of products was adequate.[65]  He advocated the opening of an account, "Factory Capacity Idle," to accumulate any avoidable loss or charges due to the fluctuations in the efficiency of the shop or commercial management.  The author would not permit the factory output to absorb this expense but would keep "the costs of the products of the factory operated and the cost of the factory idle separate from one another."

> The full operation of a factory depends upon engineering and commercial efficiency, and upon efficiency of shop management. If the cost of falling short of full operation is constantly and clearly stated, the units of idle capacity being identified and the causes traceable, there is created entirely new likelihood that effective remedies will be applied.[66]

In facilitating the recording of factory costs according to capacity actually utilized, Whitmore divided the machines into three classifications:[67]

1. Machines of full efficiency, of general use, and of constant service.--The author would ascertain what constituted full operation by determining the number of operational days per year (say 300), the working hours per day (assume 8), and the time idle for repairs (estimated at 10%).  The result of these hypothetical data, 2,160 hours in this case, would be adopted as the standard of full operation for the year.

2. Machines of full efficiency, of special use, and of less than

---

[65] Ibid., p. 256.

[66] Ibid., pp. 257-258.

[67] Ibid., pp. 439-440.

continuous operation.--After determining the special uses for which the machines were installed and the extent to which the machines have been calculated for use during the year, a percentage of full employment (assume 40%) was established.  The product (40% of 2,160), 864 in this instance, would be accepted as the standard of full employment.

3. Machines of less than full efficiency and of use only when more economically operated equipment was busy.--The standard was obtained as in the case of the machines in Classification One:  ". . . their use is certainly worth no more than the hourly rate so determined, and probably even on this basis the work is expensively done; and the actual cost of keeping such machines in the shops cannot be too plainly shown."

Applying this information to the machine costs for the year, the machine rates per hour were ascertained.  A monthly statement of charges, divided as to time charged to operation and to idle time, was prepared and formed the basis for the following journal entry:

```
            Manufacturing Account                    xxx
            Idle Capacity                            xxx
              Machine Rates                                 xxx
                  To distribute the machine expenses
                  for the period to production and to
                  idle time.
```

The debit to the Manufacturing Account represented the product of the hours operated and the machine rates, while the charge to Idle Capacity was the difference between this time so charged and the time calculated upon as full operation.

The Idle Capacity Account, according to Whitmore, was charged with

the whole expense of idle capacity and the cost figures were freed from
this fluctuating and confusing element. After profits had been determined on the basis of the resulting cost figures, the idle capacity expense was deducted from them. Therefore, for this writer, the charge
for idle capacity was a profit and loss item rather than a cost of manufacturing element.[68]

Murdoch also recognized the importance of Idle Capacity and followed the same general procedure as Whitmore but tended to simplify his
method of ascertaining the machine rates:

> . . . "Idle Capacity." The loading for profit must be made
> ample enough to cover this, as the selling department cannot
> be saddled with such expense specifically. The expense
> caused by machinery standing idle is the result of accident
> or bad management, and the proper cost figure to quote to the
> sales department for competitive purposes is the minimum at
> which the factory can produce the goods while running full
> swing, leaving it up to the executive to see that the produc-
> tion department keeps it down as near the minimum as possi-
> ble.[69]

This author provided for ascertaining the charges allocatable to
Idle Capacity and, as in the case of Whitmore, designated such expenditures as profit and loss items rather than cost of production elements.

Somewhat later, Whitmore applied some of his cost accounting principles to the shoe manufacturing industry in a lecture delivered at New
York University.[70] In defining cost, the writer declared that true or

---

[68]Ibid., III, 31.

[69]Murdoch, Andrew A., "The Proper Treatment of Machine Costs," The
Journal of Accountancy, III (December, 1906), 123-130.

[70]Whitmore, John, "Shoe Factory Cost Accounts," The Journal of
Accountancy, VI (May, 1908), 12-25.

correct cost did not necessarily include every expense incurred in producing an article:

> Accidents and blunders occur and the cost, as in some instances the cost of unused factory capacity, may be so great that it would be absurd to state it as a part of the cost of the product.[71]

After the acceptance of this concept, he would separate and disclose properly irrelevant costs from ordinary and necessary manufacturing expenditures and would establish attainable standards not only for simple work but also for complex processes.

That the author contemplated more than simple cost estimates may be evidenced from the following quotation:

> It is possible to carry the application of the principle of distinguishing between proper and improper costs so far as to use calculations of proper costs and then to direct the cost accounting to showing the variations of actual from calculated costs. This involves the setting up of complete standards for quality in materials and efficiency in working, and is not to be confused with estimates of probable cost which are arrived at by any superficial method, or except with the idea of continuously testing actual and calculated costs by each other.[72]

Whitmore found his system applicable to those industries which had so many manufacturing orders that it was not practicable to work out separate cost records for each order, and stated that it was sufficiently flexible to fulfill his suggested purposes of cost accounts--

---

[71] Ibid., p. 14.

[72] Ibid.

the bookkeeping purposes:  to state profits or losses and to value inventories; the economical purpose:  to reveal and eliminate waste, thus decreasing cost of production; and the commercial purpose:  to determine prices at which products can be sold for a profit.

In the handling of raw materials for the shoe industry, the author would issue these products at a standard price and would carry, in a surplus or deficiency account, the variations between the actual and the standard figures.  However this procedure involved only the storehouse ledger--no entry was made in the general books in connection with this operation--and served as a statistical device to indicate the variations in the cost of obtaining a given grade of leather over any period of time.[73]

With respect to labor, the author prepared "Labor Cost Sheets" which undertook to predetermine the labor cost of producing the sample shoe.  By using these labor cost sheets, the individual postings to the cost sheets for separate operations were eliminated and this economy of standard costs was recognized.  Periodically, the production, valued at calculated costs, was analyzed, departmentalized, and compared with the actual labor costs as accumulated in the general ledger accounts.[74]

In 1931, Whitmore referred to this article and suggested the cost accounting procedure as practiced in 1908:

Some of these [American manufacturers] were keeping individual manufacturing-order cost accounts; and some were merely

---

[73]Ibid., pp. 16-23.

[74]Ibid., pp. 24-25.

crediting their manufacturing accounts with the production at
costs calculated beforehand; and some were using standard
cost sheets, pure and simple, without bringing the figures
into their general account books at all.[75]

He declared that he was familiar with all of these procedures be-

fore December, 1903, and that he had described a method of using stand-

ards to credit the manufacturing accounts in those industries with manu-

facturing orders so small and numerous that the keeping of individual

cost accounts for them were not practicable. He stated that, at the

same time--May, 1903--he had disclosed the technique for determining

variances from standards in these industries.

It must be recognized that Whitmore had believed that historical

and estimating costs could be improved and that he sought an answer for

handling idle time and material use variations. However, his method of

setting standards--

The amount of net surplus or net deficiency in the upper
leather storeroom should be stated week by week, and the
standard of prices raised or lowered at any time that it is
seen to be necessary in order to keep the prices placed on
the products of the sorting, and used in issuing the sorted
leathers, in substantial agreement with actual costs[76]

--tends to remove his system from standard cost technique. Nevertheless,

his efforts deserve to be considered as a definite contribution to the

early development of standard cost procedure.

---

[75]Whitmore, John, "Poverty and Riches of 'Standard Costs,'" The
Journal of Accountancy, LI (January, 1931), 11.

[76]Whitmore, John, "Shoe Factory Cost Accounts," The Journal of
Accountancy, VI (May, 1908), 23.

When considering the evolution of standard costs, Wildman of New York University deserves to be included as one of the individuals who contributed to its early development. He stated that "predetermined costs should be technically distinguished from estimated costs, in that they are constructed from predetermined standards scientifically obtained."[77]

This author anticipated something more than estimated costs and pointed out that the "Efficiency Department," to which he devoted a chapter in his text because of the close relation which it bears to cost accounting, was "one of the most striking innovations of recent times."

He gave the efficiency engineer, who supervised the "Efficiency Department," the task of fixing standards of quantity and quality with respect to machinery, men, materials and methods; the cost accountant the task of maintaining adequate records; and both the efficiency engineer and the cost accountant the task of tying the standards and the records into the cost accounting procedure.[78]

> Standards serve to develop a predetermined cost. Taking into
> consideration the cost of material as determined by the stand-
> ards of quantity and quality, the cost of labor as determined
> by the standard time of operation, the cost of overhead as
> determined by the standard of the various elements composing
> it, it is possible to predetermine or obtain an estimated
> cost which may be used as a standard or basic cost and which
> provides for 100% efficiency.[79]

---

[77]Wildman, op. cit., p. 88.

[78]Ibid., pp. 84-87.

[79]Ibid., p. 87.

Although Wildman did not develop an accounting procedure for assisting his so-called efficiency engineer, he should be cited for so forcefully calling this possibility to the attention of the cost accountant.

W. E. McHenry, Auditor of the Cambria Steel Company, may be considered to have anticipated certain standard cost procedure in his plea for common sense in the cost department--"Logical Factory Costs."[80] This author presented several illustrations, some of which will be reproduced (modified somewhat with respect to form and content), in whole or in part, to substantiate the present writer's initial statement.

In the first place, the author assumed a manufacturer of a single product selling for $10, with a weekly demand ranging from 200 to 1,000 units. The following schedule will indicate the company's old method of treating overhead for certain months of the year:

TABLE 1.--OLD METHOD OF TREATING "OVERHEAD"[81]

| Month | Units of Product | Factory Expense | Expense Per Unit | Overhead Per Unit, Including Average Depreciation and Interest at 43¢ |
|---|---|---|---|---|
| January | 3,100 | $2,745 | $0.89 | $1.32 |
| March | 1,700 | 2,955 | 1.74* | 2.17* |
| June | 4,075 | 2,830 | 0.69 | 1.12 |
| November | 4,430 | 3,595 | 0.81** | 1.24** |
| Author's Average for the Year | | | 0.916 | 1.346 |

*Includes excess repairs of $0.40.
**Includes excess repairs of $0.14.

---

[80] McHenry, W. E., "Logical Factory Costs," The Engineering Magazine, L (February, 1916), 733-741.

[81] Ibid., p. 734.

Stating these data in another manner, McHenry prorated the foregoing overhead over the fifty-two weeks in the year at various levels of production:

SCHEDULE OF OVERHEAD AT VARIOUS PRODUCTION LEVELS[82]

|  | Production Levels | | | | |
| Explanation | 20% | 40% | 60% | 80% | 100% |
|---|---|---|---|---|---|
| Weekly Output (Units) | 200 | 400 | 600 | 800 | 1,000 |
| Weekly Overhead (Total) | $800 | $847 | $945 | $989 | $1,035 |
| Weekly Overhead (Unit) | $ 4 | $2.12 | $1.58 | $1.23 | $ 1.04 |

When the prime costs (materials and direct labor) were found to be $7.00 per unit, the writer prepared a schedule of unit operational results at these various levels of production:

SCHEDULE OF UNIT OPERATIONAL RESULTS
AT STATED PRODUCTION LEVELS[83]

|  | Production Levels | | | | | |
| Explanation | 20% | 40% | 60% | Average Last Year | 80% | 100% |
|---|---|---|---|---|---|---|
| Overhead | $ 4.00 | $ 2.12 | $ 1.58 | $ 1.35 | $ 1.23 | $ 1.04 |
| Material and Direct Labor | 7.00 | 7.00 | 7.00 | 7.00 | 7.00 | 7.00 |
| Total Unit Cost | $11.00 | $ 9.12 | $ 8.58 | $ 8.35 | $ 8.23 | $ 8.04 |
| Selling Price | 10.00 | 10.00 | 10.00 | 10.00 | 10.00 | 10.00 |
| Profit or Loss* | $ 1.00* | $ 0.88 | $ 1.42 | $ 1.65 | $ 1.77 | $ 1.96 |

Criticizing this cost procedure, he indicated two possible methods of disclosing total costs based on these respective production levels. The first method--that of the average man who "follows the conservative

---

[82] Ibid., p. 734, adapted.

[83] Ibid., p. 735.

rule of distributing what he terms 'actual' expense, and his absurd attempt to make the separation of 'unearned' expense"--would likely be this:[34]

| Explanation | Production Levels | | | | |
|---|---|---|---|---|---|
| | 20% | 40% | 60% | 80% | 100% |
| Weekly Expense | $ 800 | $ 847 | $ 945 | $ 989 | $1,035 |
| Proportion of Expense to Output | $ 160 | $ 338 | $ 567 | $ 791 | $1,035 |
| Material and Direct Labor | 1,400 | 2,800 | 4,200 | 5,600 | 7,000 |
| Total Costs | $1,560 | $3,138 | $4,767 | $6,391 | $8,035 |
| Units Produced | 200 | 400 | 600 | 800 | 1,000 |
| Unit Cost | $ 7.80 | $ 7.85 | $ 7.95 | $ 7.99 | $ 8.04 |

As an alternative, he then presented his standard technique:

We found the prorated expense, running full, about $1,035, and the output, about 1,000. For practical purposes we adopt, as a standard rate for distributing the burden in this case, $1 (instead of $1.035) per unit. (In actual practice a standard rate is seldom based on units of output, but upon time or service of equipment used; this gives an index of variation in output in a given time and the cost of such variations in efficiency of operation.)[35]

| Explanation | Production Levels | | | | |
|---|---|---|---|---|---|
| | 20% | 40% | 60% | 80% | 100% |
| Materials and Direct Labor | $1,400 | $2,800 | $4,200 | $5,600 | $7,000 |
| Expense: By Standard Rate | 200 | 400 | 600 | 800 | 1,000 |
| Total Cost | $1,600 | $3,200 | $4,800 | $6,400 | $8,000 |
| Units Produced | 200 | 400 | 600 | 800 | 1,000 |
| Unit Cost "Standard" | $ 8 | $ 8 | $ 8 | $ 8 | $ 8 |
| Weekly Expense | $ 800 | $ 847 | $ 945 | $ 989 | $1,035 |
| Expense: By Standard Rate | 200 | 400 | 600 | 800 | 1,000 |
| "Unearned Expense" | $ 600 | $ 447 | $ 345 | $ 189 | $ 35 |
| "Unearned Expense" per Unit | $ 3 | $ 1.12 | $ 0.58 | $ 0.23 | $ 0.04 |

---

[34] Ibid., p. 735, adapted.

[35] Ibid., p. 735, adapted.

Finally, as a more logical method of treating factory expense, McHenry divided the year into thirteen four-week periods and prepared a table to illustrate further his standard burden rate method of treating this production factor (Table has been reproduced only partially):

TABLE 2.--STANDARD BURDEN RATE METHOD OF TREATING "OVERHEAD"[86]

| Four Week Period | Units of Product | Earned Expense Per Unit | Earned Expense | Unearned Expense | Total Standard Expense | Actual Expense |
|---|---|---|---|---|---|---|
| 1 | 2,800 | $1.07 | $ 3,000 | $    905 | $ 3,905 | $ 3,914 |
| 3 | 1,600 | 1.00 | 1,600 | 1,845 | 3,445 | 3,439 |
| 7 | 3,575 | 1.06 | 3,800 | 285 | 4,085 | 4,053 |
| 13 | 4,000 | 1.00 | 4,000 | 130 | 4,130 | 4,140 |
| Author's Annual Totals | 37,550 | $1.048 | $39,400 | $11,130 | $50,530 | $50,596 |
| Average | | | | 66 | 66 | |
| Unearned Expense | | 0.298 | | $11,196 | | |
| Grand Total | | $1.346 | | | $50,596 | $50,596 |

The author pointed out that his methods were applicable to a factory producing one or many products. And, finally, he declared that by having the cost of idle or unproductive hours clearly disclosed as "Unearned Expense," any variation in the efficiency of work done was reflected in the costs.

> While the principles upon which the scientific method is
> based have been recognized for ten years, its introduction
> has been extremely slow. One reason for this is that, simple
> as are the principles, their application in actual practice
> is far from simple. The experience and painstaking work

---

[86] Ibid., p. 736, abridged.

necessary to an installation are considerable, and unless the work is done with an eye to the practical at all times, the "system" is apt to be top-heavy or otherwise unsatisfactory.[87]

McHenry undertook to explain his standard cost concepts in two other magazine articles--"Cost Per Ton," _The Engineering Magazine_, Volume XLVI (February, 1914), and "Is Your Cost System Scientific," _The Engineering Magazine_, Volume LI (August, 1916); however, the original article considered in this study contains the best analysis of his ideas.

In addition to portraying some concepts of standard costs, McHenry had proposed a year divided into thirteen months of four weeks each, had presented manufacturing costs at various levels of production, and had suggested the difficulties with which a scientific system of cost accounting might be undertaken.

Webner's publication, _Factory Accounting_, recognized not only estimated costs but also a rather unique technique that he termed "Standard Costs."[88] This device is not a true standard cost procedure, as understood in this study, but does indicate some advancement over the estimating method. In view of the fact that the author rejected estimating costs as wholly inadequate but recommended his "Standard Costs" as having immense practical value, the development of this scheme has been placed in this chapter, "The Background of Standard Cost Accounting."

Under his plan, the total list price, together with the departmental costs of material, labor, and overhead expense, should be computed

---

[87] Ibid., p. 741.

[88] Webner, _Factory Accounting_, pp. 187-191.

for each product manufactured.  These departmental costs were then expressed as percentages of the list price--the "standard" costs for the author.

> These standard costs are worked out in advance, are tested in
> actual practice, and no change is necessary until tests or
> balances at the close of cost periods show variations in the
> cost.[89]

In ascertaining the cost standards or percentages for the various departments, Webner made use of prior cost figures as ascertained from the records of the concern.  In order to illustrate his technique, the following data have been assumed for Product X - 3 - BT, which has a list price of $2.00 subject to a 10% trade discount, by the present writer:

STATISTICAL DATA FOR PRODUCT X - 3 - BT AS
ASCERTAINED FROM THE RECORDS OF THE
MANUFACTURING COMPANY FOR 1943

| Price Elements | Amount | Departmental Analysis | | |
| --- | --- | --- | --- | --- |
| | | No. 1 | No. 2 | No. 3 |
| Materials | $ .381 | $ .257 | $ .061 | $ .063 |
| Labor | .352 | .105 | .057 | .190 |
| Overhead | .237 | .077 | .040 | .120 |
| Factory Cost | $ .970 | $ .439 | $ .158 | $ .373 |
| Commercial Costs | .185 | | | |
| Profit | .645 | | | |
| Discount | .200 | | | |
| List Price | $2.000 | | | |

Applying the author's technique, the following Cost Standards would

---

[89] Ibid., p. 187.

be determined for this product.  The list price of $2.00 is the basis for the computation.

SCHEDULE OF STANDARD COSTS FOR
PRODUCT X - 3 - BT
(Percentages of List Price of $2.00)

| Price Elements | Totals | Departmental Standards | | |
| --- | --- | --- | --- | --- |
| | | No. 1 | No. 2 | No. 3 |
| Materials | 19.05 | 12.85 | 3.05 | 3.15 |
| Labor | 17.60 | 5.25 | 2.85 | 9.50 |
| Overhead | 11.85 | 3.85 | 2.00 | 6.00 |
| Factory Costs | 48.50 | 21.95 | 7.90 | 18.65 |
| Commercial Costs | 9.25 | | | |
| Profit | 32.25 | | | |
| Discount | 10.00 | | | |
| List Price | 100.00 | | | |

Continuing this hypothetical case, it may be assumed that two thousand units of Product X - 3 - BT are started through the factory in 1944.  Applying these percentages to the total list price of $4,000 (2,000 units x $2.00 list price), the Cost Standards, by departments, for the completion of this production order would be as follows:

SCHEDULE OF COST STANDARDS FOR TWO THOUSAND
UNITS OF PRODUCT X - 3 - BT IN 1944

| Price Elements | Totals | Departmental Standards | | |
| --- | --- | --- | --- | --- |
| | | No. 1 | No. 2 | No. 3 |
| Materials | $ 762 | $514 | $122 | $126 |
| Labor | 704 | 210 | 114 | 380 |
| Overhead | 474 | 154 | 80 | 240 |
| Total | $1,940 | $878 | $316 | $746 |

Although the author suggested the recording of Cost Standards--"the advantages of expressing the departmental costs at standard rates lies in the ease of calculation, of recording, of comparison, and of change

when necessary"[90]--he failed to develop any journalization or posting

procedure therefor.

At the end of each cost period, the total actual costs, distributed

under the same classifications as the predetermined figures, should ap-

proximate the total standard costs.  The author repeated the importance

of periodic tests to demonstrate not only the accuracy of the estimated

percentages but also any variation of costs from the standards.  Another

symptom of standard costs--something the author would classify as supe-

rior to estimating costs--may be gained from a careful analysis of the

following quotation:

> Their [standard figures] chief function is, however, to af-
> ford a basis of comparison by which fluctuations of costs,
> whether up or down, may be clearly shown, and this the fig-
> ures of a standard or list-percentage plan will do.  If effi-
> ciency operations are in progress which should reduce costs,
> the management have a standard by which any reductions at-
> tained are sharply shown.  If accidental causes increase
> costs, the test will show this increase and the percentage
> expression will show its amount, and the management may then
> take such steps as they deem best.  The cost system will in-
> dicate the conditions.  It is for the management to determine
> what these conditions demand.[91]

Thus Webner demonstrated that, between 1911 (when he published his

first book) and 1917 (the date of this text), he had been influenced by

the efficiency doctrine as propounded by Harrington Emerson and others,

who have been proposed as forerunners of standard costs.  Therefore,

---

[90]Ibid., p. 188.

[91]Ibid., p. 191.

Webner's "Standard Costs" seem justified to be classified outside of Estimating Costs.

When Church published his text, <u>Manufacturing Costs and Accounts</u>,[92] he incorporated his new machine rate scheme as "Costing Method C (Scientific Machine Rate Plan)" and employed four chapters to describe the procedure.

The author explained rather completely the method used in determining the machine rate,[93] a point that was treated inadequately in his magazine articles. In the first place, he would assemble in great detail every item of expense, expressed in annual figures and incurred when the factory was working full time as shown by the past records of the firm.

When all of these expense items had been collected in groups corresponding to production factors--space factor, power factor, stores-transport factor, supervision factor, organization factor, and individual machine factor were suggested by the writer--the distribution of each factor was made to the individual machines or production centers in accordance with principles applicable to the respective factor. The hourly machine rate for each production center, which was broken down into production factors, was computed by dividing the total expenses for said production departments by the total working hours during the year. Church described these machine rates as "standard rates, which represent

---

[92]Church, A. Hamilton, <u>Manufacturing Costs and Accounts</u>, New York, McGraw-Hill Book Company, 1917.

[93]<u>Ibid</u>., pp. 355-370.

the cost of running the machine for one hour under standard and favorable conditions."[94]

Church followed his earlier procedure with respect to costing products by applying the machine rate and by employing the supplementary rate, expressed now as a percentage of the machine earnings rather than as an hourly amount, to dispose of the wasted manufacturing capacity. However, in addition to prorating the amount representing wasted capacity over production order, he stated that this item might be charged to a Waste Account, which would be closed into Profit and Loss.

The author suggested a scheme for verification of factor schedules, which was designed as a means of control when this costing plan was employed.

Some significance should be given to Church's title to this costing method--"Scientific Machine Rate Plan"--at this time (1917).  The present writer proposes that it is indicative of the increasing attention that was being given to cost accounting procedure by those writers who were trying to make cost accounting something more than an expression of historical data.

Church was influenced by the criticism of his method and by the growing importance of standard costs to such an extent that, in 1930, he retracted the application of his Supplementary Rate[95] and made the following explanation with respect to its origin and early use:

---

[94]Ibid., p. 70.

[95]Church, A. Hamilton, _Overhead Expense_, New York, McGraw-Hill Book Company, 1930, pp. 383-385.

At the time in question, nearly twenty years ago, the idea of separating wasted capacity (idle time) from true cost of jobs was entirely new and unfamiliar. No other method than that of percentages, and, to a small degree, hourly burdens, was in use, and, in introducing the new views on overhead, it was desirable not to depart too far from established usage, which, of course, called for the prorating of all current expenditure over current jobs. By the device of the wasted ratio, or as it was termed the "supplementary rate," this complete prorating was still possible, although the author was careful to point out that it was not essential, and that the waste ratio was not and could not be part of true cost.

As it turned out, no element of the new method was more severely criticized than the "supplementary rate." It was (somewhat to the author's surprise) generally recognized that it was no part of true cost and that, therefore, wasted capacity should be charged off to profit and loss. Today, this idea is so generally accepted that there is perhaps no danger in the contrary course. But at the time of the original publication of the method, this was by no means the case, and the dangers were perhaps too much emphasized by the writer.[96]

However, Church continued to employ his production factors (now termed service factors) which, in accordance with current thinking, he undertook to standardize--

The general aim of standardization of service factors is (by means of collecting all overhead into several groups of which the annual value is then worked out) to find the cost of the manufacturing capacity of the whole plant for one year[97]

--for the ultimate purpose of the standardization of overhead expense.[98]

His procedure will be considered somewhat later in this study.

Although Church withdrew a portion of his contentions with respect

---

[96] Ibid., pp. 383-384.

[97] Ibid., p. 143.

[98] Ibid., pp. 122-144.

to the treatment of overhead expense, his general interest in the subject and his final disposition of this manufacturing cost merits this recognition of his efforts during the early development of techniques that were absorbed by and refined into standard cost procedure.

HARRINGTON EMERSON'S CONTRIBUTIONS TO STANDARD COST ACCOUNTING.--As a forerunner of standard costs, perhaps the greatest significance should be given to the expositions of Harrington Emerson.  This writer initiated his theories with a wage payment scheme, "A Rational Basis for Wages,"[99] which contained three basic principles:

1. A minimum wage, which is a matter of contract, is a consideration for the assignment of time and the loss of liberty, and is an obligatory payment as long as the laborer remains on the payroll.

2. An increment, which is equivalent to the current wages of the workman's trade or profession--a definite compensation due to the laborer because he is an engineer in charge of a train and under orders, for example.

3. An additional reward, which is the remuneration for exceptional and unusual co-operation of either mind, body or both.

Somewhat later (October, 1904), Emerson presented a paper, "Percentage Methods of Determining Production Costs," in Foundry.  These two contributions were expanded into a series of articles, "Efficiency as a Basis for Operation and Wages,"[100] which were published in The Engineering

---

[99]Emerson, Harrington, "A Rational Basis for Wages," Transactions, American Society of Mechanical Engineers, XXV (1903-04), 868-883.

[100]Emerson, Harrington, "Efficiency as a Basis for Operation and Wages," The Engineering Magazine, Vols. XXXV and XXXVI (1908-09).

<u>Magazine</u> during 1908-09.

In general, the author reviewed certain typical inefficiencies and their significance, sketched the peculiar qualities that have caused national industrial prosperity in Great Britain, Germany, France, Japan and the United States, presented the current status of existing systems of organization, explained the determination and realization of standards, introduced modern efficiency cost accounting, pointed out the means for the location and elimination of wastes, restated his efficiency method of wage payments, and submitted an illustration of the efficiency system in operation.

The author's theme was suggested early in the first article:

> It is distinctly the business of the engineer to lessen waste
> --wastes of materials, wastes of friction, wastes of design,
> wastes of effort, wastes due to crude organization and admin-
> istration--in a word, wastes due to inefficiencies. The
> field is the largest and richest into which any worker was
> ever turned. Progress--absolute, not temporary timeserving--
> will be made slowly or rapidly as the ideals and standards are
> high.[101]

To illustrate his principles of efficiency and to introduce his idea of standards, Emerson recorded an observation in a railroad shop, where large cylinder bushings, weighing about 375 pounds, were being made from 1,780-pound castings. Using a 600-pound casting in the standard procedure, he showed how the cost could be decreased by more than sixty per cent.[102]

---

[101] <u>Ibid.</u>, XXXV, 531.

[102] <u>Ibid.</u>, p. 534.

COMPARISON OF COSTS

|                                      | As Made  | Standard |
|--------------------------------------|----------|----------|
| Weight, rough                        | 1,780    | 600      |
| Cost per pound                       | $ 0.04   | $ 0.04   |
| Total cost                           | 71.20    | 24.00    |
| Labor                                | 3 days   | 1 day    |
| Cost of labor, $3.00 per day         | $ 9.00   | $ 3.00   |
| Machine charge, $2.00 per day        | 6.00     | 2.00     |
| Overhead charges, $2.00 per day      | 6.00     | 2.00     |
| Total cost                           | $92.00   | $31.00   |

After pointing out the characteristics of the principal industrial nations, Emerson ascribed

> . . . to the English the efficiency of wise anticipation and continuous persistence, to the French the efficiency due to their innovations of supreme value and merit, the efficiency of the Germans to their perfection of organization, discipline and scientific minuteness, to the Japanese the efficiency due to open-mindedness and marvelous power of assimilation, to the Americans the efficiency due to individuality.[103]

Questioning the ability of American individuality and boundless resources to maintain industrial leadership for this nation, Emerson suggested that, since standards have not been applied in the industrial world except for a few performances, this supremacy might be preserved by the setting of high standards and by thus influencing each worker to rise to the limit of his capacity.

Under Emerson's organizational scheme, the staff consisted of experts who occupied auxiliary and advisory relationships with respect to management as contrasted with Taylor's system in which the experts were

---

[103] Ibid., p. 672.

functional foremen who filled integral executive positions in the organ-

ization. Emerson, assuming that the modern company is created for a

specific purpose--a purpose which is more or less realized through the

interaction of men, materials, machines and methods--set up his organi-

zation under one chief of staff and a head of staff for each of these

four subdivisions. Of particular interest to this study, the signifi-

cance of the division of methods and conditions is suggested from the

following extract:

> A staff head as to conditions and methods including standards,
> records and accounting. It has been found practically impos-
> sible either to maintain standards or records unless they are
> tied into the accounting. This is because there are standards
> as to money entries and none as to times or performances.[104]

After enumerating the duties of the department heads and their as-

sistants responsible for the handling of men, materials, equipment, and

methods, Emerson recapitulated his efforts in the following manner:

> The result of perfected staff organization is that everything
> is well and quickly done when and where wanted, that all
> costs are predetermined, that the responsibility for any de-
> viation is immediately located, that the heads of both line
> and staff can direct far better than they are now able to,
> that costs of performance decrease, and that output from the
> same equipment and men increases.[105]

In explaining the establishment of standards in a progressive shop

--an enterprise with a steady supply of work, ample income, and experi-

enced officials but with great discrepancy between actual results and

---

[104]Ibid., p. 918.

[105]Ibid., p. 920.

reasonable possibilities, was chosen as an example--Emerson proposed
that five surveys be made to determine those factors that were not operated satisfactorily by the existing organization.  These surveys covered
the handling and checking of materials, the inspection of the machines
and tools, a labor audit for considering the relation between actual and
potential output of workmen, a study of the relationship between current
costs and standard costs, and a consideration of work moving through the
factory.

To correct the weaknesses of operation as revealed by these surveys,
a staff specialist was placed in charge of each of the five different
fields covered by the preliminary investigations--for materials, the official's duties were to establish methods which would always supply the
required material at the proper time and place and at the lowest cost;
for machines and tools, the maintenance and operation in the most efficient manner; for the standardization of every task so far as time was
concerned; for standard costs, the proper recording and comparison of
expenditures for materials, labor, and indirect expenses with the predetermined figures; and for the dispatching of work through the shop in
a rapid and efficient manner.[106]

The following statement, which has been reproduced from Emerson's
example, discloses the results that were obtained through the employment
of his procedures in this particular shop.[107]

---

[106] *Ibid.*, XXXVI, 172.

[107] *Ibid.*, p. 173.

DEPARTMENT F

Statement of Conditions for 12 Months Preceding
June 30 on Basis of Standard Volume of Output

|  | Actual | Standard | Reduction |
|---|---|---|---|
| **Costs Per Hour** | | | |
| Direct Wages .............. | $ 36.93 | $ 27.77 | 25.0% |
| Overhead or Indirect Expenses ............... | 18.98 | 11.11 | 41.5% |
| Machine Expenses | 48.94 | 29.17 | 40.0% |
| Totals .............. | $104.85 | $ 68.05 | 35.1% |
| **Total Costs Per Annum** | | | |
| Direct .................... | $ 99,794 | $ 75,000 | $24,794 |
| Overhead .................. | 51,255 | 30,000 | 21,255 |
| Machine Expenses .......... | 117,470 | 70,000 | 47,470 |
|  | $268,519 | $175,000 | $93,519 |

Under this procedure, the standard costs were, theoretically, pre-determined by standardizing the efficiency of men, machines, materials, and methods rather than the cost of work. The author did not think of these standards as fixed or permanent (basic standards) but as standards subject to change when and if the standards were attained (concept of ideal standards).

> The standard costs were those possible at the date the work was undertaken. By the time actual costs are reduced to $68.05 [as in above schedule] per hour new standards will have come into existence, making the standard costs as low, perhaps, as $60.00 per hour, so that the standard is always elusively ahead of the actual.[108]

Perhaps the most significant statement by Emerson as related to this

---

[108] Ibid., p. 174.

study is found in the following quotation:

> There are two radically different methods of ascertaining
> costs, the first method to ascertain them after the work is
> completed, the second method to ascertain them before the
> work is undertaken.  The first method is the old one, still
> used in most manufacturing and maintaining undertakings; the
> second method is the new one, beginning to be used in some
> very large plants, where its feasibility and practical value
> have already been demonstrated.[109]

In pointing out the relative merits of the two systems, Emerson
stated that the old system failed to aid in the elimination of waste
since this plan delayed information until these facts had no value and
accumulated incorrect costs by including items that had no direct connection thereto, whereas the new system ascertained costs before the
work was undertaken and tabulated these costs as divided into standard
expense and into avoidable loss.  Of greatest significance in this system, he asserted, predetermination of results, based on scientific cer-
tainties modified by experience, opened a means of determining the volume
of loss due to inefficiency and placed a responsibility on the efficiency
engineer to devise means that would eliminate the wasteful differences
between standard and actual costs.

Somewhat later, Church, in criticizing Harrington Emerson's "Efficiency as a Basis for Operation," declared that "the object of cost accounts is to register and record every stage and step of production as
they actually happened."[110]  Thus he refused to approve Emerson's state-

---

[109] Ibid., p. 336.

[110] Church, A. Hamilton, "Organisation by Production Factors," The
Engineering Magazine, XXXVIII (1909), 184.

ment which has been quoted above.  At the same time, he observed that

Emerson's estimated costs were checked subsequently with actual figures

and that any discrepancy between the two was regarded as waste.  Such

costs, Church asserted, were subject to manipulation and were condemned

since costs, according to this writer, should represent only the truth

with respect to shop operation.

Continuing the study of Emerson's thesis of efficiency, it is found

that this author placed an obligation upon the efficiency engineer to

supply methods for eliminating the difference between actual and stand-

ard costs--he would revise his standards, upward or downward, with the

fluctuations in the costs of materials, labor, and manufacturing expenses.

In order that the efficiency engineer might fulfill this obligation,

Emerson stated that the accountant would be required to furnish him with

current and correct costs:

> In accounting the auditor is responsible for correct cost
> statements as to every item of expense, and the efficiency
> engineer is responsible for correct cost attainments--namely,
> 100 per cent efficiency, as to every service, material issue,
> or equipment operation.[111]

As an illustration of his technique, this author assumed a railroad

with 1,000 locomotives which traveled 30,000,000 miles per annum at a

cost of $3,000,000.  If the efficiency engineer fixed the standard cost

at six cents ($0.06) per mile, the operating results might be shown as

follows:

------

[111] Emerson, Harrington, "Efficiency as a Basis for Operation and
Wages," The Engineering Magazine, XXXVI (1909), 342.

| Type of Cost | Cost In Total | Cost Per Mile | Per Cent |
|---|---|---|---|
| Actual Cost (30,000,000 Miles) .............. | $3,000,000 | $0.10 | 100 |
| Preventable Waste ..... | 1,200,000 | 0.04 | 40 |
| Standard Cost ........ | $1,800,000 | $0.06 | 60 |

For this author, the figure of 60% was adopted as the current efficiency factor and was selected as the index of operational results for the business executive to observe--as actual costs declined, this percentage would approach 100.  Therefore, he declared that the accountant should record the standard cost, as set by the efficiency engineer, and should provide records that would permit him to determine and present this efficiency factor monthly.

> The measuring appliances and methods of the standard-practice engineer, innumerable in their variety, are invented and applied so as to test and gauge efficiency.  As to all his own measures he seeks the co-operation of the accountant, without whose figures it is impossible to record definitely and reliably the progress made, or the reverse.[112]

In attempting to locate and eliminate wastes, the author recognized three types of costs--actual costs, which represented the costs incurred during the year; standard or efficiency costs, which were predetermined by the efficiency engineer through the use of existing standards or by a series of assays; and allotted costs, which were composed of standard costs and current waste and which were predetermined by assuming the same percentages for these factors as existed during the immediately

---

[112] Ibid., p. 346.

preceding period.

To illustrate his procedure, he assumed a railroad system in which the locomotive repairs were $0.10 per unit, the actual expenses were $487,171 for the initial year of the study, the standard costs should not exceed $0.06 per unit, and the actual annual saving should be $200,-000, and, on the basis of these data, prepared the following comparative statements of operational results for four years:[113]

### ALLOTTED COSTS, ACTUAL EXPENSES AND EFFICIENCY EXPENSES

| Explanation | 1903-4 | 1904-5 | 1905-6 | 1906-7 |
|---|---|---|---|---|
| Total Units ........ | 4,725,000 | 4,785,400 | 5,776,000 | 6,462,800 |
| Allotted Standard Costs ............. | $283,500 | $287,124 | $336,560 | $323,140 |
| Allotted Wastes .... | 189,000 | 191,416 | 57,760 | --- |
| Total Allotted Cost | $472,500 | $478,540 | $394,320 | $323,140 |
| Discrepancy between record and actual | | | | |
|    Increase ....... | 14,671 | 8,080 | --- | --- |
|    Decrease ....... | --- | --- | 18,214 | 7,296 |
| Actual Total Expense as it appears in President's report | $487,171 | $486,620 | $376,106 | $315,844 |
| Amount Forward: | | | | |
|    Debit .......... | --- | 14,671 | 22,751 | --- |
|    Credit ......... | --- | --- | --- | 4,537 |
| Efficiency Expenses | $487,171 | $501,291 | $398,857 | $320,381 |

---

[113]Ibid., pp. 679-680.

UNIT STATEMENT OF EXPENSES AND COSTS

| Explanation | 1903-4 | 1904-5 | 1905-6 | 1906-7 |
|---|---|---|---|---|
| Total Units ......... | 4,725,000 | 4,785,400 | 5,776,000 | 6,462,800 |
| Allotted Standard Cost .............. | $0.06 | $0.06 | $0.06 | $0.05 |
| Allotted Wastes ..... | 0.04 | 0.04 | 0.01 | --- |
| Total Allotted Unit Cost .............. | $0.10 | $0.10 | $0.07 | $0.05 |
| Discrepancy: Loss .............. | 0.0031 | 0.0016 | --- | --- |
| Gain .............. | --- | --- | 0.001 | 0.002 |
| Actual Unit Cost .... | $0.1031 | $0.1016 | $0.069 | $0.048 |
| Efficiency, per cent: Assumed at year's beginning ....... | 60. | 60. | 85.7 | 100. |
| As shown at year's end ............. | 58.2 | 57. | 87. | 104.2 |
| Increase of cost due to inefficiency, % Assumed at year's beginning ...... | 66.7 | 66.7 | 16.7 | --- |
| Shown year's end . | 72. | 74. | 14.9 | 4.* |
| Increase or decrease of cost, per cent: Compared with original standard | 3.1 | 1.6* | 31.* | 52.* |
| Compared with current standard | 3.1 | 1.6 | 1.4* | 4.* |

*Decrease

A careful consideration of these data--the author declared that actually the corrections would be made and standards revised monthly, thus tending to minimize differences--will disclose the workings of Emerson's efficiency scheme. In 1903-04, before the efficiency efforts were installed, the actual costs were $487,171, whereas the allotted costs (determined on a basis of $0.10 per unit) amounted to $472,500. The method of handling the discrepancy, $14,671, suggests the accounting

training and/or thinking of the author, who stated that this difference
could be cleared immediately or, preferably from the efficiency standpoint, recorded in the financial statement for 1903-04 as "Accounts
Receivable" or "Advances on Work Not Yet Performed" (both asset accounts)
and, during the following year, charged immediately or in monthly in-
stallments to the maintenance account.

During the first two years, the allotted cost remained at $0.10 per
unit--standard cost of $0.06 and current waste of $0.04. For the third
year, the allotted unit cost was lowered to $0.07 by decreasing current
wastes $0.03 per unit while, in the fourth year, the standard was lowered
to $0.05 and the current wastes were eliminated. During the same time,
the department's efficiency rose from 58.2% to 104.2%. The author's
conclusions tend to indicate his thinking with respect to this system:

> Possibly some will claim that the reduction of expense was
> not due to efficiency standards and methods. Perhaps not;
> but the diagnosis of inefficiency was made before beginning
> any work, standards of cost and waste were established before
> beginning any work, a large staff using drastic modern methods
> was exceedingly busy trying to produce results through every
> means known to efficiency engineers, and where this staff was
> most active the greatest improvement was attained.[114]

Emerson, the engineer, had presented his ideas in a rather clear-
cut manner and had furnished data to substantiate his contentions. As
he concluded this section of his dissertation, he reiterated his belief
in the mutual dependence of the efficiency engineer and the accountant:

---

[114] Ibid., p. 681.

The reduction of cost is an efficiency result compared to
which the method of stating it in the accounts would be unimportant, were it not that the ability to follow efficiency
methods and to convince others of their value and effect depends largely on clear and easily understood statements, and
these statements are difficult to obtain and do not carry
weight unless at some point they are certified by the accountants, and thus tied into the official expense reports.[115]

The author's ideas with respect to the recording of efficiency in-

formation in the cost records have been very aptly summarized in the

following statement:

It is however very important that both efficiency statements
and cost statements keep close together, that both should use
the same unit, that both should use equivalency (standard
cost) and that expense shall be stated in two terms: Standard
Cost and Waste.  It will prove convenient for the accountant
to standardize from previous records both the current percentage of waste and the general burden resulting from indirect expense, rather than to carry into the daily operative
expense statement the actual but partly accidental waste and
the actual fluctuating burden, especially as the standardization of waste permits a very close prestatement of cost which
is always of advantage and also brings back forcibly to the
accountant the great purpose for which accounts were originally evolved and developed--namely, to locate and eliminate
wastes.[116]

Subsequently, Emerson published his efficiency concepts in book

form under two titles--Efficiency as a Basis for Operation and Wages

(New York, The Engineering Magazine Company, 1909) and The Twelve Prin-

ciples of Efficiency (New York, The Engineering Magazine Company, 1911)

--but evidenced no innovations of interest to this study.  In 1914, he

---

[115]Ibid., p. 815.

[116]Ibid., p. 816.

and J. K. Mason revised the standard foundry cost system of the American Foundrymen's Association.[117] However, a careful consideration of this work revealed a uniform cost system for this industry rather than a standard cost technique.

By way of summary, it must be stated that the successful application of the Emerson plan required a scientifically developed organization with a time and motion study division, with standardized factory machine and hand operations, and with carefully determined wage rates. These requirements suggest the influence of Frederick W. Taylor and his scientific methods. However, Emerson had revealed the efficiency efforts from the standpoint of the engineer only and had recorded certain cost data that still required the refinement of an individual with accounting training before a standard cost technique could be recognized.

------

[117]Emerson, Harrington, and Mason, J. K., _Revision of American Foundrymen's Association Standard Cost System_, Chicago, American Foundrymen's Association, 1914.

CHAPTER V

G. CHARTER HARRISON'S EARLY CONTRIBUTION

TO STANDARD COSTS

G. Charter Harrison--educated in England, served as an apprentice
to a chartered accountant for five years, passed the final examination
of the Institute of Chartered Accountants in England and Wales, and came
to the United States where he operated as public accountant, comptroller,
and cost consultant--not only recognized the significance of Frederick
W. Taylor's ideas of scientific management and of Harrington Emerson's
doctrines of shop efficiency but also undertook to apply accounting
technique to a practical recording and presentation of information as
made available by the application of their methods.  He came to accept
"standard costs" as the nomenclature for his cost technique and subsequently stated that he installed the first standard cost system in the
factories of the Boss Manufacturing Company of Kewanee, Illinois, in
1911.[1]

His first recorded explanation of this new cost procedure, "Cost
Accounting to Aid Production,"[2] has been accepted by the present writer
as the initial effort to present standard cost principles in a unified
and concise series of articles.  Somewhat later, these nine periodical

---

[1]Harrison, G. Charter, _Marginal Balances_, monograph published by
American Management Association, 1937.

[2]Harrison, G. Charter, "Cost Accounting to Aid Production," _Indus-
trial Management_, Vols. LVI and LVII (October, 1918-June, 1919).

contributions, revised and enlarged, were published in book form under
the same title as the magazine publications.[3]

In his indictment of the established cost accounting methods, Harrison pointed out some of the defects of the current practice and insisted that the designing of a practical system required a fundamental training in accounting principles as might be obtained only by years of practical accounting experience.

Requirements of a Cost System.--Although Harrison knew that he could not set out definite standards for a cost accounting system that would be applicable to all concerns, he did undertake to state certain more or less general requirements:[4]

1. Accurate cost of specific articles.--The system should provide for the recording of cost data in such a manner that accurate and prompt information could be prepared for costs of parts, of work in process, and of finished products.

2. Manufacturing efficiency data.--The cost system should furnish not only complete data relative to manufacturing efficiency, as well as to the cost of idleness, but should also disclose increases or decreases in cost of material, labor, and manufacturing expenses analyzed as to purchase price and as to the efficiency of use of these productive elements.

----

[3] Harrison, G. Charter, Cost Accounting to Aid Production, New York, The Engineering Magazine Company, 1921.

[4] Harrison, G. Charter, "Cost Accounting to Aid Production," Industrial Management, LVI, 275-279.

3. Promptness in furnishing information.--Harrison thought that the
value of cost information was generally in direct ratio to the promptness with which such information was presented.  Although complete statements were declared to be impracticable, the author proposed a daily
summarized manufacturing report, a summarized payroll report, and a summarized machine report--including standard hours, actual hours worked,
employment efficiency, standard production, actual production, and operating efficiency.

4. Report for the manufacturing executive.--In addition to the
daily reports, Harrison declared that a single monthly statement should
be prepared which would disclose all of the pertinent features of the
month's operations.  When he wrote his book, he stated:

> . . . it is perfectly possible to furnish the executive of a
> large manufacturing plant with a summarized cost statement on
> a single sheet of paper of ordinary letter size from which in
> a few minutes he can learn more about the essential facts of
> his business than would be possible from spending hours in
> grappling with the usual detailed cost statements.[5]

The Summarized Manufacturing Statement, as taken from an actual
form used by the author, illustrates the principle involved:[6]

---

[5] Harrison, Cost Accounting to Aid Production, p. 13.

[6] Ibid., pp. 14-15.

SUMMARIZED MANUFACTURING STATEMENT MONTH OF
January, 1944

Total Actual Cost for Month .................. $00
Total Standard Cost for Month ...............  00

Net Increase or Decrease Comparing
    Actual with Standard* ..................       $00

Analysis of Above Variation by Causes

Variations in Fixed Charges Due to Fluctua-
    tions in Production Caused by:
  1. Calendar variations .................... $00
  2. Idle time .............................  00
  3. Variation in number of operators .......  00
  4. Variations in efficiency of operators ..  00       $00

Variations in Direct Labor Costs Due to:
  1. Rates ................................. $00
  2. Efficiency of operators ...............  00       $00

Variations in Indirect Labor Costs Due to:
  1. Rates ................................. $00
  2. Hours .................................  00
  3. Extra pay for overtime ................  00       $00

Variations in Back-Work Labor Costs Due to:
  1. Rates ................................. $00
  2. Hours .................................  00       $00

Variations in Stores and Supplies Due to:
  1. Price ................................. $00
  2. Consumption ..........................  00       $00

Variation in Power Cost Due to:
  1. Cost of producing power ............... $00
  2. Efficiency of use of power ............  00       $00

Variations in Salaries Due to:
  1. Rates ................................. $00
  2. Number of salaried persons employed ....  00       $00

Variation in Miscellaneous Expense ..........       $00

    Net Increase or Decrease as above* .....       $00

*Increase always shown in red and Decreases in black.

5. Cost of operating the system.--By coordinating the work of the

production and related departments, duplication of tasks might be avoided
and, at the same time, the efforts of executives, clerks, and shop employees might be economized by simplifying reports and procedure for
compiling material and labor cost figures.

6. Standard practice instructions for the system.--Under diagram
form, the plan of the system and the details of its operation should be
so clearly disclosed that the employees could not only understand the
routine of their own duties but could visualize also the relationship of
their contributions to the whole scheme.

After proposing these objectives as the components of an ideal
system, Harrison pointed out that the typical plan was retrospective
rather than prospective, was ineffective for tracing causes of increased
costs, and was inelastic from the standpoint of compiling and presenting
pertinent information.

<u>Standards</u> <u>and</u> <u>Standard</u> <u>Costs</u>.--Harrison pointed out that

> The application of the principle of standards to cost account-
> ing institutes the pre-determination of costs, demands that
> no work shall be undertaken without its cost have been calcu-
> lated in advance, and changes the whole viewpoint of cost
> accounting from retrospection to prospection.[7]

An analysis of this statement indicates that the author was proposing a
new cost technique--principle of standards applied to cost accounting--
as a means of gaining the reasonable requirements of a cost system and
of eliminating the weaknesses of the historical cost method.

--------------

[7]Harrison, G. Charter, "Cost Accounting to Aid Production," <u>Indus-
trial Management</u>, LVI, 391.

Already the engineer had set standards and schedules but, in the language of Gantt, "they had no means of finding out whether those schedules are lived up to or not." As Harrison had viewed such situations in practice, he pointed out that some means should be provided for disclosing the extent to which actual results conform to established standards. Since he recognized the maintenance of records as the solution for this problem, he delegated to the accountant the duty of installing and maintaining such records.

Accepting Ferguson's publication, Estimating the Cost of Work,[8] as ample testimony that costs could be predetermined, Harrison immediately answered the current objection to estimating costs--the cost accountant lacked the practical knowledge and experience to estimate the cost of work--and, at the same time, enunciated a characteristic of standard costs, by declaring that it was not the duty of the accountant to set standards but the task of the engineer or of the experienced shop official, in conjunction with the accountant, to perform this shop function.

> Such standards as the accounting division would be in a position to set must necessarily be largely based upon records of past experiences, and though data as to past performances are of interest and of value in determining the trend of costs, such data are not suitable for use as standards in the sense in which this term is used in this book.[9]

In declaring that the introduction of a system of standard costs

---

[8]Ferguson, William B., Estimating the Cost of Work, New York, The Engineering Magazine Company, 1915.

[9]Harrison, Cost Accounting to Aid Production, p. 38.

should precede the introduction of scientific shop methods, the author

enumerated the functions of the accounting division to be:[10]

1. Cooperate with the operating division by compiling standard data

as recorded in the cost department.

2. Design the cost system, together with forms, schedules, and

standard practical instructions.

3. Comply with demands of the operating division for cost informa-

tion in accordance with sound accounting and business principles.

4. Maintain complete records covering the cost of all operations:

> . . . to carry such records both at actual cost and in rela-
> tion to the standards determined by the operating division,
> and also to analyze the differences between actual and stand-
> ard cost by causes and to render periodical statements to the
> operating division in the form agreed upon and at the times
> set.

Principles of a Simple Cost System Based on Standards.--After set-

ting up the desirability and practicability of a cost system based on

standards, Harrison undertook to disclose some of the principles,

records, and procedures relative to such a technique as applied to a

factory manufacturing a single product.[11] The present writer will at-

tempt to reproduce the author's efforts by assuming an industrial enter-

prise processing a single raw material through three operations for one

standard product, which will be designated as Product X-3T-h.

_____________

[10] Ibid., p. 37.

[11] Harrison, G. Charter, "Cost Accounting to Aid Production," _Indus-
trial Management_, LVI, 391-398.

Preceding the actual manufacturing process, it was deemed necessary that a standard cost card be prepared for each product processed. The following illustration is indicative of such procedure as applied to the instance under consideration.

Form I.  STANDARD COST CARD
(Per 100 units)

Product X-3T-h

| Material | | | |
|---|---|---|---|
| Description | Standard Quantity | Standard Price (100) | Standard Amount |
| Raw Material W | 740 | $2.00 | $14.80 |

| Labor | | | |
|---|---|---|---|
| Operation | Standard Hours | Standard Rate (Hour) | Standard Amount |
| 1 | 5 | $ .60 | $ 3.00 |
| 2 | 12 | .80 | 9.60 |
| 3 | 10 | 1.00 | 10.00 |
| Total Labor | 27 | | $22.60 |

| Burden | | | |
|---|---|---|---|
| 1 | 5 | $ .40 | $ 2.00 |
| 2 | 12 | .50 | 6.00 |
| 3 | 10 | .32 | 3.20 |
| General Burden | 27 | .20 | 5.40 |
| Total Burden | | | $16.60 |

| Total Standard Cost | | | $54.00 |
|---|---|---|---|

In the case under consideration, Product X-3T-h, which sells for $0.81 per unit, was analyzed carefully with respect to operations by the industrial engineer and was ascertained to have a standard cost of $54.00

per hundred units and, therefore, a standard profit of $0.27 each, if
the monthly production was maintained at 1,200 units.

With this information before him, the manufacturer may set up his
plans based on this standard profit of $0.27 per unit.  Since the sell-
ing price is more or less fixed, this individual will direct his activities to keeping the costs at or below the standard.  The accountant's
contribution to these efforts of the manufacturer will be considered
under the following classifications:  materials, direct labor, burden,
and manufacturing efficiency statement.

1. Materials.--In order to ascertain the statistics required to
present the facts relative to the component, raw materials, Harrison
prepared a Material Account (Form B), which had the status of a statement rather than that of a ledger account.  He presented also a Summarized Material Report (Form C), which contained the significant information pertaining to the use of raw materials during the month.

| Material Account | | | | | | Form B |
| (Price quoted per _100_ ) | | | | Raw Material: _W_ | | |
| | | Actual | | Standard | | Ratio Actual to |
| Department | Units | Price | Amount | Price | Amount | Standard |
| Purchases in Month | 10,000 | $1.92 | $192.00 | $2.00 | $200.00 | |
| Freight In | | .12 | 12.00 | | | |
| Handling Expense | | .02 | 2.00 | | | |
| Total | 10,000 | $2.06 | $206.00 | $2.00 | $200.00 | 103 |
| Used | 9,102 | 2.06 | 187.50 | 2.00 | 182.04 | 103 |
| Inventory | 898 | 2.06 | $ 18.50 | 2.00 | $ 17.96 | 103 |

In the case under consideration, 10,000 units of Raw Material W were purchased at a total actual cost of $2.06 per hundred whereas the standard cost had been set at $2.00 per hundred. This discrepancy would be the basis for an investigation which should indicate whether the purchasing department had functioned inefficiently or whether the price level of products had advanced. If a price level variation existed, it might be desirable to revise the standards--a ratio of actual to standard (103 per cent) was computed for this purpose.

| | | | | | | | | |
|---|---|---|---|---|---|---|---|---|
| **SUMMARIZED MATERIAL REPORT** | | | | | | | **Form C** | |

| Description | Pieces Cut | Actual | | | Standard | | | |
|---|---|---|---|---|---|---|---|---|
| | | Units | Price | Amount | Units Per 100 | Total | Price | Amount |
| Raw Material W | 1,200 | 9,102 | $2.06 | $187.50 | 740 | 8,880 | $2.00 | $177.60 |

SUMMARIZED MATERIAL REPORT (Continued)

| | Increase* or Decrease | | | | | | |
|---|---|---|---|---|---|---|---|
| | Amount | | | | | | |
| | Due to Price Fluctuations | | | Due to Use Efficiency | | | |
| Units | Units | Price | Amount | Units | Price | Amount | Total |
| 222* | 9,102 | $0.06* | $5.46* | 222* | $2.00 | $4.44* | $9.90* |

From the Summarized Material Report (Form C) it may be noted that 1,200 units of the finished product were processed at an actual cost for raw materials of $187.50. The standard cost of such production was established at $177.60. The unfavorable difference of $9.90 was divided into two parts:

    Due to Price Fluctuations .............. $5.46
    Due to Use Efficiency Fluctuations .....  4.44
            Total Increase ................... $9.90

The increased cost due to price fluctuations may be ascertained in the following manner:

|  | Units | Price | Amount |
|---|---|---|---|
| Actual Cost of Materials Used | 9,102 | $2.06 | $187.50 |
| Standard Cost of Materials Used | 9,102 | 2.00 | 182.04 |
| Increase of Actual over Standard | 9,102 | $ .06 | $ 5.46 |

In order to determine the increased cost of materials due to the quantities used being greater than the standard, the following procedure was employed by Harrison:

|  | Units | Price | Amount |
|---|---|---|---|
| Actual Material Used Computed at Standard Price | 9,102 | $2.00 | $182.04 |
| Standard Material Used Computed at Standard Price | 8,880 | 2.00 | 177.60 |
| Increased Material Used Computed at Standard Price | 222 | 2.00 | $ 4.44 |

An analysis of these data pertaining to raw materials will indicate that the author has established a standard raw material cost for production, has provided for determining the actual raw material cost of production, and has proposed a scheme for explaining any variance that may arise when actual costs are compared with standard figures.

2. Direct Labor.--With respect to direct labor costs, Harrison

designed the Summarized Production and Payroll Report (Form D), which has been reproduced, in accordance with the case under consideration, to depict a factory with three departments and with the production calculated for both actual and standard costs.

| | | Productive Hours | | | | Average Rate Per Hour | | |
| | | | Standard | | Increase* or Decrease | | | Increase* or Decrease |
| Depart-ment | Produc-tion | Actual | Per 100 | Total | | Actual | Stand-ard | |
| 1 | 1,200 | 52 | 5 | 60.0 | 8.0 | $.62 | $ .60 | $.02* |
| 2 | 1,120 | 141 | 12 | 134.4 | 6.6* | .84 | .80 | .04* |
| 3 | 1,080 | 126 | 10 | 108.0 | 18.0* | .96 | 1.00 | .04 |
| Totals | | 319 | | 302.4 | 16.6* | | | |

SUMMARIZED PRODUCTION AND PAYROLL REPORT      Form D (heading for first table)

---

SUMMARIZED PRODUCTION AND PAYROLL REPORT (Continued)

| | Standard | | Productive Payroll | | | | | | |
| | | | Increase* or Decrease | | | | | | |
| | | | Due to Changes in Rates | | | Due to Variations in Production Efficiency | | | |
| Actual | Per 100 | Total | Hours | Rate | Amount | Hours | Rate | Amount | Total |
| $ 32.24 | $ 3.00 | $ 36.00 | 52 | $.02* | $1.04* | 8.0 | $ .60 | $ 4.80 | $ 3.76 |
| 118.44 | 9.60 | 107.52 | 141 | .04* | 5.64* | 6.6* | .80 | 5.28* | 10.92* |
| 120.96 | 10.00 | 108.00 | 126 | .04 | 5.04 | 18.0* | 1.00 | 18.00* | 12.96* |
| $271.64 | $22.60 | $251.52 | 319 | | $1.64* | 16.6* | | $18.48* | $20.12* |

A summary of this rather lengthy report, which, from necessity, has been presented in two sections, discloses more clearly the facts in the case:

|  | | | Increase* or Decrease<br>Due to | |
| Depart-<br>ment | Actual<br>Expense | Standard<br>Expense | Fluctuations<br>in Rates | Fluctuations<br>in Efficiency |
| --- | --- | --- | --- | --- |
| 1 | $ 32.24 | $ 36.00 | $1.04* | $ 4.80 |
| 2 | 118.44 | 107.52 | 5.64* | 5.28* |
| 3 | 120.96 | 108.00 | 5.04 | 18.00 |
| Totals | $271.64 | $251.52 | $1.64* | $18.48* |

To illustrate the calculation of the increases and decreases, the
following schedule has been prepared for Department One only:

| | Hours | Hourly<br>Rate | Amount |
| --- | --- | --- | --- |
| STANDARD: | | | |
| Per 100 units (Form I,<br>    Standard Cost Card ..... | 5 | $.60 | $ 3.00 |
| Per production of<br>    1,200 units (Form D) .... | 60 | $.60 | $36.00 |
| ACTUAL: | | | |
| Per Form D ............... | 52 | $.62 | 32.24 |
| | 8 | $.02* | $ 3.76 |
| INCREASE: | | | |
| Due to hourly rate<br>    increase ............... | 52 | $.02* | $ 1.04 |
| DECREASE: | | | |
| Due to efficiency<br>    increase ............... | 8 | $.60 | $ 4.80 |
| NET DECREASE ....... | | | $ 3.76 |

The variations for the other departments might be determined in the
same manner. With this information, it is possible to disclose efficiency as well as to discover the results of employing an individual
with a higher wage scale than that set in the standards for the particular job.

As an alternative method of computing and presenting data with respect to direct labor costs, Harrison designed a schedule, Analysis of Standard Labor Earnings, which has been adapted to the assumed figures in this case.[12] This schedule displays some improvement over the former technique, particularly when current statements for labor variations are taken into consideration.

ANALYSIS OF STANDARD LABOR EARNINGS

| | | | | | Analysis of Increases* and Decreases | |
| | | | (3) | (4) | Increase* | Increase* |
| | | | Net In- | Actual | or Decrease | or Decrease |
| | | | crease* | Hours | Due to | Due to |
| | (1) | (2) | or De- | Figures | Rate | Efficiency |
| Depart- | Standard | Actual | crease | at Stand- | Variations | Variations |
| ment | Labor | Labor | (2 - 1) | ard Rates | (2 - 4) | (4 - 1) |
|---|---|---|---|---|---|---|
| 1 | $ 36.00 | $ 32.24 | $ 3.76 | $ 31.20 | $1.04* | $ 4.80 |
| 2 | 107.52 | 118.44 | 10.92* | 112.80 | 5.64* | 5.28* |
| 3 | 108.00 | 120.96 | 12.96* | 126.00 | 5.04 | 18.00* |
| Totals | $251.52 | $271.64 | $20.12* | $270.00 | $1.64* | $18.48* |

3. Burden.--In the foregoing examples, it will be noted that the principles underlying the distribution of costs for material and labor are relatively simple and are applied readily to the operation or to the product manufactured. However, in the case of burden, Harrison did not recognize such direct relationship between the expenditure and the operation or the product manufactured but did foresee a complex problem in allocating a portion of such manufacturing costs to the finished good or semi-processed article.

---

[12] Ibid., LVII, 52.

As an initial step in finding a solution to this problem, the author divided the burden expenditures into two classifications--fixed charges and fluctuating expenses.

Under the first classification, fixed charges, he placed those manufacturing expenditures which tend not to vary with quantity of production--rent, insurance, depreciation, foremen's salaries, and other costs necessary to maintain an organization for the manufacturing processes. It was pointed out that this portion of the burden charge varied inversely with the volume of production and resulted in the manufacturer attempting to decrease unit costs by increasing quantity of production.

On the other hand, the writer delegated to fluctuating charges all those costs which tend to vary directly with production--cost of small tools, machine repairs, indirect materials, and power.

A consideration of these types of burden will justify Harrison's concept that variations between actual and standard fixed charges may arise from two factors--actual expenditures varying from the established standard and actual production differing from the assumed standard of production. According to Harrison, at this time, the fluctuating charges varied only because of variations in expenditures.

After recognizing these characteristics in burden expenditures, a standard monthly production rate was established (1,200 units in the hypothetical case under consideration), and a statement (Form J) was prepared for the purpose of setting the standard hourly burden rates, which were established for both fixed and fluctuating expenses.

STATEMENT SHOWING METHOD OF FIGURING STANDARD BURDEN
ON BASE OF STANDARD PRODUCTION OF 1,200 UNITS     Form J
PER MONTH IN ALL DEPARTMENTS

| Department | Standard Hours Per 100 Units (Form A) | Standard Hours Per 1,200 Units | Estimated Monthly Expense on Basis of 1,200 Units Fixed Charges | Estimated Monthly Expense on Basis of 1,200 Units Fluctuating Expense | Estimated Monthly Expense on Basis of 1,200 Units Total | Standard Burden Rate Per Hour Fixed Charges | Standard Burden Rate Per Hour Fluctuating Expense | Standard Burden Rate Per Hour Total |
|---|---|---|---|---|---|---|---|---|
| 1 | 5 | 60 | $ 3.60 | $ 20.40 | $ 24.00 | $.06 | $.34 | $.40 |
| 2 | 12 | 144 | 14.40 | 57.60 | 72.00 | .10 | .40 | .50 |
| 3 | 10 | 120 | 6.00 | 32.40 | 38.40 | .05 | .27 | .32 |
| General | 27 | 324 | 64.80 | --- | 64.80 | .20 | --- | .20 |
| Totals | | | $88.80 | $110.40 | $199.20 | | | |

As soon as the month had closed, a Summarized Burden Report (Form E) was prepared. In the case under consideration, the total of the actual expenses was $207.80, whereas the total standard expense earned--standard burden rates applied to standard hours contained in the monthly production (see Form D)--was $186.24. The variation of $21.56 was analyzed into three parts and by departments (see Form E).

SUMMARIZED BURDEN REPORT     Form E

| Department | Actual Hours | Actual Expense Fixed | Actual Expense Fluctuating | Actual Expense Total | Standard Hours (In Actual Production) | Standard Expense Fixed Charges |
|---|---|---|---|---|---|---|
| 1 | 52 | $ 4.10 | $ 18.20 | $ 22.30 | 60.0 | $ 3.60 |
| 2 | 141 | 16.00 | 58.12 | 74.12 | 134.4 | 14.40 |
| 3 | 126 | 5.20 | 34.18 | 39.38 | 108.0 | 6.00 |
| General | 319 | 72.00 | | 72.00 | 302.4 | 64.80 |
| Totals | | $97.30 | $110.50 | $207.80 | | $88.80 |

| Standard Expense Earned | | | | | | Increase* or Decrease | | | |
| | | | | | | Fixed Charges | | | |
| Fixed Charges | | Fluctuating Charges | | Total | | Due to Variations in Expenditures | Due to Variations in Production | Fluctuating Charges | Total |
| Per Hour | Amount | Per Hour | Amount | Per Hour | Amount | | | | |
| $.06 | $ 3.60 | $.34 | $ 20.40 | $.40 | $ 24.00 | $ .50* | $ .00 | $ 2.20 | $ 1.70 |
| .10 | 13.44 | .40 | 53.76 | .50 | 67.20 | 1.60* | .96* | 4.36* | 6.92* |
| .05 | 5.40 | .27 | 29.16 | .32 | 34.56 | .80 | .60* | 5.02* | 4.82* |
| .20 | 60.48 | | | .20 | 60.48 | 7.20* | 4.32* | | 11.52* |
| | $82.92 | | $103.32 | | $186.24 | $8.50* | $5.88* | $ 7.18* | $21.56* |

In order to illustrate the author's procedure, the analysis of Department Two, with a total variation of $6.92, has been recorded in the following manner:

FIXED CHARGES:

Estimated monthly expense for processing
   1,200 units of Product X-3T-h .......... $ 14.40
Actual expense for the month ............. 16.00
Increase due to fluctuations in expense ..        $1.60

Standard hours based on production of
   1,200 units per month (Form J) ......... 144.0
Standard hours earned on production of
   1,120 units (Form E) .................... 134.4
Decrease in standard hours ............... 9.6
Standard rate per hour ................... $ 0.10
Increase due to production being less
   than standard ...........................       .96

FLUCTUATING CHARGES:

Actual expense for month ................. $ 58.12
Standard expense for month--134.4 hours
   at standard rate of $0.40 per hour ..... 53.76
Increase of actual over standard ........       4.36

    TOTAL INCREASE .................... $6.92

In view of the fact that this hypothetical case covers only one product, which must ultimately absorb all expenditures, it is a rather imperfect illustration of burden distribution from the standpoint of complex conditions.  However, this instance does offer an excellent opportunity to correlate costs with causes and to distinguish between expenditures resulting in full value and those creating less than full value due to incompetence and inefficiency--an analysis of not only the debit side of the burden account (actual expenditures) but also an evaluation of the credit side (value of services resulting from such expenditures).

4. Manufacturing Efficiency Statement.--After the actual expenditures for materials, labor, and burden had been recorded in the factory records and the statistical statements, as heretofore reproduced, had been prepared, the accountant would be in position to furnish the executive with a report of operations for the month, or other fiscal period as might be agreed upon.

As an illustration of such a report, Harrison designed Form A, Summarized Manufacturing Efficiency Statement, which has been adapted to the case under consideration.

| | Actual Expense for Month | Standard Expense for Month | Increase* or Decrease | | | | Ratio Actual to Standard |
|---|---|---|---|---|---|---|---|
| Description | | | Due to Price Fluctuations | | Due to Fluctuations in Use Efficiency | Total | |

SUMMARIZED MANUFACTURING EFFICIENCY STATEMENT      Form A

| Description | Actual Expense for Month | Standard Expense for Month | Due to Price Fluctuations | | Due to Fluctuations in Use Efficiency | Total | Ratio Actual to Standard |
|---|---|---|---|---|---|---|---|
| **MATERIAL:** | | | | | | | |
| Raw Material W | $187.50 | $177.60 | $5.46* | | $ 4.44* | $ 9.90* | 105.6 |
| | | | Due to Fluctuations in Rates | | Due to Fluctuations in Efficiency | | |
| **LABOR:** (Dept.) | | | | | | | |
| 1 | $ 32.24 | $ 36.00 | $1.04* | | $ 4.80 | $ 3.76 | 89.6 |
| 2 | 113.44 | 107.52 | 5.64* | | 5.28* | 10.92* | 110.2 |
| 3 | 120.96 | 108.00 | 5.04 | | 18.00* | 12.96* | 112.0 |
| | $271.64 | $251.52 | $1.64* | | $18.48* | $20.12* | 108.0 |
| | | | Due to Variations in Expenditures | Due to Variations in Production | Fluctuating Charges | | |
| **BURDEN:** | | | | | | | |
| 1 | $ 22.30 | $ 24.00 | $ .50* | $ .00 | $ 2.20 | $ 1.70 | 92.9 |
| 2 | 74.12 | 67.20 | 1.60* | .96* | 4.36* | 6.92* | 110.3 |
| 3 | 39.38 | 34.56 | .80 | .60* | 5.02* | 4.82* | 113.9 |
| General | 72.00 | 60.48 | 7.20* | 4.32* | | 11.52* | 119.0 |
| | $207.80 | $186.24 | $8.50* | $5.88* | $ 7.18* | $21.56* | 111.6 |
| Total Cost | $666.94 | $615.36 | | | | $51.58* | 108.2 |

A consideration of this statement indicates that not only have

actual and standard expenses been presented by cost elements and by

departments for labor and burden but also variations therefrom, classified in the same manner, have been brought to the attention of the interested reader.

At the same time, the ratios of actual to standard costs have been
computed in order that adjustments to final inventories, cost of sales,
and/or other items--recorded in the financial records at standard fig-
ures--might be made without great difficulty.

For the busy executive, this condensed report would give a rather
complete picture of the operational results in the factory for the month
and would suggest the factors that needed particular attention.  For the
individual who was required to make a more detailed study of the factory
situation, there might accompany this report a complete set of schedules
and explanations of the month's manufacturing data.

5. Summary.--A review of this very simple illustration will tend to
disclose the principles that Harrison was undertaking to present.

In the first place, he designed a standard cost card (Form I) containing the data for producing one hundred units of this product during
a month when 1,200 units would be processed.  According to the author,
this information would be accumulated by the engineering department,
assisted by management and the accountant as required.  Thus, these data
would represent the exercise of scientific procedure--not the mere estimate of any individual--and would be recorded by the accountant.

And then the accounting department would provide for the recording
of actual expenditures during the month, for the ascertaining of the
production for the month, for the determining of the standard cost of

this production, and for the computing of the variation between actual

and standard figures.

And, finally, provision was made for the presentation of these data,

in rather condensed form, to the executive immediately after the close

of the fiscal period.  In this manner, inefficiencies might be recog-

nized quickly and corrections might be applied before great damage had

been done.

Principles of a Complex Cost System Based on Standards.--After pre-

senting the principles of a very simple standard cost technique, Harri-

son depicted an accounting procedure, based on standards, for an enter-

prise which manufactured a large number and variety of parts and which

assembled these parts into various kinds of standard machines.[13]  The

author stated:

> This plan has been drawn up to demonstrate that it is possi-
> ble to design a system of standards or predetermined costs
> which will meet all essential requirements, giving results not
> possible under the expensive and detailed retrospective cost
> systems and yet involving a minimum of clerical work both in
> the shops and the offices.[14]

1. The Standard Cost Card.--Just as a standard cost card was pre-

pared for the single product under the simple cost procedure, so must a

standard cost card--based on data and plans formulated by the engineers,

who may be assisted, where necessary, by management and the accountant--

be completed for each product under this cost technique.

---

[13] Ibid., LVI, 456-463.

[14] Ibid., p. 459.

In order to illustrate this procedure, Form C, Summarized Standard
Cost of Product, has been prepared for Product C - 8 (one of the finished goods of an assumed factory) which requires five different raw
materials and which passes through six manufacturing processes or departments.

| SUMMARIZED STANDARD COST OF PRODUCT C - 8 | | Form C |
|---|---|---|
| Description | Amount | Total |
| MATERIAL: | | |
| A | $3.09 | |
| B | .75 | |
| C | 1.08 | |
| D | .50 | |
| E | .36 | |
| Miscellaneous Material | 2.07 | |
| Total Material | | $ 7.85 |
| LABOR: | | |
| Department: | | |
| 1 | $ .68 | |
| 2 | .17 | |
| 3 | .05 | |
| 4 | .16 | |
| 5 | .23 | |
| 6 | .35 | |
| Total Labor | | 1.64 |
| BURDEN: | | |
| Department: | | |
| 1 | 110.0% | $ .75 |
| 2 | 165.0% | .28 |
| 3 | 137.5% | .07 |
| 4 | 137.5% | .22 |
| 5 | 165.0% | .38 |
| 6 | 121.0% | .42 |
| General Burden | 55.0% | .90 |
| Total Burden | | 3.02 |
| TOTAL COST | | $12.51 |

2. Monthly Summarized Production Report.--Before considering the
treatment of material, labor, and burden under this method, the procedure for ascertaining the monthly costs for these components in production must be presented.

At the end of the month, the production for each department was
summarized and was recorded on Form D (Monthly Summarized Production
Report) under the column Number of Pieces Finished.  In the case under
consideration, the production for the month of May, 1943, in Department 1
amounted to the following:  511 units of Part 1-x, 109 units of Part 3-y,
and 242 units of Part 5-z.

|  |  | MONTHLY SUMMARIZED PRODUCTION REPORT |  |  |  |  | Form D |
|---|---|---|---|---|---|---|---|

Department  1                                              Month of  May  194 3

| Part Number | Number Pieces Finished | Standard Labor Cost Unit Price | Standard Labor Cost Total | Standard Material Cost — Material A Unit Cost | Standard Material Cost — Material A Total | Standard Material Cost — Material ? Unit Cost | Standard Material Cost — Material ? Total | Total |
|---|---|---|---|---|---|---|---|---|
| 1-x | 511 | $0.43 | $219.73 | $1.95 | $   998 |  |  |  |
| 2-x |  |  |  |  |  |  |  |  |
| 3-y | 109 | .38 | 41.42 | 1.95 | 213 |  |  |  |
| 4-z |  |  |  |  |  |  |  |  |
| 5-z | 242 | .25 | 60.50 | 1.95 | 473 |  |  |  |
| Totals |  |  | $321.65 |  | $1,684 |  |  |  |

By applying the standard labor cost and the standard material cost
(Material A only used in the illustration) from the respective Standard
Cost of Parts Cards to these production figures, the total standard
labor cost of $321.65 and the total standard material (Material A) cost

of \$1,684.00 were determined for Department 1. In view of the fact that the standard burden for this department was established as 110 per cent of direct labor, the standard amount to be charged to work in process for this item would be \$353.82 (110% of \$321.65). These costs will be considered further under the discussion of material, labor, and burden.

3. Material.--In order to maintain a record of this cost element, materials were divided into as few classes as practicable, with the necessary subclassifications, and two sets of accounts--the controlling accounts for main classes, carried in both standard and actual figures, and the detail accounts, kept in quantities only by the storekeeper-- were maintained.

At the end of the month, the Controlling Account for Material A (Form E), which has been taken as an illustration, may be assumed to contain the information as recorded in the following account.

MATERIAL A    CONTROLLING ACCOUNT    Form E

Dr.          Cr.

| Date | Description | Actual | Standard | Ratio | Date | Description | Actual | Standard | Ratio |
|---|---|---|---|---|---|---|---|---|---|
| May 1 | Inventory | \$4,180 | \$4,000 | 104.5 | May 31 | Standard Material in Production | \$1,812 | \$1,684 | 107.6 |
| 31 | Purchases Month | 116 | 82 | 140.2 | | | | | |
| 31 | Freight Month | 96 | | | 31 | Excess Consumption of Material | 77 | (71) | 107.6 |
| | | | | | 31 | Total | \$1,889 | \$1,684 | 112.2 |
| | | | | | 31 | Inventory | 2,503 | 2,327 | |
| | Total | \$4,392 | \$4,082 | 107.6 | | Total | \$4,392 | \$4,082 | 107.6 |

A consideration of this account will indicate that the debit side contains the initial inventory valued at actual cost of $4,180.00 and at standard cost of $4,000.00, the purchases for the month valued in the same manner, and the freight for the month recorded at actual value only. Finally, the total value of Material A available for issuance during the month was indicated as $4,392.00 at actual cost and as $4,082.00 at standard figures. The ratio of actual to standard cost of total available raw materials during the month, 107.6 per cent, was regarded by Harrison as the Price Adjustment Ratio and was used subsequently to convert any raw material figures for the current month from standard to actual values or from actual to standard costs as the necessity might arise.

The credit side of the account is worthy of particular attention. In the first place, the author ascertained the standard material cost in the factory production for the month by preparing Form D, Monthly Summarized Production Report. In the case under consideration, this cost amounted to $1,684.00. By applying the Price Adjustment Ratio to this figure, he calculated the actual cost of this standard quantity of material used as $1,812.00 (107.6% of $1,684.00).

Under the author's procedure, standard requisitions were prepared for the products to be processed and were presented to the storekeeper, who delivered the required raw materials as needed. Additional materials for a job order were requested on special forms and excess consumption was ascertained readily therefrom. In the case under consideration, this item amounted to $71.00 at standard cost and, converted into actual figures by the use of the Price Adjustment Ratio (107.6% of

$71.00), equaled $77.00.  The amount of $71.00 represented the variation

in costs due to the increase in consumption--Material Usage Variation--

but failed to get the status of an actual entry in the account (as will

be noted from the addition of the items in the standard column on the

credit side).  The standard sum of $71.00 was placed therein as a memo-

randum entry only and was so indicated by encirclement.  This method of

obtaining the Material Usage Variation was superseded by another pro-

cedure, as proposed by Harrison and hereinafter presented, which is not

subject to the same degree of confusion and criticism as the technique

just reviewed.

In addition to the Material Usage Variation, as already determined,

the author provided for computing the Price Variation:

```
Actual Cost of Materials in Production ....... $1,889.00
Actual Materials in Production Computed at
   Standard Price ($1,889.00 ÷ 107.6%)[15] ......  1,755.00
Variation Due to Increase in Price ..........  $  134.00
```

The sum of this variation and the Material Usage Variation amounts to

$204.00 ($134.00 + $71.00), which represents the difference between

actual cost of materials put into production ($1,889.00) and standard

cost of standard materials in production ($1,684.00).

The final inventory of $2,503.00 (actual value) and $2,327.00

(standard value) balanced the account--any material shortage resulting

_______________

[15]Ordinarily, this figure is ascertained from Stores Issued Report,
which is priced at standard values, and the Price Adjustment Ratio is
applied for actual cost of materials in production.

from handling inefficiencies in the stores room would have been charged to a burden account before the adjusting and closing entries were recorded--and represented the initial inventory for the following fiscal period.

As an alternative method of computing raw material costs and variations, Harrison subsequently presented a material controlling account[16] as herewith reproduced with data for Material A.  The debit side of the account contained the same information as the initial account (Form E); however, the credit side recorded the actual issues at standard prices ($1,755.00 in this instance), which would be obtained from the material requisition cards, and converted this amount into actual figures ($1,889.00) by applying the Price Adjustment Factor (107.6%).  This procedure eliminated the Material Usage Variation (see Form E for the amount of $71.00 as this variation) and recorded inventories, purchases, and issues at both actual and standard values.

MATERIAL CONTROLLING ACCOUNT      Form 7 B

Material Class     Material A

| Date | Description | Actual | Standard | Ratio | Date | Description | Actual | Standard | Ratio |
|---|---|---|---|---|---|---|---|---|---|
| May 1 | Inventory | $4,180 | $4,000 | 104.5 | May 31 | Material Issues Month | $1,889 | $1,755 | 107.6 |
| 31 | Purchases Month | 116 | 82 | 140.2 | 31 | Inventory | 2,503 | 2,327 | 107.6 |
| 31 | Freight Month | 96 | | | | | | | |
| | | $4,392 | $4,082 | 107.6 | | | $4,392 | $4,082 | 107.6 |
| June 1 | Inventory | $2,503 | $2,327 | 107.6 | | | | | |

<hr>

[16]Harrison, G. Charter, "Cost Accounting to Aid Production," _Industrial Management_, LVII, 222-223.

In order to determine the variations, the author prepared Form 8 K,
Statement Showing Method of Arriving at Variations in Material Cost by
Classes of Product.  The statement is self-explanatory; however, the
information for Column (f) might be obtained by subtracting the data in
Column (b) from that in Column (e) as well as by the method suggested
and might be considered more logical than the original procedure.

STATEMENT SHOWING METHOD OF ARRIVING AT VARIATIONS
IN MATERIAL COST BY CLASSES OF PRODUCT          Form 8 K

| Material Class | (a) Standard Quantity at Standard Price | (b) Actual Quantity at Standard Price | (c) Increase* or Decrease Due to Consumption Variation (b)-(a) | (d) Price Adjustment Factor | (e) Actual Quantity at Adjusted Price (b)x(d) | (f) Increase* or Decrease Due to Price Variations (g)-(c) | (g) Net Increase* or Decrease Due to Variations from Standard (e)-(a) |
|---|---|---|---|---|---|---|---|
| A | $1,684 | $1,755 | $71* | 107.6 | $1,889 | $134* | $205* |

Before applying the procedure followed with respect to Materials in
Process, it has been deemed desirable to present Form J, Analysis of
Standard Cost of Shipments.  This statement, as may be noted from the
abridged reproduction as applied to the current case, was a summary, in
work sheet form, with columns for each type of raw material processed
and for direct labor cost by departments.  The quantity of each finished
product--in order to suggest the technique, only the data for Product
C - 8, as found in the foregoing statements, and for totals of material,
labor, and burden have been incorporated in this example--was recorded

and the standard cost figures (see Form C) were applied in determining
the information herein recorded.

---

ANALYSIS OF STANDARD COST OF SHIPMENTS     Form J

| Shipments | | | Material | | | | | |
| --- | --- | --- | --- | --- | --- | --- | --- | --- |
| | | | A | | ?? | | Total | |
| Machine Number | Part No. | Number Shipped | Each | Total | Each | Total | Each | Total |
| A - 2 | | | | | | | | |
| B - 6 | | | | | | | | |
| C - 8 | | 100 | $3.09 | $ 309.00 | | | $7.85 | $ 785.00 |
| D - 9 | | | | | | | | |
| Total | | | | $ 1,288.00 | | — | | $14,816.22 |
| Standard Burden % of Standard Labor Amount | | | | | | | | |
| Standard General Burden 55% | | | | | | | | |
| Total Standard Cost of Shipments | | | | $22,450.68 | | | | |

?? <u>Note:</u> Additional columns for Materials and Labor Departments.

===

ANALYSIS OF STANDARD COST OF SHIPMENTS (Continued)

| Legend as above | Department One | | ?? | | Total | |
| --- | --- | --- | --- | --- | --- | --- |
| | Each | Total | Each | Total | Each | Total |
| C - 8 | $ .68 | $ 68.00 | | — | $1.64 | $ 164.00 |
| Total | | $275.51 | | | | $3,422.10 |
| Standard Burden % of Standard Labor | 110% | | | | | |
| Amount | | $303.06 | | | | $2,330.21 |
| Standard General Burden 55% | | | | | | 1,882.15 |

In this illustration, it has been assumed that the standard cost of finished goods completed and shipped amounted to $22,450.68. A consideration of Form J indicates that this sum has been analyzed in the following manner:

1. Standard Material Cost of $14,816.22, which includes $1,288.00 of Material A and which consists of $785.00 in Product C - 8.

2. Standard Labor Cost of $3,422.10, which includes $275.51 for Department One and which consists of $164.00 in Product C - 8.

3. And Standard Burden Cost of $4,212.36, which includes departmental burden charges of $2,330.21 and general burden expenditures of $1,882.15. The departmental burden charge for Department One amounted to $303.06 (110% of $275.51--the direct labor for the department).

This form might have been styled "Analysis of Standard Cost of Production" and have been supplemented with similar statements for Cost of Shipments and Cost of Inventory of Finished Goods. However, Harrison neglected to include any inventory data for finished goods, and such procedure was not necessary to disclose the author's initial presentation of this particular element.

With the information, as recorded in Form J, available, Form F, Material in Work-in-Process Account, may be illustrated by employing data for Material A. In this instance, the debit side of this account contains the initial inventory and the materials processed during the month (see Form E) recorded at both actual and standard figures. The ratio of the sum of the actual costs to the corresponding figures for standard costs results in the Price Adjustment Ratio of 109.4 per cent.

The credit side of the account is posted with the standard cost of shipments, $1,288.00, as obtained from Form J.  The corresponding actual

cost of $1,409.00 is computed by applying the Price Adjustment Ratio to

the standard figure (109.4% of $1,288.00).  By balancing the account,

the final inventory of Material A in Work-in-Process is determined at

both actual and standard values.

<table>
<tr><td colspan="11" align="center">MATERIAL A    IN WORK-IN-PROCESS ACCOUNT       Form F</td></tr>
<tr><td colspan="5">Dr.</td><td colspan="6" align="right">Cr.</td></tr>
</table>

| Date | Descrip-tion | Actual | Stand-ard | Ratio | Date | Descrip-tion | Actual | Stand-ard | Ratio |
|------|------|------|------|------|------|------|------|------|------|
| May 1 | Inventory | $1,032 | $ 987 | 104.6 | May 31 | In Shipments | $1,409 | $1,288 | 109.4 |
| 31 | Used in Month | 1,889 | 1,684 | 112.2 | 31 | Inventory | 1,512 | 1,383 | 109.4 |
| | Total | $2,921 | $2,671 | 109.4 | | | $2,921 | $2,671 | 109.4 |

A review of this procedure indicates that Harrison provided for re-

cording raw materials in the stores department controlling accounts and

materials in process at both actual and standard figures and for ascer-

taining the relationship of such values by the Price Adjustment Ratio.

At the end of the period, he determined the standard material value in

production from a statement prepared for this purpose and converted this

element into actual value figures by applying the Price Adjustment Ratio.

And, finally, the author calculated the gross variation between actual

and standard values and analyzed this discrepancy into two components--

difference due to increase in consumption and variance due to increase

in price.

4. Labor.--In recording the data with respect to expenditures for labor, Harrison designed Form G, Labor in Work-in-Process for Department One. This account contained, on the debit side, the labor charges in the initial inventory of work in process at both actual ($298.16) and standard ($272.94) values, the direct payroll for the month ($338.06) at actual costs, and the standard labor costs in monthly production ($321.65) as computed on Form D, Monthly Summarized Production Report. The ratio of the sum of the actual debit column ($636.22) to the total of the standard debit column ($594.59) denotes the Price Adjustment Ratio for Labor (107.0%).

DEPARTMENT  1  LABOR IN WORK-IN-PROCESS                    Form G

Dr.                                                          Cr.

| Date | Description | Actual | Standard | Ratio | Date | Description | Actual | Standard | Ratio |
|---|---|---|---|---|---|---|---|---|---|
| May 1 | Inventory | 298.16 | 272.94 | 109.2 | May 1 | Labor in Shipments | 294.80 | 275.51 | 107.0 |
| 31 | Direct Payroll for Month | 338.06 | 321.65 | 105.1 | 31 | Inventory | 341.42 | 319.08 | 107.0 |
| | Total | 636.22 | 594.59 | 107.0 | | Total | 636.22 | 594.59 | 107.0 |

The credit side of the account contained the standard cost of shipments ($275.51) as recorded on Form J, Analysis of Standard Cost of Shipments. Applying the Price Adjustment Ratio to this figure, the actual cost of shipments (107.0% of $275.51 equals $294.80) was computed. The account was balanced with the final inventory, which was stated at both actual and standard values.

5. Burden.--Following the same general procedure for recording
burden as for direct labor, the author prepared Form H, Burden in Work-
in Process for Department One.  On the debit side, the account carried
burden charges in the initial inventory of work-in-process at actual
($326.78) and standard ($285.97) values, the actual burden charges for
the month ($387.63), and the standard burden charges in the month's
production ($353.82) as computed by applying the burden rate (110.0%)
set out in Form C, Summarized Standard Cost of Product C - 8, to the
standard labor in monthly production ($321.65) recorded on Form D.  The
Price Adjustment Ratio for Burden (111.7%) was computed as in the cases
of materials and direct labor.

|  |  | DEPARTMENT 1 | BURDEN IN WORK-IN-PROCESS | | | | | Form H |
| Dr. | | | | | | | | Cr. |
| Date | Descrip-tion | Actual | Stand-ard | Ratio | Date | Descrip-tion | Actual | Stand-ard | Ratio |
| --- | --- | --- | --- | --- | --- | --- | --- | --- | --- |
| May 1 | Inven-tory | 326.78 | 285.97 | 114.3 | May 31 | Burden in Ship-ments | 338.52 | 303.06 | 111.7 |
| 31 | Charges for Month | 387.63 | 353.82 | 109.5 | 31 | Inven-tory | 375.89 | 336.73 | 111.7 |
| | Total | 714.41 | 639.79 | 111.7 | | Total | 714.41 | 639.79 | 111.7 |

The credit side of the account contained the standard burden
charges in shipments ($303.06) as recorded on Form J.  By applying the
Price Adjustment Ratio to this figure, the actual cost of shipments

($338.52) was calculated (111.7% of $303.06).  The final inventory,
valued at both actual and standard cost figures, was sufficient to balance the account.

6. Monthly Statements for Executives.--One of the advantages of
Harrison's method may be found in the statements that were prepared im-
mediately after the close of the fiscal period for the consideration of
management.  In this system, the first schedule to be considered will be
Form M, Current Cost of Products (as applied to the data for Product
C - 8).

This statement--a similar form would be completed for each product
manufactured--contained the standard cost of the particular product as
established in Form C (Summarized Standard Cost of Product), the ratios
of actual costs for the month to the standard costs of production during
the month as recorded in the work-in-process accounts for materials,
labor, and burden, and the standards adjusted by applying the respective
ratios to the corresponding predetermined figures.  In this case, the
current cost of Product C - 8 was raised from the standard sum of $12.51
to an adjusted figure of $13.55, or by an amount of $1.04.  The data
were presented in such a manner that the variance could be ascertained
for materials, according to classifications, and for labor and burden by
departments.

CURRENT COST OF PRODUCTS     Form M

Product:   C - 8            Month of  May , 1943

|  | Standard Cost | Ratio Actual to Standard | Adjusted Standard Cost |
|---|---|---|---|
| **MATERIAL:** | | | |
| A | $ 3.09 | 112.2 | $ 3.47 |
| B | .75 | 102.4 | .77 |
| C | 1.08 | 107.8 | 1.16 |
| D | .50 | 109.7 | .55 |
| E | .36 | 126.4 | .46 |
| Miscellaneous Material | 2.07 | 111.1 | 2.30 |
| Total Material | $ 7.85 | | $ 8.71 |
| **LABOR:** | | | |
| Department: | | | |
| 1 | $ .68 | 105.1 | $ .71 |
| 2 | .17 | 107.5 | .18 |
| 3 | .05 | 98.3 | .05 |
| 4 | .16 | 94.1 | .15 |
| 5 | .23 | 112.0 | .26 |
| 6 | .35 | 88.2 | .31 |
| Total Labor | $ 1.64 | | $ 1.66 |
| **BURDEN:** | | | |
| Department: | | | |
| 1 | $ .75 | 109.5 | $ .82 |
| 2 | .28 | 103.2 | .29 |
| 3 | .07 | 101.0 | .07 |
| 4 | .22 | 90.0 | .19 |
| 5 | .38 | 105.3 | .40 |
| 6 | .42 | 88.0 | .37 |
| General Burden | .90 | 115.0 | 1.04 |
| Total Burden | $ 3.02 | | $ 3.18 |
| **TOTAL COST** | $12.51 | | $13.55 |

In the second schedule, Summarized Manufacturing Statement (Form K), the author undertook to present a complete statement of operational results for the month. The illustration (see following page) has been abridged by supplying the data for Material A and for Department One's labor and burden, as recorded in the work-in-process accounts in this case, together with assumed totals for these three cost components.

| | | SUMMARIZED MANUFACTURING STATEMENT | | | | Form K |
| | | Month of __May__ 1943 | | | | |

| | | This Month | | Increases* or Decreases | | |
| | Ratio | Actual | Standard | This Month | Last Month | Year to Date |
|---|---|---|---|---|---|---|
| MATERIAL: | | | | | | |
| A | 112.2 | $ 1,889.00 | $ 1,684.00 | $ 205.00* | | |
| B | | | | | | |
| C | | | | | | |
| D | | | | | | |
| E | | | | | | |
| Miscella-neous | | | | | | |
| Total | | $16,811.30 | $14,516.20 | $2,295.10* | | |
| LABOR: | | | | | | |
| Dept.: | | | | | | |
| 1 | 105.1 | $ 338.06 | $ 321.65 | $ 16.41* | | |
| 2 | | | | | | |
| 3 | | | | | | |
| 4 | | | | | | |
| 5 | | | | | | |
| 6 | | | | | | |
| Total | | $ 3,954.20 | $ 3,741.18 | $ 213.02* | | |
| BURDEN: | | | | | | |
| Dept.: | | | | | | |
| 1 | 109.5 | $ 387.63 | $ 353.82 | $ 33.81* | | |
| 2 | | | | | | |
| 3 | | | | | | |
| 4 | | | | | | |
| 5 | | | | | | |
| 6 | | | | | | |
| General | | | | | | |
| Total | | $ 4,629.37 | $ 4,285.19 | $ 344.18* | | |
| TOTAL COST | | $25,394.87 | $22,542.57 | $2,852.30* | | |

The required information for completing this schedule might be obtained readily from the various work-in-process accounts after the monthly postings had been recorded.  Additional columns might be added, as suggested, for comparative purposes.

And, finally, Harrison provided for the preparation of a monthly financial statement to determine the net profit, Form L--Adjusted Cost of Sales and Profit and Loss Statement.

The standard cost of shipments, analyzed by classification of materials and by departments for labor and burden, was taken from Form J, and the Price Adjustment Ratios for Material, for Labor, and for Burden were applied to these figures for an adjusted cost of shipments (which, for Harrison, amounted to actual costs).  The final result, in this case, was an actual cost of sales of $24,093.50, a gross profit of $3,031.25, and a net profit of $3,403.07.

ADJUSTED COST OF SALES AND PROFIT AND LOSS STATEMENT

Month of   May   1943        Form L

|  | Standard Cost of Shipments | Ratio Actual to Standard | Adjusted Cost of Shipments |
|---|---|---|---|
| MATERIAL: |  |  |  |
| A | $ 1,288.00 | 109.4 | $ 1,409.00 |
| B |  |  |  |
| C |  |  |  |
| D |  |  |  |
| E |  |  |  |
| Miscellaneous Material |  |  |  |
| Total Material | $14,816.22 |  | $16,218.37 |
| LABOR: |  |  |  |
| Dept.: |  |  |  |
| 1 | $ 275.51 | 107.0 | $ 294.80 |
| 2 |  |  |  |
| 3 |  |  |  |
| 4 |  |  |  |
| 5 |  |  |  |
| 6 |  |  |  |
| Total Labor | $ 3,422.10 |  | $ 3,241.62 |
| BURDEN: |  |  |  |
| Dept.: |  |  |  |
| 1 | $ 303.06 | 111.7 | $ 338.52 |
| 2 |  |  |  |
| 3 |  |  |  |
| 4 |  |  |  |
| 5 |  |  |  |
| 6 |  |  |  |
| General Burden |  |  |  |
| Total Burden | $ 4,212.36 |  | $ 4,633.51 |
| TOTAL COST | $22,450.68 |  | $24,093.50 |
| AMOUNT BILLED |  |  | $32,124.75 |
| GROSS PROFIT |  |  | $ 8,031.25 |
| SELLING AND ADMINISTRATIVE EXPENSES |  |  | $ 4,628.18 |
| NET PROFIT |  |  | $ 3,403.07 |

Thus, Harrison had provided for recording the current information during the month at both actual and standard figures, for determining the cost of goods sold at standard values in the first computation, and for adjusting these values to actual figures for the purpose of preparing the periodic financial statements.

Accounting for Scrap Under Standard Costs.--Although Harrison anticipated no great problem in recording the entries for raw materials and in ascertaining the variations between actual and standard values for the materials used, he did recognize a possible impracticability in determining the effect of the resultant variation in scrap when an attempt was made to compare actual with standard figures for this item.

In order to facilitate the solution of this problem, he designed a Material Requisition Card to accumulate the following information:  the standard cost of material issues (actual material issued valued at the standard price); the standard cost of the standard material in the product (standard weight in the production computed at standard prices); and the standard value of the standard scrap to be salvaged from the product.

In the second place, he employed the Scrap Clearance Account to record the data with respect to this item.  This account for Scrap A, as assumed to illustrate the author's procedure, indicates that the total actual weight of scrap produced during the month of May amounted to 1,242 pounds.  This figure might be obtained by periodically weighing the scrap produced or by recording weights of both the sales of scrap and the quantities reclaimed and by adding this sum to the inventory of scrap at the end of the period.  The total scrap produced, if priced at the standard value of fifty cents and the current value of fifty-one and two-tenths cents per pound, amounts to a standard value for scrap of $621.00 and an actual value for the same item of $635.90.

SCRAP CLEARANCE ACCOUNT

Class No. __Scrap A__                         Standard Value __50¢__ per pound
Dr.

| Date | Product | Actual Weight Pounds | Standard Value at Actual Weight | Current Value at Actual Weight | Ratio Current to Standard Value | Standard Scrap in Production | Excess Standard Value of Scrap Made |
|---|---|---|---|---|---|---|---|
| May 31 | C - 8 | | | | | $340.00 | |
| | D - 11 | | | | | 186.00 | |
| | E - 15 | | | | | 84.00 | |
| | | 1,242 | $621.00 | $635.90 | 102.4 | $610.00 | $11.00 |

SCRAP CLEARANCE ACCOUNT (Continued)

Cr.

| Date | Explanation | Weight Sold Pounds | Amount Realized | Standard Value | Ratio |
|---|---|---|---|---|---|
| May 11 | Sales | 300 | $156.00 | $150.00 | 104.0 |
| 16 | Sales | 200 | 100.00 | 100.00 | 100.0 |
| | | 500 | $256.00 | $200.00 | 102.4 |
| 31 | Scrap used | 160 | 81.92 | 80.00 | 102.4 |
| | Inventory | 582 | 297.80 | 291.00 | 102.4 |
| | | 1,242 | $635.90 | $621.00 | 102.4 |

In view of the fact that the Material Requisition Card contained a blank for accumulating the Standard Value of Scrap in Production, the data for this column on the Scrap Clearance Account would be determined by computing the sum of the amounts on the requisition cards for the period. In the case under consideration, the total Standard Scrap in Production was assumed to be $610.00--including $340.00 for Product C - 8 --which was $11.00 more than the standard value of scrap made. This amount was allocated to production and the adjusted value of scrap was computed by the use of a schedule, which Harrison termed "Schedule Giving Complete and Equitable Distribution of Scrap Made."

SCHEDULE GIVING COMPLETE AND EQUITABLE
DISTRIBUTION OF SCRAP MADE

| Product | Excess Cost of Material Issued | Excess Scrap Per Cent | Excess Scrap Amount | Standard Value of Scrap Made | Total Scrap (5) | Adjusted Value of Scrap Made (102.4% of Column 5) |
|---|---|---|---|---|---|---|
| C - 8 | $ 71.00 | 50 | $ 5.50 | $340.00 | $345.50 | $353.79 |
| D - 11 | 42.60 | 30 | 3.30 | 186.00 | 189.30 | 193.84 |
| E - 15 | 28.40 | 20 | 2.20 | 84.00 | 86.20 | 88.27 |
| | $142.00 | 100 | $11.00 | $610.00 | $621.00 | $635.90 |

And, finally, the Work-in-Process Account (the account for Product C - 8 only reproduced) was designed to accumulate not only the actual and standard cost of material issued and the standard cost of material in production but also the standard and actual credits for scrap produced and the standard scrap in the production for the period. A Scrap Reclaimed Account and a Scrap Inventory Account, which have not been illustrated, were used to complete the recording of information with respect to scrap.

## WORK-IN-PROCESS MAKING

Line     Product C - 8

Dr.

| Date | Standard Cost of Actual Material Issued | Material Adjustment Factor | Actual Cost of Material Issued | Standard Cost of Material in Product | Excess Standard Cost of Material Issued | Ratio Actual to Standard Material Cost |
|---|---|---|---|---|---|---|
| May 31 | $1,755.00 | 107.6 | $1,889.00 | $1,684.00 | $71.00 | 112.2 |

## WORK-IN-PROCESS MAKING (Continued)

Cr.

| Date | Explanation | Standard Cost of Scrap Made | Ratio Actual to Standard Scrap Value | Actual Credits | Standard Credits |
|---|---|---|---|---|---|
| May 31 | | $340.00 | | | $340.00 |
| 31 | Excess Scrap | 5.50 | | | |
| | | $345.50 | 102.4 | $353.79 | |

Accounting for Finished Goods Inventory in Standard Costs.--As a
means of maintaining a control over finished products, Harrison designed
Form 7 G, Inventory Controlling Account.  This account, which was prepared for each class of products, accumulated data--classified by materials, labor, and burden--for the initial and final inventories, the
charges during the month for finished products, and the credits for the
month's shipments, all of which were valued at both actual and standard

figures.  In reality, this account represented Harrison's standard cost
technique applied to the perpetual inventory system.

INVENTORY CONTROLLING ACCOUNT                                    Form 7 G

Class of Product    C - 8

| Date | Description | Material | | | Labor | | |
|---|---|---|---|---|---|---|---|
| | | Actual | Standard | Ratio | Actual | Standard | Ratio |
| May 1 | Inventory | 1,610.12 | 1,508.42 | 106.7 | 322.03 | 300.07 | 107.3 |
| 31 | Charges for Month | 1,409.00 | 1,288.00 | 109.4 | 294.80 | 275.51 | 107.0 |
| 31 | Totals | 3,019.12 | 2,796.42 | 107.9 | 616.83 | 575.58 | 107.2 |
| 31 | Shipments in Month | 2,170.33 | 2,010.33 | 107.9 | 429.81 | 401.07 | 107.2 |
| June 1 | Inventory | 848.79 | 786.09 | 107.9 | 187.02 | 174.51 | 107.2 |

INVENTORY CONTROLLING ACCOUNT (Continued)

| Burden | | | Total | |
|---|---|---|---|---|
| Actual | Standard | Ratio | Actual | Standard |
| 406.87 | 372.10 | 109.4 | 2,339.02 | 2,180.59 |
| 333.52 | 303.06 | 111.7 | 2,042.32 | 1,866.57 |
| 745.39 | 675.16 | 110.4 | 4,381.34 | 4,047.16 |
| 532.11 | 481.97 | 110.4 | 3,132.25 | 2,893.37 |
| 213.28 | 193.19 | 110.4 | 1,249.09 | 1,153.79 |

Standard Machine Rates for Allocating Burden to Production.--Harri-
son recognized the value of the method of using machine rates in the
allocation of burden to production and sought to illustrate a procedure
for setting standard rates as well as for employing these rates in the

cost records.[17]

In the first place, he explained that a machine rate was made up of the following factors:

1. A standard rate per hour for machine repairs and maintenance.
2. A standard rate per hour for power.
3. A standard rate per hour for departmental burden (over and above machine maintenance and power).
4. A standard rate per hour for general factory expense.[18]

To initiate this procedure, he proposed that the rates be based on past performance; however, as soon as standards of possible attainment could be calculated--ideal standards were recognized here--these standards should be employed. As a means of ascertaining these rates, he prepared a schedule--illustrated for departmental burden, Department X, only--for each of these four classes of burden.

DEPARTMENTAL BURDEN - DEPARTMENT X

Total Machine Hours in Department in Period __1,200__

| Account | Total Expense in Period | Rate Per Machine Hour |
|---|---|---|
| Supplies | $ 84.00 | $ .07 |
| Indirect Labor | 108.00 | .09 |
| Other Expense Accounts | 48.00 | .04 |
| | $240.00 | $ .20 |

After the rates had been computed, it was necessary to provide for determining the actual hours worked, the standard hours earned (standard

_______________

17Harrison, G. Charter, "Cost Accounting to Aid Production," _Industrial Management_, LVII (1919), 49-55.

18_Ibid._, p. 54.

hours in production for the period), and the standard machine earnings.
At the end of the period, this information was assembled and Form D,
Analysis of Standard Machine Earnings, was prepared.

ANALYSIS OF STANDARD MACHINE EARNINGS                Form D
Month of    May   , 194 3

| | | | | | Machine Efficiency Data | | | |
| | | (3) | (4) | (5) | (6)<br>Employ-<br>ment | (7) | (8)<br>Oper-<br>ating | (9) |
| (1)<br>Machine<br>Group<br>Number | (2)<br>De-<br>part-<br>ment | Number<br>of<br>Machines<br>in Group | Standard<br>Working<br>Hours in<br>Period | Actual<br>Hours<br>Worked | Effi-<br>ciency<br>%(5÷4) | Stand-<br>ard<br>Hours<br>Earned | Effi-<br>ciency<br>%(7÷5) | End<br>Effi-<br>ciency<br>%(7÷4) |
|---|---|---|---|---|---|---|---|---|
| 12 | X | 2 | 400 | 364 | 91 | 313 | 86 | 78 |
| 29 | | 1 | 200 | 166 | 83 | 182 | 110 | 91 |
| 37 | | 3 | 600 | 564 | 94 | 528 | 93 | 88 |
| Totals Department X | | | 1,200 | 1,094 | 91 | 1,023 | 94 | 85 |

ANALYSIS OF STANDARD MACHINE EARNINGS (Continued)

Standard Machine Earnings

| Total Standard<br>Machine<br>Earnings | | Repairs and<br>Maintenance | | Power | | Departmental<br>Burden | | General Fac-<br>tory Expense | |
| Per<br>Hour | Amount | Per<br>Hour | Amount | Per<br>Hour | Amount | Per<br>Hour | Amount | Per<br>Hour | Amount |
|---|---|---|---|---|---|---|---|---|---|
| $1.00 | $ 313.00 | $.12 | $ 37.56 | $.42 | $131.46 | $.20 | $ 62.60 | $.26 | $ 81.38 |
| .90 | 163.80 | .10 | 18.20 | .34 | 61.88 | .20 | 36.40 | .26 | 47.32 |
| 1.10 | 580.80 | .14 | 73.92 | .50 | 264.00 | .20 | 105.60 | .26 | 137.28 |
| | $1057.60 | | $129.68 | | $457.34 | | $204.60 | | $265.98 |

This schedule indicated the operational efficiency of Department X, divided as to machine groups and classified according to three classifications:

1. The Employment Efficiency: ascertained by dividing the actual hours worked by the standard working hours in the period (1,094 ÷ 1,200 or 91% for Department X) and suggested the ability of management to keep the factory facilities employed.

2. Operating Efficiency: computed by dividing the standard hours in production by the actual hours worked (1,023 ÷ 1,094 or 94%) and indicated the efficiency of operation of the factory facilities during the time they were actually employed.

3. End Efficiency: determined by dividing the standard hours in production by the standard working hours in the period (1,023 ÷ 1,200 or 85%) and disclosed the efficiency to which the available factory facilities were employed during the period as measured by the actual results obtained.

And, finally, the standard machine earnings were determined by applying the standard machine rates to the standard hours in production for the period. These results were compared with the actual expenditures for the period by employing a Departmental Efficiency Statement, which was so very similar to Form K (Summarized Manufacturing Statement) that it was not adapted to these data.

With respect to the significance of machine rate, Harrison made the following statement when he revised his original material for publication in the text:

There is nothing new in the use of machine rates as a medium of burden distribution but it is a somewhat remarkable fact

that apparently the leading exponents of their use have not
realized that in machine rates they have in their grasp the
means of bringing cost accounting into line with modern industrial thought as expressed in scientific management methods.
So completely has the accounting mind been obsessed by the
idea that the sole object of cost accounting is to distribute
expenses in such a manner as to obtain correct information
as to the costs of manufacture that the fact in machine rates
we have the ideal vehicle for furnishing operating efficiency
data does not seem to have been realized. . . . The advantages
gained from the use of machine rates as a medium of expense
distribution though important is not to be compared with that
resulting from their use as a means of comparing the actual
expense with standard.[19]

<u>Elasticity of Standard Costs</u>.--Harrison pointed out that standard

costs should be so compiled that they could be adjusted to the basis of

current conditions with little difficulty--the price adjustment factor

was accumulated for this purpose.  Thus it was not necessary to recom-

pute the detailed costs of the various parts entering into the standard

cost of a product in order to make adjustment for price fluctuations in

materials, labor, and burden.  However, the author would revise his

standards due to a change in the methods of manufacture in order that

the standard costs might conform to this innovation.

Although Harrison believed that standards were constantly changing,

yet he recognized a value in more or less permanent standards for com-

parative purposes:

But a great proportion of the value of efficiency information
compiled is lost if there is no way of showing the costs of
today in comparison with the standards of yesterday.  Under
the method illustrated . . . in addition to showing actual

---

[19]Harrison, <u>Cost Accounting to Aid Production</u>, pp. 106-107.

costs in relation to adjusted standards these are also shown in relation to a base standard, so that efficiency data compiled at any time is always comparable with that compiled at any other time.[20]

A careful analysis of this quotation will suggest that Harrison not only recognized and approved the use of ideal standards but also understood and accepted the value of basic standards. In order to employ basic standards for statistical purposes and to provide ideal standards for current operational purposes, the author devised a scheme for revising the standards periodically. Beginning with basic standards as scientifically established, he compared the actual and standard costs for the period and disclosed any variations as increase or decreases from the basic standard.

DEPARTMENTAL EFFICIENCY STATEMENT PREVIOUS TO
REVISION OF STANDARDS
May, 1943

| Account | Actual Cost in Period | Basic Standard Cost in Period | Increase or Decrease Comparing Actual Cost With Basic Standard | |
|---|---|---|---|---|
| | | | Increase | Decrease |
| Direct Labor | $ 5,400 | $ 5,000 | $400 | |
| Indirect Labor | 2,250 | 2,100 | 150 | |
| Machine Repairs | 1,680 | 1,750 | | $ 70 |
| Supplies | 450 | 500 | | 50 |
| Power | 927 | 900 | 27 | |
| Totals | $10,707 | $10,250 | $577 | $120 |

If it were deemed desirable to revise the basic standards for a

---

[20] Harrison, G. Charter, "Cost Accounting to Aid Production," *Industrial Management*, LVII (1919), 486.

subsequent period, the revision would be made on the basis of percentages as compiled in a Schedule of Revision of Standards.  Such a schedule
has been prepared for the case under consideration:

FIRST REVISION OF STANDARDS

| Accounts | Per Cent of Basic Standard |
|---|---|
| Direct Labor | 104 |
| Indirect Labor | 102 |
| Machine Repairs | 96 |
| Supplies | 90 |
| Power | 85 |

After the actual costs had been compiled for the subsequent period,
these figures were compared with both basic and current standards--as
indicated in the following schedule, Departmental Efficiency Statement
Made in Accordance with First Revision of Standards.

DEPARTMENTAL EFFICIENCY STATEMENT MADE IN ACCORDANCE
WITH FIRST REVISION OF STANDARDS
May, 1944

| Accounts | Actual Cost in Period | Basic Standard Cost in Period | Increase* or Decrease Comparing Actual Cost with Basic Standard | | Current Standard % of Base | Current Standard Amount | Increase* or Decrease Comparing Actual Cost with Current Standard | |
|---|---|---|---|---|---|---|---|---|
| Direct Labor | $ 5,400 | $ 5,000 | $400* | | 106 | $ 5,300 | $100* | |
| Indirect Labor | 2,210 | 2,100 | 110* | | 102 | 2,142 | 68* | |
| Machine Repairs | 1,650 | 1,750 | | $100 | 96 | 1,680 | | $30 |
| Supplies | 440 | 500 | | 60 | 90 | 450 | | 10 |
| Power | 800 | 900 | | 100 | 85 | 765 | 35* | |
| Totals | $10,500 | $10,250 | $510* | $260 | | $10,337 | $203* | $40 |

A consideration of this technique will indicate that the basic standards
might be revised annually and the actual costs compared with both the
permanent and the current standards.  Additional elasticity is thus
given to standard costs by the fact that either of these standards,
basic or current, might be employed for recording the cost data in the
accounting records.

Summary of Harrison's Early Contribution to Standard Costs.--A careful consideration of this chapter will indicate that G. Charter Harrison
had recognized the value of Taylor's and Emerson's concepts and had designed a cost procedure for the recording, the analysis, and the presentation of such data as might arise from the application of their principles.

In the first place, he accepted the engineer's computations as
standards and proceeded to provide for the recording of these figures
and for the accumulation of corresponding actual data according to sound
accounting practice.  Provision was made for classifying this information as to materials, labor, and burden and for creating such accounts
as might be needed for additional analysis of these components.

By recording the cost data in the accounts at both actual and standard figures, the author indicated one of the methods of journalizing
standard costs--Method C, Charging Work in Process at Both Actual and
Standard Values.

At the same time, he provided for computing and presenting the
variations that might arise from comparing actual and standard figures--
for materials, the Price and the Usage Variations; for labor, the Rate

and the Efficiency Variations; and for burden, the Fixed Charges Variations Due to Differences in Expenditures and Due to Differences in Production and the Fluctuating Charges Variation.

In addition to recording actual and standard costs and to compiling
variations between these two values, Harrison anticipated the significance of current reports for executives and provided for submitting
pertinent cost information in brief form immediately after the close of
a fiscal period.

And, finally, Harrison added elasticity to cost accounting by
recognizing the value of ideal standards (current standards for the
author) as well as basic standards, and by providing a means of revision
of the basic standards to current standards and of comparing actual with
either and/or both of these types of standards. As a method of converting inventories, cost of sales, and other accounting items from standard
to actual values for financial statement purposes, Harrison proposed the
Price Adjustment Factor and designated some of the conditions under
which it might be used.

CHAPTER VI

THE DEVELOPMENT OF STANDARD COST PRINCIPLES

Since G. Charter Harrison presented his initial ideas concerning

the application of the principles of standards to cost accounting in

1918, an enormous amount of literature has been written on the subject

of standard costs.  After a rather careful consideration of much of this

material, the present writer has found that most of these writings have

taken the forms of discussions of controversial issues, of case studies

of specific applications to industry, and/or of textbook presentation of

accounting procedures.  However, little effort has been given to the

task of summarizing and coordinating the many concepts that have been

proposed.  In recognition of the paucity of investigation with respect

to this phase of standard cost accounting, the writer has undertaken to

restate such principles, techniques, and/or methods that have been com-

prehended from his study.

Some Important Factors in the Early Development of Standard Costs.--

In addition to the contributions of G. Charter Harrison, who continued

to promote standard costs in theory by numerous publications and ad-

dresses and in practice by installations of cost systems, several other

forces tended to accelerate the acceptance of this philosophy of cost

keeping.

Perhaps the major force in presenting standard costs to accountants,

and in turn to industry, may be accepted as the National Association of

Cost Accountants, which was organized in 1919.  Credence is given to

271

this assertion by a restatement of the objectives of the Association as

outlined by President William M. Lybrand:

> In the first group are the collection and distribution of in-
> formation dealing with all phases of cost work, which includes
> in a broad way the publishing of cost pamphlets, the issuing
> of special bulletins, the development of research work and
> the consideration and discussion of cost topics through local
> chapters and service departments.[1]

During the next ten years (and continuing until the present time so far

as that is concerned), a portion of the annual International Cost Con-

ferences, as sponsored by the National Association of Cost Accountants,

was devoted to a consideration of some phase of standard costs while

numerous bulletins, pamphlets, and research projects were published and

distributed by this organization.

One of the most significant of these publications was a book, _De-

partmental and Standard Costs_ (1923), by William S. Kemp, Treasurer of

The Holtzer-Cabot Electric Company and Vice-President of the National

Association of Cost Accountants.[2]  Harrison has characterized this pub-

lication in a very satisfactory manner as follows:

> One of the big undertakings to be tackled by the National
> Association of Cost Accountants is the preparation of road
> maps made up by those who have traveled some of the trails
> leading to that agreeable spot called satisfactory cost ac-
> counting.  One of these road maps has been presented to this

---

[1] Lybrand, William M., "President's Report," _National Association of
Cost Accountants Yearbook_, 1921, p. 10.

[2] Kemp, William S., _Departmental and Standard Costs_, New York,
National Association of Cost Accountants, 1923.

Association by our worthy President in his book "Departmental
and Standard Costs" which gives us a complete and definite
picture of the actual methods operated by Mr. Kemp himself.
This book involved a tremendous amount of labor cheerfully
given gratis in the interests of better cost accounting and
the profession is under a deep debt of gratitude to Mr. Kemp
for his outstanding contribution to its literature.[3]

Another recognition of standard cost, as being worthy of widespread

consideration, was evidenced by the importance that was allotted to this

subject in the preparation of the program for the International Congress

of Accounting in Amsterdam (1926).  The addresses pertaining to standard

costs included the following:  C. Hewetson Nelson, "Standard Costs as a

Basis of Management and Industrial Control"; J. Anton de Haas, "Standard

Costs as a Basis of Management and Industrial Control"; Professor Johan

Gerard Charles Volmer, "Standard Costs as a Basis of Management and In-

dustrial Control"; and William S. Kemp, "Standard Costs as a Basis of

Management and Industrial Control."[4]  This distinction was repeated in

1929, when the Congress met in New York and the program included three

addresses on standard costs:  G. Charter Harrison, "Fundamentals of

Standard Costs"; Eric A. Camman, "Standard Costs Installation and Pro-

cedure"; and Horace G. Crockett, "Methods of Presentation and Managerial

Application of Standard Costs."[5]

---

[3]Harrison, G. Charter, "Standard Costs and Variations," National
Association of Cost Accountants Yearbook, 1925, p. 112.

[4]Het Internationaal Accountantscongress, Amsterdam, J. Muusses,
Uitgever te Purmerend, 1926, pp. 279-365.

[5]Proceedings, International Congress on Accounting, New York, International Congress on Accounting, 1929, pp. 859-908.

In the meantime, Thomas Downie, Jr., an English Chartered Accountant, had published a short book, The Mechanism of Standard (or Predetermined) Cost Accounting and Efficiency Records (1927).  Although he
evidenced a knowledge of this subject--defined by this author as "a system of accounting which records:  (a) the standard or pre-determined
cost of the product (or service rendered); (b) the actual cost of the
product; and (c) the relation between the standard cost and the actual
cost of the product"[6]--he failed to present his material in as concise
manner as Harrison, Kemp, Camman, and other American writers were employing at this time.

If an index of English thinking with respect to standard costs may
be assumed to have been expressed by C. Hewetson Nelson, Past-President
of the Society of Incorporated Accountants and Auditors, in his speech
before the International Congress on Accounting in 1926, another indication of that country's tardiness in accepting this cost accounting technique will be gained.  The following quotation is indicative of his
trend of thought:

> Without closer analysis we may, I suggest, say that when we
> use the phrase "standard costs" we use the term as meaning
> "standard" to a particular trade or industry.[7]

A careful analysis of this statement will disclose that the speaker
was contemplating uniform costs (a uniform cost system) rather than

---

[6]Downie, op. cit., p. 2.

[7]Het Internationaal Accountantscongress, op. cit., p. 285.

standard costs.  The same idea with respect to English cost accounting has been gained by the present writer in his investigation of cost articles in The Accountant from 1920 to 1930--that is, that the authors were undertaking to apply cost systems to various industries rather than to apply standard cost technique.

That the standard cost idea was accepted by American cost accountants is attested by the fact that the members of the National Association of Cost Accountants, at the national convention held in Chicago in 1927, went on record as advocating this cost accounting plan by adopting the following resolution:

> BE IT RESOLVED--That we deplore this practice[8] and urge every man engaged in business to adhere firmly to a price policy which shall yield a reasonable profit over normal cost;
> That we believe the true purpose of competition is to bring about a real lowering of normal costs through greater efficiency;
> That we urge every business to develop and install adequate standard cost methods so that these policies may be intelligently applied.[9]

The recognition of the subject of standard costs as worthy of consideration for texts and other publications covering the field of cost accounting tends to represent a factor in this technique's development. The following authors, who wrote prior to 1930, presented standard costs with varying degrees of treatment:  Alford (1924), Jordan and Harris

---

[8]The author had referred to practice, as herein quoted, as "selling at or below normal cost."

[9]National Association of Cost Accountants Yearbook, 1927, p. 88.

(1925), Lawrence (1925), Amidon and Lang (1928), and Maze and Glover (1929).[10]

Some Important Factors in the Later Development of Standard Costs. --In 1930, G. Charter Harrison published his concepts of this subject in a book, Standard Costs,[11] and recorded a more adequate treatment of installing standard cost systems and of analyzing cost variations than he had presented in his original publication.

Two years later, the American Institute of Accountants sanctioned standard costs by inviting Eric A. Camman to prepare a volume on this subject and by publishing, through its committee on publication, this author's efforts under the title Basic Standard Costs.[12]

In explaining the American Institute of Accountants' interest in this text, A. P. Richardson made the following statement under the section "Editor's Notes" of this publication:

> Strangely enough the phrase "standard costs" although it has been known for many years, is comparatively little understood. . . . It seemed to the committee on publication that if there could be a fairly authoritative treatise upon this constantly growing subject it would be most desirable to publish it. And, accordingly, Mr. Camman, who is known as an author throughout the country and to some extent abroad, was invited to prepare the text which is now presented by the Institute's committee. . . .

---

[10] Alford, Management's Handbook, pp. 1,321-1,325 and 1,382-1,399; Jordan and Harris, op. cit., pp. 485-492; Lawrence, Cost Accounting (1925), pp. 376-397; Amidon and Lang, op. cit., pp. 269-285; and Maze and Glover, op. cit., pp. 299-332.

[11] Harrison, Standard Costs, op. cit.

[12] Camman, Basic Standard Costs, op. cit.

The committee on publication feels a sense of peculiar gratification in presenting this book which it believes to be the most comprehensive treatise on the subject of standard costs which has yet been written.[13]

Cecil Merle Gillespie presented his text, Accounting Procedure for Standard Costs,[14] in 1935 and undertook not only to explain the principles of the three fundamental methods of operating standard costs but also to illustrate these methods with actual operating situations.  In view of the fact that the two former treatments of standard costs had presented only one method for recording costs in the accounts--Harrison and Camman had recorded both actual and standard values in their accounts--Gillespie's work tends to demand recognition in this later development of standard costs.

At this time, it seems desirable to enumerate the efforts of some of the English and Australian writers of cost literature.  Wight, English author and accountant, included a chapter, "Standard Costs and Idle Capacity,"[15] in his publication, The Fundamentals of Process Cost Accounting.  Although he anticipated standards at various levels of production, he advocated that the standard be set at a reasonable basic of attainment--"75 per cent of full capacity or even less."  Pointing out that some authors were charging the cost of idle capacity to profit and loss, Wight rejected this procedure from a practical standpoint because

_______________

[13]Ibid., pp. v-vi.

[14]Gillespie, Accounting Procedure for Standard Costs, op. cit.

[15]Wight, L. A., The Fundamentals of Process Cost Accounting, London, Sir Isaac Pitman and Sons, Ltd., 1932, pp. 91-98.

he thought that overhead charges must be earned.  Somewhat later, he

recognized both fixed and fluctuating expenses and expressed the belief

that a distinction should be made between the two in fixing standards.[16]

Kearsey, another English writer and cost accountant, published a

book, Standard Costs,[17] and evidenced an interest in setting standards

for material, labor, and overhead and in determining variations between

actual and standard figures, but failed to manifest a similar concern

for the recording of cost data in accounts.

Leslie A. Schumer, an associate in the Commonwealth Institute of

Accountants of Australia allotted Part III, "Manufacturing Costs

(Standard Cost Methods),"[18] of his publication, Cost Accounting, to

standard costs.  In view of the fact that this book was awarded the

prize in the competition conducted by the Victoria Division of the Com-

monwealth Institute of Accountants in 1934, it may be assumed to reflect

Australian thinking in this field of accounting.  The author employed a

very unique set of flow charts to illustrate his procedure, demonstrated

the recording of work in process at standard values only, recognized

variations between actual and standard costs, illustrated numerous

ledger accounts, and devised several statements for presenting cost in-

formation to management.

---

[16] Wight, L. A., "Standard Cost," The Accountant, XC (April 28,
1934), 596-598.

[17] Kearsey, H. E., Standard Costs, op. cit.

[18] Schumer, Leslie A., Cost Accounting, Melbourne (Australia), Commonwealth Institute of Accountants, 1935, pp. 201-257.

The second Australian publication, <u>Accounting Control by Use of Standard Costs</u> (1940),[19] by Gerald H. Gregory, was, according to the Preface, the first book published in Australia dealing exclusively with standard costs.  This author tended to elaborate Schumer's procedure and to improve that author's technique, particularly with respect to statements, journal entries, ledger accounts, and the flow chart for illustrating the progress of manufacturing data through the financial records.

As final evidence of the acceptance of standard costs as a part of cost literature, attention is called to the fact that authors of textbooks on cost accounting since 1930 have presented more elaborated treatments of this subject than were included in earlier publications--particularly the respective authors' original editions.  As substantiation of this assertion, the works of the following writers are cited: Reitell (1933); Dohr, Inghram and Love (1935); Lawrence (1937); Langer (1938); Van Sickle (1938); Schlatter (1939); Blocker (1940); Newlove and Garner (1941); and Neuner (1942).[20]

After presenting the significant factors that have been observed in the development of standard costs, consideration will be given to certain principles that have come to be recognized by advocates of this

---

[19] Gregory, <u>Accounting Control by Use of Standard Costs</u>, op. cit.

[20] Reitell, <u>op</u>. <u>cit</u>., pp. 357-416; Dohr, Inghram, and Love, <u>op</u>. <u>cit</u>., pp. 474-510; Lawrence (revised edition, 1937), <u>op</u>. <u>cit</u>., pp. 327-380; Langer, <u>op</u>. <u>cit</u>., pp. L 19:1 - L 22:9; Van Sickle, <u>op</u>. <u>cit</u>., pp. 435-521; Schlatter, Charles F., <u>Advanced Cost Accounting</u>, New York, John Wiley and Sons, 1939, pp. 102-154; Blocker, <u>op</u>. <u>cit</u>., pp. 552-630; Newlove, George Hillis, and Garner, S. Paul, <u>Elementary Cost Accounting</u>, New York, D. C. Heath and Company, 1941, pp. 439-455; and Neuner, <u>Cost Accounting</u>, pp. 473-543.

subject.

    <u>Standard Costs are Predetermined Costs</u>.--In considering the nature of the standard cost technique, it must be emphasized that cost standards, as employed in factory cost accounting, are predetermined allowances for each element of production cost based on planned specifications and stated objectives.  Quoting from Green, the term "standard cost" has been defined as

> . . . a predetermined cost for each operation, or each unit
> of finished product . . . intended to represent the value of
> direct material, direct labor and manufacturing burden nor-
> mally required under efficient conditions at normal capacity
> to process a unit of product.  In other words, it is that
> cost or standard which a well-operated plant ought reasona-
> bly to attain.[21]

However, not all cost figures which are prepared in advance of operations may be admitted to the category of standard costs.  Standard costs, as understood at this time, are established through a process of scientific fact finding, which, although utilizing past performance in some instances, accepts only the results of controlled experimentation-- including a careful selection of materials; time and motion studies of operations; and an engineering analysis of equipment and other manufac- turing facilities.[22]

---

[21] Green, E. A., "Practical Standards--Their Development and Use," <u>National Association of Cost Accountants Bulletin</u>, Vol. XVI, No. 11 (February 1, 1935), pp. 641-642.

[22] Camman, <u>op</u>. <u>cit</u>., pp. 1-33; and Myers, Herbert J., Keating, William L., and Metsch, J. C., <u>How to Set Standards</u>, New York, National Association of Cost Accountants, 1931, pp. 1-98.

On the other hand, those predetermined costs, which represent merely averages of past performance or simply opinions of an official without the assistance of scientific facts, may not be termed standard costs. Such predetermined costs have, as their principal object, an approximation of actual costs without the efforts and expense required to maintain detailed records. These costs are accepted generally under the classification "Estimated Costs." (Two of the preceding chapters of this study have undertaken to consider these cost methods and to suggest that the estimating cost procedure may be said to have presaged standard costs.)

Standard Costs are Not a Cost Accounting System.--Basically, there are two general types of cost accounting systems--the job cost system and the process cost system--which may be employed as the basis for either historical or predetermined costs. Maynard (1927) referred to the different kinds of cost systems "because most of the text-books and courses give, unfortunately, definite misinformation."

> There are two basic types of cost systems: (1) the job order system, in which the cost cut-off is made at the end of a given quantity of product, and (2) the process cost system, in which the cost cut-off is made at the end of a given period of time. . . . The job order system may be used with either actual or standard costs. The process cost system may also be used with either actual or standard costs; and it is the combination of the process cost system with standard costs which is the most suitable general type for all quantity of production.[23]

---

[23]Maynard, Henry W., "The Accounting Technique for Standard Costs," National Association of Cost Accountants Bulletin, Vol. VIII, No. 12, Sec. I (February 15, 1927), p. 545.

Continuing this idea, Amidon and Lang (1928) considered "standard costs . . . merely an appendage, so to speak, to either job order or process costs,"[24] while Reitell (1933) declared that standard costs were "as applicable in a job-order plant as in a process plant."[25]

Van Sickle (1938), in a section, "Comparison of a Standard Cost System with Other Cost Systems," tended to confuse the reader with the following statement:

> The standard cost plan provides for a measurement of operating efficiency through the analysis of cost variances, whereas in the older actual process cost systems the unit cost of a product is the chief measurement of efficiency. Also in the job order actual cost system, the comparison of the actual job cost and the estimate cost discloses only that the actual cost is higher or lower than the estimated cost, but does not disclose the specific reasons therefor. In a standard cost system the importance of unit cost is dwarfed and lost sight of because of the emphasis set on the analysis of variance accounts for the purpose of disclosing efficiency or inefficiency in production.[26]

On the other hand, Blocker (1940) declared that standard costs were not distinct systems of accounting--"They may be used either with the process or operation type, or with the production order type of cost accounting system";[27] Newlove and Garner (1941) pointed out that standard cost methods may be adopted under either job cost or process cost systems--"They do not take the place of the techniques connected with those

---

[24] Amidon and Lang, op. cit., p. 270.

[25] Reitell, op. cit., p. 386.

[26] Van Sickle, op. cit., p. 436.

[27] Blocker, Cost Accounting, p. 552.

systems, but supplement them";[28] and Neuner (1942) contended that a standard cost system might be used where the costing basis was a process, a department, or a specific order--"a 'standard cost system' is not a different kind of system from specific order or process costing, but represents one or the other kind of cost system, with the added feature of cost analysis built into it."[29]

And, finally, Paton (1943), in accepting this principle, stated that cost systems might be classified as "job costs with or without standards" and "process costs with or without standards."[30]

Standard Costs are Not Uniform Costs.--Some confusion of thought with respect to standard costs has developed because of the different meanings that have been applied to the word "standard" in relation to accounting. One of these meanings--a specimen--has been responsible for the concept of a standard cost as being that cost obtained when all the firms of an industry or group employ a model method of accounting for costing their production activities.

Two examples have been deemed sufficient to illustrate this conception. The American Foundrymen's Association Standard Cost System, as revised by Emerson and Mason[31] in 1914, was designed to accumulate the

---

[28] Newlove and Garner, op. cit., p. 439.

[29] Neuner, Cost Accounting, p. 478.

[30] Paton, W. A., Accountants' Handbook, New York, The Ronald Press Company, 1943, p. 218.

[31] Emerson, Harrington, and Mason, J. K., Revision of American Foundrymen's Association Standard Cost System, op. cit.

cost of operation (material, labor, and capital charges) by divisions
(metal costs, conversion cost, floor cost, and cleaning costs) for the
association's members.  The United Typothetae of America Standard Cost-
Finding System, as approved by this organization in 1918, was contemplated to record predetermined figures based on average costs for the
preceding twelve months and to provide a "reserve for overhead" to absorb the differences between actual and estimated figures.[32]  In view
of the fact that neither of these systems undertook to set standards
according to scientific methods or to analyze cost variations as a
measure of factory efficiency, two essentials of standard costs, these
cost finding plans must be classified in a category other than that of
standard costs.

This idea was expressed again in 1921 when the program of the National Association of Cost Accountants' annual conference contained a
section under the heading "Uniform Methods and Standardized Costs."  In
addition to Miller's presentation of the Printers' Standard Cost System,
the addresses during this session included descriptions of the model accounting systems for the Garment Industry, the Biscuit and Cracker Industries, the Tanning Industry, and the Laundry Industry.  A careful consideration of these papers will eliminate these accounting procedures
from standard costs.[33]

---

[32]Miller, Edward T., "Operation of the Printers' Standard Cost
System and Some Results," National Association of Cost Accountants Yearbook, 1921, pp. 143-154.

[33]National Association of Cost Accountants Yearbook, 1921, pp. 143-
196.

Somewhat later, Camman criticized this tendency of accepting standard costs as the terminology for specimen cost systems and declared that
this conception should be eliminated.[34]

When the subject of accounting systems for industries was considered a second time in a National Association of Cost Accountants Conference (1934), the title of the discussion section, "Problems in the
Application of Uniform Cost Accounting Methods," suggests a change of
thought with respect to this subject--"Uniform Cost Accounting" has
superseded "Standard Costs" as the terminology for expressing a model
cost accounting system as adopted by an industry or group within an industry.[35]

Additional credence is given to this assertion--"Uniform Cost Accounting" has replaced "Standard Cost Accounting" for designating a cost
system employed by an industry--by the definition of uniform cost accounting as expressed by the Department of Manufacture of the Chamber of
Commerce of the United States, an organization that has extended its influence to the greater adoption of such methods:

> Uniform cost accounting comprises a set of principles and in
> some cases of accounting methods which when incorporated in
> the accounting systems of the individual members in an indus-
> try will result in the obtaining of cost figures by the indi-
> vidual members of the industry which will be on a comparable

---

[34] Camman, Eric A., "Standard Costs Installation and Procedure,"
Proceedings, International Congress on Accounting, 1929, New York, International Congress on Accounting, 1930, pp. 874-877.

[35] National Association of Cost Accountants Yearbook, 1934, pp. 85-
142.

basis.  Uniform cost accounting does not mean the preparation
of average or standard cost figures for the industry, nor the
inclusion in costs of predetermined or fixed elements of cost.[36]

Since 1930, the following authors of textbooks have recognized this
distinction between uniform and standard costs and have treated both
subjects in their publications:  Dohr, Inghram, and Love (1935); Lawrence (1937); Blocker (1940); and Neuner (1942).[37]

In view of this trend of thought and for the sake of clear terminology, this study will consider "specimen cost systems" as "uniform
costs systems," a phase of accounting not contemplated by this investigation.  However, by way of explanation, it should be noted that a uniform
system might employ standard cost methods--as an example, the cost system compiled by Philip N. Miller and Company, at the request of the Wool
Institute, for the Woolen and Worsted Industry may be cited.[38]

Types of Standard Costs.--With the application of two other meanings of the word "standard"--(1) an ideal and (2) a measure--to cost
accounting, there have developed two principal systems of accounting
procedure for setting and expressing standards--(1) the current or ideal
standard, which proposes to reflect what performance should be during
the period that the standard is to be used, and (2) the basic or bogey

---

[36]Chamber of Commerce of the United States, Uniform Cost Accounting
in Trade Associations, Washington, D. C., 1933, pp. 1-2.

[37]Dohr, Inghram, and Love, op. cit., pp. 586-600; Lawrence, op.
cit., pp. 463-475; Blocker, Cost Accounting, pp. 668-678; and Neuner,
Cost Accounting, pp. 728-749.

[38]The Wool Institute, Cost Manual and Comparative Cost Records for
Woolen and Worsted Industry, New York, Brown and Wilson, Inc., 1928.

standard, which undertakes to serve as a unit of measure or as a convenient means of establishing relative values.

(1) Current or Ideal Standards. According to this procedure, which is intended to be representative of what costs should be under the prevailing (current) conditions, the manufacturing specifications are established at the present figures and are revised to reflect modifications in process methods and/or changes in material prices, labor rates, and manufacturing expenses. Such standards are regarded as real costs, which are recorded in the accounting records during the fiscal period and are employed in valuing the inventories of work in process and finished goods for financial statement purposes, with the differences between the actual and standard costs being diverted to variation accounts and being closed to the profit and loss account for the period.[39] Under this procedure, the theory is accepted that standard costs are attainable costs and that deviations therefrom are the results of inefficiencies.

In the setting of standards under the current or ideal standard theory, three distinct concepts have developed with respect to the level at which such standards should be established:

(a) Expected Actual Standards. These standards represent a short-run point of view--the cost that management expects to incur if the anticipated prices of material, labor, and burden prevail during the period, if the usage of these cost components corresponds to that efficiency

---

[39]Paton, Accountants' Handbook (1943), pp. 222-227.

level as predetermined, and if the level of production is maintained at
that volume as planned.

Blocker (1940) made the following declaration with respect to this
type of standard, which he termed "standards as representing budget
forecasts of expected production and costs":

> Standards should be reasonably attainable expectations of
> conditions within a plant, but the expression is so vague
> that it would be difficult to know at what point above actual
> costs and below ideal costs the standards should be set.[40]

Langer (1938) recognized this standard, "Expected Performance as
Standard," as one of the most common standards and offered the following
criticism of this device:

> Because of the temporary character of this standard it is im-
> perfect as an indicator of trend over a long period of time,
> but it is of high utility in a more important field, that of
> measuring operations and setting up an objective to be at-
> tained.[41]

A consideration of this exposition will indicate that deviations
from this standard will arise from three causes--(1) failure to achieve
the predetermined level of operation, (2) failure to forecast correctly
the prices of commodities and services purchased, and (3) failure to
realize the expected degree of efficiency in the employment of the productive factors--and that these differences may be either debit or
credit variations, thus reflecting performance that has been either

---

[40] Blocker, Cost Accounting, p. 555.

[41] Langer, op. cit., p. L 19-4.

better or worse than anticipated.

Other writers to include a treatment of this standard in their publications include:  Kearsey (1933), Gillespie (1935), Schumer (1935), Mannix (1938), McFarland (1939), Gregory (1940), and Neuner (1942).[42]

(b) Normal Standards.  Another type of standards refers to costs predicted upon normal operations for the concern over a complete business cycle.  Kemp (1923) anticipated this procedure but probably did not extend his efforts to the same degree as that contemplated at this time:

> In establishing normal rates there are really two normals,
> one which has to do with plant capacity and the other with
> the normal use of the plant as actually operated.[43]

Amidon and Lang accepted standard costs as normal costs but with a somewhat greater degree of permanence than is anticipated at the present time.

> . . . the concept of a . . . normal cost implies a certain
> measure of permanence.  The standards . . . are not subject
> to change from period to period in the same way that esti-
> mated costs are.
>
> Standard costs may, therefore be defined as representing
> a forecast of what costs should be under normal conditions,
> and as furnishing a basis for measuring production efficiency.[44]

---

[42] Kearsey, op. cit., p. 37; Gillespie, op. cit., p. 11; Schumer, op. cit., p. 5; Mannix, Raymond L., A Basic Course in Cost Accounting, Boston, Recording and Statistical Corporation, 1938, p. 191; McFarland, Walter B., "The Basic Theory of Standard Costs," The Accounting Review, XIV (June, 1939), 153; Gregory, op. cit., p. 64; and Neuner, op. cit., p. 501.

[43] Kemp, op. cit., p. 24.

[44] Amidon and Lang, op. cit., p. 270.

Maze and Glover likewise anticipated normal standards, somewhat in
accordance with the practice at the time of their writing.

> Standard costs should not be regarded as permanent in their
> nature, but should be flexible so as to take care of variance
> in both material and labor fluctuations. . . .
>
> . . . as a rule, standards are not chosen because they are
> considered perfect, but rather because they set a goal.[45]

Reitell (1933) presented a modified use of this plan under his
"normal capacity" level--"this means that the basis for standard costs
is a volume of production that is a fair average output based upon sales
expectancy for a typical year and adjusted to the mechanical capacity of
the plant."[46]

Current literature characterizes the normal standard as a statis-
tically determined figure intended to level the fluctuations from seasonal and cyclical causes and to eliminate erratic fluctuations. Such a
standard is difficult to establish, in view of errors connected with
predicting the extent and duration of cyclical effects. Therefore,
variances arise from performance being above or below normal conditions
or from prices and/or volume differing from normal figures and represent
causes, for the most part, beyond the control of the individual firm.
This concept has been criticized unfavorably as failing not only to
offer the proper incentive to the factory personnel but also to serve as
a measure of efficiency--during some years of the cycle the standard is

--------

[45]Maze and Glover, op. cit., pp. 304 and 315.

[46]Reitell, op. cit., p. 358.

easily surpassed while during others it is entirely unattainable.[47]

Langer, toward the close of the period, repeated Kemp's statement that initiated this trend of thought: "The normal used in setting this standard must be selected with due regard both for the capacity of the plant to produce and the normal sales expectancy."[48]

(c) Best Attainable Performance or Ideal Standard. The third level at which standards might be set represents the best performance that might be achieved under the most favorable conditions--"the most favorable prices for materials and labor, highest output with the best equipment and layout possible, and the maximum of efficiency in utilization of the resources."[49]

That ideal standards were used rather early in standard cost history is gained from George Rea's publication, "An Introduction to Predetermined Costs,"[50] which stated that the cost system must be adapted to the conditions of each factory and organization. After designing such a procedure to a textile mill manufacturing a single line of goods, but with many widths and qualities, he declared that the standard should be analyzed each year and revised for a permanent change in any manufacturing element that tended to distort the comparison between actual and

---

[47]Mannix, op. cit., pp. 191-192; McFarland, op. cit., p. 153; Blocker, op. cit., p. 554; Neuner, op. cit., pp. 501-502.

[48]Langer, op. cit., p. L 19-3.

[49]Neuner, op. cit., p. 500.

[50]Rea, George, "An Introduction to Predetermined Costs," National Association of Cost Accountants Bulletin, Vol. V, No. 7 (December 15, 1923), pp. 3-15.

standard costs.

Lawrence (1925) also tended to pioneer this concept when he wrote
the following statements:

> Standard costs are neither actual, average, nor normal
> costs, but are estimates of what the costs should be under
> as nearly perfect conditions as it is possible to secure.
> They are not necessarily fixed or permanent in their nature,
> but are subject to change from time to time as they may be
> affected by various conditions that alter ideal conditions.
> . . .
>
> While it is desirable to have the standards represent
> ideal conditions it is not always advisable to have them do
> so.  If the standards are set too high at the beginning, the
> actual costs may be so far different from them as to discour-
> age those who undertake the task of cost reduction.  If, on
> the contrary, they are not set high enough they may be so
> easy of attainment as to encourage a spirit of self-satisfac-
> tion which will destroy the incentive to greater accomplish-
> ment.  Where there is a wide divergence between actual costs
> and the standards, it is sometimes advisable to use a series
> of successive standards, starting below the true standard and
> revising them as the actual costs are brought nearer to the
> desired amounts.[51]

When this author revised his text in 1935, he recognized that standard costs might represent "ideal conditions, normally attainable conditions, or an improvement over present conditions" but tended to reject
his original ideal standard concept:

> Standards based upon ideal conditions may be practically
> valueless if those conditions are so far above present condi-
> tions as to discourage rather than encourage effort to meet
> them.  In most instances standards based upon normally attain-
> able conditions are a greater incentive to increased effi-
> ciency than are unattainable ideal standards.[52]

---

[51]Lawrence, op. cit., pp. 376 and 377.

[52]Ibid. (1935), p. 330.

Downie (1927), the English writer, accepted this concept as the basis for setting standards--"the best conditions and equipment available, the most suitable materials, the best operations and ways of doing them which can be discovered, are adopted as standards."[53]

Schlatter (1939), although failing to state clearly that the ideal standard was his chosen standard for promoting efficiency in the factory, implied such a decision by the following statement:

> It is the opinion of the writer that standards that represent a high attainment in the particular plant, with the facilities and methods of manufacture in use, prove to be the most successful in increasing efficiency and economy. By "a high attainment" is meant some high peak of productive efficiency at low cost actually reached at some time in the past. Such standards are high enough to avoid the type of satisfaction that leads to stagnation, and still low enough to be possible for reattainment, thus avoiding discouragement that deters men from trying to better some past records.[54]

On the other hand, some authors consider ideal standards as analogous to the theoretical standard recognized in engineering specifications--standards seldom attained but ideals often established in the attempt to improve efficiency. In view of the fact that these standards assume perfection, which is seldom realized, the variances will ordinarily be debits--interpreted as failure to attain the ideal level of efficiency. Therefore, as somewhat of a compensation for this contingency of the ideal standard, employees are not held responsible for the whole

---

[53]Downie, op. cit., p. 9.

[54]Schlatter, Advanced Cost Accounting, pp. 108-109.

of those variances arising from the application of this practice.[55]

In considering the practicability of these three types of standards, generally classified as "Current Standards," evidence has been found supporting "Normal Standards" as the most acceptable at the present time. Neuner termed "Ideal Standards" as "engineering standards in the strictest sense and . . . rarely used because of the difficulty of attaining such a level of performance."[56]

The Research and Technical Service Department of the National Association of Cost Accountants conducted two surveys of representative American industries during the last six years and obtained identical results, although there was relatively little duplication of enterprises in the two samples, with respect to the bases upon which the standards were calculated by these concerns. The following schedule has been prepared from the data recorded in the presentations of these studies.

-----

[55]Gillespie, op. cit., p. 11; Langer, op. cit., p. L 19-4; Mannix, op. cit., p. 191; McFarland, op. cit., pp. 153-154; Blocker, op. cit., p. 554.

[56]Neuner, op. cit., p. 500.

Bases on which Production or
Capacity is Calculated

| Explanation | 1938 Study[57] | | 1941 Study[58] | |
|---|---|---|---|---|
| | Number of Companies | Per Cent of Total | Number of Companies | Per Cent of Total |
| Companies using Normal Capacity | 127 | 65 | 154 | 65 |
| Companies using Expected Volume | 67 | 35 | 83 | 35 |
| Totals | 194 | 100 | 237 | 100 |

In view of the fact that the "Ideal Standard" was omitted from the questionnaires, evidently the research officials of the association deemed this type of standard of minor importance. Since 281 or 65 per cent of these concerns based their standards on "Normal Capacity," some credence is given to the original statement in this summary that the tendency was to apply normal standards in practice for the purpose of setting levels of operation.

(2) Basic or Bogey Standards. Basic or bogey standards are intended to serve only as measures "for the determination of cost trends over long periods, and require adjustments to current levels for valuation of inventories and compilation of current costs."[59]

These standards possess the additional nature of a statistical

---

[57] "Practice in Applying Overhead and Calculating Normal Capacity," National Association of Cost Accountants Bulletin, Vol. XIX, No. 15, Sec. III (April 1, 1938), pp. 917-932.

[58] "Accounting for Excess Labor Costs and Overhead Under Conditions of Increased Production," National Association of Cost Accountants Bulletin, Vol. XXII, No. 24, Sec. III (August 15, 1941), pp. 1551-1570.

[59] Paton, Accountants' Handbook, p. 226.

device established for some base year and employed in much the same manner as the statistician uses the commodity price indexes.  Unlike current standard costs, basic standard figures do not displace actual values in the ledgers and financial statements but are recorded in parallel columns, along with actual costs, in the ledger accounts.

That Harrison contemplated the basic standard plan in 1921 may be gained from the following quotation:

> . . . it will be noted that whatever the current cost stand-
> ard may be (whether alternate, revised basic or revised alter-
> nate) comparisons of actual costs under the plan followed are
> invariably made with both this current standard and the basic
> standard. . . .
>
> All costs being shown in relation to the base or origi-
> nal standard, it follows that statements that can be compared
> with the same thing can be compared with one another, so that
> however many changes in standards may have been made in the
> interim between two statements comparisons can readily be
> made between them.[60]

Worrall (1923) stated that, before a standard cost plan could be put into operation, it was necessary to set standard costs for all articles manufactured.  After describing a procedure for setting such standards, this writer explained that "the standard cost is now used in the accounting, in about the same manner as a price list is used for billing, for setting up the standard cost against the actual production as reports are received."[61]

---

[60] Harrison, Cost Accounting to Aid Production, p. 211.

[61] Worrall, William F., "Standard Costs--How to Establish and Apply Them," National Association of Cost Accountants Bulletin, Vol. IV, No. 16 (May 1, 1923), p. 5.

During the same year, Camman published an article, "Choosing the

Basic Cost Plan," which might be termed an antecedent of his treatment

of the subject, "Basic Standard Costs."[62]  Three years later, this

author was more specific with his explanation of basic standard costs,

as may be evidenced from the following definition:

> The standard cost of an article may be defined as that cost
> which results from computing its manufacturing specifications
> at fixed basic prices for the components of material, labor
> and manufacturing expense.[63]

Continuing this trend of thought, Camman characterized standard costs,

when extended at basic prices, as a common denominator, an indicator of

trend, and a means of showing relative values.

The following statement tends to suggest that Jordan and Harris

accepted the idea of basic standards in 1925:

> The standard costs are not changed unless there is some rela-
> tively permanent change in the method of manufacture, in the
> standard time allowance or in the basic labor rates.  The fact
> that changes in general conditions or in operating efficiency
> from month to month may occur, is no reason for changing the
> basic standard costs which should always be used as the basis
> for setting selling prices.[64]

That Camman became the chief proponent of this cost plan may be

---

[62]Camman, Eric A., "Choosing the Basic Cost Plan," National Association of Cost Accountants Bulletin, Vol. V, No. 4 (November 1, 1923), pp. 1-12.

[63]Camman, Eric A., "Uses of Standard Costs," National Association of Cost Accountants Bulletin, Vol. VII, No. 12, Sec. I (February 15, 1926), p. 439.

[64]Jordan and Harris, op. cit., p. 486.

attested by two additional contributions by this author.  In 1929, when

he appeared before the International Congress on Accounting, he advo-

cated this procedure in his address, "Standard Costs Installation and

Procedure," by illustrating only a system of cost accounting that might

be installed under Basic Standards.  And, in the second place, when he

came to write a book on this subject, he designated <u>Basic Standard Costs</u>

as the title for his publication.  In expressing his preference for this

procedure, he made the following assertion:

> There is a certain appeal in the adoption of the standard
> cost as the object of attainment, arising possibly from the
> natural human impulse to consider a standard of any kind as
> something at which to aim or to which to conform--every man
> is attracted by an ideal.  Moreover, since the beginnings of
> scientific management the word "standard" has come into wide
> usage in manufacturing circles in the sense of a par of per-
> formance.  But it should be remembered that this par is not
> the par of the golf course, which relatively few can attain;
> it must be set as a practical matter within reach of average
> ability.  It therefore follows that in business a standard
> can not be an impossible ideal, a criterion of excellence, or
> even an ultimate object; it must be reduced to the point of
> ordinary fulfilment.  Hence it becomes more a measure of par-
> ticular performance against average performance than a state-
> ment of aim, and the choice as to accounting plan in reality
> then is reduced to a question whether the measure is to be
> changed so as to approximate the desired result or is to be
> maintained constant so as to bring out the variations from
> both expected and past performances in the actual result.[65]

As additional evidence against the use of Current (Ideal) Standard

Costs, Camman proposed the necessity for continual revision of the stand-

ards, which, if not adjusted as often as the circumstances require, rep-

resent neither the predetermined cost figures nor a measure for inter-

---

[65]Camman, <u>Basic Standard Costs</u>, pp. 37-38.

preting results.

Mogel, who applied "Basic Standard Costs" to a hosiery mill, declared that this cost plan "has the advantage of giving actual costs while at the same time providing a gauge or tool of measurement in the form of standards."[66]

In accepting standard costs for accounting purposes, Heinen believed that the question for a given industry was not whether it "can use standard costs, but whether it shall attempt to keep its standards in 'ideal figures,' frequently revised, or on the basic plan without revision of the standards themselves except at such times as the manufacturing processes are altered."  The writer accepted the basic plan "on logical grounds" and because "it can do all that the current plan can do, all the while possessing advantages of its own."[67]

McEachren, partner in the firm of Ernst and Ernst and specialist in cost and budget installations, declared that the differences between the "basic" and "current" plans were primarily a matter of mechanics and were not sufficient for creating two distinct systems.

> It appears, therefore, that in actual practice the only substantial difference between the two plans in respect to the pricing of inventories is in the treatment of direct labor variances which actually may not be of major importance. With

---

[66] Mogel, Lloyd F., "Basic Standard Costs as Applied to a Hosiery Mill," National Association of Cost Accountants Bulletin, Vol. XVI, No. 17, Sec. I (May 1, 1935), p. 961.

[67] Heinen, Francis I., "Standard Costs: Current vs. Basic," National Association of Cost Accountants Bulletin, Vol. XVII, No. 7, Sec. I (December 1, 1935), pp. 359 and 363.

a current standard cost plan, these variances would be charged
or credited to profit and loss; presumably under the basic
plan they would be reflected in inventory values.  It does not
seem likely that this difference can be of major importance
except in unusual cases.

The only real major difference between the two plans is
a matter of mechanics.  The basic plan appears to carry along
a permanent set of standards which it attempts to adjust
through the use of ratios to an historical cost basis for
balance sheet purposes and to up-to-date standards for control purposes.[68]

Joseph A. Hill, a Chicago cost accountant, gave the "depression

years" credit for contributing to the consideration "of ideas that here-

tofore were considered too scholastic."

How to continue the operation of a manufacturing plant
at a profit, however small, with a greatly reduced personnel
and machine capacity curtailed, required that cost control
methods be still further refined.  Many manufacturers were
forced to practically eliminate their cost departments because of the large expense of operating an elaborate system
that gave them little assistance in controlling costs.  The
solution in many cases was basic standard cost accounting
employing the use of cost ratios.  This method of cost control is rapidly gaining favor because of the results obtaina-
ble at a much lower expense of cost department operation.[69]

Writers of cost accounting textbooks since 1930, who have consid-

ered "Basic Standard Costs" as worthy of some recognition, include:

Dohr, Inghram and Love (1935), Gillespie (1935), Lawrence (1937), Langer

(1938), Mannix (1938), Schlatter (1938), Van Sickle (1938), Blocker

---

[68] McEachren, John W., "Can Standard Costs be Standardized?," National Association of Cost Accountants Bulletin, Vol. XXI, No. 11,
Sec. I (February 1, 1940), p. 684.

[69] Hill, Joseph A., "Basic Standard Cost Accounting Employing the
Use of Cost Ratios," National Association of Cost Accountants Bulletin,
Vol. XXI, No. 11, Sec. I (February 1, 1940), p. 693.

(1940), Neuner (1942).[70]

A consideration of this development of the subject, "Types of Standard Costs," will indicate that there has been much discussion of the relative merits of the different kinds of standards. A choice between current and basic standards will depend ordinarily upon whether management desires that variances be expressed in absolute or relative form and whether it wishes the standard to serve as incentive and performance comparisons or trend indications. Current standards will satisfy the first two conditions--variances expressed as absolutes and standards acting as incentives--in a more satisfactory manner whereas basic standards will meet the requirements of the alternative cases more readily.

Standard Cost Accounting Procedures.--After the standard costs have been established, the installation of a suitable method of accounting for such costs must be considered. The scope of such an accounting system and the extent to which standard costs will be incorporated in the records will depend upon the amount and type of information desired, the capacity of management to assimilate such data, and the amount of funds that may be expended in the compilation of the cost figures.

A careful consideration of cost literature has disclosed three general classifications of procedures for employing standard costs in an accounting system: (1) incorporated as statistical data in subsidiary

---

[70]Dohr, Inghram and Love, op. cit., p. 476; Gillespie, op. cit., pp. 11-12; Lawrence, op. cit., p. 330; Langer, op. cit., p. L 19-3; Mannix, op. cit., pp. 192-194; Schlatter, op. cit., pp. 106-108; Van Sickle, op. cit., p. 449; Blocker, op. cit., pp. 554-556; Neuner, op. cit., p. 501.

records only; (2) incorporated as memorandum data in the ledger accounts

for comparative purposes; and (3) incorporated as operational data in

the accounts for valuation reasons.

Blocker has given two explanations for the lack of uniformity in

accounting methods for standard costs:

> . . . standards are a recent managerial device and . . .
> standards are superimposed upon existing cost systems which
> have been adapted to the needs of the individual concern.[71]

(1) Accounting Procedures when Standards are Incorporated as Statis-

tical Data in Subsidiary Records Only. Lawrence (1925) pointed out that

it was generally satisfactory to maintain statistical records of stand-

ard costs rather than to record such costs in the general books.[72] Al-

though he did not describe any technique for compiling such information

in his initial publication, he did recognize this feature in his revised

edition (1937) by stating that the actual costs would be recorded accord-

ing to the general accounting practices of the business while the stand-

ard costs would be accumulated in classifications similar to those used

in the ledger accounts.

> A worksheet is prepared on which the actual and standard
> costs are shown in parallel columns with the differences from
> standard shown in additional columns. The differences are
> then analyzed as to variance causes and the amount of vari-
> ance due to each cause is shown in additional columns.[73]

---

[71] Blocker, _op. cit._, p. 581.

[72] Lawrence, _op. cit._, p. 396.

[73] _Ibid._ (revised edition, 1937), p. 377.

Rea (1923), in explaining predetermined costs for a textile mill,
contemplated standard costs as statistical devices only:

> The amounts charged to goods in process are distributed in
> the factory ledger to departmental sections with accounts for
> operations and qualities. . . . These accounts are neither
> closed into total or process costs nor further distributed
> into quality costs. Therefore, it is not necessary to enter
> the credits for finished product. The factory ledger is only
> an analysis of departmental operations, agreeing in its peri-
> odical totals with the charges to the controlling accounts.[74]

John M. Bush (1924), in discussing variations from standard costs
of materials, contemplated a statistical system of standards in view of
the fact that only accounts affecting materials were carried for stores,
goods in process, and finished goods at actual costs and that necessary
data and analyses were compiled on supporting statements. Although the
author computed the variation of actual costs from standards on his statistical reports and analyzed such variances as to variations in price
and variations in use, he failed to record these variations in the
records and carried only actual figures through the general ledger.[75]

Blocker (1940) advanced the opinion that the method of delegating
standard cost data to subsidiary records rather than to general ledger
accounts probably represented the method of accounting most commonly
used for recording standard costs. He conceded that this method was
particularly adaptable to those industries manufacturing special orders

---

[74] Rea, op. cit., p. 14.

[75] Bush, John M., "Proper Treatment of Variations from Standard Costs
of Materials," National Association of Cost Accountants Yearbook, 1924,
pp. 195-202.

and having a system of production order cost accounting.  Under his

scheme, the general ledger contained actual costs only while the sub-

sidiary records accumulated both actual and standard costs.  Management

was supplied with information respecting variances between actual and

standard costs, either daily or weekly, for the purpose of controlling

factory operations.[76]

Neuner conceived of two situations in which this procedure might be

followed:

(a) The cost accounts would be kept in the usual manner--"tied in"

with the books of account.  In this case, the process accounts would con-

tain actual costs while the standards would apply for analytical pur-

poses only.  He rejected this procedure as being too expensive for exten-

sive use, in view of the fact that he thought the clerical work for

these cost account operations would be doubled.

(b) The cost system would be maintained independent of the general

accounting system.  Under this plan, the cost accounting system in gen-

eral would be operated without reference to the entries in the general

accounting records and standard costs would be used to analyze the fig-

ures appearing on the cost sheets of the detached system.[77]

Dohr, Inghram and Love (1935) and Langer (1933) recognized that

standard costs might be used as statistical devices for comparison with

the actual costs as shown by the books but failed to develop this thesis

----------------

[76]Blocker, op. cit., pp. 615-626.

[77]Neuner, op. cit., pp. 510-511.

to any extent.[78]

Although this method has been presented in this study as a scheme that might be employed by a manufacturing enterprise, it should be recognized by the reader that such a technique is really outside of the realm of accounting for standard costs but within the field of standard costs from the developmental standpoint.

(2) Accounting Procedure when Standards are Incorporated as Memorandum Data in the Ledger Accounts. Under this method, which has been illustrated in the presentation of G. Charter Harrison's contribution to standard costs, the cost information is charged into the accounts at standard costs as well as actual costs and the accounts are credited likewise with both actual and standard figures. The relationship between the actual and standard values is expressed ordinarily as a ratio, which may be applied to the standard figures for ascertaining the average actual cost of the particular cost component under consideration.

Since this method is used with basic or bogey standards, the comparisons are made of present performance with a more or less fixed standard, which may or may not be representative of present conditions. Therefore, the standard costs, as employed under this method, do not represent the current normal costs of production but serve merely as a measure of the expected proportions of the cost components--materials, labor, and burden.

Worrall (1923) employed this method in his accounting scheme, as

---

[78]Dohr, Inghram and Love, op. cit., p. 478; Langer, op. cit., p. L 22-1.

may be observed from the following quotation from this author:

> The relation between the standard and actual cost is
> also shown in this account [Work in Process] by the use of
> ratios.  These ratios are used as a means of converting the
> standard cost of the credits to actual cost.[79]

Brugger (1925) recognized only the method of recording both actual
and standard costs in the accounts when he published his article, "Standard Costs--Their Development and Use."[80]

Camman (1926) explained the plan of recording cost at both actual
and standard values in his publication, "Uses of Standard Costs."  However, in his appearance before the International Congress on Accounting
in 1929, he presented three principal methods of employing standard
costs in the records:

a. To charge work in process accounts at actual costs and to
   credit them at standard costs.
b. To charge work in process accounts at standard costs only
   (diverting differences between actual and standard to
   variance accounts) and to credit them at standard.
c. To charge work in process accounts at standard costs as
   well as at actual costs and to credit them at both standard and actual.[81]

After discussing the merits and weaknesses of the three plans, he rejected the first as inadequate and accepted the third as preferable for
recording cost information.  Although he recognized the two methods--

---

[79]Worrall, op. cit., pp. 9-10.

[80]Brugger, F., "Standard Costs--Their Development and Use," National
Association of Cost Accountants Bulletin, Vol. VI, No. 13 (March 2, 1925),
pp. 3-16.

[81]See Proceedings, International Congress on Accounting, 1929,
p. 876.

a and b above--in his text, <u>Basic Standard Costs</u> (1932), he was prima-

rily interested in the plan (Method c above) that he had sponsored

initially.

That Downie (1927), the English writer, was familiar with this

method is evidenced by his statement with respect to the second preva-

lent type of system, which he designated as Method B:

> In the second type of system, stocks and cost of sales
> are recorded in the financial books at actual cost.  In the
> factory books cost of manufacture by lines of product is re-
> corded in parallel at standard and actual values, and the
> ratio of the latter to the former cost is developed.  The
> cost of individual parts or finished goods taken from process
> and put into stores or shipped, is recorded at standard
> values, and the standard values are converted to actual cost
> values by application of group "cost ratios" developed by the
> Work-in-Process Accounts.[82]

Using the general principles employed by Method B, Downie presented,

but failed to illustrate, a third prevalent method for recording stand-

ard cost information.  Work-in-Process accounts, by cost elements, accu-

mulated the cost of the scheduled production at both actual and standard

values.  The remainder of the procedure will be quoted:

> The actual production resulting from the expenditure
> made is taken out of the Work-in-Process Accounts, and is
> charged to stores or cost of sales at standard and actual
> cost--standard cost being converted to actual cost by appli-
> cation of the cost ratios at debit of the accounts.  Other-
> wise expressed, the debit side of the Work-in-Process Account
> accumulates the expenditure at standard and at actual values,
> from which is expected a given desired quantity of production;
> the credit side shows the quantity of production (at standard

---

[82] Downie, <u>op</u>. <u>cit</u>., p. 22.

and at actual values), actually realized from the given
amount of expenditure.  The efficiency of production by cost
elements is then determined by calculating the ratio of manufacturing expense at standard value to production at standard
value.[83]

Downie not only exhibited forms that might be used in recording
Method B, but also pointed out that this method was applicable to enterprises manufacturing a very few lines of products while the third type
was adaptable to the textile industry.

That Harrison was still accepting this method when he wrote his
book, Standard Costs, in 1930 is evidenced by the following quotation:

Standard cost accounting is a method of cost accounting which
provides for all cost data being recorded on a dual basis:
(1) on an actual cost basis; (2) on a standard cost basis.[84]

Service (1931), in providing a method "for ascertaining reliable
production costs without constant repetitive calculations in detail,"
suggested the "use of basic standard costs and development from the
accounts of actual current costs, the variances to be expressed in
ratios to standard costs."

The simplest and most practical way of obtaining costs
is through the use of basic standard costs for each of the
three elements, material, labor and expense.  This means that
there should be carried into the accounts, side by side with
each dollar actually spent for material, labor and expense,
a standard dollar, less or more, that represents the estimated or expected cost of materials used, the labor performed

---

[83] Ibid., p. 23.

[84] Harrison, Standard Costs, p. 228.

and the expense which should be applied.  These basic standard costs would represent the best knowledge available from
the experience of the company and the identity of the elements would be retained, as well as the identity of variances
in the actual costs of each element, whether material, labor
or expense.[85]

Dohr, Inghram and Love (1935) characterized this method as "The

Dual Plan"--". . . in which the accounts covering the production activi-

ties are kept in terms of <u>both</u> standard and actual.  . . . each of such

accounts will contain two debit and two credit columns."[86]

Gillespie (1935) designated this standard cost procedure as "Method

C: Charging Process at Actual and Standard and Crediting at Actual and

Standard" and devoted a rather large portion of his text to the examina-

tion of this method.[87]

Lawrence (1937) termed this cost technique "Method 3--Double Column

Ledger Accounts," and presented a short problem to illustrate the "case

of double column ledger accounts, and at the same time show the use of

variance accounts."[88]

Langer (1938) explained the procedure, "Actual and Standard Costs

Carried Parallel in the Accounts," with a rather detailed illustration;

Mannix (1938) stated that the first plan for using standard costs was to

---

[85]Service, Robert B., Jr., "Accounting Through the Medium of
Standard Costs," <u>National Association of Cost Accountants Bulletin</u>,
Vol. XII, No. 13 (March 1, 1931), p. 1045.

[86]Dohr, Inghram and Love, <u>op</u>. <u>cit</u>., p. 478.

[87]Gillespie, <u>op</u>. <u>cit</u>., pp. 251-314, 325-358.

[88]Lawrence, <u>op</u>. <u>cit</u>., pp. 371-377.

incorporate both the actual and the standard costs in the ledger accounts; Schlatter (1938) treated this subject very superficially; and Van Sickle omitted this method entirely from his presentation of standard costs.[89]

Blocker (1940) and Neuner (1942) designated this technique as "Standard Costs as Memorandum Information."[90]  That these two authors were considering the recording of cost information at both actual and standard figures may be proved by the following statement from Blocker. (This quotation is identical with Neuner's trend of thought.)

> The second plan of exhibiting standard costs as memorandum information is more complicated in procedure and more costly in operation.  The plan provides for the insertion of standard costs in Memorandum money columns in journals and general ledger accounts at the same time actual costs are recorded so that a daily comparison between actual and standard costs may be made.  Journals are arranged with two sets of debit and credit columns, Actual and Standard, and ledger accounts may be prepared with three sets of debit and credit columns:  Actual, Standard, and Variance.[91]

In order to suggest that the basic standard cost procedure is accepted as practical at the present time, the following quotation is taken from an article by E. J. Hanley (1941), Secretary and Treasurer of the Allegheny Ludlum Steel Corporation:

---

[89]Langer, op. cit., pp. L 22:4-8; Mannix, op. cit., pp. 193-195; Schlatter, Advanced Cost Accounting, p. 112; and Van Sickle, op. cit., pp. 435-521.

[90]Blocker, op. cit., pp. 620-626; Neuner, op. cit., pp. 511-517.

[91]Blocker, op. cit., p. 620.

Two things were influential in determining the choice of the "basic" standard cost procedure. One was its treatment of variances. Under- or over-liquidated overhead expense or burden is the only variance that is removed currently from inventory accounts under this plan. Parallel accounts are carried for raw materials and work in process, the one at actual and the other at standard. When shipment is made, actual is cleared in the proportion that actual balances bear to standard balances, and the remaining variance rests in the actual account--in other words, inventories are carried at actual cost not at standard.

The second reason the "basic" plan was chosen was that establishing standards was a difficult problem and it was realized that some were going to be relatively quite different from others.[92]

(3) Accounting Procedure when Standards are Incorporated as Operational Data in the Accounts. When the standard cost figures are recorded in the accounts as valuation data for inventory purposes, two general methods have developed with respect to the degree that standard figures may be used--(a) Work in Process Charged at Actual and Credited at Standard, and (b) Work in Process Charged at Standard and Credited at Standard. These methods, which will be considered separately, may employ any one of the current types of standard costs--expected actual standard, normal standard, or best attainable (ideal) standard.

(a) Work in Process Charged at Actual and Credited at Standard. With respect to the accounting technique under this method, the Work in Process account is charged with the actual cost of the period's production and is credited with the standard cost of the same period's produc-

---

[92] Hanley, E. J., "An Application of Standard Costs in the Steel Industry," *National Association of Cost Accountants Bulletin*, Vol. XXII, No. 21, Sec. I (July 1, 1941), p. 1271.

tion (both finished goods and work in process inventories).  The balance
of this account represents the net variation for the period, which
serves as an index of efficiency for the concern's operation during this
time.

That this method was in somewhat of a state of confusion in 1925 is
suggested by its treatment in a pamphlet, "Cost Accounting Through the
Use of Standards," by the Department of Manufacture of the Chamber of
Commerce of the United States.  In presenting the accounting for standard costs, the author employed three plans of procedure.  Two of these
plans made use of some of the principles of this method:

Typical Plan 1 contained three Work-in-Process accounts, which were
debited and credited in the following manner:

| Accounts | Debits | Credits |
|---|---|---|
| Work in Process-<br>  Material | Actual costs | Standard costs ad-<br>  justed to actual |
| Work in Process-<br>  Labor | Actual Labor costs | Standard costs |
| Work in Process-<br>  Overhead | Standard costs | Standard costs |

Typical Plan 2 likewise employed three Work-in-Process accounts,
which were debited and credited as follows:

| Accounts | Debits | Credits |
|---|---|---|
| Work in Process-<br>  Material | Standard costs | Standard costs |
| Work in Process-<br>  Labor | Actual Labor costs | Standard costs ad-<br>  justed to actual |
| Work in Process-<br>  Overhead | Standard costs | Standard costs |

A careful consideration of these plans will indicate that neither may be classified wholly under this method; however, since at least one of the accounts is charged with actual costs, these plans have been somewhat arbitrarily presented under this classification.[93]

Camman condemned this method because he declared that it permitted cost variations to be concealed until a count of the work in process was made at the end of the period and that, in view of this lapse of time in awaiting the computation of the work in process inventory, much of the value of the information was lost.[94]

Sabin (1933), Works Accountant for the Walker Manufacturing Company, employed this method in his application of standard costs to machine shops and foundries.[95] Kearsey (1933), the English author, also accepted this accounting procedure as the basis for recording standard costs in the accounts when he published his text.[96]

Gillespie (1935) designated this procedure as "Method A: Charging Process at Actual and Crediting at Standard," while Lawrence (1937) termed this technique "Method 2--Variance Entries After Work in Process Entries."[97]

-----

[93]"Cost Accounting Through the Use of Standards," Chamber of Commerce of the United States, Washington, D. C., 1925, pp. 26-39.

[94]See Proceedings, International Congress on Accounting, 1929, pp. 876-877.

[95]Sabin, R. M., "Standard Costs for Machine Shops and Malleable Foundries," National Association of Cost Accountants Bulletin, Vol. XV, No. 7, Sec. I (December 1, 1933), pp. 393-411.

[96]Kearsey, op. cit., pp. 123-127.

[97]Gillespie, op. cit., pp. 23-37; Lawrence, op. cit., pp. 367-371.

Langer varied this method of recording standard costs with his
plan, "Segregating or Isolating Variations when the Product is Completed,"
by charging the Goods in Process account with the actual cost of material, labor, and manufacturing expense and by making the following journal entry when the finished goods were transferred from the factory to
the stock room:[98]

```
            Finished Goods (at Standard)          xxxx
            Variations--Dr. or Cr.                xxxx
               Goods in Process (at Actual)              xxxx
                  To record the transfer of finished
               goods, with actual cost divided as to
               standard and variations.
```

An analysis of this method indicates that the unfinished product is left
in the Goods in Process account at actual costs, while the variations
apply to the finished goods only.

Blocker (1940) pointed out that this method might be used in either
of the following cases satisfactorily:

a. The use of three accounts, one each for Materials in
   Process, Labor in Process and Overhead Expense in Process,
   in enterprises which are not departmentalized.
b. The use of a single work in process account for each production department or operation in departmentalized concerns.[99]

The principal merit that may be suggested for the method of charging the Work-in-Process account with actual costs and crediting this

---

[98] Langer, <u>op</u>. <u>cit</u>., p. L 22-1.

[99] Blocker, <u>op</u>. <u>cit</u>., p. 581.

account with standard figures is its simplicity and minimum daily accounting routine; however, this plan is limited as an aid to management
since the effectiveness of the standards cannot be ascertained until the
close of a fiscal period, at which time a comparison can be made of
actual and standard costs and the variances can be determined.

(b) Work in Process Charged at Standard and Credited at Standard.
Under this accounting procedure, the Work-in-Process account (accounts
may be used for each cost component--materials, labor, and burden) is
charged with the standard costs of materials, labor, and burden in operations completed and is credited with the standard cost of the finished
goods. In this way, the balance of this account represents the final
inventory of work in process valued at standard figures--the differences
between actual and standard cost of material, labor, and burden were
computed and transferred to variance accounts concurrently with the recording of charges to the Work-in-Process account.

That this procedure was employed as early as 1925 is evidenced by a
publication, "Cost Accounting Through the Use of Standards," of the
Department of Manufacture, Chamber of Commerce of the United States.
This pamphlet not only explained this method but also contained necessary ledger accounts for illustrating the routine that would be followed.[100]

Downie (1927), the English writer, designated this cost accounting
plan as "Method A"--". . . a mechanism . . . whereby . . . all factory
costs are carried in the books at standard or predetermined values"[101] --

---

[100]Op. cit., pp. 28-52.

[101]Downie, op. cit., p. 22.

and presented not only a chapter of explanation but also a section including sixteen forms for recording such factory costs.[102]

Maynard (1927), in explaining the cost system used by the Gillette
Safety Razor Company, presented a standard cost plan which required a
Work-in-Process account for each of the three cost components--material,
direct labor, and burden--and which recorded cost data in these accounts
only at standard values.[103]

When Amidon and Lang (1928) came to the accounting procedure for
their standard cost system, they employed three Work-in-Process accounts
(one each for material, labor, and manufacturing expense), which they
debited and credited with standard figures.  Maze and Glover (1929) used
one Work-in-Process (Controlling Account) account but debited and credited this account with standard values.[104]

Reitell (1933), in explaining his bookkeeping for standard costs,
presented only one accounting method--the charging and crediting of Work-
in Process accounts (he presented an account for each factory department
but not for each cost component) for standard figures only.[105]

Dohr, Inghram and Love (1935) termed this method "The Single Plan"
--". . . the ledger accounts covering the production activities are kept
in terms of standards and variances"; Gillespie (1935) devoted two

---

[102] Ibid., pp. 25-42, 64-80.

[103] Maynard, op. cit., pp. 542-563.

[104] Amidon and Lang, op. cit., pp. 273-282; Maze and Glover, op. cit.,
pp. 329-331.

[105] Reitell, op. cit., pp. 388-416.

chapters to the treatment of this technique, "Method B: Charging Process at Standard and Crediting at Standard"; and Lawrence (1937) indicated this procedure as "Method 1--Variance Entries Prior to Work in Process Entries."[106]

Although Paul E. Gnaedinger (1935), a Canadian industrial engineer, recognized the two other types of standard cost methods, he accepted "Method B" (Process Account Debited and Credited at Standard and Differences Charged to Variation Accounts) as the most comprehensive--"since the variations and manufacturing cost inefficiencies are shown up directly in the income and profit and loss statements, thereby possibly attaching greater importance and laying more emphasis on any inefficiencies which are revealed."[107]

The two Australian authors, Schumer (1935) and Gregory (1940), presented only this method for treating standard costs in the accounting records. They would charge the Work-in-Process account with the quantity of goods manufactured at Standard Cost Card Value (for material, labor and overhead) and would credit this account with the quantity of finished goods at standard cost, thus leaving in this account the standard value of the work in process.[108]

When Bennett (1936), Manager of the Cost Accounting Division of

---

[106] Dohr, Inghram and Love, _op. cit._, p. 478; Gillespie, _op. cit._, pp. 39-54 and 145-164; and Lawrence, _op. cit._, pp. 358-365.

[107] Gnaedinger, Paul E., "Standard Costs," _Cost and Management_, X (1935), 297.

[108] Schumer, _op. cit._, pp. 228-257; Gregory, _op. cit._, pp. 33-40.

Cooley and Marvin, outlined a cost plan for the knitting industry, he
accepted standard costs only for the records and declared that the cost
variances should not be made a part of the cost figures or cost of sales
at any point.[109]

Other writers of cost accounting texts to include this method in
their publications were:  Langer (1938), Schlatter (1938), Van Sickle
(1938), Blocker (1940), and Neuner (1942).[110]

A careful consideration of this method--Charging and crediting Work
in Process at Standard--will indicate that it provides the technique for
making the fullest possible use of standard costs for reducing the expense of maintaining cost records--stores records may be kept in quantities only; material requisitions may have standard costs printed on the
forms and, thus, pricing may be eliminated; and standard cost cards for
orders may remove the necessity for analyzing material requisitions and
time tickets.  And, finally, the variances are recognized and recorded
immediately, which fosters the application of corrective measures.

After this rather detailed development of the types of cost standards and of the methods employed for recording the cost information in
the accounts, it has been deemed desirable to indicate the procedures
that are followed in practice.  The data for this consideration were

------------------------------

[109]Bennett, Clinton W., "A Cost Plan for the Knitting Industry,"
National Association of Cost Accountants Bulletin, Vol. XVIII, No. 3,
Sec. I (October 1, 1936), pp. 143-166.

[110]Langer, op. cit., pp. L 22:3-4; Schlatter, Advanced Cost Accounting, pp. 114-122; Van Sickle, op. cit., pp. 476-513; Blocker, op. cit.,
pp. 609-615; and Neuner, op. cit., pp. 517-527.

taken from a study by the Research and Technical Service Department of
the National Association of Cost Accountants in 1940.[111]  The following
quotation will suggest the extent of the sample as selected by this research group:

> This report summarized the practices of 325 industrial
> companies, representing a wide variety of industries.  While
> small as well as large companies are included in this group,
> the majority of the companies would be classified as large or
> medium sized.[112]

In presenting the methods of cost accounting as used by these companies, the following schedule has been reproduced from the study with
respect to absolute figures and has been computed by the present writer
with respect to relative amounts.

Methods of Cost Accounting Used by
325 Industrial Companies

| Cost Accounting Methods | Absolute[113] | Relative |
|---|---|---|
| Job Costs ............. | 66 | 20.31 |
| Process Costs ......... | 67 | 20.62 |
| Ideal or Current<br>Standard Costs ...... | 103 | 31.69 |
| Basic or Measure<br>Standard Costs ...... | 21 | 6.46 |
| Various combinations of<br>Job, Process and<br>Standard Costs ...... | 44 | 13.54 |
| Unclassified .......... | 18 | 5.54 |
| No answer to this<br>question ........... | 6 | 1.84 |
| Totals .......... | 325 | 100.00 |

---

[111] "Finished Goods Inventory Practice," *National Association of
Cost Accountants Bulletin*, Vol. XXI, No. 14, Sec. III (March 15, 1940),
pp. 927-956.

[112] *Ibid.*, p. 927.

[113] *Ibid.*, p. 928.

Although the writer recognizes the danger of drawing conclusions from data of this nature--number of companies rather than the relative importance of such companies in the industrial world--he does deem it practicable to offer this information as evidence that standard costs are rather important in computing cost data and that the current standard methods are the more important of the two general classifications of standard costs.

_The Principle of Exceptions in Standard Costs._  Perhaps the most important and most valuable phase of Standard Cost Accounting is the comparison of the actual costs with the standard costs and the analysis of the causes of the differences--variances.  In this respect, standard cost accounting represents the application of the _principle of exceptions_ to cost accounting.

The importance of the "exception principle" was called to the attention of the industrial executive by Taylor as early as 1911 in the following manner:

> It is not an uncommon sight, though a sad one, to see the manager of a large business fairly swamped at his desk with an ocean of letters and reports, on each of which he thinks that he should put his initial or stamp.  He feels that by having this mass of detail pass over his desk he is keeping in close touch with the entire business.  The exception principle is directly the reverse of this.  Under it the manager should receive only condensed, summarized, and invariably comparative reports, covering, however, all of the elements entering into the management, and even these summaries should all be carefully gone over by an assistant before they reach the manager, and have all of the exceptions to the past averages or to the standards pointed out, both the especially good and especially bad exceptions, thus giving him in a few minutes a full view of progress that is being made, or the reverse, and leaving him free to consider the broader

lines of policy and to study the character and fitness of the important men under him.[114]

Harrison (1918) recognized the significance of this principle as is evidenced by this assertion:

> Reports to executives should be based on the principle of exceptions and in place of providing a mass of detailed and undigested information should be drawn up to indicate clearly and unmistakably where exceptional or abnormal conditions exist.[115]

In contemplation of this principle, Harrison made this statement in 1922:

> . . . cost information should be thoroughly predigested before it is handed to the executive. Information relative to cost variations in the finest detail should be available for the executive, but this detailed information should be strictly supplemental. The cost statements should be so arranged that these details can be instantly obtained when required, but at the outset the mind of the executive should not be confused by a mass of figures.[116]

And continuing this theme, Harrison wrote Section 27, "Cost and Profit Variation Formulas," of the Management's Handbook (1924).[117] In introducing his subject, the author pointed out the importance of variations between actual and standard costs as a means of disclosing inefficies:

---

[114]Taylor, Frederick Winslow, *Shop Management*, New York, Harper and Brothers, 1911, p. 126.

[115]Harrison, G. Charter, "Cost Accounting to Aid Production," *Industrial Management*, LVI (1918), 281.

[116]Harrison, G. Charter, "Working Plans for Standard Costs," *Management Engineering*, III (October, 1922), 227.

[117]*Op. cit.*, pp. 1382-1400.

In brief, this method of cost accounting is based upon the
_principle of exceptions_ and renders it possible for the cost
accountant to sift from the great mass of his cost data the
essential facts needed by the management.[118]

Following this statement, he proceeded to develop formulas for computing

thirteen cost variations--Calendar Variations, Idle Time, Production

Efficiency, Labor Rate Variations, Labor Time Variations, Material

Prices, Material Quantities, Variations in Number of Set-Ups, Variation

in Set-Up Times, Distributive Expense, Expense-Miscellaneous, Salaries-

Rates, and Salaries-Staff--and to design a "Variation Analysis Sheet"

for compiling these variations and an "Operating Efficiency Statement"

for presenting this information to the manufacturing executive.

Alford (1928) accepted this principle--the "law of exceptions" as

expressed by him--with the following statement:

> Managerial efficiency is greatly increased by concentrating
> managerial attention solely upon those executive matters
> which are variations from routine, plan, or standard.[119]

Isaacson (1932) defined the standard cost plan as "the management

of a concern by the 'Theory of Exceptions'" and undertook to support his

thesis with a series of illustrations that followed very closely G.

Charter Harrison's technique as presented in his book, _Standard Costs_.[120]

---

[118] _Ibid._, p. 1382.

[119] Alford, L. P., _Laws of Management Applied to Manufacturing_, New
York, The Ronald Press Company, 1928, p. 74.

[120] Isaacson, L. E., "A Standard Cost Layout as Planned for a Medium-
Sized Organization," _National Association of Cost Accountants Bulletin_,
Vol. XIV, No. 8, Sec. I (December 15, 1932), pp. 602-627.

Lawrence (1937), in recognizing the principle of exceptions, stated that management should undertake to correct exceptional conditions while operations that met standard should require relatively little attention.[121]

Blocker (1940) has restated the "principle of exceptions" in a very pertinent manner:

> The principle of exceptions assumes that actual perform-ance which meets the standard time or rate is satisfactory and that only those activities which fail to come up to stand-ard or which exceed standard are worthy of executive atten-tion. Thus the attention of management may be focused on important cases of exception from standards; operations which meet standard or which approach standard performance so closely that the variances are negligible may be ignored. Daily reports of labor and materials can be so arranged that the foreman of each production center and the supervisor of each department can see off-standard conditions and can in-vestigate excessive costs before they have continued for any length of time.[122]

In the application of the principle of exceptions, authors of cur-rent cost literature have provided for the compilation, presentation, and disposition of the variances between the actual costs and the stand-ard costs of production. Additional consideration of this subject will be undertaken in the following chapters on the accounting for materials, labor, and burden under standard costs.

The Relation of Standard Costs to Budgets. The relationship between standard costs and budgets has not always been clearly understood or uni-versally accepted as adhering to a single concept or principle. In view of the fact that the two terms are commonly associated together, it has

---

[121]Lawrence, op. cit., p. 351.

[122]Blocker, op. cit., p. 558.

been deemed desirable to consider briefly some of the ideas with respect
to their relationship.

McKinsey (1927), in accepting the terms "standards" and "budgets"
as practically synonymous--attention should be called to his recognition
of the possibility for some distinction--made the following statement:

> In the broadest sense, all standards are budgets and all
> budgets are standards. When a standard is established, you
> are in effect setting up a goal which you wish to reach or a
> measuring stick of your activities. When you establish a
> budget, you are doing the same thing. Whether or not your
> budgeted cost would be different from your standard cost de-
> pends upon the basis upon which you established your standard
> cost. If the standard cost is established on a basis of your
> average production over a period of years, and your budgeted
> cost is established on a basis of what you expect to do dur-
> ing the period, then there may be a difference between the
> two.[123]

Harrison (1923) expressed the same general idea in this manner:

> There is no basic difference between standard costs and
> budgets. They are both based upon the fundamental idea of
> predetermination as opposed to the old idea of reporting
> events after they have happened.[124]

However, in a later publication (*Standard Costs*, 1930), he suggested
some distinction between the objectives of these two devices when he
pointed out that "standard costs furnish the factory superintendent and
the factory foreman with this information as regards factory costs, and
standard profit or budget systems give the executive this information as

---

[123] See *National Association of Cost Accountants Yearbook*, 1927,
p. 250.

[124] *Ibid.*, 1928, pp. 289-290.

regards profits."[125]

On the other hand, Camman was emphatic in asserting that standard costs and budgets were not identical:

> There is a distinction between budgets and standard costs which is not always clearly understood. The terms are not synonymous. A budget may be used without embodying standard costs. Standard costs are not necessarily budgeted or expected costs. The only instance in which the terms are synonymous is that wherein budgeted burden rates are used for computing standard costs. For that purpose the burden budget is a necessary preliminary calculation.
>
> It is usually found when standard costs are used that budgets and budgetary methods will also be adopted, because both procedures have in common the object of better management through planning toward definite ends, regulating performance according to definite expectations, and recognizing effectiveness in accomplishment. Budgets are the logical accompaniment of standard costs.[126]

Williams (1934)--in his publication, _The Flexible Budget_--made a rather sharp distinction between standard costs and budgets.[127] MacDonald (1939)--another writer of budgetary literature, _Practical Budget Procedure_--recognized a rather close relationship between standard costs and budgeting but rejected standard costs as a substitute for budgeting. The following quotation is indicative of these two writers' trend of thought:

> The entire scheme of standard costs rests on what has been called the principle of exceptions, namely, the recording

---

[125]Harrison, _Standard Costs_, p. 28.

[126]Camman, _Basic Standard Costs_, p. 12.

[127]Williams, John H., _The Flexible Budget_, New York, McGraw-Hill Book Company, 1934, pp. 74-82.

only of variations from the standards.  The standards are adjusted to correspond to changes in operations, in piece rates,
and in standard times for day-work jobs.  They are usually
refigured periodically.  They serve as a goal or par for attainment or betterment in the actual cost of each product and
operation, and as a yardstick with which to measure the relative economy of each.  Standard costing is an ally of budgeting, ably supports it, and should really be considered a part
of it, but standard costs alone do not constitute a budget.[128]

Dohr, Inghram and Love (1935) recognized some relationship between

standard costs and budgets, as may be gained from a consideration of the

following quotation:

> The budget is essentially an instrument of financial
> "control" and in its preparation careful estimates are made
> of expected sales, factory output, and distribution, adminis-
> tration and financial costs.  Standard costs are essentially
> an instrument of efficiency measurement and in their use ac-
> tual performance is compared with a standard and the differ-
> ences between actual and standard are resolved into "vari-
> ances" based upon the cause of such differences.  While the
> objectives of standard and budgetary accounting are, at the
> outset, separate and distinct, it will be found that in
> actual operation there is a very close relationship between
> the two procedures.[129]

Neuner (1942), after characterizing budgetary control, pointed out

some distinction between this device and standard costs:

> . . . the budget adopts the same point of view as that taken
> by standard cost techniques; the attempt to set up a predeter-
> mined standard of operations in general is a budget, while
> the setting of predetermined costs per unit of various
> products is called setting standard costs.  The two proce-
> dures can be seen to be part and parcel of the same attitude

---

[128]MacDonald, John H., _Practical Budget Procedure_, New York,
Prentice-Hall, Inc., 1939, p. 14.

[129]Dohr, Inghram and Love, _op. cit._, p. 500.

and aim; the difference consists largely in technical variations of method, and the scope of the intended operation.[130]

Paton (1943) stated that "a distinction should be noted between the
standard costs as applied to budgeting and those used in standard cost
accounting."[131]

McFarland has expressed the relationship between standard costs and
budgets in a very concise manner, as may be evidenced by a consideration
of the following quotation:

> . . . Both budgeted costs and standard costs are predeter-
> mined costs and represent applications of the managerial prin-
> ciple that calls for pre-planning of activities. The princi-
> ple difference lies in the scope of the terms, for "budget"
> is a much broader word than "standard cost." Budgeting gen-
> erally comprises the setting of objectives for all aspects of
> income and expense whereas standard costs include only the
> regular operating expenses. Capital expenditures, sales reve-
> nues, and cash collections and disbursements are budgeted,
> but these figures are rarely called standards. Furthermore,
> standard costs are generally unit costs whereas budgeted
> costs are aggregate costs for a specified volume of product
> or a period of operation. This is perhaps what might be ex-
> pected when it is remembered that standard costs evolved in
> the factory whereas budgeting had its development in the
> financial, administrative, and selling divisions of business
> organizations.[132]

After presenting these contrary declarations with respect to the
relationship between standard costs and budgets, this study has adhered
to the philosophy of Camman, Paton and McFarland and, although conceding

---

[130] Neuner, _op. cit._, p. 503.

[131] Paton, _Accountants' Handbook_, p. 1170.

[132] McFarland, Walter B., "The Basic Theory of Standard Costs," _The
Accounting Review_, XIV (June, 1939), 155-156.

the importance of budgeting as a distinct managerial procedure, has
classified the presentation of that group of principles associated with
budgetary control as outside the realm of standard costs and has undertaken to develop only those techniques that are considered peculiar to
and necessary for standard costs.

<u>Advantages of Standard Costs</u>. Coincident with the development of
standard costs, a number of advantages have been proposed as available
for industrial enterprises that employ this cost procedure:

1. Standard costs facilitate the pricing of the annual inventories
--raw materials, work in process, and finished goods (Worrall, 1923).

2. Standard costs can be installed with but little change in the
general accounts, stock records, and production statistics (Rea, 1923).

3. By the use of cost formulas, in connection with standard costs,
the cost accountant is able to compile information to show not only that
inefficiencies exist, but also the cost and underlying causes of these
inefficiencies (Harrison, 1924).

4. Standard costs provide for analytical study and compilation of
data respecting detailed cost elements that furnishes valuable information for executives, engineers, and designers (Brugger, 1925).

5. The standards, although subject to revision as conditions require, are uniform in principles for all time--he was employing basic
standards (Brugger, 1925).

6. Standard costs serve as a means of controlling inventories
(Camman, 1926).

7. Reveals waste, due to spoiled work, through a variance account

(Camman, 1926).

8. Standard costs reduce the clerical work necessary for the operation of a cost system (Amidon and Lang, 1928).

9. Standard costs furnish the factory superintendent and his foremen with information regarding the relative efficiency of the operators
in the various departments (Harrison, 1930).

10. Standard costs reduce the cost of operating the cost department
of a concern as compared with job-order plan (Harrison, 1930).[133]

Reitell (1930), in considering the standard cost plan of accounting,
discussed ten advantages of this procedure.  These advantages will be
enumerated in the words of the author:

1. Standard cost place emphasis on costing performance rather
   than on costing product.
2. Standard costs produce live, dynamic data as contrasted
   with dead, static information as comes from the so-called
   actual cost systems.
3. Standard costs nip in the bud inefficiencies and leaks.
4. Standard costs offer a tool whereby management can increase the productive capacity of the plant.
5. Standard costs set up a scientific method for controlling
   overhead expense.
6. Standard costs take full advantage of "The Exception Principle" in industry.
7. By use of standard costs the sales and merchandising divisions are given more reliable data.
8. Standard costs aid the control and recording of materials.
9. Standard costs administer the psychological injection that
   makes the whole organization "cost-conscious" and "per-
   formance-minded."

---

[133] Worrall, op. cit., p. 10; Rea, op. cit., p. 15; Harrison, in
Management's Handbook, op. cit., p. 1395; Brugger, op. cit., p. 15;
Camman, Uses of Standard Costs, pp. 449 and 452; Amidon and Lang, op.
cit., p. 284; Harrison, Standard Costs, pp. 11 and 15.

10. Standard cost plans are cheaper to operate and are the
ultimate in simplicity.[134]


The _Cost and Production Handbook_ (1934) enumerated, with pertinent

comments, sixteen purposes and advantages of standard cost methods.

These enumerated merits will be reproduced as follows:


1. To aid in standardization of products, of methods, and of
processes.
2. To focus attention on variations from established standards of production cost and factory expense.
3. To provide a means of analysis of variations, by causes.
4. To simplify costing procedure and, thereby, to lower cost
of operating cost system.
5. To provide information with greater promptness.
6. To provide a common unit of comparison of labor costs.
7. To set normal plant capacities.
8. To provide a uniform base of comparison for all cost elements.
9. Determination of the rate and direction of cost trends.
10. More accurate cost, and simple costing procedure, in
evaluating investments in inventories.
11. Greater practical benefit to the sales division in furnishing more accurate, and stable, costs as a basis for
establishing selling prices.
12. Provides a basis for the determination of idle equipment
or idle capacity expense, which can then be eliminated
from current production cost.
13. Provides objectives for all divisions of business.
14. Net profits can be predicted and variations from the predicted results can be analyzed by causes.
15. Assists sales and general executives to more effective
control by concentrating on exceptions from standards.
16. Promote cooperation and coordinate the efforts of all
divisions of a business as no other agency has succeeded
in doing in the past.[135]

---

[134]Reitell, Charles, "Advantages and Disadvantages of the Standard
Cost Plan of Accounting," _National Association of Cost Accountants Year-
book_, 1930, pp. 152-157.

[135]See Alford, in _Cost and Production Handbook_, op. cit., pp. 1119-
1121.

And, finally, Van Sickle (1938) has listed some of the outstanding

advantages of a standard cost system as follows:

1. The details that accompany the operation of the older
   types of actual cost systems are largely dispensed with.
2. The costs are predetermined before production takes place
   rather than having to wait until after production is completed to obtain the actual costs.
3. The analyses of the cost variances are invaluable in disclosing to the management the details of operating efficiency or inefficiency.[136]

Weaknesses in Standard Costs. After the enumeration of the advan-

tages that may be derived from the use of standard costs, it has been

deemed desirable to consider the weaknesses, disadvantages, and/or limi-

tations that have been called to the attention of students of this sub-

ject.

Brugger (1925) suggested the following limitation that applied to

standard costs; however, a careful consideration of this statement will

tend to minimize its importance.

The standard cost plan seems best adapted for use in a
plant manufacturing a rather limited number of standard articles in very large quantities requiring very few main classes
of material. As the articles manufactured increase in number,
as articles of special design for specific customers' requirements are introduced, and as the number of classified accounts
for materials is increased, the standard cost system becomes
less attractive from the standpoint of economy.[137]

Reitell (1930) recognized two disadvantages that might be encountered

---

[136] Van Sickle, op. cit., p. 437.

[137] Brugger, op. cit., p. 14.

in the use of standard costs:

> (1) By using standard costs we substitute estimates and fore-
> casts for the results of actual experience; and
> (2) Where any industry produces a large variety of products
> it becomes almost impossible to revise standards more
> frequently than annually.  This means that standard costs
> have an average lag of six months in reflecting price
> changes in raw material, changes in labor rates, and revi-
> sions in overhead save as these changes show up in vari-
> ances.[138]

Lawrence (1930) proposed the following weaknesses in standard costs, "not because of any opposition to the theory of standard costs that is gaining widespread adoption, but because it is felt that something may be gained by looking into the opposite side of the question":

> 1. . . . the desire to use standard costs without actual
> costs as a check upon them.  Too many people look on a
> standard cost as a magic thing that you can pick out of
> the air, by means of which you can get rid of all your
> troubles.
> 2. . . . too great reliance upon an untrained and uncompre-
> hending human element that is not mentally equipped to
> carry out the work required in a proper handling of a
> standard cost system.
> 3. . . . looking upon standard costs as an easy and cheap way
> out of accounting difficulties.
> 4. . . . (1) desire for speedy reports, and (2) the wish for
> low operating expenses in connection with the accounting
> and cost department.  These two ends are exactly opposite
> to each other in their final result.  If you want speedy
> reports, you must expect to pay a price for them; if you
> want to cut down accounting expense, you cannot expect
> speedy reports.[139]

---

[138] See _National Association of Cost Accountants Yearbook_, 1930, p. 157.

[139] Lawrence, W. B., "Weaknesses in Standard Costs," _National Association of Cost Accountants Bulletin_, Vol. XI, No. 22 (July 15, 1930), pp. 1493-1494 and 1496.

And, finally, Van Sickle (1938) indicated two criticisms that might be applied to standard costs:

> Standard costs are indicted as being arbitrary and fictitious since they are not actual costs, and as being misleading when reflected in inventories and the cost of goods sold. . . .
>
> The argument cannot be refuted, that the standard cost plan results in the monthly inventory values of goods in process and finished goods being shown at an arbitrary standard cost rather than at actual cost.[140]

Summary. A consideration of this chapter will indicate that standard costs do not represent the development of a new system of cost accounting but rather the application of scientific techniques to the job order and process systems of cost accounting, which had, heretofore, been maintained on a historical basis.

In this development of the types of standards, the methods of recording standard cost data, and the treatment of variances, endeavor has been made to present adequately the broader features that are encountered in a study of standard costs. The subsequent chapters on material, labor, and burden will undertake a more comprehensive analysis of these subjects as applied to the respective cost components.

---

[140] Van Sickle, op. cit., p. 436.

CHAPTER VII

ACCOUNTING FOR MATERIALS IN STANDARD COSTS

The term "materials," as comprehended in this study, will consist
of any goods which have been purchased by a manufacturer or converter
with the intention of applying conversion operations before such commodities will be offered for sale.  Such goods may be raw materials, or
partially fabricated products secured from other processing enterprises,
and may be charged directly to specific jobs, processes, or commodities.

> For an item of raw material to be classified as direct mate-
> rial, it must be possible to measure the cost of the material
> that is applicable to each unit of product or job manufac-
> tured.  If the material cannot be charged directly to some
> production cost order number, then it cannot be classified as
> a direct material.[1]

With respect to the accounting for materials, accounts and records
may be so devised that their status may be determined at any required
stage of production from the time such materials enter raw materials,
through work in process, into finished goods, and, finally, as a part of
cost of sales.  In the case of the application of standard costs to this
procedure, the technique ordinarily provides for the measurement of the
efficiency of the character and the quality of the materials as well as
the degree of competence exhibited in their purchase, maintenance, and
utilization.  The information gathered through the use of such methods

---

[1] Van Sickle, *op. cit.*, p. 65.

furnishes not only a basis for costing the particular product but also enables management to make pertinent comparisons with respect to material conversion efficiency.

In contemplation of a system of accounting for materials that will fulfill these requirements, a procedure must be undertaken that will follow rather closely the physical steps employed in the handling of them. The designing of such a system will take into consideration the establishing of material standards for the products manufactured, the control of materials prior to their entrance into the manufacturing operations, the accounting for materials in process, the comparison of actual with standard costs, and the disposition of any variances from such standard figures.

Setting Material Cost Standards.--The determination of the standard material cost of a commodity includes at least two important factors-- the kind and quantity of the material required for the product's manufacture, and the price of such material.

As early as 1925, the setting of quantity standards was recognized to be a real problem, as has been indicated in a study published by the Chamber of Commerce of the United States.[2] This pamphlet proposed several means that might be employed in determining such standards:

> Job Cost. Where a job cost or actual cost method has previously been in use the cost sheets will present a source of data, but usually these cost sheets must be studied with care if reliable figures for the quantities of materials used are to be obtained. . . .

----

[2]Cost Accounting Through the Use of Standards, op. cit., p. 20.

   <u>Process Costs</u>. Where actual costs have previously been
obtained by the process method, as is the case where products
are made continuously, and not in lots or separate orders,
the process cost sheets should reveal information on which to
base standards for use of materials; in fact, in many cases
process cost sheets are likely to be found more satisfactory
for this purpose than similar job cost sheets where job costs
are kept.

   <u>Test Runs</u>. Where no systematic cost system has previously been in use, it may be necessary to rely for material
standards on test runs. Under this plan a certain quantity
of material is put in process, a careful record is kept, and
the quantity of the finished product obtained therefrom is
recorded. . . .

   <u>Analyses</u>. A fourth method for the obtaining of information on material quantities is afforded by mechanical and
chemical analyses and mathematical computations. . . .[3]

William L. Churchill (1927), a consulting engineer, advanced the

opinion that the compilation of standard costs for materials represented

the simplest of the major cost factors but, in his discussion, he pro-

ceeded to present only the price elements--market value on date of trans-

fer, incoming freight, carrying charges, and standard wastes--that enter

into such costs. However, his efforts at this time suggest a recogni-

tion of the problem by this writer.[4]

In recognition of the increasing importance attached to the intel-

ligent setting of standards and of the paucity of information connected

with this subject, the National Association of Cost Accountants spon-

sored a contest, which was designated as the Jordan Prize Competition,

--------

[3]<u>Ibid</u>., pp. 20-21.

[4]Churchill, William L., "Materials in Standard Cost," <u>National
Association of Cost Accountants Bulletin</u>, Vol. VIII, No. 21 (July 1,
1927), p. 984.

in 1931.  This competition, which was open only to members of the Association, provided for the selection of the three best essays on the subject, "How to Set Standards."

The winner of the first prize, Herbert J. Myers, recognized two
standards with respect to materials--quantity standards and price standards.  He suggested that the engineering department determine the standard quantity of material for each product to be made by a careful analysis of such commodity rather than by a consideration of past performance.
With respect to standards of price, he recognized two broad classes of
products--raw materials purchased in the open market at market prices
and valued for standard cost purposes at the average price for a complete business cycle; and special materials and parts required for a
definite product and valued according to the contract price at the time
manufacture was begun.  For this author, the standard price would be
changed only if some discovery, invention, or new method instituted a
permanent reduction in the price of the commodity.  William L. Keating
and J. C. Metsch, the other writers contributing winning essays in this
contest, expressed identical ideas as those advanced by Myers.  Therefore, these essays tend to establish the thinking at this time with
respect to setting standards for this cost element.[5]

In 1937, Keating again considered this subject by stating that the
determination of standards, under either the basic system of standard
costs or the expected (ideal) system, was the same in the beginning;

---

[5] Myers, Keating and Metsch, _op_. _cit_., pp. 1-98.

that is, the kind and quantity of material is specified and is priced at

the unit figure as determined for the period projected:

> Adjustment to new standards under the ideal system in-
> volves setting up new unit prices and extending new standards,
> while under the basic system, adjustment would be expressed
> as a percentage of previously established standards.  The
> kind and quantity remain permanent until engineering or de-
> signing changes compel revision.  Price changes are usually
> reflected in standards when decided trends indicate some de-
> gree of permanence at higher or lower levels.[6]

Coincident with Keating's presentation, B. M. Sayre, Controller of

Vilter Manufacturing Company, noted the importance of material specifi-

cation.[7]

> This specification should be prepared by the engineering de-
> partment and should at one time detail such information as is
> required by all departments concerned.  It should be univer-
> sally usable.  It should provide data for engineering, pur-
> chasing, manufacturing, stores, shipping, costing and selling.[8]

In contrast with some thinkers on the subject of material price

standards, Sayre placed the responsibility for the setting of this stand-

ard in the cost department rather than in the purchasing department.

If so prepared, a basis is established whereby purchase price
variance is truly indicative.  The variance should be divided

---

[6]Keating, William L., "Controversial Points in Treatment of Materials Under a Standard Cost System," _National Association of Cost Accountants Yearbook_, 1937, pp. 88-89.

[7]Sayre, B. M., "Material Control as Exercised by the Controller's
Department," _National Association of Cost Accountants Yearbook_, 1937,
pp. 64-76.

[8]_Ibid._, p. 66.

between market changes, lack of or over-production and faulty buying.[9]

In treating the subject of standards for material costs, the views of some authors of recent textbooks on cost accounting will indicate the trend of thought. With respect to the setting of quantity standards, Amidon and Lang (1928), Harrison (1930), Lawrence (1937), and Van Sickle (1938) gave this duty to the engineering department; Gillespie (1935) allotted it to the engineering and planning departments; and Blocker (1940) and Neuner (1942) placed this function in the engineering department but subject to verification by chemical and mechanical analyses or by test runs. With respect to price standards, Gillespie (1935) delegated this task to a group of marketing experts; Van Sickle (1938) placed this responsibility with the cost department; Blocker (1940) based this standard on executive judgment, assisted by statistical and forecasting data; and Neuner (1942) permitted the purchasing or stores department to set material price standards.

The Accountants' Handbook, in discussing the setting of standards for materials,[10] likewise recognized quantity and price standards for this cost element. With respect to quantity standards, this publication made the following assertion:

> Quantity standards for direct materials are based on definite
> written data set initially on engineering specifications,
> blue prints and bills of material. If not originally available

---

[9] Ibid., p. 73.

[10] Op. cit., pp. 229-234.

written <u>specifications</u> and bills of material should be prepared for each part, subassembly, major assembly, mix formula,
process, etc., showing material class, analysis, stock dimen-
sions, and quantity required.[11]

In connection with material price standards, the following quota-

tion from the same authority is indicative of the current trend of

thought:

> Material-price standards under the basic-standard cost plan
> are set at the inception of the system on the basis of mini-
> mum or long term averages and are not ordinarily revised for
> each accounting period. Material-price standards under the
> current-cost standard plan are usually set to be effective
> for a period of one year. Generally the prices are estab-
> lished by the purchasing department, with the bases approved
> by the management. . . . Where materials are purchased on
> contracts the <u>contract</u> <u>prices</u> should apply. . . . Prices of
> materials which fluctuate widely in price may be stabilized
> by long term contracts, but where such contracts are not in
> effect prices are set in accordance with current price levels
> and probable trends as forecasted for the period. . . . The
> price standard must include <u>transportation charges</u> to the
> plant . . . unless the amounts are of minor importance and
> the clerical work required for accurate allocation is exces-
> sive in the light of possible increased accuracy to be
> gained.[12]

Earl L. Green (1938) proposed a special department in the indus-

trial organization with the specific function of accumulating and corre-

lating the production and engineering data from which the standard mate-

rial specifications might be written. From these specifications, a list

of materials might be drafted and might be made the basis for a forecast

by the purchasing department as to the average unit prices to be paid

---

[11]Ibid., p. 229.

[12]Ibid., p. 234.

during the period in which the standards were to be effective.[13]

Paul E. Gnaedinger (1935), a Canadian industrial engineer, advocated that price standards, when once established, should remain unchanged during the fiscal period in order that the standard costs, as
determined during any portion of the period, might be comparable.  Furthermore, in case of new materials being added to the standard material
list during the year, this writer stated that the standard prices thereof should be set on a basis equivalent to that used when the original
standards were established rather than to current data.[14]

J. G. Blocker (1936) thought that quantity standards, when carefully and correctly set, should remain unchanged as bases for measuring
efficiency until there had been a change in the quality of materials
used, a new invention, or a variation in the processing procedure.[15]

Control of Materials.--After the quantity and price standards have
been established for each product to be manufactured, consideration
should be given to the method of control that will be employed in the
maintenance of this cost element.  This method must recognize two phases
of material control--physical requirements and accounting procedure.

Although the physical phase of material control is beyond the contemplation of this study, it may be noted that provision must be made in

---

[13]Green, Earl L., "Objectives of Standard Costs and Their Use in
Measuring Performance," Cost and Management, XIII (September, 1938),
246-247.

[14]Gnaedinger, op. cit., p. 293.

[15]Blocker, J. G., "Budgeting in Relation to Standard Costs," The
Accounting Review, XI (June, 1936), 119.

the physical layout of the plant for satisfactory space, equipment, and bins for a well planned stock room, that supervision of this department must be placed with a responsible stock-room clerk, and that adequate assistance must be given to this individual for the proper maintenance of stock and for the accurate preparation of records.

In discussing the subject, "Accounting for Materials," before the International Congress on Accounting in 1929, Rohrbach[16] stated:

> All of the authoritative writers who have discussed the sub-
> ject are in agreement as to the procedure and methods includ-
> ing the types of the various records necessary to control the
> material element, because the methods are more or less stand-
> ardized.

In view of the fact that this writer has enumerated the records required for an adequate control of materials and has included pertinent summarizations for these records, a rather lengthy quotation covering this phase of material control has been taken from his paper:

1. Purchase Requisitions, which are a definite notice from
   the individual or department requiring the material, to
   the Purchasing Department or Executive in charge of seeking out and placing the order for the material.
2. Purchase Orders, which are a definite notification from
   the Purchasing Department or the executive responsible for
   the buying, to the source of supply.  Necessary routine
   having to do with prices, terms, quantities, shipping details, dates, grade of material having been supplied and
   confirmed by the purchasing department and the shipper.
3. Reports of Material Received, which are often in the nature of Receiving Slips showing exactly the quantity,

---

[16]Rohrbach, John F. D., "Accounting for Materials," Proceedings International Congress on Accounting, New York, International Congress on Accounting, 1930, pp. 811-826.

grade and type of material which has been received in the
Receiving Department.

4. Invoices from Shippers or Creditors, which are supported
   by the previous records, that is the Purchase Requisition
   and Purchase Order and the Receiving Slip or Report of
   Material Received.

5. Purchase Invoice Record or Voucher Record Register, which
   is the recognized financial accounting record for providing for a register or compilation of all purchases so that
   the liability may be followed through intelligently.

6. Raw Stock Records, which are often kept in duplicate, a
   detailed set of controlling Stock Records being kept in
   the general office or under the supervision of the Cost
   Department, these being supported by a second set which
   are often in the nature of Stock Records which are kept
   right at the bins where the raw stock items are stored.

7. Material Requisitions or Reports of Materials Consumed,
   which are the notice to the cost office or general office
   that certain materials have been transferred from stock,
   to operating floors for a definite use. . . .

8. Credit Reports or Material Transfer Reports, which would
   show transfer of materials back to raw stock from operating floors, or transfers of material from one department
   to another.

9. Inventory Records, which would show a classification and
   list all the materials on hand at a given period of time
   when an inventory is required. . . .[17]

In applying these material records to standard costs, the receiving

of materials brings into use the first important record in the account-

ing procedure. In view of the fact that this form, Reports of Material

Received, represents the initial point of accounting for the physical

material, it not only should contain information necessary for the iden-

tification of the particular physical material but also should accumu-

late data for recording the quantities and values involved.

Urich (1936), in describing an accounting procedure for materials,

stressed the importance of the Receiving Report and pointed out that it

---

[17]Ibid., pp. 812-813.

might be prepared in as many copies as the departmentalization of the organization required.[18]  Accepting three as the minimum number to be prepared, he would retain one in the storeroom and would forward two to the cost department.  One of the cost department's copies would be used as a basis for checking the invoice for quantities and would be forwarded, together with the vendor's invoice, to the accounting department for vouchering.  The second copy, as received by the cost department, would be used as a basic accounting record and would be provided with space for accumulating both standard and actual costs.

With respect to the handling of Material Requisitions, Service (1930) presented very clearly a practical system as used by the Norton Company.[19]  After the stock room clerk had indicated on the material requisition the actual quantity issued, the accounting department recorded the actual and standard prices and the standard quantity, as stated in the standard part cost record.  Extensions were made from these data for three costs--(1) actual cost: actual quantity at actual price; (2) standard cost of actual quantity: actual quantity at standard price; and (3) standard cost of standard quantity: standard quantity at standard price.  These requisitions became not only the media for journal entries but also the means for determining material price trends and

---

[18]Urich, John E., "Accounting for Productive Materials," _National Association of Cost Accountants Bulletin_, Vol. XVII, No. 9, Sec. I (January 1, 1936), pp. 487-491.

[19]Service, Robert S., Jr., "How Should Material Cost Variations be Recorded and Treated?," _National Association of Cost Accountants Yearbook_, 1930, pp. 159-162.

material usage efficiency currently by the application of statistical

devices.

In view of the fact that the utilization of these records will vary

somewhat depending upon the standard cost method employed, any addi-

tional consideration thereof will be deferred until such need may arise

in the presentation of the various cost methods.

<u>Materials in the Records at Actual Costs</u> (<u>Work in Process Charged</u>

<u>with Actual and Credited with Standard Costs</u>).--Materials may be carried

in the stores records at actual cost, at standard values, or at both

actual and standard figures.  In a recent questionnaire by William L.

Keating,[20] as completed by 142 members of the National Association of

Cost Accountants, a preference for recording purchases at actual costs

was suggested--charged at actual cost 65%, at standard cost 28%, and at

both actual and standard costs 7%.  With respect to practice, this ques-

tionnaire disclosed a similar condition--recorded at actual cost 77%, at

standard cost 19%, and at both actual and standard costs 4%.

If this cost element is valued at actual costs in the stock records,

the accounting for the issuance of materials will vary according to

whether the issues are charged to work in process at actual or standard

values.  The results of the Keating questionnaire indicated a rather

strong preference for issuing materials at actual costs--charged at

actual costs 69% (average cost basis 32%; first-in, first-out basis 27%;

last-in, first-out basis 4%; and current market basis 6%) and at standard

---

[20]See "Controversial Points in Treatment of Materials Under a Standard Cost System," <u>National Association of Cost Accountants Yearbook</u>, 1937,
pp. 91-92.

values 31%--and a comparable situation as existing in practice--charged
to work in process at actual cost 80%, and at standard values 20%.

The first method to be considered will record the purchases of materials in the stores account at actual values, will charge the issues of
materials to the work in process accounts at actual cost, and will
credit these accounts with the standard values of the goods completed.
In order to illustrate the procedure that may be used under this method,
the following data will be assumed:

1. Five hundred units of Raw Material R, with a standard
   value of $2.00 each, were purchased for $2.10 each.
2. Four hundred ten units of Raw Material R were issued during the period.  The standard for the production during
   this time amounted to four hundred units.
3. Finished Product M required a standard quantity of four
   units of Raw Material R each.
4. The inventory of work in process at the end of the period
   amounted to twenty units of Product M, partially processed
   but fully completed with respect to materials issued.
5. Finished products transferred to the warehouse consisted
   of eighty units of Finished Product M.

To record the purchase and receipt of the raw materials, the following journal entry would be made--a general journal is used in these
illustrations; the book of initial record would depend upon the accounting records maintained--from the data supplied by the Purchase Requisition, the Purchase Order, the Vendor's Invoice, and the Report of Materials Received, all of which would comprise the support for the voucher
authorizing this particular entry:

                Materials--Raw Material R          1,050.00
                    Vouchers Payable                              1,050.00
                        To record the purchase of
                    five hundred units of Raw Mate-
                    rial R, with a standard value
                    of $2.00 each, for $2.10 each.

As the materials were issued, Material Requisitions were prepared

and were employed as the basis for the journal entry (or entries) giving

effect to the transfer of such materials from the stock room to the fac-

tory:

                Materials in Process                861.00
                    Materials--Raw Material R                      861.00
                        To record the issuance of four
                    hundred ten units (standard for
                    production four hundred units) of
                    Raw Material R at actual cost of
                    $2.10 each.

As the products were completed, the Material in Process account

would be cleared of the quantity transferred by crediting this account

with the standard value of such finished goods.  In the case under con-

sideration, it was assumed that eighty units of Finished Product M (re-

quiring a standard quantity of four units of Raw Material R each) were

transferred.  The journal entry to record this transaction would be as

follows:

                Finished Goods                      640.00
                    Materials in Process                           640.00
                        To record the completion of eighty
                    units of Finished Product M, requiring
                    three hundred twenty standard units of
                    Raw Material R at a standard cost of
                    $2.00 each.

At the close of the fiscal period, an inventory of work in process
would be taken and an adjusting entry would be made to transfer such
inventory, valued at standard cost, to a Work in Process Inventory account, according to Blocker[21]--to a Work in Process Clearing account,
according to Gillespie.[22]  In this case, it has been assumed that the
inventory contained twenty units of Finished Product M, partially processed but fully completed with respect to materials issued:

```
Work in Process Inventory                160.00
    Materials in Process                         160.00
        To record the final inventory of
    materials in process of twenty units of
    Product M, partially processed but
    fully completed as to materials--eighty
    standard units of Raw Material R at the
    standard cost of $2.00 each.
```

If these transactions may be posted to the Materials in Process
account, a clearer conception of what has occurred will be gained:

Materials in Process

| Issues at actual cost | 861.00 | Finished Goods trans-<br>ferred at Standard Cost | 640.00 |
| --- | --- | --- | --- |
| | | Materials in Process at<br>Standard Cost | 160.00 |

The balance of this account, sixty-one dollars, represents the net
difference between actual and standard costs of materials for the fiscal
period's production.  This amount may be left, until the books are closed,
in this account, may be transferred to a Material Variation account in

---

[21] Blocker, _Cost Accounting_, p. 582.

[22] Gillespie, _Accounting Procedure for Standard Costs_, p. 25.

total, or may be analyzed as to price and quantity variations and be

closed in the following manner:

```
Material Price Variation                        41.00
    Materials in Process                                    41.00
        To record the amount of variation in
    the Work in Process account for materials
    due to actual price of Raw Material R
    exceeding the standard price:
        410 units issued at actual cost of
            $2.10 each                          861.00
        410 units issued at standard cost
            of $2.00 each                       820.00
                Price Variation                  41.00


Material Quantity Variation                     20.00
    Materials in Process                                    20.00
        To record the amount of variation in
    the Work in Process account for materials
    due to actual quantity issued exceeding
    the standard quantity required for the
    period's production:
        410 units (actual) at $2.00 each        820.00
        400 units (standard) at $2.00 each      800.00
                Quantity Variation               20.00
```

Various names have been given to these variation accounts. Gilles-

pie[23] has referred to them as "Materials-Price Variation" and "Materials-

Quantity Variations"; Langer[24] as "Stores-Price Variation" and "Direct

Materials-Quantity Variation"; Neuner[25] as "Material Price Variation"

and "Material Quantity Variation"; Blocker[26] as "Material Price Variance"

---

[23]Ibid., p. 29.

[24]Langer, op. cit., p. L 22-3.

[25]Neuner, Cost Accounting, p. 526.

[26]Blocker, Cost Accounting, p. 582.

and "Material Quantity Variance"; and Van Sickle[27] as "Material Price Variance" and "Material Usage Variance."

After these entries for recording the material variations, analyzed as to quantity and price, have been posted to the Materials in Process account, it will be noted that this account will be closed.  The disposition of these variations will be considered in a subsequent section of this study.

Schlatter characterized this procedure as the "Single Manufacturing Method"[28]--he used only one manufacturing account, which was charged with materials, direct labor, and burden at actual cost and which was credited with the standard cost of these elements in the finished goods --and selected it as the simplest method of including standards in the accounts.

In preparing this analysis of recording materials in the records at actual costs, the publications by the following authors have been considered rather carefully:  Blocker, Gillespie, Langer, and Van Sickle.[29]

<u>Materials</u> <u>in</u> <u>the</u> <u>Records</u> <u>at</u> <u>Standard</u> <u>Costs</u>.--In undertaking this method of recording material costs, attention must be called to the fact that the material purchases may be charged to the accounts controlling stores at either actual or standard values; however, as the materials

---

[27]Van Sickle, <u>op</u>. <u>cit</u>., p. 507.

[28]Schlatter, <u>Advanced Cost Accounting</u>, pp. 112-115.

[29]Blocker, <u>Cost Accounting</u>, pp. 581-599; Gillespie, <u>op</u>. <u>cit</u>., pp. 23-27; Langer, <u>op</u>. <u>cit</u>., pp. L 22:1-3; Van Sickle, <u>op</u>. <u>cit</u>., pp. 435-447.

are issued, the entries to record the transfer of such materials to the
factory will be valued at standard figures under either of the alternatives for recording stores initially.

1. Stores Records Charged at Actual but Issues of Stores Charged to
Materials in Process at Standard.--Under this circumstance, the recording of purchases of materials would be identical with that of the preceding case.  If the data, as assumed for illustrating the former method of
recording material cost, may be employed for presenting this case, the
journal entries, as required for materials, may be made in the following
manner.

```
Materials--Raw Material R                1,050.00
   Vouchers Payable                                  1,050.00
      To record the purchase of five
   hundred units of Raw Material R,
   with a standard value of $2.00
   each, for $2.10.
```

In this case, the record of unit price will be kept at both actual
and standard figures.  The actual unit price will appear on the Materials Requisition in order that the material account may be credited
properly, while the standard unit price will be included thereon in
order that the Material in Process account may be charged correctly. In
the present instance, the journal entry for issuing the materials would
be as follows:

```
Materials in Process                        820.00
Material Price Variation                     41.00
    Materials--Raw Material R                            861.00
        To record the issuance of four hun-
    dred ten units of Raw Material R:
    410 units at actual cost of $2.10
            per unit                         861.00
    410 units at standard cost of
        $2.00 per unit                       820.00
            Material Price Variation          41.00
```

The subsequent entries for recording material costs would be identical with those of the former method, would reflect the final inventory
of materials in process at standard value, and would disclose the material quantity variation but not the material price variation (this variation was recorded when the materials came into process).  Therefore,
these journal entries will not be repeated.

Van Sickle found two merits in this plan--the stores inventory may
be kept at actual cost (the basis as desired by the management of some
concerns) and the price variance represents the difference between actual and standard cost that is applicable to the materials actually consumed.  This author recognized a like number of disadvantages--the price
record must be kept both at actual and at standard values, and the stores
requisitions must be priced both at actual and at standard figures.[30]

Blocker advocated that this method--the pricing of materials at
actual cost on the stores records and the issuing of them at standard
values--be adopted in order that the stores records would not have to be
adjusted each time a new standard material price was established.  He

-----------

[30]Van Sickle, op. cit., p. 443.

saw, also, an advantage in being able to compute the price variation of
materials actually processed between the materials and work in process
accounts.[31]

Langer varied this procedure somewhat by charging materials in
process at the standard cost of the standard quantity of materials in
production and by carrying any discrepancy to a Material Variation account. In the case at hand, the following entry would be made for the
issuance of the materials:

```
Materials in Process                          800.00
Material Variation                             61.00
    Materials--Raw Material R                             861.00
        To record the issuance of four hun-
        dred ten units (the standard for the
        period's production) of Raw Material R
        at cost of $2.10 each (standard $2.00
        each):
        410 units (actual) at $2.10 (actual)  861.00
        400 units (standard) at $2.00
            (standard)                         800.00
                Material Variation              61.00
```

The author stated that this Material Variation account might be
analyzed according to its primary causes--price and quantity variations.
He designated this technique as Method B.[32]

After Van Sickle's Material in Process account had been adjusted
for Material Quantity Variation (twenty dollars in this illustration)
and had been credited with the standard cost of finished goods, and after
Langer's Materials in Process account had been credited with the standard

---

[31]See The Accounting Review, XI, 121.

[32]Langer, op. cit., pp. L 22:2-3.

cost of finished goods, the balance of each of these authors' Materials

in Process account would represent the work in process inventory for

this particular cost element (direct materials) valued at standard

figures.

In the handling of direct materials, Amidon and Lang described a

rather unique method of recording this cost component under standard

costs.[33]  Although materials were recorded in the stores account ini-

tially at actual cost, the requisitions were priced both at actual

```
Stores                                    1,050.00
    Vouchers Payable                                1,050.00
        To record the purchase of five
    hundred units of Raw Material R at
    actual cost of $2.10 each.
```

and at standard values and two entries were made at the end of the cost

period to record the summary of the requisitions:

```
Variations from Standard-Material          861.00
    Stores                                            861.00
        To record the actual value of stores
    issued:  410 units (actual) at $2.10
    (actual) each.

Work in Process-Material                   820.00
    Variation from Standard-Material                  820.00
        To charge work in process with the
    standard value of stores issued:  410
    units (actual) at $2.00 (standard)
    each.
```

A consideration of the Variation from Standard-Material account,

---

[33]Amidon and Lang, op. cit., pp. 275-280.

after these entries have been posted, will indicate that its balance

represents the variation from the standard due to price differences only.

The Stores account, which has been debited and credited with actual

costs, carries a balance that represents the final inventory of mate-

rials valued at actual cost.  The Work in Process account is credited

with the standard value of the finished goods and contains a balance

equivalent to the final inventory of materials in process valued at

standard figures.

It is rather interesting to note that Maze and Glover used this

same procedure--they employed the "Material Variation Account" instead

of Amidon and Lang's "Variation from Standard-Material" account--to

record raw material variations in their presentation of standard costs.[34]

A more logical procedure for charging the Work in Process-Materials

account with only the standard cost of operations performed, so far as

materials are concerned, was designed by Henry W. Maynard (1927).[35]  In

order to illustrate his technique, the assumed data will be used as the

basis for the necessary journal entries.

```
Stores Account                            1,050.00
    Accounts Payable                                1,050.00
        To record the purchase of five
        hundred units of Raw Material-R
        at actual cost of $2.10 each.
```

---

[34]Maze and Glover, op. cit., pp. 329-331.

[35]See "The Accounting Technique for Standard Costs," National Association of Cost Accountants Bulletin, Vol. VIII, No. 12, Sec. I (February
15, 1927), pp. 547-554.

```
Scheduled Material in Process           861.00
    Stores Account                              861.00
        To record the actual value of stores
    issued: 410 units (actual) at $2.10
    actual) each.

Work in Process                         800.00
    Scheduled Material in Process               800.00
        To charge the work in process account
    with the standard cost of standard quan-
    tity of material in operations performed:
    400 units (standard) at $2.00 (standard)
    each.
```

The author stated that the balance of the Scheduled Material in
Process account represented the variance from standard cost and that
this variance would be closed to a Profit and Loss account--he suggested
"Variance from Standard Cost--Material."  That the author anticipated
the analysis of this variance is indicated by the fact that he presented
two variance accounts for materials--"Purchase Loss and Gain" and "Manufacturing Loss and Gain."[36]

Newlove and Garner (1941), in following Maynard's general concept,
exemplified the journal entries in a much clearer manner than had been
done before.[37]  The following journal entries would be made by these
authors to record the case under consideration:

```
Raw Materials                           1,050.00
    Vouchers Payable                            1,050.00
        To record the purchase of five
    hundred units of Raw Material-R at
    actual cost of $2.10 each.
```

---

[36]Ibid., pp. 546-552.

[37]Newlove and Garner, op. cit., p. 450.

| | | |
|---|---|---|
| Scheduled Raw Materials | 861.00 | |
|    Raw Materials | | 861.00 |

      To record the actual value of stores issued: 410 units (actual) at $2.10 (actual) each.

| | | |
|---|---|---|
| Materials in Process | 800.00 | |
|    Scheduled Raw Materials | | 800.00 |

      To charge the work in process account with the standard cost of standard quantity of material in operations performed: 400 units (standard) at $2.00 (standard) each.

| | | |
|---|---|---|
| Price Variations--Raw Materials | 41.00 | |
|    Scheduled Raw Materials | | 41.00 |

      To record the amount of variation in " scheduled raw material account due to actual price of Raw Material-R exceeding the standard price:

| | |
|---|---|
| 410 units issued at actual cost of $2.10 each | 861.00 |
| 410 units issued at standard cost of $2.00 each | 820.00 |
|     Price Variation | 41.00 |

| | | |
|---|---|---|
| Efficiency Variations--Raw Materials | 20.00 | |
|    Scheduled Raw Materials | | 20.00 |

      To record the amount of variation in scheduled raw material account due to actual quantity issued exceeding the standard quantity required for the period's production:

| | |
|---|---|
| 410 units (actual) at standard cost of $2.00 each | 820.00 |
| 400 units (standard) at standard cost of $2.00 each | 800.00 |
|     Efficiency Variation | 20.00 |

Under this procedure, the Material in Process account would be charged with the standard cost of production and would be credited with the standard cost of goods completed. Any balance in this account would represent the Work in Process inventory valued at standard cost figures.

Schlatter, in his Multiple Account Method, presented a somewhat different method of recording the issuance of materials and the variations from standard,[38] as may be gained from applying the data of the hypothetical case:

| | | |
|---|---|---|
| Materials Variation A | 861.00 | |
|     Materials-Raw Material R | | 861.00 |

       To record issuance of four hundred ten units of Raw Material R (four hundred units the standard for production) at actual cost of $2.10 (standard cost $2.00) per unit.

| | | |
|---|---|---|
| Materials in Process | 800.00 | |
|     Materials Variation A | | 800.00 |

       To charge the manufacturing account with the standard quantity of materials of four hundred units priced at the standard cost of two dollars per unit.

The Finished Goods account would be charged with the standard cost of the materials in the products completed during the period and the Materials in Process account would be credited with the same amount. The balance of this account would represent the Work in Process Inventory for materials valued at standard cost.

The balance of the Materials Variation A account would represent the difference between the actual and standard cost of materials put into the manufacturing process during the period. This balance, according to the author, was analyzed for price variance and for usage variance. His method for such analysis followed the customary procedure, which has been illustrated already.

2. Stores Records Charged at Standard and Credited at Standard.--If

---

[38]Schlatter, *Advanced Cost Accounting*, pp. 115-117.

the materials in the stores accounts are valued on a standard cost basis,
the purchase invoices must be priced at the standard figures before the
entry recording such purchase is recorded in the materials account.  In
the example, which has been used before, the entry to record the receipts of this purchase would be as follows:

```
Materials--Raw Material R                          1,000.00
Materials Price Variation                             50.00
    Vouchers Payable                                             1,050.00
        To record the purchase of five hun-
        dred units of Raw Material R at $2.10
        (standard value $2.00) each:
            500 units at actual of $2.10           1,050.00
            500 units at standard of $2.00         1,000.00
                    Price Variation                   50.00
```

Van Sickle recognized the difficulty of obtaining the data for this
journal entry and proposed a scheme for solving the problem as well as
two procedures for recording the facts in the accounting records.[39]  In
the first place, he prepared the following schedule for ascertaining the
standard cost and material price variation figures (data are for above
example, slightly varied, but with the totals identical with the amounts
in the original case).

PURCHASE INVOICE COST AND STANDARD COST
COMPARATIVE PRICE RECORD

| Vendor's Invoice Price | | | Standard Cost Price | | | Material |
| Quan-tity | Unit Price | Actual Cost | Quan-tity | Unit Price | Standard Cost | Price Variance |
|---|---|---|---|---|---|---|
| 100 | $2.50 | $ 250 | 100 | $2.00 | $ 200 | $50 (Dr.) |
| 200 | 1.90 | 380 | 200 | 2.00 | 400 | 20 (Cr.) |
| 200 | 2.10 | 420 | 200 | 2.00 | 400 | 20 (Dr.) |
| 500 | 2.10 | $1,050 | 500 | 2.00 | $1,000 | $50 (Dr.) |

---

[39]Van Sickle, op. cit., pp. 443-447.

After this information had been obtained, the author recorded the
invoices in the voucher register and indicated the actual cost, the
standard cost, and the material price variance.  As an illustration, his
voucher register, with the present writer's illustration, would be as
follows:

VOUCHER REGISTER

| Accounts Payable (Actual) Credit | Material Price Variance Debit or Credit | | Stores Inventory (Standard) Debit |
|---|---|---|---|
| $  250 | (Dr.) | $50 | $  200 |
| 380 | (Cr.) | 20 | 400 |
| 420 | (Dr.) | 20 | 400 |
| $1,050 | (Dr.) | $50 | $1,000 |

This author's alternative plan was to record the invoices in the
voucher register at actual cost only, to compute the price variance on
each invoice, to recapitulate these price variances at the end of the
period, and to make such adjusting entry as might be necessary to reflect the standard cost values in the materials accounts.  In the example heretofore used, the entries for such recordings, under this procedure, would be as follows:

| | | |
|---|---|---|
| Materials-Raw Material R | 1,050.00 | |
|     Vouchers Payable | | 1,050.00 |
|         To record the purchase of five hundred units of Raw Material R at actual cost of $2.10 each. | | |
| Material Price Variance | 50.00 | |
|     Materials-Raw Material R | | 50.00 |
|         To credit the materials account with the excess of actual cost over standard cost, in order to reflect the standard cost price of purchases in the materials account. | | |

Van Sickle recognized a disadvantage in this method of carrying raw materials because net profit was somewhat misstated--the price variance was based upon materials purchased during the month rather than upon the amount consumed during the corresponding period.  If it became desirable to remove this discrepancy from the records, the author outlined a technique that might be followed.  Using the current case, journal entries will be made to illustrate his concept:

```
Materials-Raw Material R                        1,000.00
Material Price Variance Adjustment                  50.00
    Vouchers Payable                                           1,050.00
        To record the purchase of five hundred
    units of Raw Material R for $2.10 (stand-
    ard $2.00) each at standard value and to
    indicate the variance in an inventory ad-
    justment account.

Materials in Process                              820.00
    Materials-Raw Material R                                     820.00
        To record the issuance of four hundred
    ten units of Raw Material R at standard
    cost of $2.00 each.

Material Price Variance                            41.00
    Material Price Variance Adjustment                            41.00
        To record the unfavorable price vari-
    ance applicable to materials used during
    the period.
```

By using this plan, both the actual and the standard costs of the materials inventory at the end of the period are known and the net profit for the period is stated more accurately than in the preceding case.  It should be noted that the Material Price Variance Adjustment account is complementary to the Materials account and, when these two accounts are taken together on the balance sheet, they tend to reflect

the actual cost of the materials inventory.  In the case under consideration, these accounts would give the following results as shown on the
balance sheet:

Current Assets:

        Material Inventory at Standard              180.00
        Material Price Variance Adjustment            9.00
            Material Inventory at Actual Cost                 189.00


Langer designated this procedure as Method C, recognized the resulting discrepancy, but failed to make any provision for an adjustment as
Van Sickle had done.[40]  Blocker and Neuner, who explained this method
rather thoroughly, neither recognized the discrepancy nor undertook to
make any adjustment for disclosing it.[41]

In addition to the initial entry in this section, these authors
would make the following journal entries to record the issuance of direct materials and the delivery of finished goods to the warehouse:

        Materials in Process                        800.00
        Material Quantity Variation                  20.00
            Materials-Raw Material R                         820.00
                To record the issuance of four hun-
                dred ten units (standard for production
                was four hundred) of Raw Material R at
                standard value of $2.00 each.

---

[40] Langer, op. cit., pp. L 22:8-9.

[41] Blocker, Cost Accounting, pp. 523-527; Neuner, Cost Accounting,
pp. 609-612.

<pre>
Finished Goods                                       640.00
    Materials in Process                                      640.00
        To record the completion of eighty
    units of Finished Product M, requiring
    three hundred twenty standard units of
    Raw Material R at standard cost of
    $2.00 each.
</pre>

After these entries had been recorded, the balance of the Materials

in Process account represented the final inventory of Work in Process,

valued at standard cost, for this cost component.  The difference be-

tween the actual and standard values would be recorded in two accounts:

(a) The Material Price Variation account, with a debit balance of

fifty dollars, indicated the excess of actual over standard cost for

materials purchased during the period rather than the variance for mate-

rials actually processed during the particular time.

(b) The Material Quantity Variation account, with a debit balance

of twenty dollars, represented the excess of actual over standard issues

of materials during the period.

Schlatter[42] would make the following entries for recording material

costs under this method:

<pre>
Materials-Raw Material R                   1,000.00
Material Price Variation                      50.00
    Vouchers Payable                                   1,050.00
        To record purchase of five hundred
    units of Raw Material R at $2.10
    (standard $2.00) and to indicate the
    variation due to price.
</pre>

---

[42] Schlatter, _Advanced Cost Accounting_, pp. 117-118.

            Materials Usage Variation A              820.00
                Materials-Raw Material R                      820.00
                    To record the transfer of the actual
            quantity of materials at standard price.

            Material in Process                        800.00
                Materials Usage Variation A                   800.00
                    To record the transfer of the stand-
            ard quantity of materials at standard
            price.

Under this procedure, the raw materials are carried at standard value, the material price variation for purchases is recorded in a separate account, the standard materials in process are stated at standard values, and the excess of actual over standard quantity of materials used is left in the Materials Usage Variation account.

A rather interesting deviation from these methods of recording materials in the accounts at standard values has been presented by John E. Urich, a cost accountant with varied phases of responsible and practical experience.[43]  His methods will be illustrated by journal entries containing the data from the hypothetical case.  When the goods have been received, the Receiving Report would accumulate both the actual and standard cost of the purchase and would form the basis for two journal entries:

            Purchasing Profit and Loss Account      1,050.00
                Vouchers Payable                              1,050.00
                    To record the purchase of five
            hundred units of Raw Material R at
            actual cost of $2.10 each.

---

[43]See "Accounting for Productive Materials," National Association of Cost Accountants Bulletin, Vol. XVII, No. 9, Sec. I (January 1, 1936), pp. 487-494.

```
Inventory of Raw Materials                      1,000.00
    Purchasing Profit and Loss Account                      1,000.00
        To charge the Materials account with
    the standard cost of purchases:  five
    hundred units at standard cost of $2.00
    each.
```

At the time the materials are transferred to the factory, the Material Requisition would be priced at standard values and would be the basis for the following journal entry:

```
Material Utilization Account                     820.00
    Inventory of Raw Materials                               820.00
        To record the transfer of four hundred
    ten units (actual) of Raw Material R to
    the factory at standard cost.
```

The Material Utilization account serves as a means for determining the use efficiency of materials.  For this author, the materials do not become a part of materials in process until they have passed through the first operation--"the operation which identifies the material with a unit or product or a shop order."  This account is charged with the total actual issues valued at standard cost, as has been seen, and is credited with the standard quantity, at the point of first operation, valued at standard cost and with the standard value of offal, by-product, and/or waste.  In this case, the standard value of standard materials in production amounted to eight hundred dollars.

```
Materials in Process                             800.00
    Material Utilization Account                             800.00
        To record the standard value of materials
    in production: four hundred units at $2.00
    each.
```

In order to continue this writer's thesis, the hypothetical case
may be amended to assume that the standard value of waste obtained at
the end of the first productive stage amounted to five dollars.

<pre>
        Waste Inventory                          5.00
          Material Utilization Account                   5.00
            To record the standard value of
          waste recovered from the first manu-
          facturing process.
</pre>

A consideration of Urich's "Material Utilization Account" indicates
that its balance represents the variance from standard due to material
usage efficiency.  The subsequent entries for recording finished goods
parallel the method already presented.

Ranald G. Rucker declared that it was logical to record materials
at standard cost and thus to eliminate the price variation at the time
of acquisition,[44] while R. E. Love, a Canadian writer, offered two reasons for keeping the material ledger at standard values:

> First--it is necessary for those working on the material
> ledger to enter in the material cost variance record the dif-
> ference between standard and actual.  This gives us a com-
> plete picture of the ability of the purchasing department or
> the trend of costs quickly.  Second--it means that the mate-
> rial requisitions for parts to be used in the manufacturing
> of the products can be entered more quickly because there is
> only one standard price. . . . The standard is set and used
> constantly.[45]

---

[44] Rucker, Ranald G., "Cost Analysis by Standards in the Accounts,"
The Accounting Review, XIV (December, 1939), 374.

[45] Love, R. E., "Standard Costs," Cost and Management, VI (1931),
261.

In discussing the basis for charging raw materials into production costs, Kemp offered the following advantages that might be gained from employing standard costs:

> 1. It furnishes a basis on which to establish standard material cost values in the finished parts and completed product inventory, the loss or gain on materials purchased for manufacture being accounted for at the time of their receipt to the extent that their cost varies from the standard prices established. Moreover, these losses and gains are easily shown for management purposes by classes of materials.
> 2. It simplifies cost accounting, as one value remains in force over a considerable period of time and can be applied to the cost of product the moment an order or part of an order is completed. This feature is of great importance when departmental accounting is carried on, as standard values permit the debits and credits between departments being made at the time the product is transferred.
> 3. It does away with the variation in material costs on production orders and puts cost on a fair comparative basis. Under this method the variation in the cost of materials shown on the comparative cost record is due only to more or less material being used on the order than the amount allowed, thereby showing conclusively manufacturing efficiency or lack of it.[46]

<u>Materials in the Records at Actual and Standard Costs</u>.--As has been pointed out in the presentation of Harrison's early treatment of standard costs, materials may be recorded in the accounts at both actual and standard prices and the relationship between such values may be indicated by percentages. In order to illustrate this method, journal entries, following Gillespie's presentation,[47] will be prepared to record the following assumed data for materials:

---

[46]Kemp, W. S., "On What Basis Should Raw Material be Charged into Production Costs?," <u>National Association of Cost Accountants Yearbook</u>, 1923, pp. 176-177.

[47]Gillespie, <u>Accounting Procedure for Standard Costs</u>, pp. 251-272.

1. The beginning inventory of Raw Material R consisted of
   five hundred units with a standard cost of $2.00 and an
   actual cost of $2.10.
2. Purchases:  Four hundred units at $2.32½ each.
3. Issues:  Six hundred twenty units (standard for production amounted to six hundred units) during the period.
4. Finished Product F requires two units of Raw Material R.
5. Two hundred forty units of Finished Product F were completed and delivered to the warehouse.

When the invoice is received, the standard price of materials would

be recorded thereon and the following journal entry would be made.  (If

a voucher system were used, proper columns for standard figures would be

provided as has been suggested by Van Sickle in the reproduction hereto-

fore presented.)

|  | Actual Debits | Actual Credits | Standard Debits | Standard Credits |
|---|---|---|---|---|
| Materials | $930 | | $800 | |
|    Vouchers Payable | | $930 | | |
|    Standard Clearing Account | | | | $800 |

     To record the purchase of
five hundred units of Raw
Material R for $2.32½ (stand-
ard cost $2.00).

After this journal entry, in dual form, had been posted, the mate-

rials account for this particular item would show the following informa-

tion:

### Materials - Raw Material R

| | Actual | Standard | Ratio | | Actual | Standard | Ratio |
|---|---|---|---|---|---|---|---|
| Inventory | $1,050 | $1,000 | 105 | | | | |
| Purchases | 930 | 800 | 116 | | | | |
| Total | $1,980 | $1,800 | 110 | | | | |

A consideration of this account will indicate that the concern had available during the period materials valued at $1,980 (actual cost) and $1,800 (standard figures) and that the ratio between these two sums was one hundred ten per cent. The journal entry to transfer the materials to the factory would contain both actual and standard values--the issues would be priced at standard and the adjustment ratio (110% in this case) would be applied to ascertain the actual amount:

|  | Actual | | Standard | |
|---|---|---|---|---|
|  | Debits | Credits | Debits | Credits |
| Materials in Process | $1,364 | | | |
| Standard Clearing Account | | | $1,240 | |
| Materials--Raw Material R | | $1,364 | | $1,240 |
| To credit materials with actual and standard cost of actual quantity of Raw Material R issued and to charge the actual column of Work in Process with the actual cost of that quantity: | | | | |
| Requisitions priced at standard: 620 units at $2.00 | | $1,240 | | |
| Price ratio from materials account applied to this figure: 110% of $1,240 | | 1,364 | | |

The posting of the credits for this journal entry to the materials account will leave a balance, which represents the final inventory valued at actual and standard figures:

Materials - Raw Material R

| | Actual | Standard | Ratio | | Actual | Standard | Ratio |
|---|---|---|---|---|---|---|---|
| Inventory | $1,050 | $1,000 | 105 | Issues | $1,364 | $1,240 | 110 |
| Purchases | 930 | 800 | 116 | Inventory | 616 | 560 | 110 |
| | $1,980 | $1,800 | 110 | | $1,980 | $1,800 | 110 |
| Inventory | $ 616 | $ 560 | 110 | | | | |

At the end of the fiscal period, the operations completed would be determined (have been assumed here to be the equivalent of finished products that would employ six hundred units of Raw Material R) and the following journal entry would be made to record the standard cost of the standard quantity of materials used:

|  | Actual | | Standard | |
|---|---|---|---|---|
|  | Debits | Credits | Debits | Credits |
| Materials in Process |  |  | $1,200 |  |
|    Standard Clearing Account |  |  |  | $1,200 |

     To charge the standard column of Work in Process account with the standard cost of operations completed --equivalent to six hundred units of Raw Material R at $2.00.

After these entries have been posted to the Materials in Process account, the debit side of this account (as may be verified below) will contain an actual cost of issues of $1,364 and a standard cost of $1,200 with a relationship between these two amounts expressed as 113.67% for the Adjusting Ratio of materials in process.

### Materials in Process

| | Actual | Standard | Ratio | | Actual | Standard | Ratio |
|---|---|---|---|---|---|---|---|
| Issues | $1,364 | $1,200 | 113.67 | Completed | $1,091 | $ 960 | 113.67 |
| | | | | Inventory | 273 | 240 | 113.67 |
| | $1,364 | $1,200 | 113.67 | | $1,364 | $1,200 | 113.67 |
| Inventory | $ 273 | $ 240 | 113.67 | | | | |

As stated in the hypothetical case, two hundred forty units of Finished Product F (requiring a standard total of four hundred eighty units of

Raw Material R) were completed and transferred to the warehouse. The
journal entry, which has been posted to the above account for Materials
in Process, for recording the finished goods would be as follows:

|  | Actual | | Standard | |
| --- | --- | --- | --- | --- |
|  | Debits | Credits | Debits | Credits |
| Finished Goods | $1,091 | | $ 960 | |
| Materials in Process | | $1,091 | | $960 |
| To record the actual and standard cost of raw materials in goods completed during the period: | | | | |
| 240 units of Finished Product F at $4.00 | | | $ 960 | |
| Adjusting ratio for materials in process applied to this factor: 113.67% of $960 | | | 1,091 | |

The Standard Clearing Account, as employed by Gillespie, served as
a balancing account and made possible a trial balance of standard debits
and credits. At the end of each fiscal period, this account was balanced
in the same manner as the inventory accounts.

It should be noted that this method employs basic or bogey standards,
which are, theoretically, permanent. In view of the fact that both
actual and standard figures are recorded in the accounts, variations do
not make their appearance as in the other methods of recording standard
costs in the books of a concern. However, provision is usually made to
present percentages of variation between actual and standard costs of
production as efficiency indexes--to be compared with comparable ratios
for previous periods. Gillespie computed three ratios[48] with respect to

---

[48] Ibid., p. 264.

materials for disclosing the operational results to management:

(a) Overall Ratio.--This ratio is taken from the debit side of the Work in Process account--113.67% in this case--and is suggestive of the price and quantity relationship.

(b) Material Price Ratio.--This figure is obtained from the debit side of the Materials account--110% in this instance--and is indicative of the relationship between actual and standard cost of materials.

(c) Material Quantity Ratio.--This percentage is computed by dividing the Overall Ratio by the Material Price Ratio--113.67 ÷ 110 or 103.34%--and is suggestive of the relationship between actual and standard quantities of materials used.  If only one material were used, this ratio might be ascertained by dividing the actual quantity by the standard quantity--620 ÷ 600 or 103.34% in this illustration.

Worrall, in disclosing the procedure for the handling of materials as practiced by the International Silver Company in 1923, stated that two sets of accounts were maintained for raw materials[49]--the controlling accounts, which were carried on the factory ledger at both actual and standard figures; and the detail accounts, which were maintained by the storekeeper in quantities only.  In recording the vendors' invoices, which had been priced at the standard cost also, the materials controlling accounts were charged with both the actual and standard values and the relationship between these two amounts was shown by dividing the actual cost by the standard.  This ratio was used (as indicated hereto-

---

[49] Worrall, William F., "Standard Costs--How to Establish and Apply Them," _National Association of Cost Accountants Bulletin_, IV, 6-8.

fore) to determine the credits to these accounts.

As materials were requisitioned by the factory, issues were made upon requisitions requiring the following information--material account number, actual quantity issued, standard cost of actual quantity issued, standard cost of material in product, class of product, and production order number. With these data recorded on the Materials Requisition, the following procedure was followed:

> Monthly or as often as may be desired the requisitions are sorted by classes of material and credits are made to the controlling account at standard cost, which is adjusted to actual cost by the use of the ratio between actual and standard cost as shown on the debit side of the account. This difference between the actual and standard cost will reflect the variation due to the actual price being more or less than standard. Inasmuch as the quantity of material in the article may vary it is necessary to provide for showing this condition. In order to do so the requisitions are now sorted by classes of product and a tabulation is made of the standard cost of the material in the product and the standard cost of material issued, the latter being adjusted to actual cost in the same manner as for the credits to the controlling account as previously explained. The actual cost of the material issued and the standard cost of the material in the product are now posted to the debit of the Material Work in Process accounts. The ratio between these two amounts is used as a means for adjusting the standard cost of credits to actual cost.[50]

Although Worrall failed to present journal entries and ledger accounts, a careful analysis of this quotation will indicate the similarity of this technique with that of G. Charter Harrison as recorded some five years earlier and reproduced already in this study.

Three years later, this author presented another explanation of this

------

[50] _Ibid._, p. 7.

method of recording materials under standard costs.[51]  Although this

article tended to parallel the former publication, he designed a working

sheet that might be valuable for ascertaining accounting information. In

order to illustrate its use, the following data will be assumed:

| Material Class | Cost Per Unit | | Actual Units Issued | Standard Units in Production |
| --- | --- | --- | --- | --- |
| | Actual | Standard | | |
| M | $1.09 | $1.12 | 516 | 500 |
| P | 2.12 | 2.15 | 834 | 820 |
| T | 3.07 | 3.09 | 632 | 610 |

MATERIAL USAGE REPORT

Factory: _____________                    Period:  Month of March, 1944

| Material Class | Actual Cost of Quantities Actually Used A | Standard Cost of Quantities Actually Used B | Standard Cost of Quantities Which Should Have Been Used Per Formulae C | Variances | | |
| --- | --- | --- | --- | --- | --- | --- |
| | | | | Material Price Ratio A/B | Material Usage Ratio B/C | Material Cost Ratio A/C |
| M | $ 562.44 | $ 577.92 | $ 560.00 | .97 | 1.03 | 1.00 |
| P | 1,768.08 | 1,793.10 | 1,763.00 | .98 | 1.02 | 1.00 |
| T | 1,940.24 | 1,952.88 | 1,884.90 | .99 | 1.04 | 1.03 |
| | $4,270.76 | $4,323.90 | $4,207.90 | .99 | 1.03 | 1.02 |

Author's note accompanying this schedule:[52]

Material Price Ratio expresses the influence of changes in material
purchase price alone.

Material Usage Ratio expresses the effect of using more or less than
quantities specified in formulae.

Material Cost Ratio is the combination of Material Price and Usage
Ratios.

---

[51] Worrall, William F., "Standard Costs--How to Get Them," _National
Association of Cost Accountants Yearbook_, 1926, pp. 148-154.

[52] Ibid., p. 126.

F. Brugger (1925), supervisor of costs at the Pittsfield Works of General Electric Company, depicted the handling of materials at both actual and standard values but made no improvement over Worrall's technique.[53]  Robert B. Service, Jr. (1931) advocated this method of recording material costs in order that a standard of measurement might be established in each material account and a means might be provided whereby the current and replacement cost of materials, parts, and finished products, so far as this cost element was concerned, could be ascertained readily.[54]

In addition to the problems that have been illustrated in connection with the standard cost method in which both actual and standard values are recorded in the accounts, several writers who have illustrated this accounting procedure have recognized that a technique for reflecting scrap in these accounts is worthy of consideration.

Harrison (1927) included "spoiled work" as one of the four reasons why actual and standard material costs do not coincide but stated that, if these exceptions were recorded in the accounts, the material cost could be computed on a standard cost basis.  In submitting a procedure for compiling the necessary information, the author designed an account, "Production Material Controlling Account," and included pertinent

---

[53]See "Standard Costs--Their Development and Use," *National Association of Cost Accountants Bulletin*, Vol. VI, No. 13 (March 2, 1925), pp. 9-13.

[54]See "Accounting Through the Medium of Standard Costs," *National Association of Cost Accountants Bulletin*, Vol. XII, No. 13 (March 1, 1931), pp. 1045-1047.

explanations for maintaining this account.[55]

As a means of presenting Harrison's contribution, this account will
be reproduced but hypothetical figures will be employed rather than
those of the author.

PRODUCTION MATERIAL CONTROLLING ACCOUNT
Month of ___April___ , 1944

| Material Class Name | Inventory 1st of Month | | | Purchases in Month | | | Standard Adjustments | |
|---|---|---|---|---|---|---|---|---|
| | Actual | Standard | Ratio | Actual | Standard | Ratio | Usage | Spoiled Work |
| A Brass | $137 | $133 | 103 | $269 | $261 | 103 | $ 6 | $22 |
| B Steel | 219 | 209 | 105 | 367 | 352 | 102 | 12 | 8 |
| Totals | $356 | $342 | 104 | $636 | $613 | 103 | $18 | $30 |

PRODUCTION MATERIAL CONTROLLING ACCOUNT (Continued)

| Total for Month | | | Used Other Than for Production | | Cost of Sales | | Inventory End of Month | |
|---|---|---|---|---|---|---|---|---|
| Actual | Standard | Ratio | Actual | Standard | Actual | Standard | Actual | Standard |
| $406 | $366 | 111 | $50 | $45 | $232 | $209 | $124 | $112 |
| 586 | 541 | 108 | | | 445 | 412 | 141 | 129 |
| $992 | $907 | 109 | $50 | $45 | $677 | $621 | $265 | $241 |

The following explanations, which represent a summary of Harrison's
explanatory notes, have been deemed necessary to convey the author's intentions:[56]

_______________

[55]Harrison, G. Charter, "Installing Standard Costs," _Manufacturing Industries_, XIV (August, 1927), 114-116.

[56]_Ibid._, p. 116.

1. One sheet of the "Production Material Controlling Account" was used each month.

2. The initial inventory figures included the cost of the unworked materials in stores, the material in work in process, and the material in finished parts and completed products.

3. Purchases at actual included the billed amount of invoices plus freight; the standard column contained the standard cost of such invoices.

4. Under the "Standard Adjustments," the "Usage" column accumulated the standard cost of material used in excess of standard quantity of production, while the "Spoiled Work" column contained the standard material cost of spoiled work.

5. Total for Month: (a) actual column represents the sum of the initial inventory and purchases valued at actual cost; (b) standard column contains sum of initial inventory and purchases at standard less the "Standard Adjustments"--in the words of the author, "The reason for this is that while these adjustments do not affect the actual cost or the money invested, they do affect the standard value of the inventory which has been reduced to the extent of the excess material usage and the spoiled work"; (c) the ratios reflect the variations from standard due to price variations, to excess material usage, and to spoiled work.

6. Used Other Than for Production--Plant maintenance and/or sales to company employees.

7. Cost of Sales: (a) standard cost obtained by applying the standard cost of commodities to the quantities of such goods sold; (b) ratios of actual to standard are applied to the standard costs for actual figures.

8. Inventory at the end of the month is the difference between "Total for Month" and sum of "Used Other Than for Production" and "Cost of Sales."

A careful consideration of this form and the explanations relating thereto will indicate the point of significance with respect to the treatment of scrap--the standard value of the scrap was deducted from the available material (initial inventory and purchases) before the ratios of actual to standard were computed.

Downie (1927), the English writer, was cognizant of a material usage variation resulting from spoiled work--"Manufacturing Spoilage," according to this author.[57] He designed a "Monthly Spoilage Schedule,"

---

[57] Downie, op. cit., pp. 48-52 and 95-98.

which accumulated the production wastes and served as the basis for adjusting the costs of "material, labor, and overhead in each of the In Progress Control Accounts and In Progress Accounts, so that the actual expenditure (at standard rates) represents the quantity of good production (at standard value)."[58]

In order to illustrate this author's technique, his "Work in Process" account has been reproduced and hypothetical data have been supplied:[59]

PARTS IN PROGRESS CONTROL ACCOUNT

Product Class ..... PS/M16

| 1944 | Material | | | Labor | | |
|---|---|---|---|---|---|---|
| | Standard | Actual | Ratio | Standard | Actual | Ratio |
| May 1 Balance | $ 50 | $ 52 | 104 | $ 48 | $ 50 | 106 |
| 31 Manufacturing Expense | 200 | 208 | 104 | 200 | 214 | 107 |
| | 12* | | | 14* | | |
| 31 Production | | | | | | |
| June 1 Balance | | | | | | |

PARTS IN PROGRESS CONTROL ACCOUNT (Continued)

| Overhead | | | Total | | | Credits | | |
|---|---|---|---|---|---|---|---|---|
| Standard | Actual | Ratio | Standard | Actual | Ratio | Standard | Actual | Ratio |
| $ 60 | $ 63 | 105 | $158 | $165 | 104 | | | |
| 250 | 275 | 110 | 650 | 697 | 107 | | | |
| 15* | | | 41* | | | | | |
| | | | $767 | $862 | 111 | | | |
| | | | 490 | 544 | 111 | $490 | $544 | 111 |
| | | | 277 | 318 | 111 | | | |

*Credits:  to be entered in red ink.

[58] Ibid., p. 51.
[59] Ibid., p. 96.

Camman (1929) pointed out that his usage variance covered both waste of raw material and loss because of spoiled or defective product:

> Sometimes it is possible to develop separate ratios, before and after defective product is taken into account. This is done when spoiled and defective work as distinct from legitimate scrap can be easily identified. In this way a very useful record can be kept of controllable waste.[60]

At this time, Camman did not pursue his concept to the extent of indicating the accounting procedure for recording scrap; however, when he wrote his book (1932), he made a more complete statement concerning this subject, as may be evidenced by the following quotation:

> In the record of production, the factor of spoiled work and scrap must be remembered. Waste of this kind should be taken into account by deducting approximately, in the work-in-process group accounts, the reclaim value of the spoilage and scrap produced. The manner of doing this depends upon the plan adopted for material work-in-process accounts. If it is feasible to set the standard material cost of net good production (including any fluctuation in work-in-process) against the actual cost of material drawn, the deduction for scrap and spoiled work need be made under actual costs only, inasmuch as the standard cost of production is net; i.e., the deduction at standard is already included. But if it is the procedure to charge work-in-process accounts at the actual and standard cost of material drawn and to credit them for net material in products finished, the deductions must be made from the charges at both actual and standard costs, taking reclaim value from "actual" and full standard material cost from "standard." This has the effect of reducing the standard charges more than the actual charges, thus increasing the cost ratio sufficiently to cover the losses, and of bringing the standard costs on the one side to the same basis as on the other. Or, if the basic standard costs are set up to derive net material after including allowance for scrap at

---

[60] Camman, Eric A., "Standard Costs Installation and Procedure," _Proceedings, International Congress on Accounting_, 1929, pp. 889-890.

basic standard scrap values, the procedure will require deductions from work-in-process charges at reclaim value under
"actual" and at standard scrap values for scrap, with full
standard material cost for spoiled work under "standard."  In
the last two cases, deviations in yield must be disclosed by
work-in-process inventory verifications at proper periods.[61]

The problem of handling scrap under the standard cost method in
which both actual and standard values are recorded in the accounts was
recognized by Gillespie (1935) as worthy of some treatment.  Under his
procedure, the scrap for the month was evaluated at the standard cost of
the raw material at the point of delivery into the work in process account and this standard scrap value was recorded in the cost ledger.[62]

If the hypothetical case, as used already in this section, may be
applied again for illustrative purposes, with the additional assumption
that twenty units of Raw Material-R were scrapped after being put into
process, Gillespie's method would disclose the following accounting
technique.  (In view of the fact that Gillespie's procedure for issuing
materials has already been illustrated by journal entries for these data,
this portion of the example will be omitted but will be posted to a
ledger account.  Only the journal entry for recording the standard scrap
value will be made.)

---

[61] Camman, _Basic Standard Costs_, pp. 181-182.

[62] Gillespie, _op. cit._, pp. 299-306.

|  | Actual | | Standard | |
| --- | --- | --- | --- | --- |
|  | Debits | Credits | Debits | Credits |
| Standard Clearing Account |  |  | $40 |  |
| Materials in Process* |  |  |  | $40 |

To record standard scrap
value of 20 units of Raw
Material-R (standard value
$2.00 each).
*Posted in red on debit
side.

### Materials in Process

|  | Actual | Standard | Ratio |  | Actual | Standard | Ratio |
| --- | --- | --- | --- | --- | --- | --- | --- |
| Issues | $1,364 | $1,200 | 113.67 |  |  |  |  |
| Scrap |  | 40* |  |  |  |  |  |
|  | $1,364 | $1,160 | 117.58 |  |  |  |  |

*Red: denotes a deduction.

Gillespie made the following explanation, after stating that the
effect of this transaction was to change the prior department's ratio
(in this instance, the raw material ratio):

There is no credit to the actual costs of the particular
department in which scrap occurs. That department accordingly
stands charged in actual expense column with the expense which
the scrapped product consumed in its last department. There
would be no labor charge in that department because no labor
would be paid in the department which caused the scrap. The
net effect, then, upon the scrapping department is an increase
in its expense ratio of actual to standard cost of production.[63]

With respect to the actual value of scrap, Gillespie would make the
following journal entry at the time the scrap was recovered (quantity of
material spoiled valued at expected price per unit to be obtained when

---

[63] Ibid., p. 304.

sold):[64]

|                                  | Actual |         |
|                                  | Debits | Credits |
| -------------------------------- | ------ | ------- |
| Scrap Raw Material Inventory     | $20    |         |
| Materials in Process*            |        | $20     |

    To record the scrap value of 20 units
of Raw Material-R (Scrap value of $1.00
each has been assumed).

    *Posted in red on debit side.


### Materials in Process

|        | Actual  | Standard | Ratio  | | Actual | Standard | Ratio |
| ------ | ------- | -------- | ------ | - | ------ | -------- | ----- |
| Issues | $1,364  | $1,200   | 113.67 | | | | |
| Scrap  | 20*     |          |        | | | | |
|        | $1,344  | $1,200   | 112.00 | | | | |

    *Red: denotes a deduction.


In evaluating Gillespie's presentation, the present writer considers the fact rather unusual that he illustrated only the "Standard Value for Scrap" procedure in his example in the text[65] whereas his problem on this subject[66] and the solution thereof[67] contained only the "Actual Value for Scrap." The author failed to use these two values for scrap in the same example or problem or to indicate their relationship in any other manner than in the points that have been cited.

-----

[64] Ibid., p. 304.

[65] Ibid., p. 299.

[66] Ibid., pp. 270-271.

[67] Gillespie, Cecil Merle, Solutions to Problems in Text, Accounting Procedure for Standard Costs, New York, The Ronald Press Company, 1935, pp. 35-36.

<u>The Disposition of Material Variations in Standard Costs</u>.--The
treatment of variations between actual and standard costs involves certain concepts upon which accountants are not in agreement.  In general,
there are two points of view with respect to this question.

In the first place, one group of cost accountants maintain that
standard costs are not the actual (true) costs of the products and that,
therefore, the variations between actual and standard values should be
spread over the cost of sales, finished goods inventory, and work in
process inventories.  The second group of accountants maintain that, if
standards are carefully determined and revised when necessary, the standard costs are the true costs and that the variation accounts represent
losses and/or gains due to the operation of efficiency factors.  Since
they believe that such manufacturing losses and gains are not normal
items in manufacturing cost, they contend that the variation accounts
should be closed to either Cost of Sales or Profit and Loss and that the
inventories should be valued at standard figures.  Thus efficiency and
inefficiency, for this group, are not value to be recorded on the balance sheet as inventories but are gain or loss to be recorded on the
profit and loss statement.

William S. Kemp (1923), in following the latter school of thought,
computed his cost of sales on a standard cost basis by carrying the difference between actual and standard costs to a Loss and Gain account instead of merging it into the cost of the product and allocating such
cost to Cost of Sales and the final inventories of work in process and

finished goods.[68]

In 1925, G. Charter Harrison stated that he had treated the difference between actual and standard costs originally as a Profit and Loss item, that, for a time, he had abandoned this method in favor of a plan under which the variations from the standard costs were contained in the costs of the products, but that, a short time before, he had returned to the plan as initially employed.

> To be specific on this point I should mention that material costs are figured in cost of sales on the basis of the prices actually paid for the material but variations . . . due to excess material consumption are not included in the cost of the goods sold.[69]

In 1928, Amidon and Lang carried the difference between actual and standard costs of materials to one account, Variation from Standard-Materials, and proposed that the balance of this account be closed to the Profit and Loss account.[70]

Gillespie (1935), assuming that the standards were attainable, presented two methods of disposing of variations from standard manufacturing costs--close all variations to profit and loss; or close all variations except materials price variation (this variation prorated over cost of goods sold and inventories) to profit and loss. This author failed to indicate a preference as to the method that should be used.

--------

[68] Kemp, _Departmental and Standard Costs_, pp. 56-58.

[69] Harrison, G. Charter, "Standard Costs and Variations," _National Association of Cost Accountants Yearbook_, 1925, pp. 114-115.

[70] Amidon and Lang, _op. cit._, p. 281.

He did state that it might be necessary to establish a reserve to reduce inventories to cost or market, whichever is the lower.[71]

As a suggestion to the procedure in 1937 with respect to the disposition of material variations, the following portion of Keating's survey of one hundred forty-two members of the National Association of Cost Accountants has been reproduced. (The figures represent actual number of answers and not percentages.)[72]

|  | Preference | Practice |
|---|---|---|
| 5. At the end of fiscal year do you prefer to charge material variation losses to-- |  |  |
| Current operations (profit and loss or cost of sales), | 92 | 55 |
| or |  |  |
| Apportion them over inventory and current operation (profit and loss or cost of sales) | 25 | 16 |
| 6. At the end of fiscal year, do you prefer to credit material variation gains to-- |  |  |
| Current operations (profit and loss or cost of sales), or | 75 | 50 |
| Apportion them over inventory and current operations (profit and loss or cost of sales), or | 22 | 12 |
| Credit to a reserve account | 17 | 7 |
| 7. At the end of fiscal year, do you prefer to-- |  |  |
| Offset all variations (labor, overhead and material) in final disposition, or | 58 | 44 |
| Accord material variations separate treatment irrespective of what labor and overhead variations may show | 40 | 9 |

---

[71]Gillespie, _Accounting Procedure for Standard Costs_, p. 187.

[72]See _National Association of Cost Accountants Yearbook_, 1937, p. 92.

An analysis of these statistics will indicate that these represent-
atives of cost accounting preferred, both in theory and in practice, to
carry material variation charges into profit and loss for the period in
which the variations occurred and that they exhibited a similar attitude,
but with a smaller percentage approving, for handling material variation
credits.

Langer (1938) recognized the two methods of closing the variation
accounts for materials--under the theory that accounting records should
show actual costs, variances were absorbed proportionally by work in
process inventory, cost of sales, and finished goods inventory; under
the theory that such records should show normal costs, variances were
closed to profit and loss as a part of the Cost of Sales account.[73]

Van Sickle (1938) considered the variation accounts as profit and
loss items and, on the Statement of Profit and Loss, used the net unfavorable cost variances as an addition to cost of sales or the net
favorable cost variances as a subtraction from cost of goods sold before
determining the gross profit.[74]

Schlatter (1939) pointed out that the variations might be apportioned over work in process inventory, cost of goods sold, and finished
goods inventory but preferred that the variation accounts be closed to
profit and loss--however, he would not carry them to Cost of Sales
account as such a procedure would not produce actual, standard, or true

---

[73]Langer, op. cit., p. L 22:9.

[74]Van Sickle, op. cit., p. 510.

cost--when the accounts and statements were shown at standard cost.[75]

Blocker (1940), in criticizing the methods employed by the two schools of thought respecting the disposition of variances as contrary to the best accounting practice, advocated that each variance be analyzed and that its disposition be made to depend upon the underlying reasons for its existence. For materials, he formulated his concepts under three classifications:

(a) Disposition of Variances Due to Incorrect Standards.--In view of the fact that products manufactured during this period have been valued incorrectly, the variances should be apportioned to work in process inventories, cost of goods sold, and finished goods inventory in proportion to the period's production represented by each of these three accounting items.

(b) Disposition of Material Price Variance.--If an analysis of this variance indicates that it has arisen from changes in market prices, which were beyond the control of the executive responsible for purchases, the balance of this account should be apportioned to work in process inventory, to cost of goods sold, and to finished goods inventory in proportion "to the material value or material quantity of the period's production remaining in each stage."

In the case of a variance due to either efficiency or inefficiency in purchasing, this balance should be transferred to profit and loss. However, in case a rather large amount of the purchases during this time

---

[75]Schlatter, Advanced Cost Accounting, p. 139.

remained in inventories, the author advocated that a portion of the
variance be set up as a deferred item and be transferred to the profit
and loss account of the period in which such raw materials were sold as
finished products.

(c) Disposition of Material Quantity Variance.--Blocker would consider this variation usually as a profit and loss item; however, in
those cases in which a large portion of the goods manufactured during
the period remained in inventories to be sold in subsequent periods, he
would transfer a portion of the variance to a deferred account to be
carried to the profit and loss accounts of such subsequent periods.[76]

Neuner (1942), in accepting standards as true costs, pointed out
that there is a distinction between cost and loss and that the question
of the disposition of variations might be resolved into a more significant investigation as to the efficiency of the cost standards.  If
standards are set intelligently and their adequacy is maintained by making revisions where uncontrollable factors upset the original estimates
and if management uses the variation data as a basis for improvement of
methods, this author thought that the variation balances would ordinarily
be very small.[77]

Newman L. Smith (1944), in considering the application of standard
costs to the aircraft industry, recognized the problem connected with
the treatment of variances between actual and standard values.  His proposals were summarized in the following manner:

---

[76]Blocker, Cost Accounting, pp. 595-597.

[77]Neuner, Cost Accounting, p. 528.

Therefore, I would like to contend arbitrarily that <u>under normal productive conditions</u> all variances arising from waste, inefficiency, or idle plant capacity should be closed to profit and loss, as incurred, not recognizing such costs as applicable to the cost of the product. All price variances should be subject to special accounting treatment indicated by an analysis of the conditions in respect thereto, and such variances may be either restored to inventories and cost of goods sold, or written off directly to profit and loss.[78]

In addition to the Material Price and Material Quantity Variations, a few writers of cost literature have recognized another type of material variance--a variation resulting from the manufacturing department failing to adhere to the standard formulas for the mixing of raw materials.

Harrison (1930) explained this variance, "Variance Due to Mix," and developed a formula for computing this variation. Using his symbols, as explained below, the formula, as applied to metal costs, will be reproduced:[79]

$B$ = Market Cost--actual metal used, figured at market price.
$B_1$ = Actual weight of metal used distributed according to standard formulas and figured at market price.

$B_1 - B$ (that is, standard mixture $=$ Saving or loss due to the
      for actual weight of      following causes
      metal used less actual     combined:
      at market price)          (a) Using transferred
                         material
                  (b) Mix

Although this formula determined variances due to two causes--

---

[78]Smith, Newman L., "Cost Determination in Aircraft Production," <u>National Association of Cost Accountants Bulletin</u>, Vol. XXV, No. 12, Sec. I (February 15, 1944), p. 628.

[79]Harrison, <u>Standard Costs</u>, p. 277.

(a) Using transferred material and (b) Mix--Harrison presented an example in which no transferred material was considered and the entire variation, as determined by the application of this formula, was attributed to "Variation Due to Mix."[80]

Camman (1932) stated that the material used might not be exactly the kind, size, and/or grade as specified in the basic standard costs and that, accordingly, there would arise another factor of variation--"Material Use-Substitution," for this author.

> Then the material cost ratio is affected, because the actual material cost is on a basis different from the standard material cost for net good production. The variation present finds its way into the use variation, inasmuch as the price variation alone is eliminated. Should it be desired to ascertain how much of the use variation may arise from this cause, it would be necessary to compute two standard costs for materials used, one for the materials actually used and another for the materials that should have been used. Ordinarily this is a refinement in analysis that is not warranted by practical benefit. It will usually be satisfactory to permit any variation from this cause to be merged with the use variation, where indeed it belongs, because any deviations from specifications in the nature of materials used will probably result in a variation in the quantity required.[81]

Gillespie (1935) also recognized that variations between actual and standard costs might arise from the substitution of a material on hand for the standard material which was not available at the time. He followed Camman somewhat in calling this variation the "Substitution of Materials Variation."[82]

---

[80] Ibid., p. 245.

[81] Camman, Basic Standard Costs, pp. 87-88.

[82] Gillespie, Accounting Procedure for Standard Costs, pp. 158-159.

In providing for the compilation of necessary facts for ascertaining this variation, the author stated that a "substitution of materials" form would be prepared and signed by the shop official authorizing the substitution. The following quotation will indicate his procedure:

1. A "substitution of materials" form . . . shows:
   (a) quantity and standard value of standard material
       10 at $10.00 = $100.00
   (b) quantity and standard value of substitute
       10 at $11.00 = $110.00
   (c) difference in standard values
       $110.00 - $100.00 = $10.00 (debit)

2. Periodically, the substitution slips are summarized and recorded:

       Work in Process                          $100.00
       Substitution of Material Variation         10.00
           To-Materials                                    $110.00
               To record summary of substitu-
           tion as follows:
           Standard cost of standard
               materials                $100.00
           Standard cost of substi-
               tuted materials           110.00
               Substitution Variation  $ 10.00

   Note that the substitution slips are requisitions which are
       honored by the stores department in lieu of the standard
       bills of material which would have been used if standard
       materials had been available.[83]

Paton (1943) observed that, in certain process industries, reports indicating the variations in mixes and in yields were required, and designed the following Material-Usage Report for this purpose:[84]

---

[83]Ibid., p. 159.

[84]Paton, Accountants' Handbook, p. 241.

MATERIAL-USAGE REPORT

Plant __________  Dept. ________  Product __________  Week Ended _______

|  | Amounts at Standard Prices | | | | | | Usage % |
|  | Standard | | | Actual | | | |
|  | Pounds | % | Amount | Pounds | % | Amount | % |
|---|---|---|---|---|---|---|---|
| Mix Variance |  |  |  |  |  |  |  |
| Material--A | 5,000 | 50.0 | \$ 500 | 5,500 | 55.0 | \$ 550 | 110.0 |
| B | 2,500 | 25.0 | 125 | 2,200 | 22.0 | 110 | 88.0 |
| C | 2,500 | 25.0 | 200 | 2,300 | 23.0 | 184 | 92.0 |
| Totals | 10,000 | 100.0 | \$ 825 | 10,000 | 100.0 | \$ 844 | 102.3 |
|  |  |  | 844 |  |  |  |  |
| Mix Cost Variance |  |  | -\$ 19 |  |  |  |  |
| Yield Variance |  |  |  |  |  |  |  |
| Usage as above | 10,000 | 100.0 |  | 10,000 | 100.0 |  |  |
| Shrinkage | 1,750 | 17.5 |  | 2,000 | 20.0 |  |  |
| Net Yield | 8,250 | 82.5 | \$ 825 | 8,000 | 80.0 | \$ 800 |  |
|  |  |  |  | 8,250 |  | 825 |  |
| Yield Variance |  |  |  | - 250 |  | -\$ 25 |  |
| Cost Per Pound |  |  | \$.1000 |  |  | \$.1055 |  |
| Total Material Cost Variance |  |  |  |  |  |  |  |
| Mix Cost |  |  | -\$ 19 |  |  |  |  |
| Yield |  |  | - 25 |  |  |  |  |
| Total |  |  | -\$ 44 |  |  |  |  |

A consideration of these four authors' contributions to the development of thought with respect to variations due to the use of materials differing from those contemplated by the standards will disclose a formula, a journal entry, and a report for handling the data in the accounting and statistical records.

As a final consideration of this subject, it should be noted that the problem of disposition of variations does not apply to the standard cost method in which both actual and standard values are recorded in the accounts. Although a Material Cost Variance, which may be analyzed into Material Price Variance and Material Usage Variance, does exist, this factor is expressed as a percentage--actual cost of actual materials consumed ÷ standard cost of standard materials in production--but is not determined in absolute amounts and is not recorded in ledger accounts. These percentages are presented to management as statistical data; however, journal entries are not required to record such information or to close any variations between actual and standard figures under this method.[85]

Summary.--By way of summarization, this treatment of the accounting for materials in standard costs has defined materials as any goods that become a part of a finished product in such a manner that the cost thereof may be allocated directly to such completed commodity.

The first problem that was recognized herein dealt with the setting of quantity and price standards for materials. With respect to the setting of quantity standards, this responsibility was assigned to the engineering department. In the case of setting price standards, this function was performed by either the purchasing department, the cost department, or management.

In the accounting for materials in the store room, records might be kept at actual, at standard, or at both actual and standard values. The maintaining of such records at actual prices tended to be preferable. With respect to charging materials to the Materials in Process account,

---

[85] Camman, Basic Standard Costs, pp. 82-89.

the amounts might be fixed at actual, at standard, or at both actual and standard figures.  The recording of standard values tended to be accepted in the majority of cases considered.  Finished goods might be transferred from work in process at either standard or at both actual and standard values.

When the disposition of material variations was considered, the investigation revealed two distinct schools of thought--the first would carry variations directly to profit and loss; the second would prorate variations over work in process inventory, cost of goods sold, and finished goods inventory.  The trend of thinking, as demonstrated by current cost accounting literature, indicated that variations, with some modification for those that might arise as the result of conditions outside of management's control, should be treated as profit and loss items.

## CHAPTER VIII

ACCOUNTING FOR DIRECT LABOR IN STANDARD COSTS

Direct labor may be considered as the labor of employees which can be identified, in the same manner as direct materials, with the production of a product or of a group of commodities by a manufacturing enterprise. If the labor cannot be charged to some particular production cost order or cannot be associated with some production operation, it may not be classified as direct labor.

Sanders, an author who has devoted much time to the study of labor costs, has defined direct labor in the following manner:

> Direct labor is that which is employed directly on productive work; it can therefore be allocated as a direct cost to that productive work.[1]

In order to adequately control direct labor expenditures under standard costs, provision must be made for setting labor standards, for recording labor costs in the accounts, for comparison of actual with standard values, and, finally, for disposition of any variance from such standard values. Some consideration will be given to each of these phases of standard cost procedure for direct labor.

Setting Labor Cost Standards.--In the development of labor standards in the factory, attention should be focused upon the fact that such standards are the products of two factors: (1) time or quantity standards,

---

[1] Sanders, Cost Accounting for Control, p. 119.

and (2) rate or price standards.  The time standards are considered ordinarily as technical functions to be performed by the Engineering Department while the price standards are classified as prerogatives to be
determined by the individual departments and the Personnel Department.

Myers, in the winning essay for the Jordan Prize on "How to Set
Standards" in 1931, recognized three steps in determining the standard
labor cost of an article--time, price (labor rates), and unit cost.  Of
these three, he characterized the setting of the standard time required
to perform the operations in making the article as the most important
and as the only real standard or fixed base to be used in dealing with
labor.  As a means of establishing the standard time, the author suggested that this element be determined by modern stop-watch time study
observations--either to determine the time required to perform all operations in making a part or to break the part into elementary operations,
to record the standard time for each, and to bring such data together
for a total cost--or by the application of formula technique, which, he
asserted, was being done successfully at that time.  With respect to
standard labor price, Myers pointed out that a study should be made of
the labor market in the concern's locality, that the basic rate should
be the same as that paid for comparable work in the vicinity, and that a
good wage incentive plan should be installed.  Once such standards were
installed, the time standards would be changed only if methods were
altered while price standards would serve for the period as originally
planned and changes in such costs, due to changes in labor costs, would
be recorded as labor price variations.[2]  That this procedure was not

_________________

    [2]Myers, Keating and Metsch, _op_. _cit_., pp. 7-11.

entirely theoretical is indicated by the fact that such a technique was also described by J. C. Metsch, cost accountant, in another of the Jordan Prize essays on the same subject.[3]

(1) Labor Quantity Standards.  Direct labor time standards--the labor hours required per unit of output or the units of output per labor hour--are more difficult to establish than material quantity standards, which have been considered already in this study.  This condition is due to labor standards being based upon human beings--workmen whose productivity from one period of time to another varies to a greater degree than the materials employed in making a finished product.

Service (1931) asserted that the standard time for direct labor might be obtained in various manners and enumerated five methods ranging from careful studies to mere guesses: "(a) time studies; (b) previous actual cost records; (c) previous estimated cost records; (d) piece work price files; (e) manufacturing estimates."[4]

Somewhat earlier, R. W. Darnell, Comptroller for Ritter Dental Manufacturing Company, declared that setting labor standards was the most important and difficult problem encountered in setting standards.  However, he believed that if set properly, labor standards represented a very profitable investment--served as incentive plans and reduced costs, permitted the workmen to earn more money, and built valuable morale in

---

[3]Ibid., pp. 53-54.

[4]See "Accounting Through the Medium of Standard Costs," National Association of Cost Accountants Bulletin, Vol. XII, No. 13 (March 1, 1931), pp. 1047-1048.

the plant. In discussing the procedure for establishing labor standards, he stated that there was only one method of setting standards properly-- scientific time-study under the supervision of competent time-study men-- and proceeded to outline rather briefly a method that might be followed in a metal working plant.[5]

Tingley (1927), in discussing the subject of labor standards, accepted Frederick W. Taylor as the originator of the scientific time study procedure and delegated the establishment of standard time to the engineering department.[6] Walker (1928), another author to consider time standards as an engineering function, proposed two stages in the work of the Time and Motion Study Engineer when determining "job time standards":

> The first may be termed Preliminary Time and Motion Studies, principally motion studies, in order to determine what is wrong with the operation and to obtain facts which may be used to correct such errors and eliminate wastes. . . .
>
> When such a standardization of motions has been made that maintenance of the same can be reasonably assured, then the Time and Motion Study Engineer is ready to determine the task or "job time standard." Naturally, each individual job or type of work in a business must be studied, as the motions performed in the multitude of various operations generally cover a wide range of diversification. However, a great deal has been done in classifying motions and establishing standards of time for their performance in individual industries. The cumulative value of information obtained through standards set in an individual industry makes the job not as difficult as it would appear at first sight.[7]

-----

[5]Darnell, R. W., "Standards as a Means of Reducing Costs," _National Association of Cost Accountants Yearbook_, 1922, pp. 192-200.

[6]Tingley, E. H., "The Group Bonus and Labor Standards," _National Association of Cost Accountants Bulletin_, Vol. VIII, No. 16, Sec. I (April 15, 1927), pp. 741-744.

[7]Walker, W. L., "Job Time Standards," _National Association of Cost Accountants Yearbook_, 1928, p. 49.

As the first step toward the reduction of cost and the improvement of quality in a hosiery mill, Allgood (1933) provided for a complete job analysis of each operation performed in the factory.  Following this job analysis, time studies were prepared for these operations in accordance with scientific methods.[8]

In addition to these writers of articles pertaining to the setting of labor quantity standards, mention should be made of the efforts of the following authors who were also proponents of fixing standard labor time by scientific time and motion studies:  Green (1935), Gardner (1935), Keogh (1937), and Knowles and Means (1938).[9]

And, finally, additional evidence of the importance of time and motion study in the setting of labor time standards may be presented in the nature of textbooks on this subject.  The works of Carroll, Holmes, and Lowry, Maynard and Stegemerten[10] have been considered in the preparation of this study.  As a summary for this particular section, the

---

[8]Allgood, Dwight M., "A Cost Accountant Reduces Cost and Improves Quality in a Hosiery Mill," _National Association of Cost Accountants Bulletin_, Vol. XIV, No. 11, Sec. I (February 1, 1933), pp. 838-839.

[9]Green, E. A., "Practical Standards--Their Development and Use," _National Association of Cost Accountants Bulletin_, Vol. XVI, No. 11 (February 1, 1935), p. 644; Gardner, Frederic V., "The Control of Direct and Indirect Labor," _National Association of Cost Accountants Yearbook_, 1935, pp. 144-160; Keogh, D. S., "The Control of Labor Through Standards," _National Association of Cost Accountants Yearbook_, 1937, pp. 123-135; Knowles, Asa S., and Means, Frederic C., "A Survey of Job Evaluation as Used by Industry in Determining Base Rates," _National Association of Cost Accountants Bulletin_, Vol. XX, No. 7, Sec. I (December 1, 1938), pp. 381-416.

[10]Carroll, Phil, _Timestudy for Cost Control_, New York, McGraw-Hill Book Company, 1938; Holmes, Walter G., _Applied Time and Motion Study_, New York, The Ronald Press Company, 1938; Lowry, Stewart M., Maynard, Harold B., and Stegemerten, G. J., _Time and Motion Study_, New York, McGraw-Hill Book Company, 1940.

following definition of the aims of time study has been deemed particularly pertinent:

> To subject each operation of a given piece of work to a
> close analysis, in order that every unnecessary operation may
> be eliminated and in order to determine the quickest and best
> method of performing each necessary operation; also to stand-
> ardize equipment, methods, and working conditions; then, and
> not until then, to determine by scientific measurement the
> number of standard hours in which an average man can do the
> job.[11]

(2) Labor Price Standards.  After the labor time standards have
been established, the subsequent problem is the setting of standard wage
rates--a problem which, according to Langer, must take into consideration "the age, skill, and length of service of a man, together with
labor market conditions and standing agreements with the laborers."[12]
Van Sickle (1938), in following the same trend of thought, stated that
"standard labor rates are set after considering past records, the
present status of labor, and the estimated future wage trend."[13]

Knowles and Means (1938), in considering the question of setting
base rates as of somewhat greater significance, classified this procedure as job evaluation or salary standardization--a technique which undertakes "to find the relative worth of each job within a plant and to
set up a schedule of these jobs, graduated according to difficulty, the

---

[11] Lowry, Maynard and Stegemerten, _Time and Motion Study_, p. 8.

[12] Langer, _op. cit._, p. L 20-3.

[13] Van Sickle, _op. cit._, p. 455.

base rates to coincide with this last."[14]  Continuing their thesis,

these authors enumerated four steps leading to the determination of fair

and proper wage compensation:

1. Motion-time study to learn standards of output and procedure.
2. Job analysis and specifications to learn job requirements.
3. Job evaluation to determine relative importance of job
   requirements.
4. Employee rating to allow for individual differences in
   fulfilling job requirements.[15]

The authors then presented an "Occupational Rating Sheet" and "A

Job Evaluation Summary," together with their explanation of the proce-

dure that would be followed in applying such a general program of job

evaluation.  Employing the same general procedure somewhat earlier,

Bedell, Factory Controller of the International Business Machines Cor-

poration, declared that wage rate standards were being given more seri-

ous thought in that they were assuming the nature of "an evaluation of

occupational factors to insure equitable distribution of the total wage

payroll in relation to the service rendered."[16]

After these factors have been given the consideration that may be

deemed desirable by a manufacturing enterprise, the method of wage pay-

ment must be selected.  The principal methods of wage payment, which

---

[14]See "A Survey of Job Evaluation as Used by Industry in Determining Base Rates," *National Association of Cost Accountants Bulletin*,
Vol. XX, No. 7, Sec. I (December 1, 1938), p. 384.

[15]*Ibid.*, p. 385.

[16]Bedell, L. V., "Measured Day Work--A Wage Plan," *National Association of Cost Accountants Bulletin*, Vol. XVIII, No. 9, Sec. I (January
1, 1937), p. 535.

will be available for management's application, have been classified by

Sanders in the following manner:

> Time wages include all wages paid in hourly, daily, or
> weekly rates, and accruing only on the basis of time put in
> by the operator.
>
> Piece wages are those in which payment is made by the
> piece or operation, without reference to the time consumed.
>
> Bonus and premium systems will be lumped together in one
> group which will include all those schemes in which some spe-
> cific standard of accomplishment is set up, the reaching of
> which will be rewarded.[17]

Time wage payment plans raise problems somewhat comparable with

those of the material prices in setting standards.  Standard labor rates

may be determined from past experience data or from statistical or sub-

jective forecasts.  For those industries in which wage contracts are

made with the unions, the contract wage rates may be taken as the stand-

ard rates.[18]

Piece wage payment plans, or the payment of a flat price per piece

or operation for the operation or unit of product completed, represents

the simplest method of wage payment from the standpoint of setting

standards.  Under this plan, the labor cost per piece or operation is a

uniform amount and the piece rate becomes the standard labor price.

Therefore, the number of pieces or operations completed multiplied by

the piece rate produces not only the actual cost but also the standard

---

[17] Sanders, Thomas H., "The Problem of Costing Under Various Wage
Systems," _National Association of Cost Accountants Yearbook_, 1923, p. 46.

[18] Schlatter, _Advanced Cost Accounting_, p. 110.

cost of production, unless some special incentive plan is attached to the "piece wages."[19]

Bonus and premium wage payment plans represent incentive wage schemes--schemes whereby increased production benefits the workmen (through increased earnings) and the manufacturing concern (through a lower unit cost of overhead).  There are several types of bonus and premium systems, most of which bear the name of their originator--The Halsey Premium Plan, The Taylor Differential Piecework Plan, The Gantt Task and Bonus Plan, The Emerson Efficiency Plan, The Production Bonus Plan, The Standard Time Wage Plan, and The Bedaux Point System.[20]  In view of the fact that several of these wage payment plans have been presented already in this study, which does not contemplate a treatment of this phase of cost accounting, further consideration of the various incentive schemes will not be undertaken.  However, when bonus and premium wage payment plans are used, there will arise two problems:  (1) whether the bonus or premium is to be accepted as direct labor cost, and (2) whether the extra compensation is to be considered in setting the standard wage rate.  Blocker has answered the latter question in this manner:

> If it is decided to include this element in the standard, the
> amount to be added must be determined by a study of bonuses

---

[19] Blocker, Cost Accounting, p. 571.

[20] Sanders, Thomas H., "The Problem of Costing Under Various Wage Systems," National Association of Cost Accountants Yearbook, 1923, pp. 46-51; Alford, Cost and Production Handbook, pp. 611-675; Van Sickle, op. cit., pp. 247-256; Blocker, Cost Accounting, pp. 101-109; and Neuner, Cost Accounting, pp. 207-218.

and premiums paid during past periods and an average amount
per labor operation must be computed.[21]

Neuner presented one other situation that might arise with respect
to wage rate standards.  His concept has been reproduced in the following
quotation:

> Where continuous operations can be maintained at a constant
> rate through the use of conveyor systems, wage rates may be
> set on a "per day" basis.  This is the plan advanced years
> ago by Henry Ford which has since become applicable to numer-
> ous other situations.  In such cases the standard rate of
> production per day is determined by the speed of the conveyor
> belt, and variations will be due only to changes in this
> speed or changes in the day rate.  A standard rate per day
> can be set with reference to forecasted labor market condi-
> tions.  The speed of the conveyor can also be set with refer-
> ence to the operations performed.  Variations from the stand-
> ard day wage will be purely price variations; variations due
> to changes in conveyor speed will be purely quantity varia-
> tions.[22]

In a final consideration of the subject of setting labor standards,
attention should be called to the fact that this problem requires a detailed study of the conditions under which the standards are to be used.
Although generalizations should be considered as inadequate for a specific situation, it has been deemed practicable for this study to be
concerned with pointing out the general methods that might be applied
for setting labor quantity and labor price standards in manufacturing
enterprises.

Accounting for Direct Labor.--After the labor price standards and

---

[21]Blocker, Cost Accounting, p. 571.

[22]Neuner, Cost Accounting, p. 490.

the labor quantity standards have been established for a manufacturing

enterprise, careful consideration should be given to a procedure for

assembling and recording direct labor costs. A system which is to per-

form such functions satisfactory for an industrial concern will have two

major objectives:  (1) the accumulation and compilation of the payroll,

with the amount earned by each employee calculated and with the classi-

fication of labor required in the particular factory disclosed; and

(2) the analyzation and distribution of such direct labor costs over the

manufactured products, with adequate accounting records for revealing

such information maintained.  All of these details necessary for attain-

ing the first objective are recognized as duties of the Timekeeping and

Payroll Department while comparable activities for maintaining the second

objective are accepted as functions of the Accounting Department.

A careful consideration of the first objective, as undertaken by

the Timekeeping and Payroll Department, will indicate that the technique

required for maintaining the essential information will vary according

to the industry, the enterprise within the industry, and the conditions

in the particular enterprise--especially the labor standards accepted,

the wage system used, and the classifications undertaken.  With so many

variables influencing the routine in the Timekeeping and Payroll Depart-

ment, an agency of rather minor importance to this study, complete treat-

ment of this subject has not been contemplated herein.  However, some

indications of this department's work will be presented and adequate

publications relating to its operation and functions will be enumerated

for further reference.

In describing the performance of its labor cost functions, Van

Sickle (1938) has allotted the following services to the Timekeeping and

Payroll Department:

> (1) Checking the workmen in and out of the plant each day.
> (2) Verifying the daily presence of the workmen in their re-
> spective departments.
> (3) Keeping a record of the wage rate and the location of
> each workman by department within the plant.
> (4) Collecting and completing the time tickets prepared by
> the workmen.
> (5) Proving the accuracy of the time worked as shown on the
> time tickets.
> (6) Preparing the factory payroll.
> (7) Compiling the total annual earnings of each workman.
> (8) Paying the workmen.
> (9) Keeping a record of the hours worked by producing depart-
> ments and cost centers.[23]

With respect to methods for performing these nine functions, the

efforts of the following authors, several of whom were describing actual

situations, have been found to be particularly valuable:  Brugger (1925),

Conn (1928), Alford (1934), Koester (1935), Smith (1935), Downie, L. W.

(1937), Whisler (1937), North (1937), Taylor (1937), Van Sickle (1938),

Henshaw (1939), Martin (1939), Totten (1941), Langer (1942), and Neuner

(1942).[24]

---

[23] Van Sickle, *op*. *cit*., p. 225.

[24] Brugger, F., "Standard Costs--Their Development and Use," *National Association of Cost Accountants Bulletin*, Vol. VI, No. 13 (March 2, 1925), pp. 3-16; Conn, W. H., "Unit-Time Standards as Exemplified by the Point System of Industrial Measurement," *National Association of Cost Accountants Yearbook*, 1928, pp. 62-73; Alford, *Cost and Production Handbook*, pp. 679-703; Koester, E. R., "Modern Time Study Methods Through Motion Study," *National Association of Cost Accountants Bulletin*, Vol. XVI, No. 24, Sec. I (August 15, 1935), pp. 1336-1346; Smith, Royal L., "Wage Incentive Methods, and Evaluation," *National Association of Cost*

After the Timekeeping and Payroll Department has performed its
services, the direct labor costs are compiled and analyzed by the accounting department.  Gardner, in attempting to set up limits of responsibility for these two departments, made the following statement:

> Though the cost executive is interested in the wage payment
> system, and though he may be vitally interested in the com-
> parative degree of looseness or tightness of that system, his
> primary responsibility for costs does not start until the
> system in use has been reflected in direct labor.  Whether
> that direct labor is in hours or dollars is not important.[25]

Although some credence may be given to this concept, too much
stress cannot be placed upon adequate internal control in the department
initiating labor cost data.  This study must necessarily assume that

___________

Accountants Bulletin, Vol. XVI, No. 24, Sec. I (August 15, 1935), pp.
1327-1335; Downie, L. W., "Payroll Accounting and Labor Control," Na-
tional Association of Cost Accountants Yearbook, 1937, pp. 101-122;
Whisler, R. F., "Operating the Piecework Plan," National Association of
Cost Accountants Yearbook, 1937, pp. 135-147; North, A. F., "A System of
Labor Cost and Payroll Accounting Used by the Allen Bradley Company,"
National Association of Cost Accountants Bulletin, Vol. XVIII, No. 9,
Sec. I (January 1, 1937), pp. 527-532; Taylor, Paul C., "Accurate Time-
keeping is Essential to Use of Standard Costs," National Association of
Cost Accountants Bulletin, Vol. XVIII, No. 9, Sec. I (January 1, 1937),
pp. 517-526; Van Sickle, op. cit., pp. 215-256; Henshaw, Frank O.,
"Labor Control in the Sign Shop," National Association of Cost Account-
ants Bulletin, Vol. XX, No. 15, Sec. I (April 1, 1939), pp. 981-990;
Martin, A., "The Control of Direct and Indirect Labor Costs," National
Association of Cost Accountants Bulletin, Vol. XX, No. 15, Sec. I (April
1, 1939), pp. 991-1012; Totten, William L., "Simplified Payroll Procedure and Labor Cost Distribution," National Association of Cost Accountants Bulletin, Vol. XXII, No. 15, Sec. I (April 1, 1941), pp. 823-836;
Langer, Charles H., Factory Payroll, Chicago, Walton Publishing Company,
1942, pp. SL 10:1-36; Neuner, Cost Accounting, pp. 171-198.

[25]Gardner, Frederic V., "The Control of Direct and Indirect Labor,"
National Association of Cost Accountants Yearbook, 1935, p. 149.

ample provision is made for accumulating the labor cost information and for disclosing the division of such labor cost figures in accordance with the classifications as decided upon in the particular accounting system.

<u>Direct Labor in the Records at Actual Cost</u> (<u>Work in Process Charged with Actual and Credited with Standard Costs</u>).--After the direct labor standards have been established and the labor costs have been compiled by the Timekeeping and Payroll Department, the direct labor costs may be charged to work in process at actual cost, at standard cost, or at both actual and standard figures, and the variations from such standards may be ascertained and/or recorded in accordance with the general method employed by the particular concern involved.

The first method to be considered will charge the work in process account for direct labor with the actual cost of direct labor incurred during the period and will credit this account with the standard labor cost of the products completed during the same time. At the close of the period, the inventory of work in process (valued at standard costs) will be set up by crediting the labor in process account and the balance in this account will be analyzed and closed to price and quantity variance accounts. In order to illustrate this procedure, the following hypothetical case has been prepared.

1. A finished product of Commodity X-45 requires fifty hours
   of direct labor at a standard rate of $0.80 per hour.
2. The payroll for the period was as follows:
   7,822 direct labor hours at an average rate of $0.78 per
      hour.
   Indirect labor amounted to $610.00.

3. The equivalent production during the time was:
    120 units of Commodity X-45 completed.
    56 units of Commodity X-45 50% completed.

The journal entries to record these data would be as follows (a Labor in Process account has been used for the manufacturing account).

| | | |
|---|---:|---:|
| Accrued Factory Payroll | 6,711.16 | |
|    Vouchers Payable | | 6,711.16 |

      To record the vouchering of the payroll, as submitted by the Payroll Department.

| | | |
|---|---:|---:|
| Labor in Process | 6,101.16 | |
| Overhead Expense | 610.00 | |
|    Accrued Factory Payroll | | 6,711.16 |

      To distribute the payroll, as per the payroll analysis:

| | |
|---|---:|
|     Direct Labor (7,822 hours at $0.78) | 6,101.16 |
|     Indirect Labor | 610.00 |
|        Total | 6,711.16 |

| | | |
|---|---:|---:|
| Finished Goods | 4,800.00 | |
|    Labor in Process | | 4,800.00 |

      To charge finished goods with the standard labor cost of 120 units of Commodity X-45: 6,000 hours at $0.80 or $4,800.00

| | | |
|---|---:|---:|
| Work in Process Inventory[26] | 1,120.00 | |
|    Labor in Process | | 1,120.00 |

      To record the standard labor element in work in process--56 units 50% completed: 1,400 hours at $0.80 or $1,120.00.

The balance in the Labor in Process account, after these entries have been posted, represents the net balance due to labor rate and

---

[26] Gillespie styles this account as "Work in Process Clearing Account." See _Accounting Procedure for Standard Costs_, p. 25.

quantity variations.  The account would be closed in the following manner,

which would disclose the two variations.

<pre>
    Labor in Process                27                    156.44
        Labor Price Variance                                       156.44
            To record the price variation in
        labor for period:
            Standard labor cost of actual hours:
                7,822 hours at $0.80        6,257.60
            Actual labor cost of actual
                    hours:
                7,822 hours at $0.78        6,101.16
                Price Variation               156.44

    Labor Quantity Variance 28                            337.60
        Labor in Process                                           337.60
            To record the quantity variation in
        labor for the period:
            Standard labor cost of actual hours:
                7,822 hours at $0.80        6,257.60
            Standard labor cost of labor
                in production: 7,400 hours
                at $0.80                    5,920.00
            Quantity variation:
                422 hours at $0.80            337.60
</pre>

If these journal entries were posted to the ledger accounts, the

Labor in Process account would contain the following information:

---

[27] Blocker termed this variation the "Labor Wage Variance" (Cost Accounting, p. 586); for Langer, this account was "Wage Rates Variation-- Direct Labor" (op. cit., p. L 22-3).

[28] Nomenclature according to other writers:  Blocker--"Labor Time Variance" (Cost Accounting, p. 586); Langer--"Labor Hours Variation" (op. cit., p. L 22-3); Newlove and Garner--"Efficiency Variation--Direct Labor" (op. cit., p. 450).

Labor in Process

| | | | |
|---|---|---|---|
| Direct Labor for Period | $6,101.16 | To Finished Goods | $4,800.00 |
| Labor Price Variation | 156.44 | To Work in Process | |
| | | Inventory | 1,120.00 |
| | | Labor Quantity Variation | 337.60 |
| | $6,257.60 | | $6,257.60 |

A consideration of this procedure will indicate that the direct labor has been charged to the manufacturing account (Labor in Process) at actual cost and that the labor charges in finished goods and in the work in process inventory have been credited to this account at standard values. The balance in this account has been analyzed as to Price Variation and Quantity Variation and has been closed to these two accounts.[29]

In his method, "Segregating or Isolating Variations when the Product is Completed," Langer failed to follow exactly the procedure that has been illustrated. Although he charged his Work in Process account (he used only one account, Goods in Process, to accumulate all three of the cost components) with actual costs, he credited this account with the actual cost of the finished goods. However, the Finished Goods account was charged with only the standard cost of these finished products, while the difference between this figure and the actual cost of the finished goods--the variation between actual and standard costs of the finished goods only--was charged to a special Variations account.

Applying the data of the hypothetical case, the journal entry to record the labor cost element only in the finished goods (the author

---

[29]Blocker, Cost Accounting, pp. 581-588; Gillespie, op. cit., pp. 23-32; Lawrence, op. cit., pp. 367-371.

would incorporate the material, labor, and burden costs together in this

entry) might be assumed to appear as follows:

```
Finished Product                                4,800.00
Variations                                        146.74
    Goods in Process                                        4,946.74
        To record the completion of 120 units of
    finished products.  Cost determined as
    follows:
```

|                          | Standard Labor Cost | Per Cent | Actual Labor Cost |
|--------------------------|--------------------:|---------:|------------------:|
| 120 Units Completed Product | 4,800.00         | 81.08    | 4,946.74          |
| 56 Units 50% Completed   | 1,120.00            | 18.92    | 1,154.42          |
| Totals                   | 5,920.00            | 100.00   | 6,101.16          |

In explaining this journal entry, Langer made the following state-

ment:

> This transfer leaves the unfinished product in the Goods
> in Process account at actual cost, and the variations apply
> to finished product only.  A common modification of this
> method is to remove to the Variations account also the varia-
> tion applicable to the goods in process.  In this way the
> Variations account applies to the total production costs, and
> not only to that part of it represented by finished product.
> This method is undesirable, however, as in the following
> month the Goods in Process account will contain a mixture of
> a beginning inventory at standard, plus additions at actual.
> It is usually not advisable to mix standard and actual ac-
> counts in a single account.[30]

Mannix also undertook to apply this general method and presented a

second deviation from the ordinary procedure for recording direct labor

charges at actual cost and credits at standard values.[31]  His technique

---

[30] Langer, _op_. _cit_., p. L 22-1.

[31] Mannix, _op_. _cit_., pp. 206-217.

will be illustrated by using the figures for the hypothetical case in
the following manner:

---
Direct Labor Actual Cost

---

Payroll for Period
  (Actual)                    $6,101.16


---
Direct Labor Standard Cost

---

|  |  |
|---|---|
| Finished Products | $4,800.00 |
| Work in Process | 1,120.00 |


At the end of the fiscal period, these two accounts, together with
comparable accounts for materials and overhead, would be closed by this
journal entry:

```
Direct Labor Standard Cost              5,920.00
Excess Costs Over Standard                181.16
    Direct Labor Actual Cost                        6,101.16
        To close the actual and stand-
    ard direct labor accounts.
```

In considering this method, it will be observed that the flow of
direct labor cost proceeds at actual figures up to and including the
debit side of the Labor in Process account and, from that point, con-
tinues at standard values. This shift from actual to standard is characteristic of standard cost procedure; however, the change does not
always occur in a work in process account, as will be demonstrated in
the following method.

Direct Labor in the Records at Standard Costs.--Another procedure
for recording the labor cost in the work in process account is to charge

this account with the standard cost of direct labor applicable to production and to credit the account with the corresponding value of labor in finished goods.  In view of the fact that this cost element goes directly into production in its entirety (except for the variations in this case, as demonstrated below), as contrasted with materials--materials go into the stores room and the Materials account before issuance--the accounting procedure is somewhat less complicated for direct labor than for raw materials.

If the data, as employed to illustrate the former method, may be applied to this technique, the following journal entries may be made to record the direct labor transactions.

```
Accrued Factory Payroll                             6,711.16
   Vouchers Payable                                              6,711.16
      To record the vouchering of the payroll,
   as submitted by the Payroll Department.

Labor in Process                                    5,920.00
Labor Quantity Variance                               337.60
Overhead Expense                                      610.00
   Labor Price Variance                                            156.44
   Accrued Factory Payroll                                       6,711.16
      To record the distribution of the payroll
   for the period, as analyzed herein:
      Standard Cost of Hours in Production:
         7,400 hours at $0.80                        5,920.00
      Labor Quantity Variation:
       Actual Hours at Standard Rate:
         7,822 hours at $0.80           6,257.60
       Standard Hours at Standard
       Rate:
         7,400 hours at $0.80           5,920.00     337.60
      Labor Price Variation:
       Actual Hours at Actual Rate:
         7,822 hours at $0.78           6,101.16
       Actual Hours at Standard Rate:
         7,822 hours at $0.80           6,257.60     156.44*
       Actual Hours at Actual Rates:
         7,822 hours at $0.78                        6,101.16
      Indirect Labor                                   610.00
         Total Payroll                               6,711.16
```

*Denotes a contra balance from other accounts.

As the commodities are completed, the Labor in Process account is credited with the standard costs of such finished goods.  In this case, one hundred twenty units of Commodity X-45--this commodity requires fifty hours of direct labor at eighty cents, according to the standard-- were completed:

```
Finished Goods                          4,800.00
    Labor in Process                                4,800.00
        To charge finished goods with
        the standard labor cost of 120
        units of Commodity X-45:  6,000
        hours at $0.80  $4,800.00
```

When these entries are posted, the Labor in Process account will contain a balance which represents the standard value of the work in process for labor cost, the two variation accounts will disclose the difference between actual and standard values, and the finished goods account will have been charged with the standard cost of products completed during the period.[32]

When the Department of Manufacture, Chamber of Commerce of the United States (1925), undertook to explain the method of recording direct labor at the standard value only in the Work in Process account (the Department called this method Plan 3), this agency used ledger accounts for illustrative purposes.[33]  These accounts will be reproduced; however the writer's hypothetical figures will be substituted for those

_______________

[32]Blocker, Cost Accounting, pp. 612-613; Gillespie, Accounting Procedure for Standard Costs, pp. 40-49; Van Sickle, op. cit., pp. 495-501.

[33]See Cost Accounting Through the Use of Standards, op. cit., pp. 30-33.

in the original publication, in order that a comparable situation may be
maintained in this chapter.

|                  ACCRUED                |                  PAYROLL                |
| --------------------------------------- | --------------------------------------- |
|                                         | May 31  Direct labor for                |
|                                         |         May            $6,101.16         |

|              WORK-IN-PROCESS            |              DIRECT LABOR               |
| --------------------------------------- | --------------------------------------- |
| May  1  Direct labor in                 | May 31  Direct labor in                 |
|         inventory      $                |         production at                   |
|      31 Payroll for May                 |         standard       $4,800.00        |
|         at standard    5,920.00         |                                         |

|              PROFIT & LOSS              |              DIRECT LABOR               |
| --------------------------------------- | --------------------------------------- |
| May 31  Direct labor                    |                                         |
|         variation for                   |                                         |
|         May            $   181.16       |                                         |

|              COST-OF-GOODS              |                  SOLD                   |
| --------------------------------------- | --------------------------------------- |
| May 31  Direct labor in                 |                                         |
|         production at                   |                                         |
|         standard       $4,800.00        |                                         |

Although the two significant entries may be discovered in these
accounts with very little difficulty, the writer, in attempting to
stress the trend of thought with respect to this problem, has deemed it
desirable to present these transactions in general journal form.

```
Work in Process--Direct Labor            5,920.00
Profit and Loss--Direct Labor              181.16
    Accrued Payroll                                  6,101.16
        To record the payroll for May, with
    analysis for standard cost of production
    and variation therefrom.
```

```
Cost of Goods Sold                          4,800.00
    Work in Process-Direct Labor                       4,800.00
        To record the standard cost of
    finished goods.
```

Maynard (1927) and Newlove and Garner (1941) continued the use of

the Scheduled _____ in Process account, as they had done in recording

raw material costs, when they presented the Scheduled Labor in Process

account[34] and the Scheduled Direct Labor account[35] respectively for ac-

cumulating the actual labor costs, according to the payroll, as debits

and the standard labor cost of production as credits. In view of the

fact that identical procedures were followed for handling both materials

and labor, journal entries or ledger accounts will not be prepared for

illustrating direct labor costs.

Amidon and Lang (1928) adapted the procedure that they had used for

recording materials to the accounting for direct labor.[36] The following

journal entries will tend to illustrate the flow of direct labor costs

through the accounts for these writers:

```
Variation from Standard--Direct Labor       6,101.16
    Payroll Accrued                                    6,101.16
        To record the actual direct labor
    earned during the period.
```

---

[34]Maynard, Henry W., "The Accounting Technique for Standard Costs,"
*National Association of Cost Accountants Bulletin*, Vol. VIII, No. 12
(February 15, 1927), p. 555.

[35]Newlove and Garner, *op. cit.*, p. 450.

[36]Amidon and Lang, *op. cit.*, pp. 278-282.

                Work in Process--Labor                        5,920.00
                    Variation from Standard--Direct Labor                5,920.00
                        To record the standard cost of earned
                    labor--labor in production.

                Profit and Loss                               181.16
                    Variation from Standard--Direct Labor                181.16
                        To close the balance in variance from
                    standard account, which represents the
                    excess of actual over standard cost.

                Finished Goods                              4,800.00
                    Work in Process--Labor                             4,800.00
                        To record the standard cost of the
                    products completed during the period.


Other writers to follow this general plan, as presented by Amidon
and Lang, include Maze and Glover (1929) and Schlatter (1939);[37] however,
their efforts do not merit additional consideration.

Neuner (1942), in recording direct labor at standard values in the
accounts, undertook two plans for the journalization of such information.
In the first method, he recorded the labor variation in only one account
--Cost Variation - Direct Labor--and failed to determine the price and
quantity variations.[38]

                Work in Process--Direct Labor               5,920.00
                Cost Variation--Direct Labor                   181.16
                    Accrued Payroll                                   6,101.16
                        To record the payroll for the period
                    and to charge production with the stand-
                    ard cost of labor in operations.

-------------------------------

[37]Maze and Glover, op. cit., pp. 328-332; Schlatter, Advanced Cost
Accounting, pp. 117-121.

[38]Neuner, Cost Accounting, pp. 517-523.

Under the second method, this author recognized both quantity and price variations but altered the journalization procedure somewhat from that heretofore presented:[39]

```
Direct Labor                                    6,257.60
   Direct Labor Price Variation                           156.44
   Accrued Payroll                                       6,101.16
      To record the wages earned, at
      both actual and standard values:
         Actual hours at standard cost:
         7,822 hours at $0.80        6,257.60
         Actual hours at actual cost:
         7,822 hours at $0.78        6,101.16
            Price Variation            156.44

Work-in-Process--Direct Labor                   5,920.00
Direct Labor Quantity Variation                   337.60
   Direct Labor                                          6,257.60
      To close the Direct Labor ac-
      count and to charge Work-in-
      Process for standard value of
      operations for the period:
         Actual hours at standard cost:
         7,822 hours at $0.80        6,257.60
         Standard hours at standard
           cost:
         7,400 hours at $0.80        5,920.00
         Quantity Variation:
         422 hours at $0.80            337.60
```

Langer (1938) had used the second procedure, as described and illustrated by Neuner, in his standard cost method, "Segregating the Variations when Materials and Labor are First Brought on to the Books."[40]

Other writers who recognized this method of recording direct labor in the accounts at standard costs include Thomas Downie, Jr. (1927),

---

[39] Ibid., pp. 523-527.

[40] Langer, Cost Accounting, pp. L 22:3-4.

Reitell (1933), Dohr, Inghram and Love (1935), Schumer (1935), Lawrence
(1937), and Gregory (1940).[41]

<u>Direct Labor in the Records at Actual and Standard Costs</u>.--Under
the third plan for recording labor costs, the accounts carry both the
actual and the standard values--an advantage of giving not only the
actual costs but also a gauge or tool of measurement in the form of
standards.  In order to illustrate this procedure, the data, as used for
exemplifying the two preceding methods, will be employed and the following additional assumption will be included:

|  | Actual | Standard | Ratio |
|---|---|---|---|
| Inventory of Work in Process--<br>Direct Labor at the beginning<br>of the period | $808.92 | $763.13 | 106 |

After the direct labor has been ascertained for the period, the
Work in Process account for direct labor would be charged with the
actual figures in the following manner:

|  | Actual | | Standard | |
|---|---|---|---|---|
|  | Debits | Credits | Debits | Credits |
| Work in Process--Direct Labor | 6,101.16 | | | |
| Accrued Payroll | | 6,101.16 | | |
| To record the actual direct labor cost for the period: 7,822 hours at $0.78. | | | | |

------

[41]Downie, Thomas, Jr., <u>op. cit.</u>, pp. 22 and 64-80; Reitell, <u>Cost
Accounting</u>, pp. 361-362 and 400-402; Dohr, Inghram and Love, <u>op. cit.</u>,
pp. 481-482; Schumer, <u>op. cit.</u>, pp. 239-245; Lawrence, <u>Cost Accounting</u>
(1937 edition), pp. 361-363; Gregory, <u>op. cit.</u>, pp. 103-107.

And, upon compilation of the standard cost of the work completed, a journal entry would be prepared to record the standard value of the direct labor in such finished goods:

```
Work in Process--Direct Labor            5,920.00
    Standard Clearing Account                        5,920.00
        To charge the standard column of Work
    in Process with the standard cost of the
    work completed:
```

| Units | % Completed | Equivalent | Hours Per Unit | Total Hours | Standard Rate | Amount |
|---|---|---|---|---|---|---|
| 120 | 100 | 120 | 50 | 6,000 | $0.80 | $4,800 |
| 56 | 50 | 28 | 50 | 1,400 | .80 | 1,120 |
| 176 | | 148 | | 7,400 | | $4,920 |

It is interesting to note that the material published by the International Accountants Society in 1936 for a course in Standard Costs recorded all of this information in the ledger accounts but journalized only the actual figures. The standard figures were computed in schedules and were carried directly to the accounts, more or less, as statistical data.[42]

Lloyd F. Mogel, Cost Accountant for the Princess Royal Hosiery Mills, in applying this method to the accounting for a hosiery mill, would make only one entry for the month for direct labor. During the month, according to this author, the direct labor cards were summarized on work sheets showing production, hours, and earnings. The summary was extended for standard hours and standard labor cost and was made the

---

[42]Standard Costs, Chicago, International Accountants Society, 1936, Lesson S10, pp. 7-11.

basis for the following journal entry:[43]

|  | Actual | | Standard | |
| --- | --- | --- | --- | --- |
|  | Debits | Credits | Debits | Credits |
| Process Inventory--Labor | 6,101.16 |  | 5,920.00 |  |
| Mill Payroll |  | 6,101.16 |  |  |
| Standard Control |  |  |  | 5,920.00 |
| To record the summary of direct labor for the month. |  |  |  |  |

These items would be posted to the ledger account and the relation-ship between actual and standard costs would be expressed in the form of a ratio.

### Work in Process - Direct Labor

|  | Actual | Standard | Ratio |
| --- | --- | --- | --- |
| Inventory | 808.92 | 763.13 | 106.0 |
| Monthly Labor | 6,101.16 | 5,920.00 | 103.0 |
| Totals | 6,910.08 | 6,683.13 | 103.4 |

After the ratio of actual to standard cost has been computed for the period--103.4 per cent in this case--the standard cost of goods com-pleted would be determined and, by the use of this ratio, this standard cost would be converted into a figure that would approximate actual cost. The following journal entry would be made at this time:

---

[43]Mogel, Lloyd F., "Basic Standard Costs as Applied to a Hosiery Mill," *National Association of Cost Accountants Bulletin*, Vol. XVI, No. 17, Sec. I (May 1, 1935), pp. 967-970.

|  | Actual | | Standard | |
| --- | --- | --- | --- | --- |
|  | Debits | Credits | Debits | Credits |
| Finished Goods | 4,963.20 | | 4,800.00 | |
| Work in Process-- | | | | |
| Direct Labor | | 4,963.20 | | 4,800.00 |
| To record the cost of | | | | |
| 120 units of X-45 at | | | | |
| actual and standard | | | | |
| values: | | | | |
| Standard cost: | | | | |
| 120 units x 50 hours x $0.80 = $4,800.00 | | | | |
| Actual Cost: | | | | |
| 103.4% of $4,800.00 = $4,963.20 | | | | |

For this entry, the writer of the International Accountants Society's material computed the standard labor cost in goods completed during the period and made a journal entry for recording this amount. The standard costs were converted into actual costs--"the most significant and most important feature of the basic standard cost system"--and a journal entry was made to record this value. However, the author of this material presented a journal with only two columns for recording both actual and standard figures as contrasted with Gillespie's and Mogel's four column journals.

Hill (1940), in recording the merchandise completed and transferred to finished stores during the period, would follow the same general procedure as that already presented but would use a journal somewhat different from that ordinarily employed.[44]

_______________

[44]Hill, Joseph A., "Basic Standard Cost Accounting Employing the Use of Ratios," _National Association of Cost Accountants Bulletin_, Vol. XXI, No. 11, Sec. I (February 1, 1940), pp. 695-702.

| Debit | | Description | Credit | |
| Actual | Standard | | Actual | Standard |
| 4,963.20 | 4,800.00 | Finished Stock Account | | |
| | | Work in Process--Labor | 4,963.20 | 4,800.00 |
| | | To record the actual and standard cost of 120 units of Product X-45 completed. | | |

In addition to a method for determining inventories and cost of
goods sold and a fixed base for disclosing cost trends, basic standard
costs also provide a procedure for analyzing variances between actual
and standard labor costs--and the other two cost components as well.  As
has been shown already in the discussion of materials, both actual and
standard costs are recorded in the accounts and, consequently, the variations are not journalized as in the other standard cost procedures.  However, these variations may be computed and may be presented as either
ratios or absolute figures.

Camman (1929) recognized the value of analyzing the difference between actual and standard labor costs--Labor Cost Variance for this
writer.[45]  In the first place, he computed the Labor Cost ratio[46] by
dividing the actual payroll for a period by the standard labor cost of
production for such period.  In the case under consideration, this ratio
would be 103.0 per cent--$6,101.16 (actual labor cost) ÷ $5,920.00 (standard labor cost in production)--and would be indicative that the actual

---

[45]See *Proceedings*, *International Congress on Accounting*, 1929,
pp. 885-887.

[46]Gillespie, *op*. *cit*., pp. 264-265, termed this ratio "the Labor
Overall Ratio"; International Accountants Society, *op*. *cit*., Lesson
S 10:21, called this ratio "the Actual Labor-Cost Ratio."

costs were 3.06 per cent greater than standard or that 97.03 per cent

(100.0 ÷ 103.0) of the expected results were realized for the wages paid.

When Camman came to the analysis of the labor cost variance, he

recognized the effects of two factors--the variation in output per man

hour and the variation in wage rates paid. In computing the Man Hour

ratio,[47] he presented two methods that might be applied with identical

results.

In the first place, he computed this ratio by dividing the actual

labor hours by the standard hours in production. For the hypothetical

case as used in this study, the Man Hour ratio would amount to 105.7

per cent--7,822 (actual hours) ÷ 7,400 (standard hours). This procedure

was followed by Gillespie in computing his Labor Quantity ratio and by

the writer of the International Accountants Society's material in deter-

mining his Time Ratio.

Under the second plan, which he called "a shorter way," Camman made

use of the following data (budget figures have been assumed, while the

other data have been taken from the hypothetical case):

| | |
|---|---|
| Standard Direct Labor Cost Budget at Capacity | $6,600.00 |
| Standard Direct Labor Cost of Production | 5,920.00 |
| Budget, Man Hours, at Capacity | 8,250 |
| Actual Man Hours | 7,822 |

The author stated that the budget data would be available, while the

---

[47] Gillespie, _op. cit._, p. 265, called this ratio the "Labor Quantity Ratio"; International Accountants Society, _op. cit._, Lesson S 10:21,
termed this ratio the "Time Ratio."

actual hours would be derived through the usual payroll procedure.  Using

these figures, he calculated the following ratios:[48]

  1. Ratio of Use to Capacity (in man hours):
     Actual Man Hours ÷ Budget, Man Hours, at Capacity
     7,822 ÷ 8,250 = 94.8 per cent.

  2. Ratio of Output to Capacity (in standard dollars):
     Standard Direct Labor Cost of Production ÷ Standard
     Direct Labor Cost Budget at Capacity:
     $5,920.00 ÷ $6,600.00 = 89.7 per cent.

  3. Ratio of Actual to Standard Man Hours for what was
     Produced:
     94.8% ÷ 89.7% = 105.7 per cent.

According to his reasoning, it took 94.8 per cent in time to pro-

duce 89.7 per cent in quantity, with both ratios being computed on the

common base of the budget.  Man effectiveness, according to this writer,

would be determined as 94.6 per cent (100.0 ÷ 105.7).  When Camman pub-

lished his text, Basic Standard Costs, he omitted the second method and

employed the first plan only for determining his Time Ratio.[49]

In computing the Wage Rate ratio, Camman considered the Labor Cost

ratio as an end ratio representing the product of two other ratios--the

Time ratio and the Wage Rate ratio.  Therefore, if either of these two

ratios could be determined, the other might be computed by dividing it

into the Labor Cost ratio.  In the case under consideration, the Labor

Cost ratio was found to be 103.0 per cent and the Time ratio to be 105.7

per cent.  Accordingly, the Wage Rate ratio would be 97.36 per cent

---

[48] Camman, Proceedings, pp. 885-886.

[49] Camman, Basic Standard Costs, pp. 53-68.

(103.0 ÷ 105.7).  Camman incorporated this procedure for computing the Wage Rate ratio in his text,[50] while Gillespie and the International Accountants Society followed identical routines for ascertaining this ratio in their publications.[51]

If the absolute variance figures are desired also, the ratios may be applied to the standard labor costs, as in the following schedule, to determine such amounts:[52]

SCHEDULE OF THE ABSOLUTE LABOR COST VARIATIONS

| Labor Variations | Standard Per Cent | Actual Per Cent | Differences Loss-Gain* | Standard Cost | Variations Amount |
|---|---|---|---|---|---|
| Quantity | 100.00 | 105.70 | 5.70 | $5,920.00 | $337.60 |
| Price (Rate) | 100.00 | x 97.36 | 2.64* | 5,920.00 | 156.44* |
| Cost | 100.00 | 103.06 | 3.06 | 5,920.00 | $181.16 |

Lawrence (1937), in recording the direct labor cost, not only made his journal entry carry the actual and standard values for labor in process and accrued wages but also disclosed the absolute variations in the standard columns:[53]

---

[50] Ibid., p. 57.

[51] Gillespie, op. cit., p. 265; International Accountants Society, op. cit., Lesson S 10:21.

[52] Camman, Basic Standard Costs, pp. 56-59.

[53] Lawrence, Cost Accounting (1937 edition), pp. 372-377.

|                              | Debits       |          | Credits      |          |
| ---------------------------- | ------------ | -------- | ------------ | -------- |
|                              | Standard     | Actual   | Actual       | Standard |
| Work in Process              | 5,920.00     | 6,101.16 |              |          |
| Direct Labor Quantity        |              |          |              |          |
|  Variance               | 337.60       |          |              |          |
|   Variance from Standard |        |          |              | 181.16   |
|  Direct Labor Cost      |              |          |              |          |
|   Variance         |              |          |              | 156.44   |
| Accrued Payroll              |              |          | 6,101.16     | 5,920.00 |

    To record accrued pay-
roll at actual cost,
standard labor cost in
production, and the vari-
ance divided as to cost
and quantity differences.

He explained this procedure by stating that "the actual and standard amounts can be compared by inspection of various items while the
reasons for the variances can be found in the standard cost columns opposite the variance account titles."[54]

The Disposition of Labor Variations in Standard Costs.--An analysis of the methods of recording standard costs in the accounts will indicate that variations arise from the first two methods--"Recording Labor
at Actual Costs as Debits and at Standard Costs as Credits to Work in
Process" and "Recording Labor at Standard Costs"--whereas, since the
third method records both actual and standard values in the accounts and
uses the actual figures for inventory and statement purposes, the problem
of variances in the accounts does not exist.  These variations, under
the first two plans, may be considered to arise from price or quantity
factors and may be disposed of by prorating over the cost of sales,

---

[54]Ibid., p. 376.

finished goods inventory, and work in process inventory or by charging
to Profit and Loss.

Carl P. Immekus, in discussing this problem in 1924, proposed that
Work in Process be charged with the standard cost of the total amount
paid for direct labor and that the difference between actual and standard cost be recorded in a "Variation Reserve for Direct Labor in Process"
account. As goods are completed, the Work in Process-Direct Labor account would be credited with the standard cost of goods completed and
the Variation Reserve account would be charged or credited with "the
proper amount to be transferred with the cost of production." The Finished Goods account would be charged with the algebraic sum of these two
items, which amounted to approximate actual labor cost in production. It
should be stated that the balance of the Work in Process-Direct Labor
account would represent the work in process at standard values and that
the balance of the Variation Reserve for Direct Labor in Process account
would serve as a valuation reserve to adjust this inventory to actual
cost. The actual result of this procedure was to accumulate the net
variation in one account, to analyze this account for management, and to
allocate its balance over the inventories and cost of sales.[55]

Henry W. Maynard, in considering the same point in 1927, accumulated the difference between actual and standard labor costs in one account, "Variance from Standard Cost--Direct Labor," and closed this

---

[55]Immekus, Carl P., "Proper Treatment of Variations from Standard
Cost--Direct Labor," _National Association of Cost Accountants Yearbook_,
1924, pp. 202-205.

account, which he termed an efficiency variance account, monthly to the Profit and Loss account.[56]

Another accountant, J. T. Foerth, recognized labor variances, when in excess of the standard, as the result of waste, inefficiency, or some other deficiency and declared that such variances should be written off to profit and loss in the month in which they occurred.[57]

Harry C. Nichols, in describing the standard cost procedure for labor cost variations in the Arrow-Hart and Hegeman Electric Manufacturing Company (a concern which manufactured 17,000 different completed devices ranging in price from 1 1/4¢ to $85.00 each), presented a procedure for ascertaining the direct labor costs and the variations from standard through the use of tabulating equipment. In an attempt to eliminate or reduce variations, an analysis of the main causes was made and these causes were found to be: Special and Repair Operations, Added Operations, Operations Performed Day Work Because of Small Volume, Standards Out of Line, and Low Piece-Work Ratio. By breaking the labor variances down into these classifications weekly, an analysis could be made and an adjustment devised. With responsibility delegated for these variances resulting from controllable factors, reduction or elimination was possible. Variations resulting from Added Operations (usually special orders from customers) and Standards Out of Line would be trans-

---

[56] See "The Accounting Technique for Standard Costs," National Association of Cost Accountants Bulletin, Vol. VIII, No. 12, Sec. I (February 15, 1927), pp. 554-555.

[57] See "How Should Labor and Burden Variances be Analyzed and Treated in the Accounts?," National Association of Cost Accountants Yearbook, 1930, p. 193.

ferred to cost of sales; other variations represented inefficiencies and would be closed to profit and loss.[58]

Schlatter would carry the difference between actual and standard labor costs in one account, Labor Variation, and would dispose of this account in one of two manners, depending upon the method in which the accounting records were maintained:

1. When the accounts and statements are shown at standard, the Labor Variation account would be closed to Profit and Loss. This action was based on the assumption that the variation represented waste or inefficiency.

2. If the accounts are maintained at standard costs but statements are shown at actual figures, then a journal entry must be made to adjust the Cost of Sales for this account's portion of the Labor Variation. The balance in the Labor Variation account, after the adjustment to Cost of Sales, pertains to the inventories still on the books; however, the author would not make a journal entry to adjust these inventory accounts.[59]

A consideration of the literature treating the disposition of labor variations indicates that such variations are either prorated over the inventories and cost of sales or are closed to profit and loss, with the majority of the writers, as in the case of material variations, favoring the profit and loss debit or credit. In view of the fact that labor

---

[58]Nichols, Harry C., "Direct Labor Variation Control," *National Association of Cost Accountants Bulletin*, Vol. XXII, No. 15, Sec. I (April 1, 1941), pp. 837-850.

[59]Schlatter, *Advanced Cost Accounting*, pp. 139-140.

variations are disposed of in the same manner as material variances and
that material variations have been developed adequately in the preceding
chapter, additional consideration will not be given to this subject.

Incidental Variations in Direct Labor Costs.--In addition to the
customary analyses of the difference between actual and standard direct
labor costs--price variations and quantity variations, which have been
treated in this chapter already--special conditions in a manufacturing
enterprise may require, for adequate control purposes, that this variance from standard be broken down even more minutely.  Some of the more
common variations and/or allowances will be considered.

1. Variations arising from multi-wage rates on the same operations.
This situation may develop from the transferring of laborers from one
department to another for the convenience of either the transferor--this
department may have surplus labor, which the management desires to re-
tain--or the transferee--this department may require additional assistance because of an emergency.  Sanders recognized this problem in 1929
by stating that the department receiving the benefit from such transfer
might be charged with the variation; however, he preferred that this difference be segregated from the regular price variation and be disclosed
to management as a separate item.[60]  When he published his textbook in
1934, he treated this variation as a separate item of overhead.[61]

---

[60] Sanders, Thomas Henry, "Accounting for Labor," Proceedings, International Congress on Accounting, 1929, New York, International Congress
on Accounting, 1930, p. 837.

[61] Sanders, Cost Accounting for Control, p. 125.

2. Variations arising from use of apprentices or new workers. . This variation occurs in those instances involving the use of new employees, who must undergo a period of training during which their production may be below normal and their rate of pay may be accordingly greater than their output justifies.  Sanders asserted that, if the excess charges were clearly disclosed and were considered by management as properly and profitably incurred, the accounting department had performed its function.[62]  When he wrote his textbook, he considered this variance as a cost of maintaining the labor force and, therefore, as a separate overhead item.[63]

The author of the material for the International Accounting Society (1936) accumulated this variance in a special account, "Labor Allowance-Training New Workers," and treated this account as part of the factory burden.[64]

A recent research study, under the direction of R. P. Marple for the National Association of Cost Accountants, investigated the policies of 263 companies with respect to excess labor and overhead costs.  Of particular significance to this investigation is the practice of these concerns in disposing of the cost of apprenticeship programs.  Of the 134 companies conducting such programs, 59 (44 per cent) treated such

---

[62]Sanders, Thomas Henry, "Accounting for Labor," _Proceedings, International Congress on Accounting_, 1929, p. 837.

[63]Sanders, _Cost Accounting for Control_, p. 125.

[64]See _Standard Costs_, Lesson S 6:9.

costs as charges to be absorbed in inventories while 75 (56 per cent) wrote these expenditures off as charges against current income.[65]

3. Variations arising from idle time labor payments. Idle time labor costs may occur in a factory when workers are paid for time spent waiting for work to be brought to their department, for a machine to be repaired, or for defective materials to be exchanged or serviced. Myers (1931), in explaining labor variations, stated that such variations fell under two classes--(1) "In-efficiency," and (2) "Labor Rates"--and that "in-efficiency" might be subdivided as desired. He suggested the following possible classifications:

> 1. Falling below standard (real in-efficiency).
> 2. Lost Time . . . (an exception of standard).
>     a. Machine break-down.
>     b. Out of material.
>     c. Re-operation, etc.[66]

Gillespie recognized this variance as "Lost labor time," which he computed by subtracting the "standard cost for actual hours worked" from the "standard labor cost for working hours paid."[67] Neuner (1942) treated this cost as an indirect labor charge but recorded it in a separate account in order that management might be presented with a comparative figure covering the amount of loss due to poor factory planning or

_____________

[65]"Accounting for Excess Labor Costs and Overhead Under Conditions of Increased Production," National Association of Cost Accountants Bulletin, Vol. XXII, No. 24, Sec. III (August 15, 1941), p. 1564.

[66]Myers, Herbert J., "The Installation of Standard Costs," National Association of Cost Accountants Bulletin, Vol. XII, No. 23 (August 1, 1931), p. 1850.

[67]Gillespie, Accounting Procedure for Standard Costs, p. 151.

to inefficient materials and equipment.[68]

Blocker (1942), in presenting a plan for accounting for idle time, proposed that each time ticket disclose the amount of time expended on each production order, the amount of time used in performing indirect labor as a regular or special assignment, and the amount of time classified as non-productive or idle time. If idle time represented a normal condition, this writer would charge factory overhead expense and would maintain a separate standing order for idle time in order that management's attention might be directed to the idle time factor and to the responsible department. On the other hand, if idle time was the result of abnormal conditions, which were beyond the control of the production department, he would treat such cost as a general profit and loss charge.[69]

4. Variations arising from overtime labor costs. As a result of the federal Wage and Hour law, new significance has been added to overtime bonuses for direct labor. Neuner stated that the treatment of extra overtime costs varied with the conditions under which such costs were incurred: (1) regular overtime (due to general business conditions or labor shortage) would be treated as either a charge to the factory burden account or a part of the direct labor costs as an increased rate of pay; (2) special overtime (due to some unusual condition or a particular order) would be charged directly to such order as a part of the direct labor cost or as direct manufacturing expense.[70]

---

[68] Neuner, Cost Accounting, p. 29.

[69] Blocker, Essentials of Cost Accounting, pp. 166-167.

[70] Neuner, Cost Accounting, p. 194.

Langer (1942), in his supplementary lecture on Factory Payroll,
made the following statement with respect to this subject:

> The overtime excess compensation paid for overtime on
> work orders, where the work orders are not charged with the
> overtime excess compensation, is part of the manufacturing
> costs and is generally distributed as a debit to Manufactur-
> ing Expense--Overtime Excess Compensation.[71]

The current practice of disposing of overtime compensation is suggested by the following data, which have been reproduced from the afore-
mentioned National Association of Cost Accountants' survey of 1941:[72]

Number and Per Cent of Companies Including in and
Excluding from Inventory Values the Overtime
Premiums on Direct Labor

| | Companies Using Standard Costs in Whole or Part | | Companies Using Actual Costs | | All Companies | |
|---|---|---|---|---|---|---|
| | Number | Per Cent | Number | Per Cent | Number | Per Cent |
| Premiums Included in Inventory Values | 39 | 26 | 83 | 73 | 122 | 46 |
| Premiums Excluded from Inventory Values | 64 | 43 | 14 | 12 | 78 | 30 |
| Normal Allowance in Inventory Values | 46 | 31 | 17 | 15 | 63 | 24 |
| Totals | 149 | 100 | 114 | 100 | 263 | 100 |

5. Variation arising from extra allowances and fall-downs.  In some

---

[71] Langer, *Factory Payroll*, p. SL 10-21.

[72] "Accounting for Excess Labor Costs and Overhead Under Conditions
of Increased Production," *National Association of Cost Accountants Bulletin*, Vol. XXII, No. 24, Sec. III (August 15, 1941), p. 1554.

instances, additional time, in excess of the standard, may be allowed
because the materials being processed are inferior to standard, because
the machinery being used is inefficient, or because some other obstacle,
beyond the control of the workers, is recognized as the cause of labor
operating below standard.  In such cases, the additional time will be
approved by a responsible factory official and the written authoriza-
tions, vouching for such approval, will be accumulated as "Extra Allowances" for necessary analytical purposes.

After the "Extra Allowances" have been added to the original standards, labor may still fail to attain this new--modified or adjusted--
standard.  In such instances, the variance will represent an unauthor-
ized difference between actual and standard labor costs, which has been
termed a "fall-down."

Reitell (1933) recognized this situation and, in his analysis of
direct labor variance, provided for the computation of "Time Allowances"
as well as both Time and Rate Fall-Downs."  His procedure may be illustrated by reproducing his "Direct Labor Variance" schedule, however,
hypothetical figures have been substituted for the author's example.[73]

---

[73]Reitell, Cost Accounting, p. 401.

## DIRECT LABOR VARIANCE

| | | Analysis of Productive Hours | | | Standard Costs | | |
| | a | b | c | d | e | f | g |
| De-<br>part-<br>ment | Net<br>Allowed<br>Hours | Gross<br>Allowed<br>Hours | Actual<br>Hours<br>Taken | Standard<br>Hourly<br>Rates | Cleared-<br>in Labor<br>Cost<br>a x d | Gross<br>Allowed<br>Labor<br>Cost<br>b x d | Standard<br>Cost at<br>Actual<br>Time<br>c x d |
|---|---|---|---|---|---|---|---|
| A | 10 | 14 | 16 | $0.50 | $ 5.00 | $ 7.00 | $ 8.00 |
| B | 12 | 12 | 14 | 0.60 | 7.20 | 7.20 | 8.40 |
| C | 17 | 20 | 24 | 0.40 | 6.80 | 8.00 | 9.60 |
| Total | 39 | 46 | 54 | | $19.00 | $22.20 | $26.00 |

## DIRECT LABOR VARIANCE (Continued)

| | | Analysis of Direct Labor Variance | | | | |
| | | Time | | | Rate | |
| h | i | j | k | l | m |
| Actual<br>Pay-<br>roll | Total<br>Variance<br>e - h | Allow-<br>ances<br>f - e | Fall-<br>Downs<br>g - f | Make-<br>Outs<br>g - h | Fall-<br>Downs<br>h - g |
|---|---|---|---|---|---|
| $ 9.18 | -$4.18 | $2.00 | $1.00 | $ .00 | $1.18 |
| 6.87 | + .33 | .00 | 1.20 | 1.53 | .00 |
| 9.88 | - 3.08 | 1.20 | 1.60 | .00 | .28 |
| $25.93 | -$6.93 | $3.20 | $3.80 | $1.53 | $1.46 |

A consideration of the data for Department A will indicate that the
actual payroll for the period was $9.18, the "Cleared-in Labor Costs"--
"costs which, under a standard system, are allowed"[74]--was $5.00, and
the total variance between such actual and standard figures amounted to
$4.18.  His analysis of this variance may be summarized in the following
manner:

---

[74] Ibid., p. 400.

```
Allowance (Time):
    Gross hours allowed                    14
    Less: Net allowed hours                10
      Extra Time Allowance in hours         4
    Application of the Standard
      Hourly Rate                       $0.50
      Extra Allowance (Time)                        $2.00

Fall-Downs (Time):
    Actual hours taken                     16
    Gross hours allowed                    14
      Unauthorized variance in hours        2
    Application of the Standard
      Hourly Rate                       $0.50
      Fall-Downs (Time)                              1.00

Fall-Downs (Rate):
    Actual Payroll                      $9.18
    Actual hours taken at Standard
      Hourly Rate
      16 hours at $0.50                  8.00
      Fall-Downs (Rate)                              1.18

  Total Variance for Period                        $4.18
```

In addition to the Time and Rate Fall-Downs, Reitell conceived of
favorable variances, as has been illustrated by Department B, Column 1.
He termed these differences "Make-Outs," which would occur when the
actual rates paid were less than the standard rates.[75] When this textbook was revised by Johnston in 1937, evidently no changes merited the
attention of the writers as this portion was published exactly as presented in the original edition.[76]

Gillespie (1935) prepared a worksheet, somewhat comparable with
Reitell's, for computing the "Analysis of Labor Variation." He provided

---

[75] Ibid., pp. 400-401.

[76] Reitell, Charles, and Johnston, C. E., _Cost Accounting_, Scranton,
Pa., International Textbook Company, 1937, pp. 309-310.

for the following variances:  (1) Extra Allowances, (2) Fall-Down,
(3) Make-Out Only, and (4) Fall Down and Day Work.  His definition of
"Make-Out"--"task completed within standard time plus extra allowance"[77]
--differs slightly from Reitell's meaning, as quoted in the preceding
paragraph.

6. Variation arising from set-up labor costs.  The actual time consumed on a production order, under some conditions, may be made up of
two factors--the time to adjust and apply the tools or machinery to the
particular product being processed and the operation time of the machinery on this order.  The first time element, which is the subject
under consideration, has been designated as "Preparation, Make-Ready, or
Setting Up."[78]

Harrison (1930) recognized the factor of set-up cost as of extreme
importance in analyzing the variations between actual and standard figures and stated that "manufacturing parts in too small quantities owing
to defective planning methods and other causes often results in exces-
sively high costs, owing to the set-up cost per unit of production being
increased, due to the constant changing of set-ups."[79]  In proposing a
standard set-up cost per hour, he recognized three factors as entering
into such cost--"the standard number of set-ups per hour, the standard
hours per set-up, and the standard rate per hour for the set-up man."[80]

---

[77] Gillespie, Accounting Procedure for Standard Costs, pp. 169-171.

[78] Alford, Cost and Production Handbook, p. 219.

[79] Harrison, Standard Costs, p. 88.

[80] Ibid.

In accepting these factors as possessing qualities that were subject to variation, this author devised formulas for determining the
variations resulting from their operation in a manufacturing enterprise.
His illustration will be reproduced as a means of exhibiting his procedure.[81]

|  | | Increase |
|---|---|---|
| 1. Net increase or decrease: | | |
|     H, Standard set-up cost of month's pro-<br>        duction obtained from Form EE | $250.00 | |
|     Minus A, Actial cost of set-ups in<br>        department obtained from payroll<br>        distributed | 351.00 | $101.00 |
| 5. Variation in labor rates: | | |
|     B, Actual set-up hours at standard rate | $324.00 | |
|     Minus A, as above | 351.00 | 27.00 |
| 9. Variations due to number of set-ups: | | |
|     H, as above | $250.00 | |
|     Minus E, Standard cost of actual set-<br>        ups in month; that is 600 x 0.50, as<br>        shown in the insert on the diagram | 300.00 | 50.00 |
| 10. Variation in time taken on set-ups: | | |
|     E, Standard cost of actual set-ups in<br>        month as above | $300.00 | |
|     Minus B, Actual set-up hours at<br>        standard rate as above | 324.00 | 24.00 |

Camman (1932), in outlining the accounting plan for a manufacturing
enterprise, observed that frequently the operation of setting up the
machinery for production involved a substantial portion of the manufacturing cost and indicated the importance of this factor in the following
manner:

---

[81] Ibid., pp. 116-117.

It will follow, therefore, that if the quantity of products
to be made is less than an economical lot, when the necessary
preparation is taken into consideration, a grave variation in
costs may ensue.  It will be evident that if it costs as much
to make ready to run as it does to run a given number of articles, the running costs varying with the number, and only
half the quantity is manufactured, the cost of the lot is one
and one-half times what it would be if the given number were
run.  Hence set-up or make-ready may be an important factor
and, if so, it will be desirable to treat it as a separate
item of production.  In other words, the basic standard costs
will include separate calculations for the making-ready operations.  In manufacture, such operations will be reported as
production and priced at standard cost as if "make-ready"
were a separate product.  It will then be possible to show,
not only the effectiveness with which preparatory operations
are conducted, but also the influence upon costs of deviations from economical manufacturing lots.[82]

Whisler (1937), head of the Standards Department of the National

Cash Register Company, has described a standard for set up as practiced

by this company:

> . . . this may interest you from an accounting standpoint, we
> set a separate standard for setup.  This means that after a
> man punches the last piece out of a strip of steel, the time
> required to (a) turn in his order, (b) get his next order and
> die in the machine, (c) set it up if he does his own setting
> up, (d) get that machine operating and produce the first
> piece, and (e) secure the approval of supervision, is taken
> care of by a separate standard.  This becomes a setup allow-
> ance which we keep separate for several reasons, but princi-
> pally because we have a variable quantity problem in our
> plant.  As I will show you later on, we are manufacturing
> actively some 70,000 items involving a great variety of opera-
> tions.  As you men know, it is a custom built product, manu-
> factured to suit your needs.  We are making only ten or twenty
> of some pieces a month, while other pieces are produced at
> the rate of ten or twenty thousand a month.  To eliminate the

---

[82] Camman, _Basic Standard Costs_, p. 182.

variance due to setup costs we have a setup standard and
carry it as a burden item.[83]

Paton (1943) stated that time standards should be established for
set-ups and, in further elaboration, made the following comments:

> . . . and in cases of job shops, or plants manufacturing a
> wide variety of products, the set-up should be included in
> costs as a direct-labor item on the basis of normal runs. In
> instances where set-ups are of major importance, as in spe-
> cialty order plants, the standard set-up costs allowed may be
> collected against each order or part number.[84]

Summary.--This analysis of the accounting for direct labor in standard costs has defined direct labor as that compensation to workmen whose
services have been used directly in converting direct materials into the
finished products.

The initial problem, which was considered, involved the setting of
direct labor standards--time or quantity standards and rate or price
standards. Time standards may be set satisfactorily through time and
motion studies while price standards will usually be established after
some consideration has been given to past records, the present status of
labor, and the trend of wage conditions.

As in the case of the accounting for materials, direct labor may be
recorded in the accounts at actual, at standard, or at both actual and
standard values. The recording of standard values tends to be accepted
in the majority of cases considered.

---

[83]Whisler, R. F., "Operating the Piecework Plan," _National Association of Cost Accountants Yearbook_, 1937, p. 141.

[84]Paton, _Accountants' Handbook_, p. 236.

In the disposition of price and quantity variations in direct labor costs, the possibility arises of allocating such costs to the inventories and cost of sales or of charging the same to profit and loss. Current practice seems to favor the treatment of these variations as profit and loss items.

CHAPTER IX

ACCOUNTING FOR BURDEN IN STANDARD COSTS

Burden may be accepted as a term which designates all those manu-

facturing costs that cannot be charged directly to the processed products,

or, stated in another manner, which includes all those production costs

that cannot be classified as direct materials or direct labor.  Church

(1930), an authority on this subject--"Overhead expense" for this author

--offered the following definition for this cost element:

> Overhead expense in manufacturing is defined usually as
> consisting of the so-called "fixed" charges (such as rent,
> interest, depreciation, insurance, taxes, etc.) plus all that
> large class of expenditure on labor and materials which can- [1]
> not be charged definitely to any given job or lot of product.

Of the three components of factory cost--direct material, direct

labor, and burden--burden presents the most complex problems for the

accountant who undertakes to apply standard cost procedure to the activ-

ities of a manufacturing enterprise.  This difficulty arises from the

fact that he must attempt to predetermine two distinct variables--the

amount of the burden elements (indirect materials, indirect labor, depre-

ciation, taxes, and power, for example), and the volume of production at

which such burden costs will be allocated to processed commodities.

However, this situation is somewhat counterbalanced by the fact

that, in the development of historical costs, the procedure for recording

---

[1] Church, Overhead Expense, p. 1.

burden has received more attention than that for materials and direct
labor. Furthermore, a predetermined burden rate has been employed for a
number of years to allocate such costs to production. As early as 1887,
Garcke and Fells mentioned three methods of charging burden to completed
operations: (1) cost of wages expended on the job, (2) cost of wages
and materials used on the job, and (3) the time of laborers spent on the
job. Twelve years later, H. L. Arnold stated that each machine should
be loaded with its own cost factors as well as an arbitrary sum for general factory charges and die-room expenses.[2]

Somewhat later, Church developed his production center technique
for allocating burden to production "on a more scientific basis than any
of his predecessors." In 1917, Webner not only described the pertinent
features of each important method of burden allocation but also recommended the conditions under which each plan might be used.[3]   Other
writers to evidence interest in this subject during this developmental
period included J. L. Nicholson (1909), C. H. Scovell (1916), William
Kent (1918), and D. C. Eggleston (1918).[4]

In view of the fact that predetermined burden rates, as based on
historical cost procedure, had been understood and accepted both in

---

[2] Arnold, _The Complete Cost-Keeper_, p. 18.

[3] Webner, _Factory Costs_, pp. 299-315.

[4] Nicholson, _Nicholson on Factory Organization and Costs_; Scovell,
Clinton H., _Cost Accounting and Burden Application_, New York, D. Appleton and Company, 1916; Kent, William, _Bookkeeping and Cost Accounting
for Factories_, New York, John Wiley and Sons, 1918; Eggleston, DeWitt
Carl, _Problems in Cost Accounting_, New York, D. Appleton and Company,
1918.

theory and in practice for some time, the transition from such procedure
to the application of standard burden rates did not represent as great
an innovation as the application of standard cost technique to the compilation of direct material and direct labor costs.

Setting Burden Cost Standards.--That the problems of setting burden
standards and of distributing burden to production were considered important as the second decade of the twentieth century opened is suggested
by the fact that a large portion of the Second International Cost Conference at Cleveland, Ohio, in 1921 was devoted to a discussion of these
subjects.[5] Perhaps C. B. Williams expressed the practice of the time
and indicated the trend of thought for the future when he proposed, in a
paper read before this conference, that the normal burden rate be used
to allocate burden to production.[6]

This speaker defined the normal burden rate as that rate which,
during a period of normal production and normal expense, would absorb
all the burden for that period, and stated that this normal rate would
result from dividing a normal amount of expense by a normal volume of
business for the period.

Recognizing the setting of the normal volume of production as the
most difficult part of the rate determination, this author suggested
that, for concerns lacking scientific methods for determining the

---

[5]National Association of Cost Accountants Yearbook, 1921, pp. 199-
229.

[6]Williams, C. B., "The Distribution of Overhead Under Abnormal Conditions," National Association of Cost Accountants Yearbook, 1921,
pp. 199-206.

possible output from which to deduct allowances for possible interruptions (a recognition of standard technique as highly desirable but impracticable by many enterprises at the time), the normal be established as the average of a certain number of years which might be deemed by management as representative of the enterprise's activities. This normal volume of production would be converted into burden allocation units--direct labor hours, machine hours, or other denominator--as might be required to obtain such volume.

And, finally, Williams would ascertain the normal operating expenses for the period by considering past records and by consulting the factory superintendent, as well as other officials with information and responsibility concerning such costs. By dividing such normal operating expenses by the normal burden allocation units, the normal burden rates, which would be used for the subsequent period, would be obtained. It should be mentioned also that the author understood the meaning of fixed costs and pointed out the value of departmentalizing the various expenses.

Van Zandt (1922), in considering normal burden rates in the same general trend of thought as Williams, recognized that two factors--normal production and normal burden expenditures--must be known before normal burden rates could be computed. In determining normal production, he distinguished between theoretical capacity--"the number of units a machine can produce in a given time under ideal conditions"--and practical capacity--"85% of theoretical capacity," which represented an arbitrary allowance of 15 per cent for operational contingencies--and stated

that such production should represent a per cent of practical capacity
and, under ideal conditions, should be so set that the Profit and Loss
account would never be affected by under-absorbed or over-absorbed
burden.[7]

> That is to say, normal production should be so low, and con-
> sequently normal burden rates so high, that in times of com-
> parative good business burden would be over-absorbed.  This
> over-absorbed burden should be carried to a reserve account
> and held there until the day when business again falls off
> and under-absorbed burden results, which should be charged
> against the reserve.[8]

In determining the normal burden, this author recognized three
general classes of burden items:  "(1) those which should fluctuate in
direct ratio to the volume of production, (2) those which should fluctuate partially with production, and (3) those that are fixed."[9]

As a means of computing and disclosing the burden expenditures, Van
Zandt devised a burden statement, which, although rather elementary, is
significant because of the information that it contained:

> . . . the theoretical capacity, practical capacity and normal
> hours, both for machines and men, the actual man hours worked
> and percentage of normal each month, classifications of
> burden, code numbers of the accounts, normal charge, basis of
> variation from normal according to percentage operated, burden
> earned, and actual burden.[10]

---

[7]Van Zandt, Charles, "Normal Burden Rates," National Association
of Cost Accountants Bulletin, Vol. III, No. 19 (July 1, 1922), pp. 1-12.

[8]Ibid., pp. 4-5.

[9]Ibid., p. 5.

[10]Ibid., pp. 5-6.

Fletcher (1922), in applying burden standards to the shoe industry,

advocated that the factory be divided into burden centers or departments

and that each burden item be applied directly or indirectly to the

burden center in which such expense was incurred:

> Direct burden charges include indirect labor, supplies,
> repairs, purchased power, gas, superintendence, and sundry
> items. Indirect burden charges include items of fixed ex-
> pense such as insurance, taxes, interest on investment, and
> depreciation, which are applied to centers on the basis of
> floor space, and on the value of equipment. Light, heat, and
> power charges must be determined and applied to centers on
> the basis of service rendered. General expenses such as
> superintendence, factory office, etc., must be apportioned to
> centers with regard to the service rendered.[11]

This author, after distributing the various estimated burden

charges to the respective cost centers, would compute the burden rate as

a percentage of the normal direct labor cost. As the factory operated,

this burden rate would be applied to the total cost of direct labor

charged to Work in Process to determine the burden earned--burden

charged to Work in Process. The difference between this amount and the

standard burden, as established originally, would represent unearned or

overearned burden and would be transferred to Loss or Gain on Standard

Costs. As work was completed, the Finished Goods account would be

charged and the Work in Process account would be credited with the

standard cost of such completed products. And, finally, the variation

between actual cost of burden and standard burden would be closed to

---

[11]Fletcher, F. Richmond, "An Outline of the Use of Standards in Shoe Manufacturing," National Association of Cost Accountants Yearbook, 1922, pp. 177-178.

Burden Variances.[12]

Harrison (1922) declared that the machine rate was the most accurate method which had been devised for the distribution of burden.  In
determining this rate, he figured the standard month as containing 212
working hours and made allowances from this standard for machine repairs,
set-ups, and other operational difficulties.[13]

C. W. Bennett (1922), who applied cost standards to the woolen mill,
predetermined the burden expenditures for each cost center--described by
the writer as a scientific analysis of burden expenses--and pointed out
that either the machine hour, the man hour, the direct labor, or the
percentage on labor method might be employed to apply burden to such
cost centers.[14]

Worrall (1923) rejected the use of burden rates based on direct
labor as a means of judging a department's efficiency--if one department
produced with a minimum of direct labor, he declared its burden rate
might be higher than that of the inefficient department which used more
labor.  In setting his standard burden rates for a manufacturing enterprise, this author determined its standard production--the capacity of
the plant running full time for one month--which was translated into the
number of man hours for each department, and computed the expenses,

---

[12] Ibid., pp. 157-191.

[13] Harrison, G. Charter, "Working Plans for Standard Costs," Management Engineering, II (June, 1922), 334.

[14] Bennett, C. W., "Some Phases of Woolen Mill Cost Accounting,"
National Association of Cost Accountants Yearbook, 1922, pp. 336-337.

which were divided into fixed and fluctuating charges, for operating the
particular department at such capacity.  The standard rate was ascertained by dividing the expenses by the standard man hours.  At the end
of the month, the standard burden rate was applied to the standard hours
in the department's production and the result was compared with the
actual expenditures.  Any difference was analyzed into the following
variations:  "labor rates, efficiency of labor, quantity of supplies,
price of supplies, loss in fixed charges due to the plant operating at
less than standard time, price and quantity of material."[15]

Three years later, Worrall, in setting standard burden rates, rejected his standard man hour method and employed standard machine rates
based on normal capacity--determined by reducing the practical plant
capacity by a percentage, which was not indicated, to allow for repairs
and other emergencies.  In addition to this innovation, the manufacturing expenditures were classified according to whether they were or were
not controllable by the department foreman.  Although these two types of
expenses were combined for the purpose of establishing the standard cost
of each product, they were recorded separately in the accounting procedure.  In this manner, an index to departmental efficiency, as measured
in controllable burden charges, was established.[16]

C. Howard Knapp (1924) recognized two groups of burden accounts--

---

[15] Worrall, William F., "Standard Costs--How to Establish and Apply
Them," *National Association of Cost Accountants Bulletin*, Vol. IV,
No. 16 (May 1, 1923), pp. 8-9.

[16] Worrall, William F., "Standard Costs--How to Get Them," *National
Association of Cost Accountants Yearbook*, 1926, pp. 143-154.

fluctuating burden items, which vary with the amount of production; and fixed burden items, which do not tend to vary with production--and described a method that might be employed for setting burden standards and burden rates (which, according to this writer, should be based on direct labor cost).

In computing the fixed burden rate, the fixed burden items were forecast for each department on the basis of the best information available and the sum of such expenditures was divided by the departmental productive capacity expressed in direct labor dollars. The quotient obtained by this process represented the standard fixed burden rate based on direct labor cost for the department involved.

With respect to the fluctuating items of burden, an attempt was not made to predetermine the annual expenditures in view of the fact that the total of such costs would depend upon the amount of production for the period. After considering the cost figures for the preceding year and the expected changes for the succeeding year, a standard percentage cost of direct labor was established for each item of fluctuating burden as required in the respective departments. These various percentages were totaled for a standard fluctuating burden percentage, which, when added to the standard fixed burden rate, gave the standard departmental burden rate based on direct labor cost.[17]

P. T. Skove (1927) approved the idea of flexible standards and

_______________

[17]Knapp, C. Howard, "Variations from Predetermined Standards of Burden in Manufacturing Costs," _National Association of Cost Accountants Yearbook_, 1924, pp. 206-218.

stated that his company's standards were being changed continuously as
the results of suggestions and efforts of the engineering and efficiency
departments.  In setting standard burden rates for the year, three distinct levels of production--normal or standard level, abnormal level of
peak months, and subnormal level of low operating months--were recognized and rates were set based on these levels of production.[18]

Henry W. Maynard (1927), Factory Accountant for the Gillette Safety
Razor Company, called attention to the fact that there were three types
of manufacturing expenses--100% fixed, 100% variable, and partial or
stepped variability--and that his company was experimenting with standard burden rates based on this knowledge, together with a procedure by
which a comparison might be made between the actual expenses of each
department for a fiscal period (one month was suggested by the writer)
and the amounts that should have been spent for the actual production of
the period.[19]

A year later, Maynard addressed the annual meeting of the National
Association of Cost Accountants and described the refinements of the
standard cost system of the Gillette Safety Razor Company.  Again recognizing the principle of "variability of expenses," he declared that

> . . . some expenses are wholly fixed and . . . have "zero
> variability"; others change in exact proportion to production

---

[18]Skove, P. T., "How Perfection Stove Company Figures Standard Costs
and how Actual Performance is Checked Against the Standards," *National
Association of Cost Accountants Yearbook*, 1927, pp. 189-201.

[19]Maynard, Henry W., "Standard Costs," *National Association of Cost
Accountants Yearbook*, 1927, pp. 225-226.

and are "100% variable"; other items are intermediate--we estimate that in most direct departments of the Gillette Company,
supplies are "80% variable" as production rises and falls, and
that repairs are "70% variable."[20]

A consideration of Maynard's procedure indicates that the standard

burden rates were computed on normal costs during normal activity periods.

These standards, called "accounting standards," were the basis for the

journal entries in the accounting records and for the valuation of inven-

tories; they were changed only twice each year.  At the same time, "cur-

rent standards"--standards based on the actual length of the particular

working month and the actual production of the month--were computed and

were made the basis for managerial reports.

> The difference between the "accounting" and "current"
> standards are written off each month as variances due to
> change in method, design of product, or budget allowance.
> Every six months the inventories are to be recalculated at
> both the "accounting" and the then "current standards" and
> the latter become the new basis for inventory calculation.[21]

Another feature of setting burden cost standards, which should be

investigated somewhat at this time, relates to tabulating the expenses

at varying levels of production and, on the basis of such computations,

to setting the cost standards.  Lawrence (1925) suggested such a proce-

dure as may be evidenced by the following quotation:

-------

[20] Maynard, Henry W., "What the Standard Costs and the Flexible
Budget are Doing for the Reduction of Costs in the Manufacturing Department," _National Association of Cost Accountants Yearbook_, 1928, p. 302.

[21] _Ibid._, p. 303.

The standard expenses of each department should be shown
in separate tabulations for different production conditions
and should present both total amounts for each expense and
standard rates per unit of product or per direct labor hour
or machine hour.  By this arrangement it is possible to determine the total expense which should apply in any department under various conditions and the rate per unit of product
or hour of time.  Comparison of the actual cost, either in
totals or unit rates, with the standard for that production
condition, will disclose where and why a variation has occurred.[22]

Stock and Coffey (1925), Industrial Department of Lybrand, Ross

Brothers and Montgomery, were cognizant of such a technique and prepared

a Burden Cost exhibit in which three levels of production--actual,

Increase 25%, and Increase 50%--were illustrated.  Although these writers

used the actual costs for a three months' period as the basis for their

computations, the fact that they illustrated fixed, variable, and par-

tially variable expenses at three possible points of production tends to

lend significance to their efforts at this time.[23]  In order to illus-

trate their trend of thought, a portion of their Burden schedule will be

reproduced.

---

[22] Lawrence, Cost Accounting, pp. 381-382.

[23] Stock, A. F., and Coffey, J. M., "Overhead During Low-Volume Production," National Association of Cost Accountants Bulletin, Vol. VI,
No. 12 (February 16, 1925), pp. 5-8.

BURDEN COST ACCOUNT[24]

| Description | | Increase 25% | Increase 50% |
|---|---|---|---|
| **Labor** | | | |
| Foremen and Assistants | 1,200 | 1,200 | 1,200 |
| Clerical Expense | 450 | 450 | 450 |
| . . . | | | |
| Trucking | 420 | 530 | 600 |
| . . . | | | |
| Sick and Accident Expense | 200 | 250 | 300 |
| Total[25] | 3,445 | 3,805 | 4,085 |
| | | | |
| **Maintenance** | | | |
| Building | 500 | 540 | 560 |
| Machinery | 1,200 | 1,300 | 1,350 |
| . . . | | | |
| Tools | 2,100 | 2,400 | 2,500 |
| Total[25] | 4,975 | 5,485 | 5,725 |
| | | | |
| **Supplies** | | | |
| Oils and Waste | 40 | 45 | 55 |
| . . . | | | |
| Small Tools | 70 | 85 | 95 |
| . . . | | | |
| Total[25] | 230 | 270 | 310 |
| | | | |
| **Apportioned** | | | |
| Proportion of: | | | |
| Power Expense | 2,310 | 2,440 | 2,480 |
| General Expense | 2,780 | 3,475 | 4,170 |
| Insurance | 800 | 800 | 800 |
| Taxes | 700 | 700 | 700 |
| Depreciation | 2,800 | 2,800 | 2,800 |
| Total | 9,390 | 10,125 | 10,950 |
| Total Burden | 18,040 | 19,775 | 21,070 |
| No. Direct Labor Hours | 13,900 | 17,375 | 20,850 |
| Actual Rate Per Hour | 1.30 | 1.13 | 1.02 |

---

[24] Ibid., p. 6.

[25] Although some of the authors' accounts have been omitted, the totals have been reproduced as originally recorded.

Other writers who contributed to the development of theories and
techniques related to setting burden cost standards during this period
were George Rea (1923), William S. Kemp (1923), Nelson J. Bowne (1924),
F. Brugger (1925), Clinton H. Scovell (1927), Amidon and Lang (1928),
Maze and Glover (1929), and Walter S. Gee (1929).[26]

Reitell (1931), in accepting the problem of setting burden standards as being more difficult than that connected with materials and
direct labor, initiated his procedure by differentiating between direct
and general burden expenditures--direct burden costs, which were incurred
in a particular costing center, would be accumulated in a schedule for
such center; and general burden items, which were applicable to the
whole factory, would be compiled in a general schedule and would be apportioned among the cost centers according to some method that would
tend to reflect the manner in which such expenses arose.[27] These sched-
ules--which were prepared for various volumes of production, ranging
from 40 per cent to 140 per cent--will be illustrated with somewhat
abridged examples as compared with Reitell's presentation.

---

[26]Rea, George, "An Introduction to Predetermined Costs," National
Association of Cost Accountants Bulletin, Vol. V, No. 7 (December 15,
1923); Kemp, Departmental and Standard Costs; Bowne, Nelson J., "Dis-
tributing the Overhead," National Association of Cost Accountants Bulle-
tin, Vol. VI, No. 4 (October 15, 1924); Brugger, F., "Standard Costs--
Their Development and Use," National Association of Cost Accountants
Bulletin, Vol. VI, No. 13 (March 2, 1925); Scovell, Clinton H., "Cost
Accounting Practice with Special Reference to Machine Hour Rate," Na-
tional Association of Cost Accountants Bulletin, Vol. VIII, No. 19,
Sec. I (June 1, 1927); Amidon and Lang, Essentials of Cost Accounting;
Maze and Glover, How to Analyze Costs; Gee, Walter S., "Accounting for
Burden," Proceedings, International Congress on Accounting, 1929, New
York, International Congress on Accounting, 1930, pp. 847-858.

[27]Reitell, Cost Accounting, pp. 357-376.

## DIRECT OVERHEAD[28]

Cost Center No. __1__                          Foreman _______________

Normal Capacity __2,500 standard hours__

| Expense Item Account | Direct Overhead Various Volumes of Production | | | | | |
|---|---|---|---|---|---|---|
| | 40% | 60% | 80% | 100% | 120% | 140% |
| Foreman | $ 200 | $ 200 | $ 200 | $ 200 | $ 200 | $ 200 |
| Assistant Foreman | | 100 | 180 | 180 | 180 | 250 |
| Inspector | 80 | 120 | 160 | 160 | 200 | 220 |
| Repairs | 200 | 290 | 380 | 400 | 440 | 460 |
| Defective Work | 20 | 60 | 100 | 160 | 250 | 360 |
| Overtime Bonus | 100 | 150 | 200 | 250 | 300 | 350 |
| Totals | $ 600 | $ 920 | $1,220 | $1,350 | $1,570 | $1,840 |

## GENERAL OVERHEAD[29]

Normal Capacity __50,000 standard hours__

| Expense Item Account | General Overhead Various Volumes of Production | | | | | |
|---|---|---|---|---|---|---|
| | 40% | 60% | 80% | 100% | 120% | 140% |
| General Manager and Assistants | $ 700 | $ 700 | $ 700 | $ 700 | $ 700 | $ 700 |
| Rate Setters | 1,800 | 1,940 | 2,100 | 2,610 | 2,960 | 3,460 |
| Fuel | 200 | 225 | 245 | 280 | 360 | 415 |
| Works Accounting | 2,100 | 2,450 | 2,800 | 2,920 | 3,000 | 3,060 |
| Depreciation, Machinery | 2,000 | 2,000 | 2,000 | 2,000 | 2,000 | 2,000 |
| Totals | $6,800 | $7,315 | $7,845 | $8,510 | $9,020 | $9,635 |

In setting his expense rates, Reitell accepted the 100 per cent level of production as normal. If his technique may be applied to the hypothetical case, the direct overhead rate for Cost Center Number 1 would be $0.54 ($1,350.00 ÷ 2,500). The general overhead expense at

-------

28 __Ibid.__, p. 371.

29 __Ibid.__, p. 372.

normal capacity ($8,510.00 in this case) would be apportioned among the
cost centers as the second step in setting the standard rate.  If it may
be assumed that $1,600.00 of the general overhead applied to Cost Center
Number 1, then the rate for general overhead would be $0.64 ($1,600 ÷
2,500).  The sum of these two rates--$0.54 and $0.64 = $1.18--represents
the standard overhead rate[30] for operating Cost Center Number 1 during
one productive hour.  As a final statement, attention is called to the
fact that this author understood the variability of burden costs--fore-
man's salary and depreciation were fixed, overtime bonus was variable,
and fuel and repairs were partially variable.

When this text was revised in 1937, the illustrations pertaining to
setting burden standards--now termed Flexible Budgets--were reproduced
intact.  This action suggests that the authors considered the original
publication still reflected the theoretical procedure for setting standard burden rates.[31]

Myers (1931), in his prize-winning essay on How to Set Standards,
proposed the "break-even basis" as the best plan for establishing a
standard of burden.

> By this basis is meant how much business at prevailing sales
> prices will be required to carry all fixed expenses, both
> factory and administrative.  Actual performance probably will
> vary considerably from this kind of a standard but it is
> agreed among most accountants that it is hard to determine a

---

[30]Reitell computed a standard cost rate for running a department by
including the standard direct-labor rate, the standard direct-overhead
rate, and the standard general-overhead rate in such rate.

[31]Reitell and Johnson, Cost Accounting, pp. 278-292.

real capacity for a plant and capacity is usually used as a
base for budgeting burden.  Therefore, it being easier to
determine the break-even point, a standard built on this as a
base is much more definite, more accurate, and will come
nearer being a real standard.[32]

In executing this plan, the fixed expenses were computed and the
volume of business, at current sales prices, that would absorb such fixed
expenses was determined.  Then the standard hours required to produce this
volume was ascertained.

These standard hours must carry the factory fixed expense,
but the variable expense must be determined by adjusting them
in the same ratio that standard hours required bears to
standard hours produced in the period from which the actual
expenses used as a basis is drawn.[33]

As a means of illustrating his procedure, Myers presented a schedule
of operations at six different levels of production.  A portion of this
schedule--only two of the author's levels of production--will be reproduced:[34]

---

[32]Myers, Keating and Metsch, How to Set Standards, p. 11.

[33]Ibid., p. 12.

[34]Ibid., p. 18.

|                      | Break-Even |            | 30% Increase |            |
|----------------------|-----------:|-----------:|-------------:|-----------:|
|                      | Amount     | % of Sales | Amount       | % of Sales |
| Material-Variable    | $44,840.00 | 64.78      | $58,292.00   | 64.78      |
| Labor-Variable       | 7,806.00   | 11.27      | 10,147.80    | 11.27      |
| Burden-Variable      | 7,197.50   | 10.40      | 9,356.75     | 10.40      |
|    -Fixed | 2,700.00 | 3.90     | 2,700.00     | 3.00       |
| Total Factory Cost   | $62,543.50 | 90.35      | $80,496.55   | 89.45      |
| Admin. & General (Fixed) | 4,600.00 | 6.65    | 4,600.00     | 5.12       |
| Direct Selling (Variable) | 2,076.60 | 3.00   | 2,699.58     | 3.00       |
| Total Operat. Cost   | $69,220.10 |            | $87,796.12   | 97.57      |
| Profit (Variable)    |            |            | 2,190.00     | 2.43       |
| Total Sales Value    | $69,220.10 | 100.00     | $89,986.12   | 100.00     |

In a subsequent article on Standard Costs, Myers presented his formula, together with an explanation, for determining the "Break-Even Sales Volume":[35]

$$\frac{\text{Total Fixed Expense}}{100\% - (\text{Sum of all Var. Exp. \%})} = \text{Break-Even Sales Volume.}$$

A restatement of the customary formula for determining the Break-Even Sales Volume, as illustrated by Newlove, Smith and White (1939), has been deemed desirable. This formula assumes that the fixed items are 100 per cent fixed and that the variable items are 100 per cent variable.[36]

---

[35] Myers, Herbert J., "The Installation of Standard Costs," National Association of Cost Accountants Bulletin, Vol. XII, No. 23 (August 1, 1931), p. 1853.

[36] Newlove, George Hillis, Smith, C. Aubrey, and White, John Arch, Intermediate Accounting, New York, D. C. Heath and Company, 1939, pp. 546-547.

$$\text{Break-even sales volume} = \frac{\text{total fixed items}}{1 - \dfrac{\text{total variable items}}{\text{corresponding sales}}}$$

These writers also presented the following formula--an interpolation procedure--which will determine the correct Break-Even Sales Volume if the variable expenses have a constant rate of variability. Attention is called to the fact that this formula will give a reasonable approximation of the Break-Even Sales Volume even though the variable expenses do not have a constant rate of variability.[37]

$$\text{Break-even sales volume} = S - \left( \frac{S - S'}{P - P'} \times P \right)$$

(S and S' are two different sales volumes
and P and P' are the respective net
profits realized thereon.)

Service (1931), in computing the standard burden rate, compiled the departmental manufacturing expenses--classified as controllable and fixed expenses--for a capacity of 100 per cent and determined the maximum direct labor hours per annum (number of producing employees x number of normal working hours per week x 52 weeks). The following quotation will explain the remainder of his procedure:

By dividing this amount of expense by the number of direct
labor hours, 100% capacity Burden Rate per hour is computed.
In order to obtain a practical, normal capacity rate, it is
necessary that we make allowances for:  Breakdowns, holidays,
interruptions, lack of orders, etc.  For illustration, let us
say, a discount of 3% and an additional discount of 17% for

---

[37] *Ibid.*, p. 547.

over-capacity (a lesser number of operators employed than
equipment or machines provide for) a total discount of 20%.
Having thus obtained the normal burden rate per labor hour,
we now record it on the Standard Part Cost Record.[38]

Sabin (1933), in treating the question of standard burden rates for
machine shops, accepted a standard capacity machine rate--"a standard
capacity rate is based on the number of machines in the plant increased
by a certain percentage for known idle time"[39]--as the basis for his
procedure.

Chubbuck (1934), staff cost accountant of Patterson, Teele and
Dennis of Boston, explained the varying levels of production method--
"The Flexible Budget," according to this author--for setting burden
standards.  Although he computed the Break-Even Sales Volume, he accepted 100 per cent of single-shift capacity as normal capacity for the
purpose of setting burden standards.[40]

Gillespie (1935), Langer (1938), Van Sickle (1938), Blocker (1940),
and Neuner (1942) accepted the flexible budget procedure--"a flexible
budget is an analysis of the overhead expenses required to operate a
cost center at varying percentages below and above the standard produc-

---

[38] Service, Robert B., Jr., "Accounting Through the Medium of Standard Costs," National Association of Cost Accountants Bulletin, Vol. XII,
No. 13 (March 1, 1931), p. 1054.

[39] Sabin, R. M., "Standard Costs for Machine Shops and Malleable
Foundries," National Association of Cost Accountants Bulletin, Vol. XV,
No. 7, Sec. I (December 1, 1933), p. 397.

[40] Chubbuck, Arthur C., "The Flexible Budget and Standard Costs in a
Business of Moderate Size," National Association of Cost Accountants
Bulletin, Vol. XV, No. 14, Sec. I (March 15, 1934), pp. 852-857.

tion output"[41]--as the basis for setting manufacturing expense standards.
These authors also recognized the importance of departmentalizing the
factory into service and production centers for the purpose of properly
distributing the burden expenditures.[42] Blocker has expressed this procedure, which tends to repeat elementary cost technique to such an extent that it has not been treated further in this study, in the following manner:

> In departmentalized concerns the estimates of overhead are
> classified by service and production departments, and the
> service department estimates are reallocated to the produc-
> tion departments; the production expected from each produc-
> tion department is estimated; and the estimated overhead ex-
> pense for each production department is divided by the
> estimated production of that department, expressed in terms
> of direct labor hours, direct labor cost, or machine-hours,
> to obtain an overhead expense distribution rate for each de-
> partment.[43]

In order to illustrate the various points at which the volume of
production may be established for the purpose of setting burden cost
standards, the following Schedule of Factory Operations has been prepared from assumed data:

---

[41] Van Sickle, Cost Accounting, p. 456.

[42] Gillespie, Accounting Procedure for Standard Costs, pp. 101-130;
Langer, Accounting Principles and Practices, p. L - 20:4; Van Sickle,
Cost Accounting, pp. 457-470; Blocker, Cost Accounting, pp. 571-579;
Neuner, Cost Accounting, pp. 491-504.

[43] Blocker, Cost Accounting, p. 572.

SCHEDULE OF FACTORY OPERATIONS

| Items | Theoretical Capacity | Practical Capacity | Average or Normal Capacity | Break-Even Sales Volume |
|---|---|---|---|---|
| Level | 100% | 80% | 60% | 58.4245%[f] |
| Working Hours | 20,000 | 16,000 | 12,000 | 11,685 |
| Net Sales | $100,000 | $80,000 | $60,000 | $58,424.50[e] |
| Cost of Sales: | | | | |
|   Materials | $ 10,000 | $ 8,000 | $ 6,000 | $ 5,842.45 |
|   Direct Labor | 20,000 | 16,000 | 12,000 | 11,684.90 |
|   Burden: | | | | |
|     Fixed | 5,000 | 5,000 | 5,000 | 5,000.00 |
|     Variable | 4,000 | 3,200 | 2,400 | 2,336.98 |
|     Semi-Variable (75% Variable) | 2,000 | 1,700[a] | 1,400[b] | 1,376.37[g] |
| Total Cost of Sales | $ 41,000 | $33,900 | $26,800 | $26,240.70 |
| Gross Profit | $ 59,000 | $46,100 | $33,200 | $32,183.80 |
| Non-Manufacturing Expenses: | | | | |
|   Fixed Charges | $ 20,000 | $20,000 | $20,000 | $20,000.00 |
|   Variable Expenses | 12,000 | 9,600 | 7,200 | 7,010.94 |
|   Semi-Variable Expenses (85% Variable) | 8,000 | 6,640[c] | 5,280[d] | 5,172.86[h] |
| Total Non-Manufacturing Expenses | $ 40,000 | $36,240 | $32,480 | $32,183.80 |
| NET PROFIT | $ 19,000 | $ 9,860 | $ 720 | $ 0.00 |

[a] $2,000 + ($2,000 x .75 x (−.20)) = $1,700

[b] $2,000 + ($2,000 x .75 x (−.40)) = $1,400

[c] $8,000 + ($8,000 x .85 x (−.20)) = $6,640

[d] $8,000 + ($8,000 x .85 x (−.40)) = $5,280

[e] Break-Even Sales Volume $= S - \dfrac{(S - S')}{(P - P')} \times P$

$$= \$100,000 - \frac{(\$100,000 - \$60,000)}{(19,000 - \$720)} \times \$19,000$$

$$= \$58,424.50$$

[f] $\dfrac{\$58,424.50}{\$100,000.00} \times 100\% = 58.4245\%$

[g] $2,000 + ($2,000 x .75 x (−.415755)) = $1,376.37

[h] $8,000 + ($8,000 x .85 x (−.415755)) = $5,172.86

A consideration of this schedule will indicate that not only has
the Flexible Budget procedure and the variability of expenses been illustrated but also the Theoretical Capacity, the Practical Capacity, the
Average or Normal Capacity, and the Break-Even Sales Volume have been
computed.  In continuation of this problem, the following Schedule of
Burden Rates has been prepared in order to disclose the standard burden
rates as ascertained according to each of the suggested volumes of production.

Schedule of Burden Rates Illustrating
Rates at Various Production Levels

| Level of Production | Working Hours a | Burden b | Burden Rates b ÷ a |
|---|---|---|---|
| 1. Theoretical Capacity | 20,000 | $11,000.00 | $0.55000 |
| 2. Practical Capacity | 16,000 | 9,900.00 | .61875 |
| 3. Average Capacity | 12,000 | 8,800.00 | .73333 |
| 4. Break-Even Sales Volume | 11,685 | 8,713.35 | .74569 |

A summary of this section, Setting Burden Cost Standards, will
point out that two problems are involved in setting such standards--an
estimation of the burden expenditures for the period and a forecast of
the volume of production during the same time.  With respect to the second factor, the industrial engineer, the cost accountant, and management
will ordinarily determine a level of production which tends to reflect
the objective of this particular enterprise in the most satisfactory
manner.  After this level of production has been established, each burden

item will be studied carefully and its amount will be predicted upon the basis of such operation. And, finally, the Standard Burden Rate will be computed as the quotient of the sum of the burden expenditures and the selected basis of allocation (number of standard labor hours, standard machine hours, or other basis).

Accounting for Burden.--In the usual discussion of burden in connection with standard costs, little provision has been made for accumulating the actual cost of the various burden expenditures. The writer of such literature ordinarily assumes one account for this cost component and the reader, who is not able to visualize the situation, may not comprehend this account as representing various types of costs--fixed, variable, and semi-variable, for example. In view of the confusion that tends to arise from this incomplete portrayal, some attention will be given to a few writers who have varied from this procedure.

Maynard (1927) recognized that some consideration should be given to actual costs and made the following explanations with respect to such costs:

> The accounting procedure for burden is far more complex than for either of the others, because of the different factors involved. To begin with, each expense is charged to an expense account on the general ledger (not the factory or cost ledger) before any accounting distribution is made. . . . The charges are "washed through" these expense accounts each month, and passed through the General and Cost Ledger Controlling Accounts (assuming that a separate cost ledger is maintained), and the expenses are distributed and charged in the burden ledger.

> After the debits are posted, the total burden of indirect

and service centers . . . are redistributed, until all the
expenses are carried by the direct centers. . . .[44]

Although the author failed to present journal entries, ledger ac-

counts, and financial statements containing actual cost data, he did

prepare "flow charts" suggesting the accounting procedure for such costs.

Reitell (1931), in undertaking to exhibit the whole accounting pro-

cedure, presented a detailed illustration of recording burden items.

This illustration--"Bookkeeping for Standard Costs," a chapter in his

textbook--included a Factory Journal, with columns for Direct Overhead

Expense (subdivided for three departments) and General Overhead Expense,

and ledger accounts, which had received the actual cost data and had

been closed in a systematic manner.[45]

Van Sickle (1938) realized the importance of disclosing a complete

situation and presented a set of summary transactions, "Standard Cost

System, An Illustration," in order to clarify the operation of standard

costs. He exhibited general journal entries, with necessary schedules

and computations, and general ledger accounts, including all factory ac-

counts, that might be required to summarize such journal entries.[46]

In view of the fact that actual manufacturing expenses must be re-

corded under either the job order or the process cost system based on

---

[44]Maynard, Henry W., "The Accounting Technique for Standard Costs,"
_National Association of Cost Accountants Bulletin_, Vol. VIII, No. 12
(February 15, 1927), pp. 554-556.

[45]Reitell, _Cost Accounting_, pp. 388-416.

[46]Van Sickle, _Cost Accounting_, pp. 476-521.

historical costs and that techniques have been devised for adequately
performing such functions, this phase of cost accounting has not been
deemed of such consequence to this study as to require a complete development.  However, attention is directed to the requirement, under standard cost procedure, that proper means be made to ascertain the various
actual costs, to recognize currently these costs and the liabilities
therefor as incurred, to record the transfer of indirect materials and
other cost elements between departments, and to make adjustments for
fixed costs and accrued expenses at the end of a fiscal period.  With
adequate provision made for the compilation of the actual costs, consideration can be extended to the accounting for burden costs under standard cost procedures.

Burden in the Records at Actual Costs (Work in Process Charged with
Actual and Credited with Standard Costs).--After the standards for burden
have been established, the amounts of the burden items have been forecast, and the standard burden rates have been determined, provision must
be made to record the actual and standard burden figures in the accounts.
As has been suggested in the preceding section, the actual costs will be
recorded through a scheme that meets the requirements of the particular
business.  The standard data, on the other hand, may be recorded at
actual costs (i.e., charges are at actual costs and credits are at
standard figures), at standard values, or at both actual and standard
figures in the Work in Process account.

The first method to be considered will charge the Work in Process

account for burden with the actual cost of the burden incurred during
the period and will credit this account with the standard burden cost of
the products completed during the same time.  At the close of the period,
the inventory of work in process (valued at standard burden figures)
will be set up by crediting the Work in Process account and the balance
in this account will be analyzed and closed to variation accounts.

In order to illustrate this procedure, the following data have been
assumed:

1. A concern manufactures Commodity X-45, which requires
   forty standard machine hours at a standard rate of $0.60
   (Fixed $0.36; Variable $0.24).
2. During the current period, the amount of burden was predicted to be $720.00 and the standard machine hours for
   the period were set at 1,200.
3. Production completed during the period:  21 units of Commodity X-45.
4. Work in Process at the end of the period:  20 units of
   Commodity X-45, which were 40 per cent completed so far as
   burden was concerned.
5. Actual machine hours operated during the period amounted
   to 1,172.
6. The actual factory expenses for the period were:

   | | |
   |---|---:|
   | Indirect Materials | $ 60.00 |
   | Indirect Payroll (unpaid) | 140.00 |
   | Rent | 200.00 |
   | Heat, Light and Water | 103.00 |
   | Depreciation of Machinery | 80.00 |
   | Taxes for the Period (unpaid) | 90.00 |
   | Insurance Expired | 62.00 |
   | Repairs | 40.00 |

The journal entries to record these data, according to this
method, might be as follows, if an Overhead Expense in Process account
were maintained for the manufacturing account.  (The accounting technique and account titles have been taken from Blocker's illustration of

this method.)[47]

    Overhead Expense[48]                     60.00
      Materials                              60.00

        To record the transfer of indirect materials to the factory from the stores room.

    Overhead Expense                  140.00
      Accrued Payroll                    140.00

        To record the indirect wages for the period, which were unpaid.

    Overhead Expense                  343.00
      Vouchers Payable                 343.00

        To make a summary entry for three vouchers recording the following:[49]

| | | |
|---|---|---|
| Rent | 200.00 | |
| Heat, Light and Water | 103.00 | |
| Repairs | 40.00 | |
| Total | 343.00 | |

    Overhead Expense                  232.00
      Reserve for Depreciation of
        Machinery                       80.00
      Accrued Taxes                      90.00
      Prepaid Insurance                62.00

        To record the depreciation on machinery, the accrued taxes, and the expired insurance for the period.

    Overhead Expense in Process        775.00
      Overhead Expense                 775.00

        To transfer the total actual overhead expense to Overhead Expense in Process account.

---

[47] Blocker, Cost Accounting, pp. 582-588.

[48] Gillespie designated this account as Factory Expense, while Lawrence termed it Manufacturing Expense.

[49] In practice, a voucher would be made for each of these items and each voucher would be recorded separately in the voucher register; in view of the fact that general journal entries are being used in this study, the summary entry is made for the sake of brevity.

Finished Goods                                      504.00
    Overhead Expense in Process                              504.00
        To record the standard burden cost
    of products completed during the
    period:
        21 (units) x 40 (standard machine
            hours) x $0.60 (Standard
            machine hour rate).

Work in Process Inventory                           192.00
    Overhead Expense in Process                              192.00
        To transfer work in process inven-
    tory at standard burden rates from
    Overhead Expense in Process to the
    Work in Process Inventory account:
        20 (units) x .40 (40% completed) x
            40 (standard machine hours) x
            $0.60 (Standard machine hour
            rate).

Overhead Expense--Budget Variance[50]               55.00
    Overhead Expense in Process                               55.00
        To record difference between
    actual overhead expense and standard
    overhead expense, as budgeted:
        Actual Overhead Expense          775.00
        Standard Overhead Expense
            per the budget               720.00
                                          55.00

Overhead Expense--Under Capacity
  Variance[51]                                      16.80
    Overhead Expense in Process                               16.80
        To record the variance in over-
    head expense due to actual produc-
    tion (machine hours) being less
    than standard production:
        Standard machine hours per
            the budget                   1,200
        Actual machine hours per the
            records                      1,172
        Excess of standard hours
            over actual                     28
        28 (hours) x $0.60 (Standard
            overhead expense rate) = $16.80

---

[50]Gillespie called this account "Factory Expense--Budget Variation."

[51]Gillespie termed this account "Factory Expense--Idle Time and
Overtime."

```
Overhead Expense--Production
   Efficiency Variance[52]                                        7.20
      Overhead Expense in Process                                      7.20
         To record the loss due to excess hours
      of overhead expense--machine hours were
      used in excess of standard machine hours
      for production during the period:
         Actual machine hours per the
            records                                    1,172
         Standard machine hours in
            production:
         Finished Goods:
            21 (units) x 40 (standard
               hours each)                      840
         Work in Process:
            20 (units) x .40 (40%
               completed) x 40                  320   1,160
         Excess of Actual over
            Standard (Machine hours)                      12
         12 (machine hours) x $0.60
            (Standard burden rate)                     $7.20
```

Gillespie followed the same general procedure as Blocker; however,
he maintained only one Work in Process account, which accumulated the
amounts of all the cost components, and varied his account titles as indicated in the footnotes on the preceding pages.[53]

Mannix (1933) varied this procedure somewhat by dividing his factory expenditures into fixed and variable items, which were recorded in
separate accounts, and by employing special accounts for actual and
standard values. His procedure will be suggested through the use of
General Ledger accounts (this author presented both journal entries and
general ledger accounts).[54]

---

[52] Gillespie designated this account as "Factory Expense--Quantity
Variation."

[53] Gillespie, Accounting Procedure for Standard Costs, pp. 23-35.

[54] Mannix, op. cit., pp. 206-211.

Fixed Factory Overhead--Actual Cost

| | | | |
|---|---|---|---|
| Rent | 200.00 | | |
| Depreciation of Machinery | 80.00 | | |
| Taxes | 90.00 | | |
| Insurance Expired | 62.00 | | |
| (Total $432.00) | | | |

Fixed Factory Overhead--Standard Cost

| | | | |
|---|---|---|---|
| | | Finished Stock Inventory | 302.40 |
| | | Work in Process Inventory | 115.20 |
| | | (Total $417.60) | |

Variable Factory Overhead--Actual Cost

| | | | |
|---|---|---|---|
| Indirect Materials | 60.00 | | |
| Indirect Payroll | 140.00 | | |
| Heat, Light and Water | 103.00 | | |
| Repairs | 40.00 | | |
| (Total $343.00) | | | |

Variable Factory Overhead--Standard Cost

| | | | |
|---|---|---|---|
| | | Finished Stock Inventory | 201.60 |
| | | Work in Process Inventory | 76.80 |
| | | (Total $278.40) | |

Mannix did not undertake to analyze the difference between the actual and standard figures, but, at the end of the fiscal period, closed this difference--concurrently with closing the differences between the actual and standard figures for the other cost components--to an account, "Excess Costs Over Standards." This account, in turn, was used to offset a portion of Sales in determining the net profit for the period.[55] The journal entry for recording the difference in the Excess Costs Over Standards account will be made:

---

[55] Ibid., p. 217.

Excess Costs Over Standards                 79.00
Fixed Factory Overhead Standard Cost       417.60
Variable Factory Overhead
  Standard Cost                            278.40
    Fixed Overhead Actual Cost                        432.00
    Variable Overhead Actual Cost                     343.00
        To close the actual and standard
    factory overhead accounts and to
    record the difference between these
    two costs in the Excess Costs Over
    Standards account.

Newlove and Garner (1941), in presenting Method A ("In Process"

Accounts are Debited for Actual Costs and Credited for Standard Costs),

employed a working sheet for disclosing their journal entries.[56]  The

portion of this working sheet that applies to the hypothetical case

under consideration will be illustrated.  (The variation accounts have

not been closed, as the disposition of variations between actual and

standard burden costs will be considered in a subsequent section of

this chapter.)

---

[56] Newlove and Garner, _Elementary Cost Accounting_, p. 449.

Working Sheet Showing Journal Entries
Under Standard Cost Method A

|  | Journal Entries | | | |
|  | Dr. | | Cr. | |
| Burden Incurred . . . . . . . . | A$ | 775.00 | B$ | 720.00 |
| . . . . . . . . . . . . . . . . . | | | C | 55.00 |
| Burden in Process Inventory . | G | 192.00 | | |
| Burden in Process . . . . . . | D | 703.20 | F | 504.00 |
| . . . . . . . . . . . . . . . . . | | | G | 192.00 |
| . . . . . . . . . . . . . . . . . | | | H | 7.20 |
| Burden Applied . . . . . . . . | B | 720.00 | D | 703.20 |
| . . . . . . . . . . . . . . . . . | | | E | 16.80 |
| Budget Variations--Burden . . | C | 55.00 | | |
| Idle Time Variations--Burden | E | 16.80 | | |
| Efficiency Variations--Burden | H | 7.20 | | |
| Finished Goods . . . . . . . . | F | 504.00 | | |
| General Ledger | | | A | 775.00 |
| | | $2,973.20 | | $2,973.20 |

A. Burden actually incurred was $775.00.
B. Original burden budget was $720.00
C. $775.00 (Burden actually incurred) - $720.00 (Standard
     burden per budget) = $55.00
D. 1,172 (actual machine hours) x $0.60 (standard burden
     rate) = $703.20.
E. $720.00 (Standard Burden per the budget) - $703.20
     (actual hours at standard burden rate) = $16.80.
F. 21 (units completed) x 40 (standard machine hours per
     unit) x $0.60 (standard burden rate) = $504.00.
G. 20 (units partially completed) x .40 (40% completed)
     x 40 (standard machine hours per unit) x $0.60
     (standard burden rate) = $192.00.
H. $703.00 (actual hours at standard rate) - $696.00
     (standard cost of equivalent production) = $7.20.


Lawrence (1937), in his "Method 2 - Variance Entries After Work in

Process Entries," and Langer (1938), in his "Method A - Variations Sepa-

rated When the Goods are Finished,"[57] also employed this procedure for

---

[57]Lawrence, Cost Accounting, pp. 367-371; Langer, Accounting Principles and Procedure, p. L 22 - 1.

recording standard burden costs in the accounts.

Burden in the Records at Standard Costs.--A second method for recording the burden costs in the Work in Process account is to charge this account with the standard cost of burden applicable to production and to credit this account with the corresponding value of burden in the finished goods.

Maynard (1927) explained this method as used by the Gillette Safety Razor Company to record burden.[58] In order to illustrate the early accounting procedure under this method, this author's technique will be applied to the assumed data as employed in the preceding section of this study.

In the first place, Maynard maintained a General Ledger and a Cost Ledger.  The General Ledger contained expense accounts for each class of expenses and a Cost Ledger Control account.  If it may be assumed that the required entries have been made to record the actual expenses in the General Ledger accounts, then the following entry would be made to charge these actual expenses to the Cost Ledger:

| | | |
|---|---|---|
| Cost Ledger Control | 775.00 | |
| Indirect Material | | 60.00 |
| Indirect Labor | | 140.00 |
| Rent | | 200.00 |
| Heat, Light and Water | | 103.00 |
| Depreciation of Machinery | | 80.00 |
| Taxes | | 90.00 |
| Expired Insurance | | 62.00 |
| Repairs | | 40.00 |
| To charge the Cost Ledger with the actual burden charges for the period. | | |

---

[58] Op. cit., pp. 554-560.

The Cost Ledger contained a General Ledger Control account, a Burden Ledger account (a controlling account)--with a separate account for each operating department or burden center in a subsidiary ledger--and other accounts as might be required.  The expenses would be charged to the proper accounts and the service centers' costs would be redistributed until all the expenditures were carried by the direct or production departments.  In the case under consideration, only one operating department (Department 1) has been assumed for this factory.  The journal entry, therefore, to record such expenditures on the Cost Ledger would be:

```
Burden Ledger Control--Department 1         775.00
    General Ledger Control                              775.00
        To charge Department 1 with the
    actual burden expenditures for the
    period.
```

At the end of the period, the following entries would be required to reflect the burden costs for the period:

```
Scheduled Burden in Process                 703.20
    Burden Ledger--Department 1                         703.20
        To record the standard value of
    the actual hours of production:
        1,172 (hours) x $0.60 = $703.20

Work in Process--Burden                     696.00
    Scheduled Burden in Process                         696.00
        To record the standard value of
    burden in goods processed:
    Finished Goods:
        21 (units) x $24.00         $504.00
    Goods in Process:
        20 (units) x .40 (40%
        completed) x $24.00          192.00
            Total                   $696.00
```

Finished Goods                                          504.00
    Work in Process--Burden                                    504.00
        To record the standard value of
    burden in goods completed during
    the period:
        21 (units) x $24.00              $504.00


Cost of Idle Facilities                                  71.80
    Burden Ledger Control--
        Department 1                                           71.80
        To close the unabsorbed actual
    expenses for the period to the
    variance account.


Variances from Standard Cost--Burden                      7.20
    Scheduled Burden in Process                                 7.20
        To close the balance of the
    Scheduled Burden in Process account
    --"which represents the comparison
    of efficiency or speed"--to the
    variance account.


The author prepared the following monthly burden schedule, which

has been reproduced (with the assumed data included rather than the

author's figures) as a means of suggesting a step in the development of

the technique for disclosing burden variations from standard.


Departmental Monthly Burden Statement[59]

| Burden Center | Budget of Expenses which Should be Necessary for Actual Extent of Activity | Actual Expenses | Earned Burden (Value of Machine Activity) | Expense Variances | Unearned Burden (Cost of Idle Facilities) | Unearned Burden and Variance |
|---|---|---|---|---|---|---|
| | 1 | 2 | 3 | 2 - 1 | 1 - 3 | 2 - 3 |
| 1 | $720.00 | $775.00 | $696.00 | $55.00 | $24.00 | $79.00 |

---

[59]Ibid., p. 559.

Although Maynard did not journalize the burden variations further,
he did prepare a "Monthly Operating Statement" that disclosed three
burden variations.[60] The portion of this statement that pertains to
this cost component will be reproduced (the figures are taken from the
assumed problem).

Monthly Operating Statement

Burden:

(5) Expense Variance:

| Actual Expense | Budget for Actual Amount of Activity | |
|---|---|---|
| $775.00 - | $720.00 | $55.00 |

(6) Cost of Idle Facilities:

| Budget for Actual Amount of Activity | Value of Machine Activity (Active hours at hourly rates) | |
|---|---|---|
| $720.00 - | $703.20 | 16.80 |

(7) Efficiency Variance:

| Value of Machine Activity | Standard Cost Value of Burden in Production | |
|---|---|---|
| $703.20 - | $696.00 | 7.20 |

Total Burden Variances     $79.00

Amidon and Lang (1928) followed this general procedure in recording
burden costs in the accounting records, as may be evidenced from the following reproduction of their accounts pertaining to this cost component:[61]

---

[60] Ibid., pp. 548-549.

[61] Amidon and Lang, op. cit., pp. 280-281.

## Work in Process--Manufacturing Expense

| | |
|---|---|
| 1. With amount of inventory at standard cost at beginning of period. | 3. With standard cost of product completed; at same time debit Finished Goods account. |
| 2. With amount of standard manufacturing expense for the period; at the same time credit Variation from Standard-Expense. | |

Balance represents standard cost of manufacturing expense inventory on hand.

## Actual Manufacturing Expense

| | |
|---|---|
| 1. Indirect Material. | 5. Total closed out to Variation from Standard-Expense. |
| 2. Indirect Labor. | |
| 3. Voucher Register Charges. | |
| 4. Fixed Charges. | |

## Variation from Standard--Manufacturing Expense

| | |
|---|---|
| 1. With actual cost of manufacturing expense; at same time credit actual Manufacturing Expense. | 2. With standard rates applied to production; at same time debit Work in Process-Expense. |

Balance closed to Profit and Loss.

These authors did not analyze the difference between actual and standard values. Maze and Glover, who had followed Amidon and Lang's technique for handling materials and labor, varied their burden procedure however. This statement may be substantiated by the following quotation from their publication:

There are three controlling accounts set up on the general ledger for manufacturing expense. The first account is known as Manufacturing Expense. This account is the controlling account of the subsidiary factory ledger kept by the cost accounting department. This account always has a debit balance and is the record of actual manufacturing expense incurred. The second controlling account is known as Standard Manufacturing Expense. This account is credited with all expense applied to the product in "work in process." The third

controlling account is known as the Over or Under-applied
Manufacturing Expense account, which is credited or charged
with the amount of underapplied or overapplied expense.  This
account is cleared to Profit and Loss at the end of each
month.[62]

Gillespie (1935), when recording burden costs under Method B, would

make the following journal entries for the example that has been as-

sumed:[63]

```
Factory Expense                                775.00
    To - Accounts Payable (and other
      credits)                                               775.00
        Actual factory expense incurred
    during the period.

Work in Process                                696.00
Factory Expense--Idle Time and Overtime         16.80
Factory Expense--Quantity Variation              7.20
    To - Factory Expense                                     720.00
        To charge work in process with
    standard factory expense in operations
    completed, to credit factory expense
    account with budget for month, and to
    record idle time and quantity varia-
    tions:
    Budget for Period:
      1,200 machine hours at $0.60                720.00
    Idle Time Variation:
      Budget hours at standard       720.00
      Less actual hours at standard:
        1,172 hours at $0.60         703.20      16.80*
    Quantity Variation:
      Actual hours at standard:
        1,172 hours at $0.60         703.20
      Less standard hours at
        standard:
        1,160 hours at $0.60         696.00       7.20*
    Standard factory expense in
      operations completed                       696.00
          *Debit balances
```

---

[62] Maze and Glover, _op. cit._, pp. 313-314.

[63] Gillespie, _Accounting Procedure for Standard Costs_, pp. 38-42.

```
Factory Expense - Budget Variation          55.00
    To - Factory Expense                              55.00
        To charge variations from budget
    account with excess of actual over
    budget factory expense for the
    period:
        Budget factory expense      720.00
        Actual factory expense      775.00
        Excess                       55.00

Finished Goods                              504.00
    To - Work in Process[64]                          504.00
        To charge finished goods account
    with standard cost of goods com-
    pleted during the period:
        21 units of Commodity X-45
            at $24.00               504.00
```

Schlatter (1938), in illustrating his Multiple Account Method of recording standard costs in the accounts, recorded the actual expenses in a Burden account. This account was credited with the standard cost of the work accomplished and, at the same time, the Burden in Process account was debited with this amount. Although he did not record the difference between actual and standard values of Burden--the balance in the Burden account--he did analyze such variation according to these classifications:[65] (1) the Expense Variation, (2) the Activity Variation, and (3) the Burden Efficiency Variation.[66]

---

[64] Inventory of work in process equals balance of Work in Process account; no entry would be required for this inventory.

[65] Schlatter, Advanced Cost Accounting, pp. 122-123.

[66] These variations are comparable with Gillespie's variations, which have been illustrated already. In order to present a comparable situation, Gillespie's variations have been repeated and have been numbered to correspond with the respective Schlatter variation as above-- (1) Factory Expense-Budget Variation, (2) Factory Expense-Idle Time and Overtime, and (3) Factory Expense-Quantity Variation.

Newlove and Garner (1941) planned their accounting technique for recording burden under this method (Method B, according to these writers) so that the variations were computed automatically as the cost data flowed through the accounts.[67] In order to illustrate their procedure, the assumed problem has been solved by employing the journal entries that these authors would make.

| | | |
|---|---|---|
| Burden Incurred | 775.00 | |
|     General Ledger | | 775.00 |
|         To record the actual factory expenses incurred during the year. | | |
| | | |
| Burden Applied | 720.00 | |
|     Burden Incurred | | 720.00 |
|         To record the budgeted figures for burden. | | |
| | | |
| Scheduled Burden | 703.20 | |
|     Burden Applied | | 703.20 |
|         To record the standard burden cost of actual hours worked: 1,172 hours at $0.60   $703.20 | | |
| | | |
| Burden in Process | 696.00 | |
|     Scheduled Burden | | 696.00 |
|         To record the standard burden cost of operations completed: 1,160 hours at $0.60   $696.00 | | |
| | | |
| Finished Goods | 504.00 | |
|     Burden in Process[68] | | 504.00 |
|         To record the standard burden cost in goods completed during period. | | |

---

[67] Newlove and Garner, op. cit., p. 450.

[68] The balance in the Burden in Process account represents the standard cost of burden in the Work in Process inventory at the end of the period.

| Budget Variations--Burden | 55.00 | |
|---|---|---|
| Burden Incurred | | 55.00 |

To record the burden budget variation,
which represents the difference between
the actual burden costs $775.00) and
the budgeted burden for the period
($720.00).

| Idle Time Variations--Burden | 16.80 | |
|---|---|---|
| Burden Applied | | 16.80 |

To record the burden idle time variation, which is the difference between
the budgeted burden for the period
($720.00) and the burden applied to pro-
duction during the period ($703.20).

| Efficiency Variations--Burden | 7.20 | |
|---|---|---|
| Scheduled Burden | | 7.20 |

To record the burden efficiency variation, which is the difference between the
burden actually applied for the period
($703.20) and the standard burden cost of
production ($696.00).

Other writers of standard cost literature who recognized this method
of recording burden in the accounts include:  Department of Manufacture
of the Chamber of Commerce of the United States (1925), Thomas Downie,
Jr. (1927), Reitell (1933), Dohr, Inghram and Love (1935), Schumer
(1935), Lawrence (1937), Van Sickle (1938), Blocker (1940), Gregory
(1940), and Neuner (1942).[69]

<u>Burden in the Records at Actual and Standard Costs</u>.--The third
method of recording burden in the records provides for the Work in

-------

[69]Chamber of Commerce of the United States, <u>Cost Accounting Through
the Use of Standards</u>, pp. 34-37; Downie, Thomas, Jr., <u>op</u>. <u>cit</u>., pp. 32-
38; Reitell, <u>Cost Accounting</u>, pp. 388-409; Dohr, Inghram and Love, <u>op</u>.
<u>cit</u>., pp. 480-483; Schumer, <u>op</u>. <u>cit</u>., pp. 206-209 and 246-250; Lawrence,
<u>Cost Accounting</u> (1937), pp. 358-365; Van Sickle, <u>op</u>. <u>cit</u>., pp. 496-501;
Blocker, <u>Cost Accounting</u>, pp. 609-615; Gregory, <u>op</u>. <u>cit</u>., pp. 101-148;
and Neuner, <u>Cost Accounting</u>, pp. 517-527.

Process - Burden account to be charged with the actual and standard costs of this cost component and to be credited with the actual and standard costs of burden in operations completed during the period.

Brugger (1925), in explaining the accounts to be maintained in a Cost Ledger when "Standard and Actual costs are tied in with the books of account," made the following statement with respect to the Burden Control accounts:

> The Burden Control Accounts are charged in the "actual" column with the actual burden as determined from the burden ledger records and in the "standard" column with amounts calculated by applying the standard burden rates to the standard hours or amounts shown on the summaries of Labor Operation Cards. . . . Credits to these accounts are determined from the Monthly Analysis of Standard Cost of Shipments . . . and ratios on the debit side of the respective accounts in precisely the same way as described in connection with the operation of the Material Work in Process accounts.[70]

The author presented his Cost Ledger accounts, in blank but with pertinent explanatory statements. In order that a clearer conception of the writer's purpose may be transmitted, his illustration relating to Burden will be reproduced:[71]

---

[70] Brugger, F., "Standard Costs--Their Development and Use," _National Association of Cost Accountants Bulletin_, Vol. VI, No. 13 (March 2, 1925), p. 11.

[71] _Ibid._, p. 10.

<u>Burden - Control Account</u>

Distributed to "work in process" accounts by
departments or production centers-example

| Dr. | | | Press Department | | | | | Cr. |
|---|---|---|---|---|---|---|---|---|

| Date | Descrip-tion | Actual | Standard | Ratio | Date | Descrip-tion | Actual | Standard | Ratio |
|---|---|---|---|---|---|---|---|---|---|

Charged with

Standard - Standard rates applied
      to Standard time or
      direct Labor
Actual    - From sub-ledger showing
      charges by classifica-
      tion of burden

Credited with "Burden" in
  Shipments:

Standard - From analysis of stand-
      ard cost of shipments
Actual    - Standard multiplied by
      the ratio shown on the
      debit side of this
      account

The Department of Manufacture of the Chamber of Commerce of the

United States (1925) undertook to illustrate the recording of Burden,

which was divided into fluctuating expenses and fixed charges, under a

scheme that possessed some of the characteristics of the method under

discussion. In the first place, the fluctuating expenses were made a

direct charge to production, regardless of the amount of such expendi-

tures; on the other hand, the fixed charges were absorbed by Work in

Process - Overhead through the medium of standard rates, while the varia-

tion between actual fixed overhead expenses and the amount absorbed was

transferred to Profit and Loss - Idle Capacity.[72] In order to demon-

strate the intentions of this publication, the Burden and related ac-

counts have been adapted to the assumed problem, which has been amended

to fit this particular situation:

---

[72]Chamber of Commerce of the United States, <u>Cost Accounting Through</u>
<u>the Use of Standards</u>, pp. 37-38.

7. Initial Inventory of Work in Process:

|                        | Actual   | Standard |
|------------------------|----------|----------|
| Fluctuating expenses   | $157.00  | $121.60  |
| Fixed expenses         | 195.40   |          |

### Fluctuating Expenses

| | | | | |
|---|---|---|---|---|
| May 31 | Indirect Materials | 60.00 | May 31 Fluctuating expenses for May | 343.00 |
| | Indirect Payroll | 140.00 | | |
| | Heat, Light and Water | 103.00 | | |
| | Repairs | 40.00 | | |

### Fixed Expenses

| | | | | |
|---|---|---|---|---|
| May 31 | Rent | 200.00 | May 31 Fixed expenses for May | 432.00 |
| | Depreciation of Machinery | 80.00 | | |
| | Taxes | 90.00 | | |
| | Insurance expired | 62.00 | | |

### Work in Process - Overhead

| | Actual | Standard | | Actual | Standard |
|---|---|---|---|---|---|
| May 1 Fluctuating expenses in inventory | 157.00 | 121.60 | May 31 Fluctuating expenses in production at standard | | 201.60 |
| 31 Fluctuating expenses for May | 343.00 | 278.40 | 31 Adjustment to actual (201.60 x 1.25) | 252.00 | |
| | 500.00 | 400.00 | | | |
| Ratio: 500/400 = 1.25 | | | | | |
| May 1 Fixed expenses in inventory | 195.40 | | 31 Fixed expenses in production at standard | | 302.40 |
| 31 Absorption fixed expenses at standard rates | 417.60 | | | | 554.40 |
| | 613.00 | | | | |

Profit and Loss - Idle Capacity

---

May 31 Under absorption of
     fixed expenses     14.40

Cost of Goods Sold

---

May 31 Variable and fixed
     expenses in pro-
     duction     554.40

In considering these accounts, some explanations, together with pertinent journal entries, may clarify the obscure features. In the first place, the burden expenditures were analyzed as to fluctuating and fixed expenses and were recorded initially in two accounts--Fluctuating Expenses and Fixed Expenses. At the end of the period, the Fluctuating Expenses account was closed to the actual debit column of the Work in Process - Overhead account. At the same time, the standard value of Fluctuating Burden in work in process for the period ($278.40 in this case) was incorporated in the Work in Process - Overhead account under the standard debit column--"The columns headed Standard are for the introduction of statistical figures, and these figures do not appear in the accounting."[73] The initial inventory was added to the period's cost of production, valued at both actual and standard figures, and the relationship between these two values--$500.00 ÷ $400.00 = 1.25--was ascertained. The standard cost of fluctuating burden in goods completed was computed--21 (units) x 40 (hours) x $0.24 (standard fluctuating expense rate) = $201.60--and was entered in the standard credit column of the

---

[73]*Ibid.*, p. 27.

Work in Process - Overhead account. By using the ratio (1.25) of actual to standard fluctuating expenses, this standard value was converted into actual value ($201.60 x 1.25 = $252.00).

In closing the Fixed Expenses account, the standard fixed expense rate ($0.36 per hour) was applied to the standard hours in production (1,160 hours) and the following journal entry was made:

```
Work in Process - Overhead
  (Fixed Expenses)                          417.60
Profit and Loss - Idle Capacity             14.40
    Fixed Expenses                                      432.00
      To close the fixed expenses to
    Work in Process - Overhead and Profit
    and Loss - Idle Capacity accounts.
```

And, finally, the standard value of fixed burden in finished goods was calculated--21 (units) x 40 (standard hours) x $0.36 (standard fixed expense rate) = $302.40) and, together with the actual value of fluctuating burden in finished goods, was made the basis for a journal entry recording such completed commodities:

```
Cost of Goods Sold                          554.40
    Work in Process - Overhead
      (Fluctuating Expenses)                            252.00
    Work in Process - Overhead
      (Fixed Expenses)                                  302.40
        To record the cost of goods com-
      pleted and sold during the period.
```

A careful analysis of this procedure will indicate that the allotted value of completed goods contained two types of costs--fluctuating costs determined under the actual and standard cost method, and fixed charges ascertained under the standard cost method.

Gillespie (1935) has presented both journal entries and ledger accounts for recording manufacturing expenses at both actual and standard
values.[74]  In order to illustrate the current procedure for treating
Burden expenditures in the accounts, this author's technique will be
applied to the assumed problem.

|  | Actual | | Standard | |
| --- | --- | --- | --- | --- |
|  | Debits | Credits | Debits | Credits |
| Work in Process-Factory Expense |  |  | 696.00 |  |
|   To - Standard Clearing |  |  |  |  |
|     Account |  |  |  | 696.00 |
|      To charge standard column |  |  |  |  |
|   of work in process with |  |  |  |  |
|   standard cost of operations |  |  |  |  |
|   completed: |  |  |  |  |
|   Finished Goods: |  |  |  |  |
|    21 (units) x $24.00 $504.00 |  |  |  |  |
|   Goods in Process: |  |  |  |  |
|    20 (units) x .40 |  |  |  |  |
|     (40% completed) x |  |  |  |  |
|     $24.00      192.00 |  |  |  |  |
|             $696.00 |  |  |  |  |
| Factory Expense | 775.00 |  |  |  |
|   To - Accounts Payable |  | 775.00 |  |  |
|     Actual factory expense |  |  |  |  |
|   incurred during the period. |  |  |  |  |
| Work in Process - Factory |  |  |  |  |
|  Expense | 775.00 |  |  |  |
|   To - Factory Expense |  | 775.00 |  |  |
|     To charge work in |  |  |  |  |
|   process with actual factory |  |  |  |  |
|   expenses. |  |  |  |  |

If the journal entries affecting the Work in Process - Factory
Expense account may be posted to a ledger account, the data for recording

[74]Gillespie, *Accounting Procedure for Standard Costs*, pp. 251-264.

the cost of the finished goods may be obtained more readily.

Work in Process - Factory Expense

| | Actual | R | Standard | | Actual | R | Standard |
|---|---|---|---|---|---|---|---|
| Factory Expense | 775.00 | 111.3 | 696.00 | | | | |

After the ratio of actual to standard debits (111.3%) has been computed, the actual and standard costs of goods completed during the period may be determined and the following journal entry may be made:

| | Actual | | Standard | |
|---|---|---|---|---|
| | Debits | Credits | Debits | Credits |
| Finished Goods | 560.95 | | 504.00 | |
| To - Work in Process- | | | | |
| Factory Expense | | 560.95 | | 504.00 |
| To charge finished goods with actual and standard cost of goods completed: | | | | |
| Standard cost of goods finished:  21 (units x $24.00      $504.00 | | | | |
| Apply ratio of actual to standard debits        1.113 | | | | |
| $560.95 | | | | |

In addition to the method of charging factory expense into work in process at actual and standard cost of production, Gillespie stated that the charge might be at normal and standard cost of production.[75]

> It may be desirable to charge work in process ("actual" column) by means of normal factory expense rates in order that current product costs and costs of sales be not distorted by fluctuations in actual level of production.[76]

---

[75] Ibid., pp. 275-289.

[76] Ibid., p. 275.

When this method is applied, the amount in the actual debit column of the Work in Process - Factory Expense account is the product of the actual hours operated and the normal factory expense rate--1,172 (actual hours) x $0.60 (normal rate) = $703.20, in the assumed case. If the ledger account for Work in Process may be prepared with this amount for the actual value, the result will be as follows:

Work in Process - Factory Expense

|  | Actual | R | Standard |  | Actual | R | Standard |
|---|---|---|---|---|---|---|---|
| Factory Expense | 703.20 | 101.0 | 696.00 |  |  |  |  |

If this procedure is used, the actual cost of finished goods would be computed as $509.04--101.0% (conversion ratio) x $504.00 (standard cost of finished goods) = $509.04--as compared with $560.95 when actual and standard burden figures were recorded in the accounts.

As a result of using normal and standard cost of production, a balance will usually result in the Factory Expense account after the normal charges have been transferred to the Work in Process account. This balance--unabsorbed factory expense--may be analyzed into spending variation and operating variation, according to Gillespie.[77]

---

[77]Ibid., pp. 283-286.

Analysis of Unabsorbed Factory Expense

1. Spending Variation:
    Actual Factory Expense                       $775.00
    Less - Normal Factory Expense
    for Period:
    1,200 (hours) x $0.60                        720.00    $55.00

2. Operating Variation:
    Normal Factory Expense                       $720.00
    Less - Absorbed Factory
    Expense                                      703.20    16.80
                Net Underabsorbed                          $71.80

In the first two methods of recording Burden in the accounts, an

index of the efficiency of factory operations, so far as burden is con-

cerned, was gained from the absolute amounts recorded in the accounts

representing variance between actual and standard values.  In the method

under consideration, such efficiency indexes are usually reported as

percentages of variation between actual and standard costs of production

and are intended to serve the same purpose as dollar variations in the

other methods.  Some of these ratios, as computed by Gillespie,[78] will

be determined:

1. Factory Expense: Overall Ratio.  This ratio combines prices and

quantities and is taken from the debit side of the Work in Process Ac-

count.  In this problem, this ratio is 111.3%.

2. Factory Expense: Budget Ratio.  This ratio is computed by divid-

ing the actual factory expense by the budgeted factory expense--$775.00

÷ $720.00 = 107.6%.

3. Factory Expense: Idle Time Ratio.  This ratio is determined by

---

[78]Ibid., pp. 264-265.

dividing the budget hours by the actual hours--1,200 ÷ 1,172 = 102.4%.

4. Factory Expense: Quantity Ratio. This ratio is ascertained by
dividing the actual hours by the standard hours in production--1,172 ÷
1,160 = 101.0%.

Gillespie observed that the product of the three component ratios
amounted to the overall ratio. He stated that, if several products were
being produced, it might not be feasible or desirable to compute the
budget ratio and the idle time ratio for each product; however, departmental ratios might be computed in this case as a means of judging the
operational efficiency of such departments.

Camman, another author to advocate Basic Standard Costs and to
record costs at both actual and standard figures, realized the importance of analyzing the Burden Cost Variance. In presenting Standard
Costs to the International Congress on Accounting in 1929, this author
computed the following burden ratios (the data in the assumed problem
have been repeated for illustrative purposes):[79]

1. Burden Cost Variance. This ratio was computed by dividing the
actual burden charges and accruals by the standard burden cost of pro-
duction--$775.00 ÷ $696.00 = 111.3%. This ratio corresponds with Gillespie's Factory Expense: Overall Ratio. Camman stated that this ratio
signified that the total charges, when applied to production, were
111.3% of the budgeted allotments in the standard costs but that it was
not equitable to allocate the total burden to a reduced production. He

_______________

[79]See *Proceedings, International Congress on Accounting*, 1929,
pp. 886-888.

pointed out that two influences prompted this variance--(1) the rate of expenditure and (2) the degree of capacity utilized--and provided for the computation of ratios disclosing the effects of such forces.  However, it was necessary, under his procedure, to determine three preliminary ratios:

(1) Ratio of Output to Capacity.  This ratio was determined by dividing the standard burden cost of production by the standard burden budget at capacity--$696.00 ÷ $720.00 = 96.7%.

(2) Ratio of Use to Capacity.  This ratio was computed by dividing the actual hours (machine hours according to Camman's illustration) by the budgeted machine hours at capacity--1,172 ÷ 1,200 = 97.7%.

(3) Ratio of Machine Running Time.  This ratio was computed as the quotient of the Ratio of Use to Capacity divided by the Ratio of Output to Capacity--97.7% ÷ 96.7% = 101.0%.  This ratio corresponds with Gillespie's Factory Expense: Quantity Ratio, as already computed.

If it is desirable to determine the machine effectiveness, Camman stated that another ratio might be computed at this time.  This ratio--the Machine Effectiveness Ratio--might be determined as the reciprocal of the Machine Running Time Ratio (100.0 ÷ 101.0 = 99.0%).  After these ratios have been computed, the other relationships between actual and standard figures may be determined.

2. Burden Level Variance.  This variation in the rate of expenditure was determined as a ratio, which might be computed by dividing the Burden Cost Ratio by the Ratio of Machine Running Time--111.3% ÷ 101.0% = 110.2%.  This ratio represented the relationship between expenditures

and operations.

3. Idle Capacity Variance. This variance, expressed as a percentage, represented the difference between capacity (accepted as 100%) and the per cent of hours employed during the period (97.7% in this case)--100.0% - 97.7% = 2.3%. The author thought that the trend of this variance would tend to influence the policies of an industrial enterprise.

When Camman wrote Basic Standard Costs in 1932, he devoted a chapter in this publication to the analysis of burden cost variations.[80] In introducing this chapter, he made the following assertion with respect to the application of burden to production:

> The procedure as to burden is to absorb in current costs only an amount equivalent to current operations, taking the number of hours run at normal burden rates set up in the budget for operations at normal capacity. The difference between the amount so derived, if the actual expenses are greater, is carried to profit-and-loss as unabsorbed burden. . . . the primary reason for doing this is to avoid inflating costs when operating conditions are below normal, for the variation from this cause is not properly a part of cost of products made under these conditions. . . . Over-absorbed burden, if the actual is less than the amount absorbed at normal rates, is likewise carried to profit-and-loss. . . . [81]

Applying the author's procedure to the assumed problem, with one amendment--spoiled work amounted to one unit of X-45 or $24.00 of standard burden--then the burden absorbed by production would be $703.20 and the profit and loss charge would be $71.80 ($775.00 - $703.20). Camman would make the following schedule of burden cost variations:

---

[80] Camman, Basic Standard Costs, pp. 69-81.

[81] Ibid., p. 69.

Analysis of Burden Cost Variations[82]

### Burden Absorbed

|  | Actual | Standard | Ratios |
|---|---|---|---|
| Burden absorbed in costs, at normal machine rates for the hours run | $703.20 | | |
| Production, at standard burden cost (including spoiled work) | | $696.00 | 101.0 |
| Machine Effectiveness (S : A) | | | 99.0 |
| Less - Spoiled Work, at Standard Burden Cost | | 24.00 | |
| Standard Burden, Net | | $672.00 | |
| Burden Cost Ratio | | | 104.6 |
| Spoilage Ratio (104.6 ÷ 101.0) | | 103.5 | |

In this case, employing Camman's reasoning, the burden absorbed in costs on the basis of the actual machine time stands at a ratio of 101.0 to the aggregate standard burden derived by pricing production at standard unit burden costs. In view of the fact that the standard hourly rate was identical in both cases, the ratio represents the relationship between actual and standard machine time. The machine effectiveness of 99.0 is really the reciprocal of this ratio. The burden cost ratio was employed to compare current results with past performance and to disclose the trend.

Camman also provided for an analysis of the unabsorbed burden, which was charged to profit and loss. His schedule will be adapted to the data in the hypothetical case:

---

[82]Ibid., p. 70 (adapted).

Analysis of Unabsorbed Burden[83]

Burden Unabsorbed

|  | | Controllable Expenses | Fixed Charges |
|---|---|---|---|
| Actual Controllable Expenses | | $343.00 | |
| Actual Fixed Expenses | | | $432.00 |
| Burden Absorbed in Costs | $703.20 | | |
|   Contained in Burden Rates: | | | |
|     Controllable Expenses | 40% | 231.28 | |
|     Fixed Expenses | 60% | | 421.92 |
| Unabsorbed Burden | $ 71.80 | $ 61.72 | $ 10.08 |

Camman stated that these analyses of burden costs were useful, not only because the expenses were different in nature and in points of responsibility but also because the distribution of fixed charges between operating departments was eliminated.

In addition to these writers, whose efforts have been treated in this section, the following authors also recognized the method of recording burden costs in the accounts at both actual and standard values: Thomas Downie, Jr. (1927), Lawrence (1937), Langer (1938), Blocker (1940), and Neuner (1942).[84]

The Disposition of Burden Variations in Standard Costs.--When burden expenditures are recorded in the records under the first two methods--(1) "Recording Burden at Actual Costs as Debits and at Standard Costs as Credits to Work in Process" and (2) "Recording Burden at Stand-

---

[83]Ibid., p. 73 (adapted).

[84]Downie, Thomas, Jr., The Mechanism of Standard (or Predetermined) Cost Accounting and Efficiency Records, pp. 46-52; Lawrence, op. cit., pp. 371-377; Langer, Accounting Principles and Procedures, p. L: 4-8; Blocker, Cost Accounting, pp. 615-625; Neuner, Cost Accounting, pp. 511-517.

ard Costs"--variations, which may be analyzed according to several classifications, will arise in the ledger accounts.  These variations have
been disposed of according to two rather definite patterns:  (1) prorated over the cost of sales, finished goods inventory, and work in
process inventory, or (2) transferred to profit and loss for the period
in which such variations developed.

A. S. Merrifield (1921), in explaining the use of normal burden
rates, recognized that differences between actual and normal burden--
underearned or overearned, according to this writer--would arise through
the application of such rates and declared that the variation resulting
from such procedure should not be considered a part of the manufacturing
cost but should be charged to a subdivision of Profit and Loss.[85]

Fletcher (1922) stated that "the difference between the burden
standard as originally established, and the amount earned . . . is
debited or credited, as unearned or overearned burden, to Loss or Gain
on Standard Costs."[86]  On the other hand, the increase or decrease in
actual cost of burden items was treated as a debit or credit to Burden
Variations.  Both of these variance accounts were considered as Profit
and Loss items.[87]

---

[85] Merrifield, A. S., "The Distribution of Overhead Under Abnormal
Conditions," National Association of Cost Accountants Yearbook, 1921,
pp. 218-219.

[86] Fletcher, F. Richmond, "An Outline of the Use of Standards in
Shoe Manufacturing," National Association of Cost Accountants Yearbook,
1922, p. 189.

[87] Ibid., p. 169.

Knapp (1924), who recognized both fixed and fluctuating burden
items, believed that the variation between standard fixed burden costs
and actual fixed burden charges should be charged to Profit and Loss as
idle capacity while the variations from standard on fluctuating burden
items should be carried to cost of sales and inventories--work in
process and finished goods inventories--as real rather than accidental
variations.[88]  In 1928, Knapp stated that this plan of handling burden
variations was still being used by his company, Waitt and Bond, manufacturers of cigars.[89]

Bowne (1924), who divided burden expenditures into operating or
variable charges and fixed expenses, provided for the variable charges
to be absorbed by production through rates based on actual operating
time; however, the fixed charges, which were charged into production at
normal rates, would ordinarily not be entirely absorbed--actual production would vary from the normal as set for determining the burden rate.
Under this circumstance, the unabsorbed burden would be carried to the
Profit and Loss account.[90]  The Department of Manufacture of the Chamber
of Commerce of the United States (1925), in treating overhead under

---

[88] Knapp, C. Howard, "Variations from Predetermined Standards of
Burden in Manufacturing Costs," National Association of Cost Accountants
Yearbook, 1924, pp. 216-218.

[89] Knapp, C. Howard, "What Standard Costs and Budgets are Doing for
the Reduction of Costs in the Sales and Operating Departments," National
Association of Cost Accountants Yearbook, 1928, p. 294.

[90] Bowne, Nelson J., "Distributing the Overhead," National Association of Cost Accountants Bulletin, Vol. VI, No. 4 (October 15, 1924),
p. 8.

Typical Plan 3, followed this procedure, as has been demonstrated already in this chapter.[91]

The publication by the Chamber of Commerce of the United States presented two other procedures for treating overhead. Under Typical Plan 1, the Work in Process-Overhead account was charged with standard costs, while the variation between actual expenditures and the amount absorbed through standard costs by the Work in Process-Overhead account was transferred to a Reserve for Overhead Variation account. Under the second plan, the Work in Process-Overhead account was charged with standard costs, while the difference between actual and standard values was segregated in two variation accounts--(1) Profit and Loss-Idle Capacity, which received the variation between budgeted expenses and amount absorbed through standard costs, and (2) Profit and Loss-Overhead Variance, which accumulated the difference between actual expenses and budgeted expenses. As is indicated by the titles, these accounts were considered to be profit and loss items.[92]

Williams (1927) stated that his company, the American Safety Razor Corporation, applied burden to production at standard rates and that the difference between actual burden and the standard was transferred to the Unabsorbed or Over-absorbed Expense account--"This account is not applied to the Statement of Income and Expenses, except at the end of the year, the balance being usually too small to appreciably affect the

---

[91]Chamber of Commerce of the United States, Cost Accounting Through the Use of Standards, pp. 37-38, 52.

[92]Ibid., pp. 34-38.

monthly results."[93]

Amidon and Lang (1928) accumulated the difference between the actual cost of manufacturing expenses and the standard cost of production in one account, which was closed to Profit and Loss at the end of the period.[94] Maze and Glover (1929) transferred the difference between the actual manufacturing expenses incurred--compiled in the Manufacturing Expense account--and the manufacturing expenses applied to production--credited to the Standard Manufacturing Expense account--to the Over or Underapplied Manufacturing Expense account, which was closed to Profit and Loss at the end of each month.[95]

Foerth (1930) considered that variations, when in excess of standard, represented inactivity, waste, or inefficiency, and, therefore, legitimate charges to profit and loss.[96] Cornell (1930), who divided burden costs into fixed and fluctuating expenses, accepted standard rates for the valuation of inventories and transferred both fixed and fluctuating burden variances to profit and loss.[97]

Reitell (1933) divided the manufacturing or overhead expenditures

---

[93] Williams, Charles A., "Some Practical Aspects of Standard Costs," National Association of Cost Accountants Yearbook, 1927, pp. 147-148.

[94] Amidon and Lang, op. cit., pp. 280-281.

[95] Maze and Glover, op. cit., pp. 313-314.

[96] Foerth, J. T., "How Should Labor and Burden Variances be Analyzed and Treated in the Accounts?," National Association of Cost Accountants Yearbook, 1930, p. 193.

[97] Cornell, C. H., "How is Over- or Under-Absorbed Burden to be Applied with Regard to Inventory at the End of the Fiscal Year?," National Association of Cost Accountants Yearbook, 1930, pp. 195-197.

into two classifications--Direct and General Overhead.  In applying his

standard cost technique to these classifications of overhead, he ana-

lyzed the differences between actual and standard values into two divi-

sions--(1) volume, or capacity, variance, and (2) controllable, or effi-

ciency, variance--and, therefore, accumulated his variations in four

accounts.  These accounts were closed at the end of the month to the

Profit and Loss account.[98]

Sanders (1934), in discussing the disposition of burden variances,

advocated that variations arising from controllable expenses be treated

as adjustments to the Cost of Goods Sold while such differences develop-

ing from noncontrollable expenses be transferred to Profit and Loss.

> The reason for this distinction is that variations on
> controllable expenses consist mostly of increases and de-
> creases in the amounts of expense items; in other words, they
> are parts of the actual current costs of operations.  Varia-
> tions in the noncontrollable expenses, on the other hand, are
> more likely to be due to changes in volume of business done
> and the inability of the fixed charges to adapt themselves to
> these changes.  It is therefore natural to regard the former
> group of variations as elements in the Cost of Goods Sold or
> in inventory if they are not sold.  The latter group, on the
> other hand, are due to external conditions and have nothing
> directly to do with the manufacturing operations going on in
> the shops.[99]

The author observed that some accountants were recording monthly

discrepancies between burden incurred and burden applied to production

in a Reserve for Burden Adjustment account, which was closed at the end

---

[98]Reitell, _Cost Accounting_, pp. 379-381, 415.

[99]Sanders, _Cost Accounting for Control_, pp. 377-378.

of the year to Cost of Goods Sold.[100]

Gillespie (1935), who computed three Factory Expense Variations--
(1) Idle Time, (2) Quantity, and (3) Budget--disclosed these variations
on the Statement of Profits as adjustments to Net Profit (standard basis)
and made the following summarized remarks in his discussion of Disposition of Variations:

> Several opinions exist as to the method of disposing of
> variations from standard manufacturing costs.  Assuming that
> standards are attainable, two opinions are:
>
> (a) Close all variations except materials price to
>     profit and loss; prorate materials price variation
>     over cost of goods sold and inventories.
> (b) Close all variations to profit and loss.
>
> In either case, it may be necessary to set up a reserve
> to reduce inventories to cost or market, whichever is lower.[101]

Lawrence (1937), Van Sickle (1938), Mannix (1938), and Blocker
(1940) considered burden variations as proper charges or credits to
Profit and Loss, either directly to the Profit and Loss account or indirectly through Cost of Sales.[102]  Although Neuner recognized that some
authors believed that burden variations should be prorated over cost of
sales, finished goods inventory, and work in process inventories, he
stated that, from a theoretical point of view, there was much to be said
for closing such variations to Cost of Sales or Profit and Loss accounts.

---

[100] Ibid., pp. 379-380.

[101] Gillespie, Accounting Procedure for Standard Costs, p. 187.

[102] Lawrence, Cost Accounting, pp. 362-365; Van Sickle, op. cit.,
pp. 508-518; Mannix, op. cit., pp. 215-217; and Blocker, Cost Accounting,
pp. 598-599.

His arguments tended to favor the second procedure.[103]

An analysis of the literature on this subject, Disposition of Burden Variations in Standard Costs, suggests that, although there is some inclination by a few writers to prorate such variances over cost of sales, finished goods inventory, and work in process inventory, the majority of the writers advocate that the variation accounts be closed to Profit and Loss and be disclosed on the Profit and Loss statement accordingly.

Analysis of Burden Variations by G. Charter Harrison.--G. Charter Harrison not only presented the first unified and concise series of articles pertaining to standard costs but also developed the most comprehensive formulas and work sheets for the analysis of cost variations. Although he contemplated variations for all of the cost components--materials, labor, and burden--this study will undertake to reflect his treatment of burden variations primarily.

The first attempt by this author to consider the differences between actual and standard burden expenses was expressed in a Summarized Burden Report,[104] which presented actual and standard expenses, analyzed as to fixed and fluctuating expenses, and which computed Increases or Decreases (variations) as follows: Fixed Expenses Due to Variations in Expenditures, Fixed Expenses Due to Variations in Production, Fluctuating Charges, and Total. This report was reproduced in Chapter V of this

---

[103]Neuner, Cost Accounting, pp. 527-529.

[104]Harrison, G. Charter, "Cost Accounting to Aid Production," Industrial Management, LVI (November, 1918), 394.

study--Form E, Summarized Burden Report--to which reference is hereby
given.

A second attempt to present cost variation data was in the form of
a Cost Variation Sheet for the Pickling Department of a steel mill and
formulas for obtaining the variations.[105] In order to suggest Harrison's
conception of burden variation analysis at this time, the columnar headings of this schedule will be reproduced.

| | | | A | | | B | | C | | | | D | |
| | | | Actual | | | | | Standard Cost | | | | Standard | |
| | For- | | Quantities | | | Actual | | of Standard | | | Cost of | |
| | mula | | of Actual Rates | | | Quantity | | Production | | | Actual | |
| Ac- | Combi- | Quan- | | | | at Stand- | Quan- | | | | Production | Quan- | |
| count | nation | tity | Rate | Amount | | ard Rates | tity | Rate | Amount | | | tity | Amount |

COST VARIATION SHEET   PICKLING DEPARTMENT   Month of ____

---

COST VARIATION SHEET (Continued)

| 1 | 2 | 3 & 3a | 4 | 5 & 5a | 6 | 7 & 7a | 8 & 8a | 9 |
|---|---|---|---|---|---|---|---|---|
| Com- | | Labor | | Material | | | Service Accounts | |
| pari- | | Variations | | Variations | | Expense | | |
| son in | Idle | Time | Rates | Quantity | Price | | Quantity | Price |
| Total | Time | 3 = D-B | | 5 = D-B | | 7 = D-B | 8 = D-B | |
| D - A | D-C | 3a = C-B | B - A | 5a = C-B | B - A | 7a = C-B | 8a = C-B | B - A |

---

[105]Harrison, G. Charter, "Cost Accounting in the 'New Industrial
Day,'" Industrial Management, LIX (January, 1920), 15-17.

Harrison stated that his analysis of variations could be obtained
by a proper combination of four factors:  (A) the actual expense for the
month; (B) the actual expense figured at standard rates or prices;
(C) the standard cost for standard production; and (D) the standard cost
for actual production, this being the standard cost for production (C)
divided by the standard production and multiplied by the actual production.[106]

These factors--segregated as to material, labor and burden items--
were accumulated on the work sheet and the variations were computed by
the application of the following formulas:

1.  Comparison of actual and standard in total: D - A.
2.  Cost of idle time: D - C.
3.  Time efficiency, expense varying directly with the production:
    D - B.
3a. Expense in nature of a fixed charge: C - B.
4.  Variations in labor rates: B - A.
5.  Variations in the quantities of material used when expense
    varies directly with production: D - B.
5a. Ditto when expense is in nature of a fixed charge: C - B.
6.  Variation in the price of material: B - A.
7.  Variation in expense when expense varies directly with
    production: D - B.
7a. Ditto when expense is in nature of a fixed charge: C - B.
8.  Variation in the consumption of service production (steam,
    electricity, etc.) when expense varies directly with pro-
    duction: D - B.
8a. Ditto when expense is in nature of a fixed charge: C - B.
9.  Variations in the price of service production: B - A.[107]


Two months later, Harrison referred to this illustration of the use
of formulas as "showing their application to meet a simple example" and

---

[106]Ibid., p. 16.

[107]Ibid.

stated that he had "recently compiled tables of formulas covering a wide range of conditions."[108]

These complete formulas were embodied in two tables--Table A, Formulas to Apply in the Determination and Analysis of Cost Variations for the Different Classes of Expense; and Table B, Formulas to Apply for the Various Classes of Expense in the Determination and Analysis of Cost Variations from Basic, Alternative, Revised, and Revised-Alternative-Standards--which were used in conjunction with each other.  In view of the significance of these formulas, it has been deemed desirable to reproduce the author's initial presentation of such formulas;[109] however, the use of these tables requires an understanding of the author's system of symbols, which will be quoted first.

> The capital letters A to H are used to indicate the different classes of accounting data which enter into the various formulas, as follows:
>
> A Indicates the actual time or material expended figured at the actual rates of pay or actual price of the material.
>
> B indicates the actual time or material expended figured at the standard rates of pay or standard price of the material.
>
> C indicates the standard cost for a standard working month, say of 25 working days.
>
> D indicates the standard cost for the number of working days in the month--for instance, if there were 23 working days in the month D would equal 23/25ths of C.

---

[108] Harrison, G. Charter, "Scientific Basis for Cost Accounting," Industrial Management, LIX (March, 1920), 238.

[109] Harrison, Standard Costs, p. 230:  "The first publication of a table of formulas to apply in the determination and analysis of cost variations was in an article by the author under the title of 'Scientific Basis for Cost Accounting.'"

E indicates the standard cost for the days actually worked in the month; for instance, if a plant or a department were closed down for two out of the 23 working days in the month assumed above, E would represent 21/25ths of C or 21/23rds of D. . . .

F indicates the alternate standard cost of the actual production in the month, which is obtained by dividing the alternate standard cost for a standard month by the standard production for such standard month and multiplying the quotient so obtained by the actual production. By the term "alternate standard cost" is meant a standard varying from the base or original standard and set up as a gage of operating efficiency when there is some variation from the operating methods on which the base standard is formulated. For instance, the base standard may be founded on the use of coal in a furnace, the alternate standard being introduced to bring into account the change in operating standard when fuel oil is substituted for coal.

G indicates the revised standard cost of the actual production in the month when a revised standard has been introduced for the purpose of bringing comparisons for the determination of operating efficiencies into line with correct operating standards. This is figured by dividing C by the standard production in the standard working month and multiplying the quotient by the actual production for the month.

H indicates the basic or original standard cost of the actual production in the month.

The numbers 1 to 13 are used to indicate the various divisions of cost variation analysis as follows:
1. The variation in total.
2. The variation due to the revision of the standard.
3. The variation due to the use of an alternate standard.
4. The variation in cost resulting from the number of working days in the month being more or less than the number of working days in the standard month used as a basis for figuring standard costs.
5. The variation in cost owing to idle time.
6. The variation due to the production per day or hour being more or less than standard.
7. The variation due to fluctuations in rates of pay.
8. The variation due to fluctuations in the hours worked as compared with standard.
9. The variation due to differences between the actual and standard price paid for material.
10. The variation in the quantity of material used.
11. The variation in the price of service such as power, light, etc.
12. The variation in the quantity of service consumed.
13. The variation in expense.

The small letters $p$, $b$, $c$ and $d$ are used to indicate the character of the expense being dealt with:

$p$ indicates an expense tending to vary directly with the production such as most forms of producing labor.

$b$ indicates an expense which is in the nature of a monthly fixed charge such as the salary of a superintendent, or fire insurance premiums.

$c$ indicates an expense which is a fixed charge per working day as, for instance, a time-keeper paid on an hourly basis.

$d$ indicates a fixed charge per day worked as, for instance, a cleaner paid an hourly rate while his department is working, but not paid if his department is not operating even though the rest of the plant is working.

The small letters $a$ and $r$ indicate that some other than the basic standard is being used as a means of determining the current operating efficiency:

$a$ indicates that an alternate standard is being used.

$r$ indicates that a revised standard is being used, and $ra$ that a revised alternate standard is being used.[110]

---

[110] Harrison, G. Charter, "Scientific Basis for Cost Accounting," Industrial Management, LIX (March, 1920), 238-239.

Table A.  Formulas to Apply in the Determination and
Analysis of Cost Variations for the Different
Classes of Expense[111]

(To be used in conjunction with Table B)

|  | Charge varying with production (p) | Fixed charge per month (b) | Fixed charge per working day (c) | Fixed charge per day worked (d) |
|---|---|---|---|---|
| 1. Comparison in total | H-A | H-A | H-A | H-A |
| **Standard variations** | | | | |
| 2. Revised standard | H-G | H-G | H-G | H-G |
|  | (ar) F-C | (ar) F-G | (ar) F-G | (ar) F-G |
| 3. Alternate standard | H-F | H-F | H-F | H-F |
| **Production variations** | | | | |
| 4. Working days |  | D-C |  |  |
| 5. Idle time |  | E-D | E-D |  |
| 6. Daily production |  | H-E | H-E | H-E |
|  |  | (a) F-E | (a) F-E | (a) F-E |
|  |  | (ar&r) G-E | (ar&r) G-E | (ar&r) G-E |
| **Labor variations** | | | | |
| 7. Rates | B-A | B-A | B-A | B-A |
| 8. Time | (p) H-B | (b) C-B | (c) D-B | (d) E-B |
|  | (a) F-B |  |  |  |
|  | (ar&r) G-B |  |  |  |
| **Material variations** | | | | |
| 9. Price | B-A | B-A | B-A | B-A |
| 10. Quantity | (p) H-B | (b) C-B | (c) D-B | (d) E-B |
|  | (a) F-B |  |  |  |
|  | (ar&r) G-B |  |  |  |
| **Service variations** | | | | |
| 11. Price | B-A | B-A | B-A | B-A |
| 12. Quantity | (p) H-B | (b) C-B | (c) D-B | (d) E-B |
|  | (a) F-B |  |  |  |
|  | (ar&r) G-B |  |  |  |
| **Expense variations** | | | | |
| 13. Amount | (p) H-A | (b) C-A | (c) D-A | (d) E-A |
|  | (a) F-A |  |  |  |
|  | (ar&r) G-A |  |  |  |

---

[111] Ibid., p. 240.

Table B.  Formulas to Apply for the Various Classes of Expense
in the Determination and Analysis of Cost Variations
from Basic, Alternative, Revised and
Revised-Alternative-Standards[112]

(To be used in conjunction with Table A)

| Class of<br>Expense | Basic Standard[113] |
|---|---|
| (p) Expense varying with production | |
|     p-1 Labor | $1 = 7+8(p)$ |
|     p-2 Material | $1 = 9+10(p)$ |
|     p-3 Service | $1 = 11+12(p)$ |
|     p-4 Expense | $1 = 13$ |
| (b) Fixed monthly charge | |
|     b-1 Labor | $1 = 4+5+6+7+8b$ |
|     b-2 Material | $1 = 4+5+6+9+10b$ |
|     b-3 Service | $1 = 4+5+6+11+12b$ |
|     b-4 Expense | $1 = 4+5+6+13b$ |
| (c) Fixed charge per working day | |
|     c-1 Labor | $1 = 5+6+7+8c$ |
|     c-2 Material | $1 = 5+6+9+10c$ |
|     c-3 Service | $1 = 5+6+11+12c$ |
|     c-4 Expense | $1 = 5+6+13c$ |
| (d) Fixed charge per day worked | |
|     d-1 Labor | $1 = 6+7+8d$ |
|     d-2 Material | $1 = 6+9+10d$ |
|     d-3 Service | $1 = 6+11+12d$ |
|     d-4 Expense | $1 = 6+13d$ |

Harrison revised his analysis of variation procedure occasionally,
as may be attested by the following examples:

---

[112] Ibid., p. 241.

[113] Formulas were presented in this table for Alternate standard,
Revised basic standard, and Revised alternate standard; however, it has
not been deemed necessary to present these formulas also in this blank
illustration.

1. In 1922, he supplemented his classification of expenses with a
fifth class: "e - indicates an expense which is in the nature of a
fixed charge per week or per calendar day, as for instance, the salary
of the stenographer to the superintendent."[114]

2. Subsequently, in the same series of articles, he included
another class of accounting data which entered into the variation formulas:[115]

B - 1 indicates the standard salary for the actual weeks and
fractions of a week in the month. To obtain it the following
formula is used:

$$B - 1 = \frac{C \text{ (standard cost for standard month)}}{\text{Number of weeks in standard month}} \times \begin{array}{l}\text{Actual number}\\ \text{of weeks in}\\ \text{month}\end{array}$$

3. In the latter article, he omitted the following classes of accounting data--F (Alternate standard cost of the actual production in
the month) and G (Revised standard cost of the actual production in the
month)--but failed to indicate any reasons for such omission. At the
same time, he substituted hours for days in D and E classes of accounting data.

4. This article also contained for the first time the Cost Sheet
and Variation Analysis[116] as subsequently employed by the author for computing cost variations and as presented in his text, Standard Costs, in

---

[114] Harrison, G. Charter, "Working Plans for Standard Costs," Management Engineering, III (July, 1922), 5.

[115] Ibid., p. 162.

[116] Ibid., p. 163.

1930.[117]

When Harrison published his book, <u>Cost Accounting to Aid Production</u>,
in 1924, he employed the identical classifications of expenses, classes
of accounting data, and formulas as presented in the original presentation in 1920.[118]

In 1924, he wrote Section 27, "Cost and Profit Variation Formulas,"
for the <u>Management's Handbook</u> and repeated his formula technique for
analyzing cost variations.[119] He added another classification according
to class of expense:

> <u>f</u> indicates a distributive expense. The various ele-
> ments entering into the cost of a distributive expense, as
> power, for instance, would be classified on the power cost
> sheet in the same manner as the expenses of a producing de-
> partment; a weekly salary paid an engineer would be placed in
> class <u>e</u>. On the cost sheets of producing departments which
> would be charged with a proportion of the power costs dis-
> tributed from the power cost sheet, this power expense would
> be placed in class <u>f</u>.[120]

He also changed the term for Production Variation Number 4 -
Working Day--computed as D (Standard cost for number of working days in
month) - C (Standard cost for a standard working month)--to Calendar
Variations but made no change in the computation of such variation.[121]

---

[117] Harrison, <u>Standard Costs</u>, p. 105.

[118] Harrison, <u>Cost Accounting to Aid Production</u>, pp. 205-220.

[119] Alford, <u>Management's Handbook</u>, pp. 1381-1393.

[120] <u>Ibid.</u>, p. 1391.

[121] <u>Ibid.</u>, pp. 1387-1388.

In order to illustrate Harrison's mature conception of variations

and their analyses, the following data have been assumed, have been

analyzed, and have been exhibited according to his cost variation formu-

las[122] and his Cost and Variation Sheet,[123] as presented in his latest

publication, <u>Standard Costs</u>.

Manufacturing Data for Month of April, 1944

1. The standard month during 1944 was estimated to contain 200 working hours.

2. April, 1944, was estimated to contain 195 working hours.

3. The factory actually operated 192 working hours during April, 1944.

4. The standard hours in production for April, 1944, amounted to 188 working hours.

5. The estimated burden expenditures for a standard month, the actual expenditures for April, 1944, and the actual quantities or hours valued at standard rates were as follows:

| Name of Expenditure | Actual | Standard | Actual at Standard |
|---|---|---|---|
| Foreman's Salary | $300.00 | $280.00 | $280.00 |
| Depreciation | 240.00 | 220.00 | |
| Timekeeper | 100.00 | 100.00 | |
| Electrician | 197.00 | 200.00 | |
| Truckers | 120.96 | 120.00 | 115.20 |
| Inspector | 237.50 | 261.43 | 250.00 |
| Power | 240.00 | 214.00 | |
| General Factory Expense | 100.00 | 80.00 | |
| Set-up Labor | 53.90 | 50.00 | 49.00 |
| Supplies | 56.00 | 60.00 | 54.00 |

Before preparing the Cost Sheet and Variation Analysis schedule,

the writer must compute the data for three other columns--Column D,

---

[122] Harrison, <u>Standard Costs</u>, pp. 49-72.

[123] Ibid., pp. 65, 105.

Possible Hours in Actual Month Valued at Standard Costs; Column E, Hours
Actually Worked Valued at Standard Costs; and Column H, Standard Cost of
Production.  In the case under consideration, this additional informa-
tion would be computed by using the following fractions:

Column D $\quad\dfrac{195 \text{ (Actual hours in April)}}{200 \text{ (Hours in standard month)}}$ x Data in Column C

Column E $\quad\dfrac{192 \text{ (Hours worked in April)}}{200 \text{ (Hours in standard month)}}$ x Data in Column C

Column H $\quad\dfrac{188 \text{ (Standard hours in production)}}{200 \text{ (Hours in standard month)}}$ x Data in Column C

When this information has been ascertained and recorded in the
columns designated by capital letters on the Cost and Variation Sheet
(see two subsequent pages), the variations may be computed by applying
the formula in the respective cost variation analysis columns.

COST SHEET AND VARIATION ANALYSIS　　　　　　　　　　　Month of ___April___, 1944

| | | | A | B** | C | D | E | H |
|---|---|---|---|---|---|---|---|---|
| | | | | | Monthly Standard Costs | | | Standard |
| | Account | | Actual | Actual | For Possible Hours | | Hours | Cost |
| | | | at | at | Standard | Actual | Actually | of Pro- |
| Line | Name | Class | Actual | Standard | Month | Month | Worked | duction |
| 1 | Foreman Salary | b | 300.00 | 280.00 | 280.00 | 273.00 | 268.80 | 263.20 |
| 2 | Depreciation | b | 240.00 | | 220.00 | 214.50 | 211.20 | 206.80 |
| 3 | Timekeeper | c | 100.00 | | 100.00 | 97.50 | 96.00 | 94.00 |
| 4 | Electrician | c | 197.00 | | 200.00 | 195.00 | 192.00 | 188.00 |
| 5 | Truckers | d | 120.96 | 115.20 | 120.00 | 117.00 | 115.20 | 112.80 |
| 6 | Inspector | e | 237.50 | 250.00 | 261.43 | 254.88 | 251.97 | 245.74 |
| 7 | Power | f | 240.00 | | 214.00 | | | 201.16 |
| 8 | General Fac-<br>tory Expense | f | 100.00 | | 80.00 | | | 75.20 |
| 9 | Set-up Labor | g | 53.90 | 49.00 | 50.00 | | 51.00 | 47.00 |
| 10 | Supplies | p | 56.00 | 54.00 | 60.00 | | | 56.40 |
| | Total | | 1,645.36 | | 1,585.43 | | | 1,490.30 |

**"Column B'- Standard Staff Salaries" has not been used in this illustration.

COST SHEET AND VARIATION ANALYSIS (Continued)

Cost Variation Analysis

| Line | 1** | 2** | 3** | 4** | 5** | 7** | 8** | 9** | 10** | 11** | 12** | 13** |
| | | D - C | | | | | | | | | C - A | |
| | H - A | D - B | E - D | H - E | B - A | B - A | H - B | H - E | E - B | H - A | H - A | B - A |
|---|---|---|---|---|---|---|---|---|---|---|---|---|
| 1 | 36.80* | 7.00* | 4.20* | 5.60* | | | | | | | | 20.00* |
| 2 | 33.20* | 5.50* | 3.30* | 4.40* | | | | | | | 20.00* | |
| 3 | 6.00* | 2.50* | 1.50* | 2.00* | | | | | | | | |
| 4 | 9.00* | 5.00* | 3.00* | 4.00* | | | | | | | 3.00 | |
| 5 | 8.16* | | | 2.40* | 5.76* | | | | | | | |
| 6 | 8.24 | 4.88 | 2.91* | 6.23* | | | | | | | | 12.50 |
| 7 | 38.84* | | | | | | | | | 38.84* | | |
| 8 | 24.80* | | | | | | | | | 24.80* | | |
| 9 | 6.90* | | | | 4.90* | | | 4.00* | 2.00 | | | |
| 10 | .40 | | | | | 2.00* | 2.40 | | | | | |
| | 155.06* | 15.12* | 14.91* | 24.63* | 10.66* | 2.00* | 2.40 | 4.00* | 2.00 | 63.64* | 17.00* | 7.50* |

*Indicates red figures signifying increase.
**Explanation of columnar headings - Cost Variation Analysis:

1. Net increase or decrease (H-A).
2. Calendar Variations (D-C or D-B).
3. Idle Time (E-D).
4. Production Efficiency (H-E).
5. Labor - Due to Rates (B-A).
7. Material - Due to Prices (B-A).
8. Material - Due to Use (H-B).
9. Number of Set-ups (H-E).
10. Setting-up Time (E-D).
11. Distributive Expense (H-A).
12. Expense (C-A or H-A).
13. Salaries Due to Rates (B-A).

The following columns, as presented by Harrison, have not been required in this illustration:

6. Labor - Due to Time (E-B).
14. Salaries - Due to Staff (C-B or B'-B).

After these analyses have been determined, Harrison would prepare a
Summary of Variations for disclosing the operational results for the
period.

Summary of Variations in Cost for
Month of April, 1944[124]

| | |
|---|---:|
| Total Actual Cost for Month | $1,645.36 |
| Total Standard Cost of Month's Production | 1,490.30 |
|    Net Increase | $ 155.06 |
| | |
| Analysis of Above Net Increase by Causes: | |
|    Calendar Variations | $ 15.12 |
|    Idle Time | 14.91 |
|    Production Efficiency Variation | 24.63 |
|    Labor Variation Due to Rates | 10.66 |
|    Material Variation Due to Prices | 2.00 |
|    Material Variation Due to Use | 2.40* |
|    Variation Due to Number of Set-ups | 4.00 |
|    Variation Due to Setting-up Time | 2.00* |
|    Distributive Expense Variations | 63.64 |
|    Expense Variations | 17.00 |
|    Salary Variations Due to Rates | 7.50 |
|    Net Increase as Above | $ 155.06 |

*Indicates a decrease.

A careful consideration of the information relating to Harrison's
analysis and presentation of cost variations will indicate that he began
with a relatively simple working sheet, which disclosed three expense
variations, that he amended this cost sheet as new variations appeared,
and that, finally, he designed a device that was capable of adequately
revealing fourteen variations between actual and standard costs.

Summary.--In accepting Burden as a term that designates all those

---

[124]Ibid., p. 236 (adapted to information in illustration).

manufacturing costs which cannot be charged directly to the product or to a manufacturing process, recognition has been given to the fact that this cost element involves the most complicated problems of the three cost components. However, this inherent characteristic of complexity has been alleviated somewhat, so far as the application of standard cost procedure is concerned, by the fact that predetermined burden rates have been used for some time in connection with historical costs.

The first problem confronted by the accountant in designing a standard cost technique for recording burden expenditures is the setting of burden cost standards. The difficulty of this problem tends to be increased by the fact that two variables must be forecast--the volume of production for the period and the burden expenditures for the same time.

After the standards have been set and the standard burden rates have been computed, provision is made for recording the actual expenditures in the accounting records. Subsequently, the treatment of the standard burden costs in the records may be selected from three methods--Charging Process at Actual and Crediting at Standard, Charging Process at Standard and Crediting at Standard, and Charging Process at Actual and Standard and Crediting at Actual and Standard--which have been presented from both a theoretical and practical standpoint.

And, finally, consideration has been given to the analysis and disposition of differences (variances) that arise between actual and standard values. Under ordinary circumstances, these differences are divided into three classifications: (1) Budget variation or difference between the actual expenditures for a period and the amount originally set in the standards; (2) Idle time variation or difference between the amount originally set in the standards and the burden applied to production; and (3) Quantity (Efficiency) variation or difference between the burden applied to production and the standard burden allowed for such production during the period. After the necessary analyses of burden variances have been made, such variances may be prorated over cost of sales, finished goods inventory, and work in process inventory or may be made a part of the profit and loss data, either indirectly through cost of sales or directly to the profit and loss account. The second alternative tends to be preferable according to the literature on this subject.

CHAPTER X

CONCLUSIONS

The significant aspects of the evolution of the theories and techniques commonly associated with standard costs have been considered and
have been presented in as concise a manner as practicable.  With this
treatment consummated, certain general observations and inductions have
been deemed justified by the rather extensive investigation that has
accompanied this study.  At the same time, cognizance has been given to
the rather natural limitations that assertions of the following nature
must be subject to.[1]

1. Concurrently with the development of industry in England and
America, certain estimating procedures arose and grew into a body of
techniques generally recognized as estimating costs, cost estimates, or
predetermined costs.

2. The recording of accounting data under the estimating method
disclosed differences between actual expenditures and estimated values
and created the stimuli for the cost estimate variation concepts.

3. The industrial engineer, rather than the cost accountant, recognized the need for a revolution in the industrial order and initiated
ideas that grew into improved predetermined cost techniques.

4. The cost accountant's treatment of burden represented an important phase in the development of more proficient means of ascertaining

---

[1]See above, p. 6.

cost information.

5. G. Charter Harrison consolidated the industrial engineer's theories and the cost accountant's techniques into a scientific method of treating cost data and termed his procedure "standard costs."

6. Standard costs may be considered as scientific, predetermined costs.

7. Standard costs may be classified as an American contribution to cost accounting procedure.

8. Standard costs may be superimposed upon the process cost system or the job order cost system; however, standard costs should not be considered as a distinct cost accounting system.

9. Standard costs may be treated as either basic standard costs or as current standard costs.

10. Standard costs may be recorded in the accounting records.

11. The analysis, presentation, and disposition of variances between actual costs and standard figures represent very significant phases of standard costs.

12. Standard costs, which synthesize the efforts of the industrial engineer and the cost accountant, may be considered as dynamic and elastic rather than as static and inflexible.

The subsequent pages of this study will be devoted to a brief explanation of these inductions.

1. Although the cost estimate, as a well defined technique, may not be said to have existed under the guild and domestic systems of English industrial development, evidence of the use of an elementary

estimating procedure for setting wage scales, for price fixing, and for
preventing the embezzlement of materials has been detected. As the factory system came into operation and the engineer undertook the responsibility for costing, the estimate continued to serve as a means of checking the output from raw materials and assumed the additional function of
becoming the basis for predetermining the cost of production and for
tendering bids of potential contracts. Toward the close of the nineteenth century, production tended to overtake the demand for commodities
and competitive practices caused the rather perfunctory estimating procedure, as practiced by the engineer, to be replaced by cost accounting
methods or by estimates compiled with a greater degree of care. By
1896, the cost estimate served three functions for the manufacturer--to
set prices, to determine whether the factory could make those products
with fixed prices, and to compare actual costs with estimated figures.
In 1909, J. Lee Nicholson, an American writer, provided for recording
estimated cost data in the records. Subsequently, the cost estimate--
non-scientific, predetermined cost procedure--was refined until a rather
definite method came into practice. This cost estimate, which has been
traced rather carefully through industrial development and cost accounting literature, has been represented in this study as one of the factors
that contributed to an innovation in cost accounting technique.

2. Under the guild and domestic systems, the estimate served as a
means of checking the integrity of handicraftsmen, and, in cases of
variations arising between the actual and estimated amounts, the workman
was rewarded for output in excess of the estimate and was penalized for

deficits. During that period of industrial development in which the demand for products exceeded the supply, differences were found to exist in those instances in which any comparisons were made between the actual and estimated costs; however, these variations were not considered seriously. In 1887, Garcke and Fells, the English authors, recognized the possibility of cost variations arising from the recording of cost estimates and suggested that such variations be closed into the final inventory of finished goods or be transferred to cost of sales. In 1900, Goode, an English chartered accountant, presented cost estimate variations and apportioned the raw material differences under three classifications--Errors in Pricing, Errors in Estimates of Different Proportions of Materials Used, and the Actual Waste in Excess of the Estimate. In 1919, Nicholson and Rohrbach, American writers, provided for clearing the differences between actual and estimated figures through cost of sales or profit and loss. Other American writers, who have treated the cost estimate since 1920, have usually considered variances as indexes of accuracy in computing the original cost estimates and have allocated such variances to work in process inventories, finished goods inventories, and cost of sales. The cost estimate variation has been considered in this study as of significance in the evolution of more or less scientific cost procedure.

3. In view of the fact that the engineer had performed functions of planning and estimating projects for subsequent periods of time and had observed frequently the inaccuracies of his forecasts, as well as the growing importance of competition and of productive facilities, his

trend of thought was conducive to the creation of theories and techniques that tended to influence the development of improved predetermined procedure.  Attention is called again to the engineer's efforts with respect to incentive wage plans, methods for time and motion studies, and recognition of the "principle of exceptions," as concrete examples of such contributions.

4. Although the cost accountant developed in an environment marked by commercial transactions, which were recorded and analyzed as historical data, he acquired, in undertaking to handle burden expenditures, a sense for one phase of predetermined costs.  His efforts in computing predetermined burden rates and in disposing of over- or under-absorbed burden have tended to have significance, comparable with the industrial engineer's treatment of labor costs, in the evolution of improved predetermined procedure.

5. In 1918, G. Charter Harrison published a series of articles, "Cost Accounting to Aid Production," and therein recorded initially a unified and concise treatment of certain principles that developed into standard cost procedure--the engineer's computations of the cost components were accepted as the standards (considered as measures and more or less permanent); actual and standard costs were recorded in parallel columns in the accounts; variations from the standards for material, labor, and burden were computed; and standards, based on current operational information, were provided for--the Price Adjustment Factor represented a means for converting the permanent standards into such current standards.

6. In undertaking to define or delimit the subject of this study, without indicating certain procedures commonly associated therewith, the term "standard costs" has been considered as scientific, predetermined costs. The word "scientific" has been employed to characterize such costs in order to imply the use of engineering procedure, statistical data, and carefully prepared forecasts rather than estimates based on averages or perfunctory guesses in setting the standards. "Predetermined" differentiates this type of costs from historical costs or costs ascertained after the productive effort has been spent.

7. In view of the fact that certain concepts and techniques, which influenced the development of standard costs, were initiated by American industrial engineers, that other significant theories were proposed and refined by American cost accountants, and that the synthesis of these contributions was made by Harrison, a resident of the United States for approximately ten years before such publication, this procedure may be considered a product of the modern industrial era in America, and, therefore, an American contribution to cost practice.

8. This study has recognized the process cost system and the job order cost system, which have been employed for some time to record historical costs, as the basic procedures for treating cost accounting data in the accounting records. Standard costs, on the other hand, represent a method that may be employed in connection with either of these cost accounting systems and not an independent cost accounting system.

9. With respect to setting and expressing standards, two general procedures have been recognized--the Basic or "Bogey" Standard and the

Current or Ideal Standard. The Basic Standard contemplates a more or less permanent standard, which serves as a measure or means of establishing relative values; on the other hand, the Current Standard intends to reflect present conditions, which are assumed to exist during the time that the standard will be used. Current Standards are recorded in the accounts and are used to value inventories for balance sheet purposes; whereas, Basic Standards are recorded in the records concurrently with the actual costs and are used only as a means of measuring the operational efficiency for the period.

10. Four general relationships, so far as the accounting records and standard costs are concerned, have been observed in this study. In the first place, the standard cost data may be accumulated as statistical information, separate and apart from the records, and may be compared with the actual costs, which are recorded in the accounts. Secondly, the actual data may be recorded in the records as far as the charges to the Work in Process account; subsequently, standard figures will be used to value the work in process inventory, finished goods inventory, and cost of sales. In the third instance, standard figures may be recorded as both charges and credits in the Work in Process account, and inventories and cost of sales may be valued at such standard costs. And, finally, as initiated by Harrison, the actual and standard figures may be recorded in parallel columns in the accounts, with the inventories and cost of sales valued at actual costs for financial statement purposes.

11. The application of the "Principle of Exceptions"--recognition,

analysis, and presentation of differences between actual and standard values--tends to be one of the most important principles associated with standard costs.  These variances, so far as material and labor are concerned, result from two causes--using a different quantity than set by the standard, and paying a different price per unit than anticipated. In the case of burden, there are three variance possibilities--incurring burden expenditures greater or less than anticipated in the standards; operating at a level varying from that set in the standard; and producing at a degree of efficiency differing from the standard for such production.  When Basic Standards are employed, these variances are expressed as relative values; under Current Standards, such variances are disclosed as absolute amounts and are ordinarily treated as profit and loss items, although some writers prefer to allocate such differences over cost of sales, finished goods inventory, and goods in process inventory.

12. Standard costs, which have tended to fulfill a requirement as recognized by the industrial engineer and the cost accountant for current and reliable information, have developed within an industrial environment marked by expansion and progress.  If, from the information that has been presented, it may be concluded that standard costs have moved with this industrial trend, then the logical induction seems to be that these scientific, predetermined costs possess characteristics that are capable of continuing to advance and expand with the industrial movement.

This dissertation proposed to present, in a chronological succession, those related events, forces, individuals, and/or ideas that have contributed to and/or have developed into a group of theories and techniques that have been commonly referred to as "standard costs." With this task consummated, this study comes to a conclusion.

BIBLIOGRAPHY


## Books


Alford, L. P., editor. Cost and Production Handbook. New York, The
Ronald Press Co., 1934.

Alford, L. P. Laws of Management Applied to Manufacturing. New York,
The Ronald Press Co., 1928.

Alford, L. P., editor. Management's Handbook. New York, The Ronald
Press Co., 1924.

Allen, G. C. British Industries and Their Organization. London,
Longmans, Green and Company, 1933.

Amidon, L. Cleveland, and Lang, Theodore. Essentials of Cost Accounting.
New York, The Ronald Press Co., 1928.

Arnold, Horace Lucian. The Complete Cost-Keeper. New York, The Engineering Magazine Press. First edition 1899; Third edition
1901.

Ashton, Thomas Southcliffe. Iron and Steel in the Industrial Revolution.
Manchester (England), University of Manchester Press, 1924.

Babbage, Charles. On the Economy of Machinery and Manufactures. London,
Charles Knight and Company. First edition 1832; Fourth edition
1841.

Bangs, John R., Jr. Industrial Accounting for Executives. New York,
McGraw-Hill Book Company, 1930.

Blocker, John G. Cost Accounting. New York, McGraw-Hill Book Company,
1940.

Blocker, John G. Essentials of Cost Accounting. New York, McGraw-Hill
Book Company, 1942.

Burton, Francis G. Engineering Estimates and Cost Accounts. Manchester,
The Technical Publishing Co., Ltd., 1900.

Camman, Eric A. Basic Standard Costs. New York, The American Institute
Publishing Company, 1932.

Carroll, Phil. Timestudy for Cost Control. New York, McGraw-Hill Book
Company, 1938.

Chamber of Commerce of the United States. Cost Accounting Through the
          Use of Standards. Washington, D. C., 1925.

Chamber of Commerce of the United States. Uniform Cost Accounting in
          Trade Associations. Washington, D. C., 1933.

Church, A. Hamilton. Manufacturing Costs and Accounts. New York,
          McGraw-Hill Book Company. First edition 1917; Second edition
          1929.

Church, A. Hamilton. Overhead Expense. New York, McGraw-Hill Book Com-
          pany, 1930.

Clapham, J. H. An Economic History of Modern Britain. Cambridge,
          Cambridge University Press, 1930.

Consitt, Frances. The London Weavers' Company. Volume I. Oxford,
          Clarendon Press, 1933.

Cooke-Taylor, R. W. The Factory System. London, Methuen and Company,
          1912.

Cronhelm, F. W. Double Entry by Single (A New Method of Bookkeeping,
          Applicable to All Kinds of Business; and Exemplified in Five
          Sets of Books). London, Longman, Hurst, Rees, Orme, and Brown,
          1818.

Diemer, Hugo. Factory Organization and Administration. New York,
          McGraw-Hill Book Company, 1910.

Dohr, James L. Cost Accounting Theory and Practice. New York, The
          Ronald Press Co., 1924.

Dohr, James L., Inghram, Howell A., and Love, Andrew L. Cost Accounting
          Principles and Practice. New York, The Ronald Press Co., 1935.

Downie, Thomas, Jr. The Mechanism of Standard (or Predetermined) Cost
          Accounting and Efficiency Records. London, Gee and Company,
          Ltd., 1927.

Eddis, Wilton C., and Tindall, William B. Manufacturers' Accounts.
          Toronto (Canada), Warwick Brothers and Rutter, Ltd., 1902.

Eggleston, DeWitt Carl. Business Accounting. Volume III. New York,
          The Ronald Press Co., 1920.

Eggleston, DeWitt Carl. Problems in Cost Accounting. New York, D. Ap-
          pleton and Co., 1918.

Emerson, Harrington. _Efficiency as a Basis for Operation and Wages._
New York, The Engineering Magazine Company, 1909.

Emerson, Harrington. _The Twelve Principles of Efficiency._ New York,
The Engineering Magazine Company, 1911.

Emerson, Harrington, and Mason, J. K. _Revision of American Foundrymen's
Association Standard Cost System._ Chicago, American Foundrymen's Association, 1914.

Ferguson, William B. _Estimating the Cost of Work._ New York, The Engineering Magazine Company, 1915.

Fleming, A. P. M., and Brocklehurst, H. J. _A History of Engineering._
London, A. & C. Black, Ltd., 1925.

Garcke, Emile, and Fells, J. M. _Factory Accounts._ London, Crosby,
Lockwood and Son. First edition 1887; Fourth edition 1893.

Garry, H. Stanley. _Multiple Cost Accounts._ London, Gee and Company,
1906.

Garry, H. Stanley. _Process Cost Accounts._ London, Gee and Company,
1908.

Gillespie, Cecil Merle. _Accounting Procedure for Standard Costs._ New
York, The Ronald Press Company, 1935.

Gillespie, Cecil Merle. _Solution to Problems in Text, Accounting Procedure for Standard Costs._ New York, The Ronald Press Co.,
1935.

Gregory, Gerald H. _Accounting Control by Use of Standard Costs._ Sydney
(Australia), The Law Book Company of Australasia Pty Ltd.,
1940.

Harrison, G. Charter. _Cost Accounting to Aid Production._ New York, The
Engineering Magazine Company. First edition 1921; Second
edition 1924.

Harrison, G. Charter. _Marginal Balances._ New York, American Management
Association, 1937.

Harrison, G. Charter. _Standard Costs._ New York, The Ronald Press Co.,
1930.

_Het Internationaal Accountantscongres_, Amsterdam, 1926. J. Muusses,
Uitgeverte Purmerend.

Holmes, Walter G.  Applied Time and Motion Study.  New York, The Ronald
          Press Co., 1938.

Jordan, J. P., and Harris, Gould L.  Cost Accounting Principles and
          Practices.  New York, The Ronald Press Co.  First edition 1920;
          Second edition 1925.

Kearsey, H. E.  Standard Costs.  London, Sir Isaac Pitman and Sons,
          Ltd., 1933.

Kemp, William S.  Departmental and Standard Costs.  New York, National
          Association of Cost Accountants, 1923.

Kent, William.  Bookkeeping and Cost Accounting for Factories.  New York,
          John Wiley and Sons, 1918.

Knowles, L. C. A.  The Industrial and Commercial Revolution in Great
          Britain During the Nineteenth Century.  London, George Rout-
          ledge and Sons, Ltd., 1930.

Krepp, Frederick Charles.  Statistical Book-keeping.  London, Longman,
          Brown, Green, Longmans, and Roberts, 1858.

Kydd, Samuel.  The History of the Factory Movement.  London, Simpkin,
          Marshall and Company, 1857.

Langer, Charles H.  Accounting Principles and Procedures.  Chicago,
          Walton Publishing Company, 1938.

Langer, Charles H.  Factory Payroll.  Chicago, Walton Publishing Company,
          1942.

Lawrence, W. B.  Cost Accounting.  New York, Prentice-Hall, Inc.  First
          edition 1925; Revised edition 1937.

Lawrence, W. B.  Cost Accounting for War Production.  New York, Prentice-
          Hall, Inc., 1942.

Lewis, J. Slater.  The Commercial Organisation of Factories.  London,
          E. & F. N. Spon, 1896.

Lipson, E.  The History of the Woolen and Worsted Industries.  London,
          A. & C. Black, Ltd., 1921.

Lisle, George.  Accounting in Theory and Practice.  Edinburgh, William
          Green and Sons.  First edition 1899; Revised edition 1909.

Littleton, A. C.  Accounting Evolution to 1900.  New York, American
          Institute Publishing Co., 1933.

Lowry, Stewart M., Maynard, Harold B., and Stegemerten, G. J.  Time and
     Motion Study.  New York, McGraw-Hill Book Company.  First
     edition 1927; Third edition 1940.

MacDonald, John H.  Practical Budget Procedure.  New York, Prentice-Hall,
     Inc., 1939.

Mannix, Raymond L.  A Basic Course in Cost Accounting.  Boston, Record-
     ing and Statistical Corporation, 1938.

Maze, Coleman L., and Glover, John G.  How to Analyze Costs.  New York,
     The Ronald Press Co., 1929.

Metcalfe, Captain Henry.  The Cost of Manufactures.  New York, John
     Wiley and Sons.  First edition 1885; Third edition 1907.

Milner, Frederic.  Economic Evolution in England.  London, Macmillan and
     Company, Ltd., 1931.

Mitchell, George A.  Single Cost Accounts.  London, Gee and Company,
     1907.

Myers, Herbert J., Keating, William L., and Metsch, J. C.  How to Set
     Standards.  New York, National Association of Cost Accountants,
     1931.

Neuner, John J. W.  Cost Accounting.  Chicago, Richard D. Irwin, Inc.,
     1942.

Neuner, John J. W.  Industrial Cost Accounting.  Chicago, Richard D.
     Irwin, Inc., 1942.

Newlove, George Hillis.  Cost Accounts.  Washington, D. C., The White
     Press Company, 1922.

Newlove, George Hillis, and Garner, S. Paul.  Elementary Cost Accounting.
     New York, D. C. Heath and Company, 1941.

Newlove, George Hillis, Smith, C. Aubrey, and White, John Arch.  Inter-
     mediate Accounting.  New York, D. C. Heath and Co., 1939.

Nicholson, J. Lee.  Cost Accounting Theory and Practice.  New York, The
     Ronald Press Co., 1913.

Nicholson, J. Lee.  Nicholson on Factory Organization and Costs.  New
     York, Kohl Technical Publishing Company.  First edition 1909;
     Second edition 1911.

Nicholson, J. Lee, and Rohrbach, John F. D.  Cost Accounting.  New York,
     The Ronald Press Co., 1919.

Nisbet, Andrew Gow.  Terminal Cost Accounts.  London, Gee and Company,
        1906.

Norton, George Pepler.  Textile Manufacturers' Book-keeping.  London,
        Simpkin, Marshall, Hamilton, Kent, and Co., Ltd.  First
        edition 1889; Fourth edition 1900.

Paton, W. A., editor.  Accountants' Handbook.  New York, The Ronald
        Press Co., 1943.

Proceedings, International Congress on Accounting, 1929.  New York, The
        Knickerbocker Press, 1930.

Reitell, Charles.  Cost Accounting.  Scranton (Pa.), International Text-
        book Company, 1933.

Reitell, Charles, and Johnston, C. E.  Cost Accounting.  Scranton, Inter-
        national Textbook Company, 1937.

Sanders, Thomas Henry.  Cost Accounting for Control.  New York, McGraw-
        Hill Book Company, 1934.

Schlatter, Charles F.  Advanced Cost Accounting.  New York, John Wiley
        and Sons, 1939.

Schlatter, Charles F.  Elementary Cost Accounting.  New York, John Wiley
        and Sons, 1927.

Schumer, Leslie A.  Cost Accounting.  Melbourne (Australia), Common-
        wealth Institute of Accountants, 1935.

Scovell, Clinton H.  Cost Accounting and Burden Application.  New York,
        D. Appleton and Co., 1916.

Seligman, Edwin R. A., editor-in-chief.  Encyclopaedia of the Social
        Sciences.  New York, The Macmillan Company, 1931-1935.

Sherwood, J. F., and Chase, Franklin T.  Principles of Cost Accounting.
        Cincinnati, South-western Publishing Company, 1942.

Taylor, Frederick Winslow.  Shop Management.  New York, Harper and
        Brothers, 1911.

Unwin, George.  The Guilds and Companies of London.  London, Methuen and
        Company, Ltd., 1925.

Van Sickle, Clarence L.  Cost Accounting.  New York, Harper and Brothers,
        1938.

Webner, Frank E.  Factory Accounting.  Chicago, La Salle Extension University, 1917.

Webner, Frank E.  Factory Costs.  New York, The Ronald Press Co., 1911.

Wells, F. A.  The British Hosiery Trade.  London, George Alle & Unwin, Ltd., 1935.

Wight, L. A.  The Fundamentals of Process Cost Accounting.  London, Sir Isaac Pitman and Sons, Ltd., 1932.

Wildman, John R.  Principles of Cost Accounting.  New York, New York University Press, 1911.

Williams, John H.  The Flexible Budget.  New York, McGraw-Hill Book Company, 1934.

Woods, Clinton E.  Unified Accounting Methods for Industrials.  New York, The Ronald Press Company, 1919.

Wool Institute (The).  Cost Manual and Comparative Cost Records for Woolen and Worsted Industry.  New York, Brown & Wilson, 1923.


## Periodicals


The Accountant.  London, Gee and Company, Ltd.  Vol. XIX (1893)-Vol. CVII (1942).

American Machinist.  New York, McGraw-Hill Publishing Company.  Vol. XXXV (1911).

Cost and Management.  Toronto, Canadian Society of Cost Accountants.  Vol. II (1927)-Vol. XVI (1941).

The Engineering Magazine.  New York, The Engineering Magazine Company.  Vol. I (1891)-Vol. LI (1916).

Factory and Industrial Management.  New York, McGraw-Hill Publishing Company.  Vol. LXXV (1928)-Vol. LXXXIII (1932).

Industrial Management.  New York, The Engineering Magazine Company.  Vol. LII (1916-17)-Vol. LXXIV (1927).

The Journal of Accountancy.  New York, American Institute Publishing Company.  Vol. I (1905)-Vol. LXXVII (1944).

The Journal of Economic and Business History.  Cambridge, Harvard University Press.  Vol. II (1930).

Management Engineering.  New York, The Ronald Press Company.  Vol. II (1922)-Vol. III (1922).

Manufacturing Industries.  Chicago, Ahrens Publishing Company.  Vol. IV (1927).

National Association of Cost Accountants Bulletin.  New York, National Association of Cost Accountants.  Vol. I (1920)-Vol. XXV (1944).

National Association of Cost Accountants Yearbook, 1921-1943.  New York, National Association of Cost Accountants.

Transactions, American Society of Mechanical Engineers.  New York, American Society of Mechanical Engineers.  Vol. I (1880)-Vol. LXV (1943).

Transactions, American Society of Civil Engineers.  New York, American Society of Civil Engineers.  Vol. II (1874).